WORLD WIDE WEED

World Wide Weed

Global Trends in Cannabis Cultivation and its Control

Edited by

TOM DECORTE
Ghent University, Belgium

GARY POTTER
London South Bank University, UK

MARTIN BOUCHARD
Simon Fraser University, Canada

Routledge
Taylor & Francis Group
LONDON AND NEW YORK

First published 2011 by Ashgate Publishing

Published 2016 by Routledge
2 Park Square, Milton Park, Abingdon, Oxfordshire OX14 4RN
711 Third Avenue, New York, NY 10017, USA

First issued in paperback 2016

Routledge is an imprint of the Taylor & Francis Group, an informa business

British Library Cataloguing in Publication Data
World wide weed : global trends in cannabis cultivation and
its control by Tom Decorte, Gary Potter and Martin Bouchard.
1. Cannabis – Social aspects. 2. Marijuana industry.
3. Marijuana abuse. 4. Marijuana – Law and legislation.
I. Decorte, Tom. II. Potter, Gary. III. Bouchard, Martin,
1981–
362.2'95–dc22

Library of Congress Cataloging-in-Publication Data
Potter, Gary R.
World wide weed : global trends in cannabis cultivation and its control /
by Tom Decorte, Gary Potter and Martin Bouchard.
p. cm.
Includes bibliographical references and index.
ISBN 978-1-4094-1780-4 (hbk)
1. Marijuana industry. 2. Marijuana. 3. Drug control. I. Decorte, Tom.
II. Potter, Gary, III. Bouchard, Martin, 1981–
Title.
HD9019.M38P68 2010
363.45—dc22

2010053758

ISBN 13: 978-1-138-25684-2 (pbk)
ISBN 13: 978-1-4094-1780-4 (hbk)

Contents

List of Figures

List of Tables

List of Contributors

Kenza Afsahi is a post-doctoral researcher at the International Center of Comparative Criminology at the University of Montreal, and member of Clersé (Lille Centre of Sociological and Economic Research) in Lille (France). She wrote her doctoral thesis on the economy of drugs at the University of Lille 1. Kenza also participated in the first two official investigations into cannabis in Morocco in 2003 and 2004 with UNODC and the Moroccan government. Kenza's research interests relate to cannabis cultivation, drug use in urban and rural environments, and the problems of development related to drug production. She is an economist but emphasizes ethnographic fieldwork to collect empirical data.

Xabier Arana has worked as a researcher in the Basque Institute of Criminology at the University of the Basque Country (Spain) since 2002, conducting research related to the social phenomenon of drugs and periodically organizing international symposiums, congresses and workshops related to the drugs issue. His areas of interest include alternative drug policies, analysis of drugs legislation and the rights of drug users.

Pablo Arroyo is currently a postdoctoral researcher at McGill University (Canada). He is a tropical forester by training and throughout his graduate studies at the University of Alberta, Edmonton and the University of Connecticut in the US, has developed expertise in GIS/Remote Sensing and Tropical Ecology, respectively. His main interests range from field studies in ecology to the use of hyperspectral data to detect different types of vegetation, identify single species and quantify species richness.

Vibeke Asmussen Frank is an anthropologist and associate professor at the Centre for Alcohol and Drug Research, Aarhus University, Denmark. She is also the head of the Centre for Alcohol and Drug Research. Her research builds mainly on qualitative methods and covers drug policy, drug consumption, and drug treatment. The main analytical focus has been on user perspectives, marginalization, organization and policy. She has edited several books and published research results in international journals. Besides the study of cannabis cultivation, she currently works on a project on drug treatment in prisons.

Martin Bouchard is Assistant Professor at the School of Criminology, Simon Fraser University, Canada. Prior to this appointment, he received his PhD in Criminology from University of Montreal, and completed postdoctoral work at the

University of Maryland. His work specializes in the organization of illegal drug markets and on the role of social capital in criminal careers. Other interests include criminal achievement and social network analysis. Recent work appeared in *Addiction, Contemporary Drug Problems, Global Crime, Journal of Quantitative Criminology, Journal of Criminal Justice, International Journal of Drug Policy, Journal of Drug Issues*, and *Justice Quarterly.*

Helle Vibeke Dahl is an anthropologist and a senior researcher at the Centre for Alcohol and Drug Research, Aarhus University, Denmark. Her research includes studies on hard drug and polydrug users in various treatment settings (residential, prison and out-patient drug treatment programs). She has published several articles based on an ethnographic study on the everyday life of methadone users and on policy and gender issues within the drug field. She is also the co-editor of an anthology on the relationship between drugs and crime.

Tom Decorte is a Professor of Criminology at the University of Ghent, Belgium. He is also head of the Institute for Social Drug Research (ISD). His primary research is focused on the different aspects of the use of drugs (regardless of their legal status). His work on (long term patterns of) cocaine use and cannabis cultivation has been published in international academic journals, and he has edited books on qualitative research methods, cannabis markets, and (local) drug policies. In recent years, Tom's research includes drug use among sex workers, drug use and drug distribution in prisons and local monitoring systems.

Pekka Hakkarainen, PhD, Adjunct Professor in Sociology at the University of Turku, is working as the director of the Department of Alcohol, Drugs and Addiction at the National Institute for Health and Welfare (THL) in Helsinki, Finland. He has published several studies on the epidemiology of illicit drugs, drug culture, drug policy, treatment issues and social problems.

Margaret Kalacska is an Assistant Professor at the Department of Geography, McGill University. Her main research interests include forensic and ecological applications of remote sensing, spatial modeling and tropical ecology. Her research has also included examination of cannabis cultivation in Canada.

Axel Klein is a social anthropologist with a particular interest in the consumption and social control of licit and illicit drugs. He has conducted fieldwork in the English speaking Caribbean looking at cannabis production and the convergence of cannabis and cocaine markets. Other projects include the globalization of *khat*, the repatriation of foreign national drug couriers and the systemic nature of drug control. Axel has worked for the European Commission, the United Nations Office on Drugs and Crime and is currently lecturing at the Centre for Health Science Studies at the University of Kent, United Kingdom.

Dirk J. Korf is a Professor in Criminology and director of the Bonger Institute of Criminology at the University of Amsterdam. His main fields of research are patterns and trends in drug use and drug trafficking, female and male prostitution, and crime and crime prevention among ethnic minorities. He has published numerous qualitative and quantitative papers, reports and books on these issues.

Simon Lenton is a Professor and Deputy Director at the National Drug Research Institute, at Curtin University in Perth, Western Australia. He also works as a clinical psychologist in private practice. He has published more than 30 scientific articles, book chapters, and reports on cannabis, health and the law and presented on the topic at numerous national and international conferences. He is a co-author of *Cannabis policy: Moving beyond stalemate* published by OUP in 2010. Lenton's research interests include: translation of research into policy, harm reduction, impact of legislative options for cannabis, and drink and drug driving.

Aili Malm is an Assistant Professor at the Department of Criminal Justice at California State University Long Beach. Generally, Dr. Malm's published research centers on the intersection between policing and social policy. Her publications appear in *Crime and Delinquency*, *Journal of Research in Crime and Delinquency* and *Justice Quarterly*, among others.

Virginia Montañés Sánchez is researcher in the Institute of Women Studies, University of Granada, Spain. She has been involved in the drug research field since 1999, working in different institutions and coordinating international research projects. She uses mainly qualitative research methods and her current research interests include the analysis of European drug policies, alternative drug policies, gender issues and drug users' organizations.

Rebecca Nash is a Ph.D. student at Simon Fraser University's School of Criminology, Vancouver, Canada. Becky's research uses social network analysis to explore criminal opportunities.

Holly Nguyen is a Ph.D. student at the Department of Criminology and Criminal Justice, University of Maryland. Her research interests include illegal drug markets, groups and crime, criminal careers, and quantitative methods. Recent work appeared in *Justice Quarterly*, *International Journal of Drug Policy*, and *Journal of Drug Issues*.

Rick Parent is an Assistant Professor at Simon Fraser University, School of Criminology: Police Studies located in Vancouver, BC, Canada. Dr. Parent recently completed over 25 years of service as a police officer in the Vancouver area. He is also a former police recruit instructor at the Justice Institute of British Columbia – Police Academy and a trained hostage negotiator, assigned to a regional Emergency Response Team.

Jussi Perälä is currently finishing his Ph.D. study on drug markets in Helsinki at the University of Helsinki. Previously he has conducted ethnographic research with drug addicts and on drug treatment in prison. His next research will be about cannabis cultivation and cultivators in Finland.

Gary R. Potter is Senior Lecturer in Criminology and a Senior Researcher at the Crime Reduction and Community Safety Research Group, London South Bank University (UK). The culmination of ten years of research into cannabis cultivation in the UK, *Weed, Need and Greed: a study of domestic cannabis cultivation* was published in 2010 by Free Association books.

Eva Snirer recently graduated from Simon Fraser University with degrees in Physical Anthropology and Criminology where she worked as a lab technician for the last 3 years. As an acknowledged black thumb she has stopped trying to grow any plants in her house. She is an MSc student in Geography at McGill University.

Paul Sweetsur is a statistician at SHORE (Social & Health Outcomes Research & Evaluation), Massey University, New Zealand. He has a Masters in Medical Statistics from the University of Auckland. Paul has worked in the drugs research team at SHORE for the past six years providing expertise on survey design and statistical analysis for a number of drugs projects including the 2003, 2006 and 2009 New Zealand National Household Drug Survey, 2005-2009 Illicit Drug Monitoring System (IDMS) and 2010 New Zealand Arrestee Drug Abuse Monitoring (NZ-ADAM).

Samuel Vickovic has a master's degree in criminal justice from California State University Long Beach. Sam's research focuses on medical marijuana in the United States. His work explores the various affects of the legalization of medical marijuana on the social controls of marijuana use, as well as the cultivation of marijuana.

Ralph A. Weisheit is a Distinguished Professor of Criminal Justice at Illinois State University (USA). He is the author of eight books, including *Methamphetamine: Its History, Pharmacology, and Treatment,* and *Domestic Marijuana: A Neglected Industry.* In addition to his research on illicit drugs, Dr. Weisheit has conducted extensive research on rural crime and rural justice. He has published more than 40 journal articles, and numerous book chapters and solicited essays.

Chris Wilkins is a senior researcher and leader of the illegal drug research team at SHORE (Social & Health Outcomes Research & Evaluation), Massey University, New Zealand. Dr. Wilkins has a doctorate in Economics and particular expertise in illegal drug markets and policy. He led the 2001, 2003, 2006 and 2009 New Zealand National Household Drug Surveys and developed the New Zealand Arrestee Drug Abuse Monitoring (NZ-ADAM) and Illicit Drug Monitoring System (IDMS) research programs. Chris has published over 25 peer reviewed academic articles in international drug journals.

Preface

Peter Reuter[1]

Cannabis use is now a staple of the adolescent process in most Western nations. For example, about half of everyone born since 1980 in Britain will have used the drug at least once by age 21; the same statement is true for birth cohorts since 1960 in the United States. A surprisingly large fraction of users, perhaps one third, will have used it regularly for a few years before quitting. It is not yet a universal drug; much Asia, including wealthy countries such as Japan and Korea have very low rates of use, a reminder that drug use is a social and cultural phenomenon.[2]

So where does this prohibited but ubiquitous drug come from? As the editors note, the supply is increasingly located in the Western countries themselves rather than in developing countries; this contrasts sharply from cocaine and heroin and even a number of important synthetic drugs like methamphetamine. It is a large industry in terms of the numbers of participants. For example, Bouchard (2007) estimates that over 50,000 persons work in cannabis growing in Quebec province (or 1% of the general population (15+)).

This collection of essays presents a major contribution to understanding of the dynamics of cannabis cultivation. The range and number of countries represented is impressive and indicative of how much this activity has spread among nations. The United Nations in its *World Drug Report* 2009 notes that 172 countries report some level of cannabis production in their territory. The essays here cover not just the economics of the industry but also motivations of the participants, enforcement and the response to enforcement. It is uniquely rich in its coverage of the phenomenon, particularly in the developed world, though it does cover Morocco and the Caribbean as well.

Understanding the supply side of the industry is important now because there is rising interest in the creation of regulated markets, encompassing production as well as consumption. Even though the voters of California rejected Proposition 19 in November 2010, which would have created a regulated legal market for a state with over 35 million inhabitants, the closeness of the vote (46% in favor) makes it likely that a better crafted version of the initiative might pass in the near future. Indeed, even the spokesman for the opposition to Proposition 19 conceded that the issue was when, rather than if, a legal marijuana market would be created. The state-level exemption for medical use of marijuana in about a dozen states in the

1 School of Public Policy and Department of Criminology, University of Maryland, College Park.

2 For a recent review of cannabis use and policy, see Room et al. 2010.

U.S. has generated active regulation of a quasi-legal production sector; the federal government continues to prohibit production and can always crack down on open cultivation. The Netherlands is always exploring the possibility of legal production, to remove the "front door back door" inconsistency that Dirk Korf refers to in Chapter 11.

Distinctive features of cannabis production

Thus there is a policy reason for being interested in the characteristics of cannabis cultivation, in addition to the longstanding criminological curiosity. Though some criminals from all specializations no doubt take pleasure in doing their tasks well, there is still something distinctive about the commitment of many marijuana growers to their craft. Bouchard and Nguyen describe how one offender started cultivation at age 13 with the implicit encouragement of his mother, not for the money it might yield but because of the satisfaction at mastering a craft challenge surely not oft repeated for other income generating, let alone violent offenses. The emergence of formal competitions for growing cannabis in the Netherlands (as described by Korf in chapter 11) is hard to match with any other offense. Forgers, whatever their craft pride, don't mount annual competitions for the cleverest document counterfeited.

Nor is cannabis cultivation as an individual activity so strongly and positively associated with failure in legitimate activities. Even substantial involvement in cultivation is compatible with middle class careers, without the two being intertwined, as in white collar crime.

Does this mean that criminal sanctions are doomed to failure in suppressing cannabis cultivation, a topic dealt with by Gary Potter in Chapter 15? Craft dedication might be very insensitive to criminal enforcement. Or exactly the opposite; middle class cannabis cultivators may be very responsive to the risk of a criminal conviction. We are now in the realm of pure speculation. There have been no efforts to estimate the elasticity of supply of cannabis with respect to enforcement and how that varies across countries. The variation in price per gram across countries, is substantial ($US3.36 in the UK as compared to $12.30 in the United States around 2005) may be accounted for by any of a variety of factors, including the intensity of enforcement rather than differences on the supply side.

How would current growers be affected by legalization?

A legal marijuana market will certainly generate lower retail pre-tax prices, even if there are restrictions on how large and open production can be (Kilmer et al. 2010). Is it likely that the current growers would be able to operate in the new environment?

Craft love provides a non-monetary incentive for operation, as noted in chapters of this book (Hakkarainen and Perälä [Chapter 5] and Decorte [Chapter 6]). In the standard economic model, it is possible that a producer who derives non-monetary satisfaction from the activity could undercut the purely commercial producer. Moreover the supply curve of the craft producers may be very elastic with respect to legal status; removing the criminal penalty may introduce many more growers into the market. One possibility then is a cultivation industry dominated by small producers with a differentiated product, what is called monopolistic competition.

The orchid industry may provide a model. Describing orchid growing in Taiwan (now a major exporter, accounting around 2009 for about one third of the world's production) one observer reported on the dominance of enthusiasts in the 1980s: "They had this group of people who met every few days to share opinions on varieties, techniques and everything about the orchid. There wasn't any reward when someone developed a unique variety except for the praise and envy of other members, which apparently was enough to keep them obsessed." (Hwang 2010) A rare plant could sell for many thousands of dollars.

Over the next 30 years, nursed by the government of Taiwan, the industry saw major technological innovation as well as the development of new breeds. A co-operative has been organized that allows many small producers to collaborate in ways that reduce the capital requirements of each one. The industry still seems to allow for craft operators (Hwang 2010).

The final configuration of the cannabis market will depend substantially on whether promotion is allowed. The U.S. beer industry consisted many small and regional brewers until television permitted national marketing in the 1960s. It was then transformed into an industry in which the top two producers (Miller and Anheuser-Busch) now dominate, taking advantage of the ability to create brand loyalty. Even with the development of technologies that allow for niche advertizing via the Internet, the microbreweries now account for just three percent of total sales. Brewing beer has some of the craft orientation of cannabis cultivation, with producers proud of their distinctive product, though more of its roots in tradition than of its innovativeness. But the economies of large scale promotion have confined the craft brewers to a small share of the market.

The ubiquity of cannabis use, the emergence of quasi-legal markets and the imminence of wholly legal markets make cannabis production a topic of great interest. This book provides a unique set of insights about the dynamics of the cultivation trade. That it reflects the research of scholars in so many countries who entered this topic independently is itself an indicator of the increasing urgency of understanding the causes, characteristics and consequences of those cultivating the world wide weed.

List of references

Bouchard, M. 2007. A capture-recapture model to estimate the size of criminal populations and the risks of detection in a marijuana cultivation industry. *Journal of Quantitative Criminology*, 23, 221-241.

Hwang, J. 2010. Orchids Blossom into Big Business. *Taiwan Review.* Available at: *http://taiwanreview.nat.gov.tw/ct.asp?ctNode=1446&xItem=117676&mp=1.* [accessed: 8 November 2010].

Kilmer, B., Caulkins, J., Pacula R., MacCoun, R. and Reuter, P. 2010. *Altered State? Assessing how marijuana legalization in California could influence marijuana consumption and public budgets.* RAND Drug Policy Research Center, Occasional Paper. Available at: http://www.rand.org/pubs/occasional_papers/OP315/.pdf

Room, R., Fischer, B., Hall, W., Lenton, S. and Reuter, P. 2010. *Cannabis Policy: Moving Beyond Stalemate.* Oxford, UK: Oxford University Press.

Acknowledgements

In October 2007 at the 18th annual conference of the European Society for Social Drug Research (ESSD) in Krakow (Poland), a number of participants (Tom Decorte and Gary Potter) presented their empirical work and thoughts on cannabis cultivation in Belgium and the UK. Other social scientists in Finland (Pekka Hakkarainen and Jussi Perälä) and Denmark (Vibeke Asmussen Frank and Helle Dahl) presented their work on cannabis cultivation at the next annual ESSD-conference (October 2008 in Budapest, Hungary), and somewhere in a Budapest bar, the idea of a joint work on cannabis cultivation was born. In March 2009 the third annual conference of the International Society for the Study of Drug Policy (ISSDP) provided an ideal opportunity for further discussions with other international experts on the topic, including Peter Reuter and Martin Bouchard. These events were the direct impetus for the creation of a network of scientists from all over the world who have worked on cannabis cultivation and cannabis policies, the Global Cannabis Cultivation Research Consortium (GCCRC). With the financial support of the Nordic Centre for Welfare and Social Issues (NVC) two expert meetings were held, in Helsinki and in Copenhagen, to further discuss available empirical data and their interpretation among the members of the network.

All participants to the GCCRC expert meetings were invited to submit a chapter for this book, and we extended the invitation to other scholars as well. Submitted papers were peer reviewed by experts in the field, and the book only contains chapters that successfully passed this peer review process.

We would like to express our appreciation to the European Society for Social Drug research (ESSD) and the International Society for the Study of Drug Policy (ISSDP) for bringing us together and letting us piggy-back their annual conferences for editorial discussions and parties.

Our gratitude extends to many people who have helped launch this book. Pascual Moreno and Damián Zaitch were especially helpful in the early stages of the project. We are particularly grateful to Adriaan Jansen, Craig Reinarman, and Neil Boyd, who provided valuable comments and who, like us, saw the need for a broad analysis of trends in cannabis cultivation around the world.

We also thank the authors for their diverse and interesting contributions to this book, their painstaking responses to the editors' and peer reviewers' queries and comments, and their adherence to deadlines.

Our most sincere gratitude to Peter Reuter for his close reading of the book, incisive comments and thoughtful foreword. Rarely have we encountered a scholar of Professor Reuter's intellectual stature who is as gracious, supporting and generous.

Furthermore, we want to express our gratitude towards Claire Jarvis and Jude Chillman at Ashgate Publishing, for their patience and generous assistance throughout the process of completing the manuscript. At the final phase of publication, we were fortunate that the manuscript was in the capable hands of Nick Wain. He devoted great care to the editing and to the lay-out and design. The skill and experience of Tom Norton is evident in the preparation of the Index.

We gratefully acknowledge the financial support of the Nordic Welfare Centre, which funded the meetings of our network. We would especially like to thank Pia Rosenqvist from the Helsinki office for believing in the network/consortium/idea from the very onset.

We thank the many interview respondents whose voices are heard in several of these chapters for their participation in these studies and their honesty. This work would not have been possible without their willingness to share not only their experiences but also many other intimate details of their lives. All these people deserve much credit for whatever is worthwhile in these pages. As for whatever flaws remain, the editors and authors deserve full credit.

Tom Decorte
Gary R. Potter
Martin Bouchard

Chapter 1
The Globalization of Cannabis Cultivation[1]

Gary R. Potter, Martin Bouchard and Tom Decorte

When internationally renowned cannabis activist Marc Emery was arrested in July 2005 by the Drug Enforcement Administration on charges of exporting cannabis seeds to the United States, it marked the end of one of the largest and most successful cannabis seed businesses in the world. Emery's ambitions were, literally, to "overgrow the government"[2]: sell as many seeds to as many customers as possible so that cannabis cultivation becomes simply too large and widespread to be eradicated by law enforcement efforts. Emery was probably aware that, independent of his own actions, cannabis cultivation was already spreading around the world, a trend that has accelerated at an impressive pace over the past 25 years. Beginning in the 1980s in some countries and the 1990s in others, gradually smaller quantities of cannabis were being intercepted in many of the major ports and airports of the industrialized world. At the same time, the police and the media in dozens of different countries were reporting the discovery of more and more cannabis plants over more and more cultivation sites – first in outdoor, then in indoor settings. Researchers slowly but surely became interested in the phenomenon, aiming to describe, and potentially explain, the rapid switch from importation to domestic production in their own countries.

As we start the second decade of the 21st century, the new cannabis industry continues to fascinate both casual and meticulous observers of the drug scene. At least two characteristics make this fundamental change in cannabis markets particularly interesting from an empirical point of view. Firstly, the trend is *drug specific*. For the majority of its history, the cultivation of cannabis did not stand out, at least compared to the cultivation of other illegal plants. Cannabis plantations, like coca bush or opium poppy plantations, were typically large in size, grown by local farmers in a handful of developing (producing) countries, processed and then exported to industrial (consuming) nations. While cocaine and heroin are still produced in a handful of developing countries, cannabis is now cultivated the world over. This brings us to the second point: cannabis cultivation is increasingly *universal*. From Europe to the Americas and Oceania, import substitution in the

1 The authors would like to thank Kenza Afsahi, Vibeke Asmussen Frank, Helle Dahl, Pekka Hakkarainen, Axel Klein, Simon Lenton, Ralph Weisheit and Chris Wilkins for their valuable comments on an earlier draft of this chapter.

2 http://www.marcemery.ca [accessed: 25 July 2010]

cannabis market has been noticed in almost every developed country around the world, with a notable aversion for discrimination.

This book has emerged within the context of this remarkable phenomenon. In it, we have brought together scholars from around the world who are each involved in original research on cannabis cultivation from a variety of angles. The stories told are as captivating as they are important to the field, covering both the macro (e.g. national trends in cultivation and distribution) and the micro (e.g. the methods and motivations of individual cultivators) patterns, the developed and the developing world, and societal responses to growing and the counter-responses of growers. Researchers working in Australia, Belgium, the Caribbean, Canada, Denmark, Finland, Morocco, the Netherlands, New Zealand, Spain, the United Kingdom and the United States are represented, each locating their studies within their country's particular social and political context. This geographical spread of research reflects the spread and diversity of cannabis cultivation worldwide, hence the title *World Wide Weed*. It should be emphasized early on that this book was not meant to be a comparative analysis of the cultivation industry in those countries. Instead, each author was asked to provide an empirical analysis on cannabis cultivation reflecting their own research interests and expertise, the objective being to provide an original contribution to the existing body of knowledge in the field. Before we introduce each of those chapters and how they fit within the broader context of the book, we provide a brief review of what is already known on cannabis cultivation and its modern history.

Cannabis: a plant and a drug

It is worth spending a few moments discussing some of the features of cannabis that make it so special as an illegal drug, and that help us to understand why contemporary patterns of cannabis cultivation are, as mentioned above, unique among drug production. We need to recognize firstly that cannabis is a drug, but we need also recognize that cannabis is a plant.

The term cannabis is used to cover a range of products derived from the cannabis plant and that go by many different names. There are two major forms of cannabis the drug – cannabis resin (commonly known as hash, or hashish) and herbal cannabis (often known as marijuana[3]) – and a number of less common products such as cannabis oil and pollen. Herbal cannabis consists of dried material from the plant – usually the flowers or buds and leaves of the plant. Cannabis resin is the harvested resinous secretions of the plant. Cannabis oil, pollen and other variations involve more specific parts of the plant, or more complicated processes

3 The names by which the different cannabis products are known are numerous, and vary by geographical and historical fashions. Various books offer discussions on the different names and types of cannabis products, of which Forsyth (2000) is particularly comprehensive.

of harvesting and refining the plant and the psychoactive chemicals found within it (known collectively as cannabinoids). For the purposes of this book we use the term cannabis to cover all forms of the drug (unless otherwise stated), recognizing that the herbal and resinous forms are by far the most common and that it is herbal cannabis that is most strongly associated with new patterns of production related to the globalization of cannabis cultivation.

A key characteristic that distinguishes cannabis from other drugs is that it is derived directly from the plant, with minimal processing required to produce a consumable and effective drug product[4]. There is a clear distinction between cannabis and the non-plant based drugs such as amphetamine type substances (ATSs) which are wholly manmade. There is also a clear distinction between cannabis and the other common plant-based drugs: cocaine and heroin both involve a degree of processing to convert the parent plant (the coca bush and opium poppy respectively) into the commonly recognized end product. Coca and opium are the natural products of their parent plants, and there are other plant-based (and fungus-based) drugs that are as "natural" as cannabis, but the use of coca, opium and the others is not as wide-spread as cannabis. Cocaine and heroin are the widely used 'problematic' substances, the ones that, alongside cannabis and ATSs, are the focus of coordinated international drug control efforts and the annual United Nations World Drug Report. The production of these involves the processing and refining of the raw plant material. Most cannabis products – and all marijuana and hashish – are harvested direct from the plant and are more-or-less immediately ready for human consumption (and distribution through the illicit market)[5].

Most experts agree that cannabis probably evolved in central Asia (Booth 2003, Abel 1980), but it now grows wild on every continent except Antarctica and is cultivated in most countries around the world (UNODC 2008). The spread of the plant around the globe is associated with human economic activity stemming from recognition of the various useful properties of the plant: cannabis was probably one of the earliest plants to be domesticated by man (Booth 2003). Throughout history, humanity has recognized many, many uses of the cannabis plant: as an industrial product, a medicine, a foodstuff, and even as an agent in reversing ecological damage (see Herer 2000 for a detailed overview of all of these claimed benefits). Cannabis is also a highly adaptable plant capable of growing in a range of climatic and agronomical conditions: where cannabis has been cultivated by humans it has also established itself as a weed. It is grown as an agricultural product, hemp, across much of the world (with the US being a notable exception); it is cultivated as a drug crop in at least 172 countries and territories around the world (UNODC

4 Although we can also recognise some preparations of cannabis, such as the extraction of cannabis oils using solvents, or the preparation of cannabis in alcohol, which do involve a degree of processing.

5 It should be noted that being 'natural' and easy to harvest, prepare and consume does not mean that cannabis is harmless, any more than that other widely-used, 'natural' drug, tobacco is harmless.

2008). It is, of course, this cultivation as a drug crop that is of primary interest to us here.

The demand for cannabis

To gain a full understanding of contemporary cannabis cultivation it is helpful to start with a consideration of the demand for cannabis products. Demand is, after all, the ultimate driver of cultivation. There are at least three important things to say about cannabis *demand* that are of central importance for understanding cannabis *cultivation*.

First, cannabis is the most widely and universally used illegal drug in the world. The United Nations estimates that there were between 143 and 190 million users of cannabis around the world in the year 2007, representing between 3.3% and 4.4% of the adult population. Although cannabis use is a truly global phenomenon, reported consumption rates are particularly high in North America, Western Europe and Oceania (UNODC 2009). Considering this level of demand, it is perhaps less of a surprise to discover that cannabis cultivation now occurs at a significant level in so many developed nations. With such demand, there is a clear incentive to those who seek to make money through illegal enterprise. At the same time, with such a large user population, we should not be surprised that so many have tried to figure out ways of providing themselves and their friends with a steady, home-grown quality product while avoiding the traditional illicit market.

Second, cannabis is embedded within a particular culture. While drug use is often related to particular cultural landscapes with different patterns of drug use (like different genres of music, styles of clothing or wider lifestyle choices) being integral to different sub-cultural scenes, cannabis stands out from other illegal drugs in a number of ways. For one thing, cannabis, like alcohol, cuts across a wide range of (sub-)cultures in the contemporary world – a factor illustrated in part by the previous discussion on the prevalence of cannabis use. The roots of the contemporary spread of recreational cannabis use in the developed world are strongly associated with the counter-culture of the 1960s and 1970s, as epitomized by the stereotype of the "hippie" pot-smoker. However, modern patterns of use suggest that cannabis consumption is no longer limited to a particular sub-culture, but is instead widespread and even "normalized" in many industrialized countries (see e.g. Room et al. 2010, Parker et al. 2002, Shiner and Newburn 1997). Here cannabis, like alcohol, is a feature of contemporary culture *in general* whereas most other illegal drugs are associated with more limited sub-cultural pockets.

However, there are other, more pertinent (in relation to the current discussion) aspects of the cultural significance of cannabis. As well as cannabis being ubiquitous within and as part of broader cultural scenes, it is meaningful to talk specifically of cannabis culture – a (sub-)culture centered on the drug or plant itself. Evidence for this comes from the existence of numerous cannabis clubs, societies, campaign groups and festivals around the world and from the many thousands of books and magazines dedicated to cannabis, not to mention the millions of web pages. This "cannabis culture" is particularly relevant to the emergence and spread of cultivation in developed nations. A sizeable proportion of the on- and off-line literature devoted to cannabis discusses the plant itself – and how to grow it. Most cannabis-themed magazines and internet sites carry adverts for cannabis seeds and cultivation equipment. Numerous websites are specifically devoted to cannabis cultivation, offering tips and advice to amateurs and more experienced growers alike. As well as providing basic information on how to grow cannabis they offer more advanced information on how to achieve desired results in terms of the quality, quantity and potency of cannabis produced. Sites like these often have a monthly "cream of the crop" competition where growers send in photos of their crops to be judged, on aesthetic grounds, by other members of the website community. This idea of judging the efforts of individual growers is found elsewhere in the world of cannabis culture, with the annual "High Times" Cannabis Cup in Amsterdam perhaps the best known of such competitions. Products at the Cannabis Cup are rated for quality of the drug produced as well as aesthetic properties of the plant, with prizes awarded for those responsible for growing the best crops.[6] All this further illustrates how cannabis differs from heroin or cocaine, or the opium poppy or coca bush. It would be hard to imagine anything comparable for these "harder" drugs: there is no "Heroin Cup" nor are there books or magazines with titles such as "Heroin Times" or "Cocaine Culture".

An important point here is that cannabis culture is not *just* about the use of cannabis as a recreational drug. Aesthetics play an important part in the competitions just mentioned, and growers cite the pleasures inherent in the act of cultivation and the successful production of a good *plant* rather than just the production of the drug (Decorte 2008, Potter 2010a, 2010b, Weisheit 1991, 1992). The cultural significance of cannabis as a plant is further reaffirmed for many devotees through recognition of the uses of cannabis *beyond* its recreational drug properties. The well-documented medical and industrial uses of the plant, alongside more contentious claims around the ecological and spiritual benefits of cannabis cultivation, lead many cannabis users to see the plant in an almost ideological light – such reverence for the plant as well as for the drug provide further motivation to many cannabis growers in the industrialized world (Weisheit 1991, 1992, Decorte 2008, Potter 2010a, 2010b). Given the importance of the plant for many users, it is much less of a surprise to realize that many have found it important to extend the culture surrounding the final product to the actual process of growing it.

The third aspect of the demand for cannabis that is relevant to our understanding of cannabis cultivation is that there is a social tolerance surrounding cannabis use, certainly compared to other illegal drugs (and arguably compared to the legal drugs alcohol and, particularly, tobacco). The effects of cannabis are generally seen to be pleasant, even beneficial in some instances (such as for medical use), with less harmful health consequences compared to the majority of other drugs

6 http://cannabiscup.net [accessed: 25 July 2010].

(see e.g. Nutt et al. 2010). Many countries have some degree of official tolerance to cannabis use – various examples of less punitive legal regimes for the drug are evident in many countries in Western Europe (with the Netherlands de facto legalization being the most established example) and an increasing number of states in the US. This tolerance is undoubtedly related to the fact that cannabis is widely used and increasingly normalized (in terms of cultural acceptance if not in terms of levels of use) with relatively few associated problems compared to other (legal and illegal) drugs. Although it varies from place to place such tolerance can make it easier for cultivation to flourish – growers have less to fear when their actions are less likely to be policed either formally (by the state) or informally (by neighbors reporting their activities).

In summary, cannabis cultivation is encouraged through there being high demand for the product, with users being both potential growers and potential customers to other growers. The fact that cannabis is a plant-based drug which, unlike cocaine or heroin, involves no processing of the plant to produce the final drug, and which has many other widely-recognized and clearly beneficial uses probably encourages both use of the drug and tolerance among non-users. This tolerance, especially when reflected in relatively liberal laws (or relatively liberal law enforcement), makes would-be growers all the more likely to grow.

A brief history of cannabis cultivation

Global patterns of cannabis cultivation have followed a fascinating development, from highly concentrated production in certain developing countries to quasi-perfectly decentralized production in almost every country around the world (UNODC 2008). It should be reiterated that here the focus is on the cultivation of cannabis as a drug plant, rather than as an industrial or agricultural crop, although it is impossible to completely separate out these different reasons for cultivating cannabis (see Potter 2010b). We offer here a brief description of – and explanation for – this historical evolution of cannabis cultivation, divided into three broad phases: 1) Historic and traditional production; 2) Cultivation in the developing world for the expanding markets in the developed world, and; 3) Production in the developed world, firstly in outdoor, then (and increasingly) in indoor settings. Taken together, we see a trend that truly fits the term "globalization".

Historically cannabis has been grown for a variety of reasons; it is only since the middle of the last century that the plant's drug properties have been the major driver in cultivation. Early uses of agricultural cannabis were largely centered on cannabis fibres, with archaeological evidence of hempen cord dating back to between 10,000 and 3,000 B.C. (Herer 2000, Booth 2003, Abel 1980). Throughout history cannabis has been one of the most useful – and important – plants known to man. Primarily used as a fibre crop for making cloth, paper and rope, it can also be used in construction (as an alternative to concrete), in a wide range of chemicals, dyes, fuels and cosmetics (as an alternative to petro-chemicals), and a whole host of other products (some sources cite over 25,000 known uses of the plant; see especially Herer 2000). Cannabis – hemp – originally spread across the world as an agricultural crop, moving from China to India to the Middle East and North Africa and then on into Europe, finally crossing the Atlantic to the Americas.

Focusing on cannabis as a drug crop, we can argue that there has been a historic spread of "traditional" cultivation and use that spans large chunks of the planet. The ancient Chinese and Indians, the Scythians, Greeks and Romans, the Arabians and others in the Middle-East, the Afghanis and their neighbors in Central and Southern Asia, and, later, African and Caribbean peoples all have well established histories of cannabis use with their supplies of the drug drawn from their own cultivation activities, accompanied by some exportation as cannabis use begins to take-off in other, non-producing countries. There are a number of books that offer more detail on the long history of cannabis use and cultivation around the world (e.g. Abel 1980, du Toit 1980, Clarke 1998, Herer 2000, Booth 2003). Our job here is not to repeat these histories: it is the more recent developments in cultivation patterns that are the main focus of this book. For current purposes we need only recognize the existence of traditional patterns of cultivation to provide for traditional use across large areas of what is generally referred to as the developing world.[7]

The widespread use of cannabis as a recreational drug did not extend into Europe until much later, and it is with the emergence of modern patterns of cannabis use in the developed world that we see a major and rapid shift in patterns of cannabis production. As demand for cannabis increased globally, fuelled by the developments of the "counter-culture" of the 1960s and 1970s, so cultivation in the developing world began to take on a new dimension. No longer were traditional producer nations just growing for themselves: exportation to the consumer markets of the industrialized world now became an attractive option. Not only do we see increased cultivation in many traditional growing regions, but we also see cultivation emerging in other developing world nations in response to global demands. In this way, countries such as Morocco and Mexico, major suppliers to, respectively, European and American consumers, become large-scale producers of cannabis despite not having the traditions of widespread cannabis cultivation found in Asia, the Middle-East or the Caribbean.

The explanations for this stage in the globalization of cannabis cultivation seem fairly straightforward. Demand for cannabis in the developed world began to expand rapidly from the 1960s onwards. At the same time, international efforts at drug control began to take a more coherent form with the 1961 United Nations Single Convention on Narcotic Drugs bringing together a number of earlier treaties and setting a clear framework for global anti-drug strategies. Stemming from this we see the beginnings of internationally organized eradication efforts directed at the three narcotic plants outlawed by the convention: cannabis, coca and opium.

7 Of course at the relevant points in history, many of these countries and regions hosted the most advanced civilizations of the time.

Demand for cannabis provides an obvious economic incentive which may explain some of the spread of cultivation of the drug. The global ban on cannabis may, perversely, have further encouraged cultivation in the developing world with world-wide prohibition effectively creating "non-tariff-trade barriers" around drugs.[8] Illegal goods can attract a premium through the very fact of being illegal, and bans on production and trade are more easily enforced in some countries than others. Eradication efforts are least effective in those countries or regions that are hard to access due to geographical remoteness, political unrest, or limited economic development and infrastructure. Those involved in cultivation have a tendency to respond to eradication efforts by planting more crops in the first place, by moving their operations to ever more remote wilderness areas, or by actively resisting (socially, politically or even militarily) attempts to destroy a particularly lucrative source of income. Drug cultivation is attractive to under-developed countries as a source of income. Cultivation of all the major drug crops has been strongly associated with developing world nations; cannabis, as a plant that can be grown easily in a wide range of conditions has become particularly widespread in such countries (for further insights into the difficulties of drug crop eradication see Farrell 1998, Vellinga 2004, Mansfield and Sage 1998).

The third phase in our conceptual evolution of contemporary cannabis cultivation has been the increase in cannabis cultivation across the developed world. This development has itself occurred in different phases, at different times in different countries. Outdoor cultivation has a longer history than indoor cultivation in developed countries. Although small scale cultivation probably has almost as long a history as cannabis use in the west, larger scale commercial cultivation only begins to appear towards the end of the twentieth century. Warner (1986) argues that cannabis cultivation in the US was not officially recognized as a problem until 1982. Canada, New Zealand and Australia have also reported large scale outdoor cultivation since the 80s and 90s (Bouchard 2007, Wilkins et al. 2002, Willis 2008). Large scale outdoor cultivation in Western Europe is less common, but not unheard of (Jansen 2002, Potter 2010b). Indoor cultivation, employing artificial lighting, hydroponic and irrigation technologies and climate control techniques has a fairly long history itself, dating back to the 1970s (Bouchard and Dion 2009). Leggett points out that development of these technologies along with techniques of plant husbandry and selective breeding have 'been revolutionized by breeders and cultivators working in Canada, the Netherlands and the United States' (2006:13, see also Jansen 2002). More recently, significant levels of indoor cultivation have been reported in Canada (Bouchard 2008, Malm and Tita 2006, Plecas et al. 2005) and the UK (Hough et al. 2003, Potter and Dann 2005, Potter 2008, 2010b), and widespread cultivation (both indoor and outdoor) is increasingly reported elsewhere in Western Europe (Jansen 2002, Korf 2008, Decorte 2010a, EMCDDA 2009, UNODC 2008, 2009).

8 Thanks to Adriaan Jansen for this particular point and for others in this section (personal communication, 10 January, 2010).

In some countries the levels of domestic cultivation have reached the stage where self-sufficiency in cannabis markets has largely been attained. Leggett tells us that '[a]lmost all the cannabis consumed in Australia and New Zealand is domestically produced...' (2006:41, citing Abel 1997 and Alpers 2005), and Bouchard (2008) makes the same claim for Canada. Jansen argued back in 2002 that 75% of the cannabis consumed in the Netherlands and Switzerland was internally produced, and similar levels of self-sufficiency have been reported more recently in the UK (Potter 2010b, 2008).

The emergence of domestic cultivation has been explained largely in economic terms. Reuter et al. discussed "import substitution" in relation to the US cannabis market in 1988, and Jansen used the term to describe the cannabis situation in the Netherlands in 2002. Import substitution is a term used to describe the emergence of domestic production of commodities that have traditionally been imported. The basic idea is that import substitution will occur as and when it is economically viable to do so, subject to any practical or legal constraints on domestic production efforts. With high levels of demand there is clearly an economic incentive behind domestic cannabis cultivation, with numerous studies citing financial motivations as a major factor driving cannabis cultivators (see, for example, Hafley and Tewksbury 1996 and Weisheit 1992 in the US, Nguyen and Bouchard 2010 in Canada, Potter 2010b in the UK and Jansen 2002 for Switzerland and the Netherlands). However it has also been noted that a significant number of cannabis growers in the industrialized world are also motivated by *non*-financial reasons (as discussed further, below), and Potter is keen to remind us that 'while economic considerations (as relevant to an illicit-market economy) lead to a broad understanding of domestic cannabis cultivation in the west, the existence of a non-economic "ideological" side to cannabis cultivation confuses the issue' (2010a: 148).

The earliest instances of domestic production in the developed western world were predominantly in rural and wilderness locations where geographical features (agronomical and climatic conditions, and also remoteness as a factor in avoiding law-enforcement) provided the opportunity for cultivation (Weisheit 1992, Potter et al. 1990, Hafley and Tewksbury 1996). With the development and spread of technological expertise, the opportunity for domestic cultivation in the form of indoor growing has meant that geographical factors are no longer key constraints on where cannabis can be grown. Much of the commercial cultivation in Canada (Bouchard 2007, Malm and Tita 2006, Plecas et al. 2005) and the UK (Potter 2010b), for example, occurs in major urban centers.

More detailed discussions on the explanation for import substitution can be found elsewhere (Weisheit 1992, Jansen 2002, Potter 2008, 2010a, 2010b); the important points to note for current purposes are that cannabis cultivation has spread across both the developing and the developed worlds. Cannabis is a versatile plant, and with the development of indoor growing techniques it really can be grown almost anywhere, as long as there is electricity and water available. With high levels of demand for the drug there are clear economic incentives driving domestic cultivation. Unlike for coca or opium, cannabis cultivation can be profitable even on a small scale as the drug-product return per plant is much higher (Kilmer et al. 2010). There is also much evidence of non-economically driven domestic cultivation stemming not just from the high levels of demand but also from the particular cultural or ideological status that cannabis has for many of its users.

The contemporary cannabis grower

So where does this leave us? In the modern world all three patterns of cultivation described previously co-exist: the three phases of global cannabis cultivation outlined above should not be seen as replacing each other; each successive pattern of cultivation is found alongside those that preceded it. Cultivation along traditional lines for local traditional use still occurs across large parts of the developing world. Cultivation in the developing world for exportation to western consumer markets still occurs on a very large scale. Cultivation in the developed world is becoming increasingly significant in the global market. The coexistence of these different patterns of production is clearly illustrated by a list of 'the major producing countries 2008' taken from the World Drug Report 2009 (UNODC 2009: 91). Seven of the countries – Morocco, Mexico, Paraguay, Kazakhstan, South Africa, Colombia and Lebanon – represent the developing world, some with a long history of cannabis production and some that have become global players relatively recently. The other three nations in the table – Canada, the US and the Netherlands – demonstrate the increasing role of production in the industrialized world.

What this means is that contemporary cannabis cultivation takes many different forms with variations in approach identifiable not just across different countries, as outlined in the previous section, but also within different countries. Over the years a number of writers have produced typologies of cannabis cultivators within the countries they have studied. This section attempts to bring those typologies together and to add to them, to give us a framework for identifying and understanding the different approaches to cannabis cultivation found in the modern world.

A starting point would be to build on the previous section and recognize that cultivation of cannabis (and the way cultivation fits into the global cannabis market) varies on a global scale. A simple typology of modern cannabis cultivation might therefore be "old" or "traditional" cultivation, occurring in the developing world for exportation to the developed world and "new" cultivation occurring in the developed world, primarily for domestic production (although evidence of cultivation in the developed world for exportation to other developed world countries also exists; Bouchard 2008, see also the discussion in Potter 2010a: 137-138). A primary purpose of this book is to recognize this "new" cultivation, and to explore it further. As such we shall now consider what is known about those involved in this "new" cultivation in some more detail.

As we have already observed, "new" cultivation can be divided into indoor and outdoor growing, although which form cultivation takes depends primarily on opportunity and is of limited further analytic use. We have also hinted already at a potentially more useful differentiation: the motivation behind cultivation. It is clear that economic incentives play a part for many cannabis growers, but we should be aware of the increasing body of work describing cannabis growers who are not motivated by making money. Not that profit/non-profit is a clear dichotomy: many authors recognize the interplay between financial and other motivational drivers, with some growers having purely financial concerns, others having no interest in profit whatsoever, and many (probably most) driven by a mixture of financial and non-financial interest.

Table 1.1 provides for an overview of existing typologies of contemporary developed-world cannabis growers. The interplay between financial and non-

Table 1.1 Typologies of contemporary developed-world cannabis growers

Study	Types of cannabis grower identified
Weisheit 1991, 1992 (US)	*1. Hustlers* – motivated by the challenge and the trappings of success. Usually large scale cultivators. *2. Pragmatists* – motivated by economic necessity. Size of operation varies. *3. Communal growers* – grow for own consumption as well as to sell. Motivated by "intangible rewards" as well as financial benefits. Economic necessity may push to grow larger crops.
Hafley and Tewksbury 1996 (US)	Expanded on Weisheit's typology with two additional categories: *1. Young punk* – young men (18-35 yrs) who usually occupy low level roles (e.g. mules). *2. Entrepreneur* – grow for economic benefits. Develop new methods of growing and avoiding detection.
Bovenkerk and Hogewind 2002 (Netherlands)	*1. Small home growers* – grow up to five plants (tolerated by Dutch guidelines). Produce for own use; sell surplus to friends and, sometimes, to coffeeshops. *2. Large independent home growers* – produce primarily for sale to coffeeshops or wholesalers or an established clientele. Size depends on available space. *3. Large industrial producers* – grow hundreds, thousands or even tens of thousands of plants in large agricultural areas or empty industrial buildings. Organizational structure shows clear division of labor. Probably export as well as supplying domestic markets. *4. Organizers of industrial cultivation* – contracts with several individuals who provide locations for growing. Highly organized with clear divisions of labor. Links to other criminal activity.
Hough et al. 2003 (UK)	*1. Sole use growers* – money-saving hobby. Personal consumption only. *2. Medical growers* – perceived therapeutic value of cannabis for those with medical conditions. *3. Social growers* – ensure a supply of good quality cannabis for themselves and friends. *4. Social/commercial growers* – grow for friends, but may sell cannabis to supplement their incomes. *5. Commercial growers* – grow to make money and will sell to any potential customer.

Table 1.1 cont.

Study	Types of cannabis grower identified
Potter and Dann 2005, Potter 2010 (UK)	Not-for-profit: *1. Personal use* – personal consumption rather than financial motivation. Supply friends. Motivated by "pride, practicality and/or personal ideology and ethics". *2. Medical grower* – to benefit themselves or others with medical conditions. *3. Activist growers* – political statement, promotion of cannabis. For-profit: *4. One-off opportunists* – start with intention of personal use, but realize potential for profit. Grow for specific economic goal (e.g. pay off debt). *5. Self-employed grower* – grow regularly for personal use, but selling surplus to friends. *6. Corporate growers* – entrepreneurial approach, maybe along organized crime model. Large scale, financially motivated. May be involved in other criminal activity. Group Enterprises: *7. Cooperatives* – joint efforts, mutual benefits, equal partners. Usually a group of friends with pooled resources, love for bud, left-wing ideology. *8. Franchises* – experience for profit exchange. Large scale operatives can minimize risk by spreading their activities over a number of smaller grow-ops.
Nguyen and Bouchard 2010 (Canada)	Focused strictly on young growers (13-17 years old) in Quebec, Canada *1. Entrepreneurs* – Few are heavy cannabis users, involved for tangible rewards on larger, commercial sites. *2. Generalists* – Involved in a myriad of other crimes, grow cannabis to make money and finance own cannabis use. *3. Hobbyists* – Almost strictly involved in cultivation of very small, mostly outdoor sites with few tangible rewards. *4. Helpers* – Participation limited to a helping role at harvest stage, few actually use cannabis. Many females belong to that group.

Source: Adapted and expanded from Nguyen and Bouchard 2010.

financial motivational factors is clear in all these studies. Weisheit (1991, 1992, later built on by Hafley and Tewksbury 1996) focuses specifically on those growers he defines as "commercial" – that is to say those seeking to make money (and growing a minimum of 20 plants at a time) – but recognizes the existence of many growers who do not fall into this category. Even for commercial growers, non-financial drivers play an important role, with "communal growers" (the largest group in Weisheit's study) citing the numerous "intangible rewards" associated with cultivation. These intangible rewards include "spiritual", "social" and "intrinsic" benefits from growing cannabis: the enjoyment and satisfaction of growing a good plant, producing good cannabis from it, and being able to share this with friends. The UK studies (Hough et al. 2003, Potter and Dann 2005, Potter 2010b) similarly recognize those motivated by financial concerns, those motivated by non-financial concerns and those motivated by a combination of the two (see also Decorte 2010b). Bovenkerk and Hogewind (2002), working in the Netherlands (and, like Weisheit, concentrating primarily on commercial cultivation), recognized different organizational approaches to growing relating to growers' preferred financial outcomes. Nguyen and Bouchard's (2010) recent Canadian study provided similar findings from a sample of adolescents as opposed to adults, confirming the pattern of a complicated interplay of motivational drivers behind cannabis cultivation in the developed world.

The heterogeneity of the set of participants to the cannabis cultivation industry – including adolescents and otherwise law-abiding individuals – contribute to making cannabis cultivation a difficult object of policy intervention. Recognizing such diversity is central to understanding how the industry has spread and developed to reach countries and individuals who we would not have considered could be involved in drug production as traditionally defined.

Outline of the book

We have outlined, briefly, the current global situation with regards to cannabis cultivation, identifying and offering some explanation for some key patterns and trends. It is now time to hand over to our contributors to flesh out some details and offer deeper analysis of particular aspects of the contemporary cultivation scene. We have divided these contributions into three parts.

Part I of the book looks at cultivation in the developing world. The aim here is not to provide a comprehensive analysis of cultivation in such countries – that would take a dedicated volume much larger than this one. Instead we illustrate some of the issues relating to these "traditional" patterns of cultivation as they persist in the (post-)modern world. The Caribbean is a region that has gained an international reputation based on assumptions that cannabis is widely available, universally appreciated, and culturally embedded – and that its consumption is largely unhindered by legal restrictions. In Chapter 2 Axel Klein analyzes and critiques these (largely European) representations, describing the political and economic processes that led to the introduction of *ganja* from east India into Jamaica and the other Caribbean islands, where ganja use formed a critical part of the social nexus with important ramifications for the economy, social life, individual well being and cultural identity. Although cannabis remains a contested symbol, often now associated with violence and organized crime groups, its use is approaching normalization and ganja cultivation provides an economic safety net for many. Cannabis stands in contrast to cocaine (including crack), also common in the region, but seen as wicked and detrimental, and thus legitimately prohibited.

In Chapter 3 Kenza Afsahi focuses on another region in the world where cannabis has been cultivated traditionally for several centuries: the Moroccan Rif. Based on her own empirical qualitative data, she describes how cannabis cultivation started to develop from the sixteenth century in the Rif region, and how *kif* production became industrialized from the 1960s onwards. Afsahi describes the organization of family-based cannabis operations: cultivation tasks and stages, the transformation process of the cannabis plant into hashish, and the sale of cannabis.

The author details benefits of cannabis production to the local economy and the individuals working within it, as well as the social, economic and environmental consequences associated with this activity.

Part II of the book moves the focus from "traditional" producing regions to the more recent development of the "new" cultivation industry in industrial countries. The seven chapters included in this part cover a wide range of countries – Denmark, Finland, Belgium, Canada, the US, and Spain. Chapters 4 to 6 can be seen as complementing each other, as each initially collected data using a similar web survey research design where hundreds of small-scale growers were recruited to answer a detailed questionnaire on their activities. Each also explored specific issues further using face-to-face interviews with a smaller subset of respondents, which led to three contributions with very different focuses. Helle Vibeke Dahl and Vibeke Asmussen Frank (Chapter 4) draw on a sub-sample of 19 Danish respondents who reported growing and using cannabis for medical reasons, aiming to examine the therapeutic qualities of cannabis as perceived and reported by growers (and users) themselves. Their respondents identified two main benefits of cannabis for self-medication, the first for pain related conditions, and the second mental distress issues. Not only is cannabis perceived as effective for either one of those issues, but the growers interviewed also preferred cannabis over conventional medicines. Pekka Hakkarainen and Jussi Perälä (Chapter 5) follow by moving the attention towards the more general conflict between growers and the law in Finland, and how their respondents negotiate those disputes. The authors show that the variety of justifications used by growers illustrates the complexity and the heterogeneity of the phenomenon, and hence the difficulty of having a one-dimensional policy that fails to take such diversity into account. In Chapter 6 Tom Decorte draws on an even larger sample of small-scale growers to analyze a recurrent theme in Belgian growers' narratives, namely their preoccupation with the strength and quality of the cannabis available on the market – including the cannabis they grow themselves. His findings show that the two phenomena are related: many respondents reported choosing home growing over buying their cannabis on the market because they were dissatisfied with the cannabis available. Respondents perceived their homegrown cannabis as healthier and (comfortably) milder than that sold on the market. The chapter emphasizes an important point in regards to cannabis quality, namely that "stronger is not always better".

Chapters 7 and 8 are both concerned with the social environment of growers, and how contacts are created, mobilized and used by growers as they progress in their cultivation careers. The chapters nicely complement each other by looking at this issue from two extremes – while Aili Malm, Rebecca Nash and Samuel Vickovic draw on a large sample of co-offending networks of arrested growers in British Columbia, Canada to analyze the general co-offending patterns found in the data, Martin Bouchard and Holly Nguyen were concerned with the micro details and social encounters in the careers of two Canadian growers in particular who came within reach of a milieu of "professionals". Bouchard and Nguyen start their chapter by trying to bring some conceptual order in the definitions of "professional" and "amateur" criminals, especially (though not exclusively) in the context of cannabis cultivation. The qualitative material then analyzed by Bouchard and Nguyen serves as an illustration of the importance for growers to be exposed to a social opportunity structure in order to make it as a professional grower. Aili Malm et al., for their part, frame their contribution within the literature on social network analysis of criminal phenomena, analyzing the stability of co-offending cannabis cultivation networks. Not only do they identify and describe the variety of networks patterns found in their sample (dyads, open triads, common pairs, kite-shaped), but they also demonstrate that growers have a tendency to choose co-offenders of similar ethnicity – yet different in age and gender. In other words, Malm et al. show that the complexity and skills required for cannabis cultivation have a tendency to produce unique co-offending patterns not typically found for other types of crimes.

Part II ends with two chapters providing a broader overview of cannabis cultivation in their respective countries. Ralph Weisheit (Chapter 9) first provides an important update of the situation of cannabis cultivation in the US, almost two decades after publication of his seminal study (Weisheit 1992). He shows that the industry underwent a period of change over the past twenty years where new groups got involved, and different methods to grow cannabis were gradually introduced over time. Importantly, the industry continued to expand and Weisheit shows that much of the growth has been attributed to the state of California, the one state that has come closest to considering a major change in cannabis policy. The chapter by Xabier Arana and Virginia Montañés Sánchez (Chapter 10) concludes this section (and introduces the next part of the book) by providing an analysis concerned with both sides of the coin: on the one hand, the legal regulation of cannabis in Spain; on the other hand, the responses of cannabis users and growers to those policies. After providing an overview of the legal regime and the insecurity it produced for users, the authors describe how users created groups and associations to reduce that uncertainty related to the illegal market. In particular, the authors examine the case of cannabis social clubs as a cannabis supply regulation alternative.

For Part III, we shift the focus on to the official responses to cannabis cultivation: the trends in "control" mentioned in the subtitle of the book. Our next two chapters look at two countries with different experiences of a policy of official tolerance, or decriminalization, of some aspects of cannabis use, distribution and cultivation. In Chapter 11, Dirk Korf discusses the situation in the Netherlands, well-known for tolerating the buying of cannabis through the coffeeshop system. In recent years the Dutch authorities have increasingly targeted the domestic cannabis cultivation operations that supply the coffeeshops, motivated by concern over the involvement of organized crime in these operations. Korf analyzes the changes in drug policy on the Dutch cannabis market, in terms of both desired and actual impacts on the market, and on the cannabis found within it. In Chapter 12, Simon Lenton talks us through the implementation and impact of the Cannabis Infringement Notice scheme in Western Australia. The discussion demonstrates how decriminalization of small scale cultivation may have positive harm-reduction benefits (for users) and crime-control implications (separating organized crime and commercial cultivation from personal use and supply among friends). The discussion also highlights, however, the way that political concerns can and do influence policy developments in directions other than those suggested by professional and academic advice.

The next two chapters look at eradication efforts directed against cannabis cultivation. In Chapter 13 Margaret Kalacska, Pablo Arroyo-Mora, Eva Snirer and Rick Parent review the literature on the eradication of cannabis with a particular focus on biological controls. It becomes clear that cannabis eradication is not an easily achievable goal through any currently known methods, although suggestions are made for possible future tactics. Chris Wilkins and Paul Sweetsur, Chapter 14, consider cannabis eradication efforts in New Zealand. They find that ongoing crop eradication efforts have achieved some surprisingly high seizure rates over the past ten years. However, the effectiveness of eradication efforts appears to have declined over recent years and there are a number of possible reasons for this including efforts by cultivators to make cannabis plots harder to detect.

Section III finishes with Chapter 15, where Gary Potter explores the idea of "adaptive response" amongst cannabis cultivators. Drawing on qualitative data from ethnographic research with cannabis cultivators in the UK, Potter outlines a number of strategies that growers employ to minimize the risks associated with law enforcement activity. Cannabis cultivation, even on a large commercial scale, becomes difficult to detect because cannabis growers actively try to minimize their risks, a situation helped by certain properties of cannabis that make it inherently easy to cultivate – and therefore hard to police.

Our fourteen original chapters from 24 contributors representing five continents and regions across the world can only scratch the surface of contemporary cannabis cultivation. Nevertheless the range of issues discussed and the variety of perspectives taken allows for more than just a surface understanding of the nuances of this increasingly globalized illegal activity. Each chapter stands alone as a valuable study, yet the value of the book (we hope) is greater than the sum of its parts. In the conclusion (Chapter 16) we strive to bring the different threads together to offer an explanation for the globalization of cannabis cultivation, an analysis of the challenges inherent in efforts to control cultivation and some tentative predictions – and suggestions – for the future.

A note on terminology

Individual contributors do not always use the same terminology, a situation that reflects the wider literature on cannabis. Different words are used for the same thing both within and between different countries, cultures or social groups, and the same word can have different meanings in different contexts. Authors' preferences reflect the culture they are working in, or the data they are working with. There are two areas in particular where terminology varies both by preference and by context – terms used for cannabis and its derivatives, and terminology relating to particular cultivation techniques.

Cannabis covers all forms of the drug cannabis (herbal cannabis, cannabis resin and other, less common preparations), and the cannabis plant. Marijuana and ganja are commonly used for the plant and herbal forms of the drug, but not normally for the resin. Hash and hashish are used to cover cannabis resin, but not herbal cannabis. Kif (also Kief, Keif, Keef), pollen, nederhash/nederwiet, charas, skunk etc are terms for particular cannabis preparations or varieties, often associated with particular countries or regions, that may also be used (purists would say incorrectly) more generically to cover a range of cannabis preparations. Hemp is usually used to refer to varieties of the cannabis plant grown for industrial purposes rather than as a drug crop, but hemp and cannabis are the same plant.

Growing terminology also varies. Hydroponics, technically, means cultivation with roots suspended in water. Some growers – and commentators – use a broader interpretation to cover all non-soil growing mediums. Organic, for some, means grown in soil. For others it means grown without the use of chemicals (as pesticides, fungicides, nutrients etc). For purists it encompasses both of these criteria.

List of references

Abel, E.L. 1980. *Marijuana: The first twelve thousand years*. New York: Plenum Press.

Abel, S. 1997. Cannabis policy in Australia and New Zealand. *Drug and Alcohol Review*, 16(4), 421-28.

Alpers, P. 2005. *Gun-running in Papua New Guinea: from arrows to assault weapons in the Southern Highlands, Special Report No. 5*. Geneva: Graduate Institute of International Studies, Small Arms Survey.

Booth, M. 2003. *Cannabis: A history*. London: Doubleday.

Bouchard, M. and Dion, C.B. 2009. Growers and facilitators: probing the role of entrepreneurs in the development of the cannabis cultivation industry. *Journal of Small Business and Entrepreneurship*, 22(1), 25-38.

Bouchard, M. 2007. A capture-recapture model to estimate the size of criminal populations and the risks of detection in a marijuana cultivation industry. *Journal of Quantitative Criminology*, 23, 221-41.

Bouchard, M. 2008. Towards a realistic method to estimate the size of cannabis cultivation industry in developed countries. *Contemporary Drug Problems*, 35, 291-320.

Bovenkerk, F. and Hogewind, W.I.M. 2002. *Hennepteelt in Nederland: het probleem van de criminaliteit en haar bestrijding*. [Cannabis cultivation in the Netherlands: the problem of criminality and the struggle against it]. Utrecht: Willem Pompe Instituut voor Strafwetenschappen.

Clarke R.C. 1998. *Hashish*. Los Angeles, CA: Red Eye Press.

Decorte, T. 2008. Domestic marihuana cultivation in Belgium: on (un)intended effects of drug policy on the cannabis market, in *Cannabis in Europe: dynamics in perception, policy and markets*, edited by D.J. Korf. Lengerich, Pabst Science Publishers, 69-86.

Decorte, T. 2010a. The case for small-scale domestic cannabis cultivation. *The International Journal of Drug Policy*, 21(4), 271-75.

Decorte, T. 2010b. Small scale domestic cannabis cultivation: an anonymous web survey among 659 cannabis cultivators in Belgium. *Contemporary Drug Problems,* 37 (Summer 2010), 341-70.

du Toit, B. 1980. *Cannabis in Africa*. Rotterdam: Balkema.

EMCDDA 2009. *Annual report on the state of the drugs problem in Europe*. Lisbon: EMCDDA. Available at: http://www.emcdda.europa.eu/publications/annual-report/2009 [accessed: 10 April 2010].

Farrell, G. 1998. A global empirical review of drug crop eradication and United Nations' crop substitution and alternative development strategies. *Journal of Drug Issues*, 28(2), 395-436.

Forsyth, A. 2000. *Psychoactive drugs*. London: The Stationery Office.

Hafley, S.R. and Tewksbury, R. 1995. The rural Kentucky marijuana industry: organization and community involvement. *Deviant Behavior*, 16(3), 201-21.

Hafley, S.R. and Tewksbury, R. 1996. Reefer madness in Bluegrass County: Community structure and roles in the rural Kentucky marijuana industry. *Journal of Crime and Justice*, 19(1), 75–92.

Herer, J. 2000. *The emperor wears no clothes*. Newcastle-upon-Tyne: Green Planet Books.

Hough, M., Warburton, H., Few, B., May, T., Man, L-H., Witton, J. and Turnbull, P.J. 2003. *A growing market: The domestic cultivation of cannabis*. York: Joseph Rowntree Foundation.

Jansen, A.C.M. 2002. The economics of cannabis cultivation in Europe. Paper presented at the 2nd European Conference on Drug Trafficking and Law Enforcement. Paris, 26th and 27th September, 2002. Available at http://www.cedro-uva.org/lib/jansen.economics.html. [accessed: 9 April 2010].

Kilmer, B., Caulkins, J.P., Pacula, R.L., MacCoun, R.J. and Reuter, P.H. 2010. *Altered State? Assessing how marijuana legalization in California could influence marijuana consumption and public budgets*. Santa Monica, CA: RAND Corporation.

Korf, D.J. (Ed.) 2008. *Cannabis in Europe: Dynamics in perception, policy and markets*. Lengerich: Pabst Science Publishers.

Leggett, T. 2006. Review of the world cannabis situation. *Bulletin on Narcotics*, 58 (volumes 1 and 2).

Malm, A.E. and Tita, G.E. 2006. A spatial analysis of Green Teams: A tactical response to marijuana production in British Columbia. *Policy Sciences*, 39(4), 361-77.

Mansfield, D. and Sage, C. 1998. Drug crop producing countries: a developmental perspective, in *The control of drugs and drug users,* edited by R. Coomber. Boca Raton, Florida: CRC Press, 161-82.

Nguyen, H. and Bouchard, M. 2010. Patterns of youth participation in cannabis cultivation. *Journal of Drug Issues*, 40(2), 264-93.

Nutt, D., King, L. and Phillips, L. 2010. Drug harms in the UK: a multicriteria decision analysis. *The Lancet*, 376(9752), 1558-65.

Parker, H., Williams, L. and Aldridge, J. 2002. The normalisation of "sensible" recreational drug use: Further evidence from the North West Longitudinal Study. *Sociology*, 36(4), 941-64.

Plecas, D., Malm, A. and Kinney, B. 2005. *Marihuana growing operations in British Columbia revisited (1997-2003).* Abbotsford: Department of Criminology and Criminal Justice, University of the Fraser Valley.

Potter, G. 2008. The growth of cannabis cultivation: Explanations for import substitution in the UK, in *Cannabis in Europe: Dynamics in perception, policy and markets*, edited by D.J. Korf. Lengerich: Pabst Science Publishers, 69-86.

Potter, G. 2010a. You reap what you sow: profit, pleasure and pain in domestic cannabis cultivation, in *Pleasure, pain and profit: European perspectives on drugs*, edited by T. Decorte and J. Fountain. Lengerich: Pabst Science Publishers, 134-51.

Potter, G. 2010b. *Weed, Need and Greed: a study of domestic cannabis cultivation*. London: Free Association Books.

Potter, G. and Dann, S. 2005. Urban crop circles: Urban cannabis growing in the north of England, in *Cocktails and dreams: Perspectives on drug and alcohol use*, edited by W. Palacios. Upper Saddle River, New Jersey: Pearson Prentice Hall, 89-109.

Potter, G., Gaines, L. and Holbrook, B. 1990. Blowing smoke: An evaluation of marijuana eradication in Kentucky. *American Journal of Police*, 9(1), 97-116.

Reuter P., Crawford J. and Cave J. 1988. *Sealing the borders: the effects of increased military participation in drug interdiction*. Santa Monica: Rand.

Room, R., Fischer, B., Hall, W., Lenton, S. and Reuter, P. 2010. *Cannabis policy: moving beyond stalemate*. Oxford, UK: Oxford University Press.

Shiner, M. and Newburn, T. 1997. Definitely, maybe not? The normalisation of recreational drug use amongst young people. *Sociology*, 31(3), 511-29.

UNODC 2008. *World Drug Report, 2008*. Vienna: UNODC.

UNODC 2009. *World Drug Report, 2009*. Vienna: UNODC.

Vellinga, M. (ed.) 2004. *The political economy of the drug industry: Latin America and the international system*. Gainsville, Florida: University Press Florida.

Warner, R. 1986. *Invisible hand: The marijuana business*. New York: Beech Tree Books.

Weisheit, R.A. 1991. The intangible rewards from crime: the case of domestic marijuana cultivation. *Crime and Delinquency*, 37(4), 506-27.

Weisheit, R.A. 1992. *Domestic marijuana: a neglected industry*. New York: Greenwood Press.

Wilkins, C., Bhatta, K. and Casswell, S. 2002. The effectiveness of cannabis eradication operations in New Zealand. *Drug and Alcohol Review*, 21, 369-74.

Willis, K. 2008. *Cannabis supply into and within Australia*. Canberra: Australian Institute of Criminology.

PART I
Traditional Producer Nations

Chapter 2

Peculiar and Perplexed – The Complexity of Ganja Cultivation in the English speaking Caribbean

Axel Klein

The Caribbean basin comprising the coastal states along the Central American Isthmus and northern shoulder of South America, and an assemblage of islands of varying political status, emerged in the 1980s as a major transit zone for illicit drugs bound for North American markets (Bagley and Walker 1994, Griffith, 1993, 2002). In the parlance of US law enforcement agencies, the US Virgin Islands and Puerto Rico were designated High Intensity Drug Trafficking Areas (Beruff and Cordero 2005, Griffith 1997). In the 1990s, the risk emanating from these activities was upgraded to a security threat, leading to the militarization of counter trafficking measures (Zirnite 1997). Since the attacks on the New York Twin Towers, drug control has become enmeshed with counter insurgency, leading yet again to new investments and a shift in the focus and definitions, particularly the reclassification of the organized groups involved in Colombia's rural insurrection as terrorist organizations. Since the FARC obtain a good slice of their funds from taxes on coca farmers, the war on drugs, with its panoply of measures from aerial fumigation to fast boat intercepts, became part of the war on terror (Armenta et al. 2003, Youngers and Rosin 2005, Vargas 2005).

The redeployment of US assets from drug control to home land security related counter terrorism operations initially raised concern among drug control agencies worried about leaving the Caribbean transit route unguarded. But these anxieties proved ill founded as drug trafficking was rerouted through Mexico, where the clash between organized crime and government agencies is threatening to push the state to the edge of stability (Meyer et al. 2007). The Obama administration has strengthened border security and bilateral cooperation, in an attempt to shore up support for its southern neighbor. One consequence of these more pressing preoccupations has been to relegate international support for counter trafficking operations in the Caribbean. Law enforcement agencies on both sides of the Atlantic may justify this withdrawal as a victory dividend. In the UK, for instance, operation "Airbridge", a combined services operation against cocaine traffickers working out of Jamaica has been celebrated as a success (HOCSC 2009, SOCA 2008). Equally in the Netherlands, the targeted operations against trafficking groups operating out of the Netherlands Antilles and Suriname have been evaluated as successes and wound up. In the islands, however, drug availability is unaffected, high rates of drug consumption prevalence persist, and the threat posed by traffickers to the security of small island states is undiminished (World Bank/UNODC 2007). It is evident that the priorities of governments in the region differ from those of North American and European partners. Officially, all are equal parties that have acceded to global and hemispheric treaties that define drugs as an "evil" threatening "humanity" at large, for which international cooperation is needed. But different governments may have very different ideas as to what measures are needed to best safeguard the health of their citizens and the stability of their states.

For the past five hundred years the history of the Caribbean islands has been framed by the struggle of external powers. At the centre of trans-oceanic trading networks, the islands have been too small and poorly resourced to withstand the pressure from overseas empires. European colonial powers were replaced in the early 20th century by the US as the hemispheric hegemon with great political power, economic sway and cultural influence. There have been efforts, pursued with varying degrees of intensity by different US administrations, to move towards a partnership approach. In the particular sphere of drug control, efforts have been made to incorporate collective interests in hemispheric organizations such as the CICAD, to move towards mutuality in the evaluation of drug control efforts via the Mutual Evaluation Mechanism, and draw up a joint program under the 1994 treaty. How limited such cooperation was to particular areas of supply repression becomes clear from a closer analysis of treaty provisions. Throughout the 1990s the US was primarily concerned with extracting concessions from Caribbean partners on the extradition of suspects and the rights of US naval vessels to enter territorial waters, intelligence sharing between law enforcements and joint operations (Klein 2004a). When Caribbean governments sought to push into new territory to address domestic health and governance problems relating to drugs they soon found out how strictly that room had been limited. In August 2001, one day after the publication of the Ganja Commission recommendations including the decriminalization of cannabis possession, a spokesman for the US embassy warned that "the US government will consider Jamaica's adherence to its commitment under the 1988 UN Convention when making its determination under the annual certification review" (Klein 2001). The report has remained on the shelf ever since.

Drug control as a policy issue is a many headed hydra, with new substances always appearing on the borders of the classification system, often designed specifically to avoid the control criteria of treaty provisions (Shulgin 1991). The drugs of concern in the case of the Caribbean, however, are cannabis and cocaine. These are the latest in a long list of mind altering, pleasure producing, habit forming luxuries supplied to metropolitan markets by producers and traders from this region. Most of these, sugar, spices, coffee, were transplanted from other parts of the world, and grown on fertile island soils by slave labor. Once emancipated, former slaves and their descendents, incorporated these diverse foods and stimulants into the Creole tradition. Given the diversity of origin and a history of large scale population movement, the evolving Creole culture has developed a ready predisposition towards assimilating and acculturating products and ideas (Mintz 1985b). In a situation where authenticity cannot be reduced to an encompassing story of historical origin and / or the mythical assertion of blood ties, the role of consumption has become all the more important as a symbolic marker of, first, what is associated with the good life, and second, what it is to be Caribbean. Critical here is the role of the peculiar substance (Sherrat 1995) taken into the body not for the purpose of nutrition or medication in the contemporary western sense, but for that compound of leisure, pleasure, sociability, relaxation or as they say in Jamaica, "meditation".

In many European representations of Caribbean life prominence is given to the role of cannabis, which, it is assumed, is widely available, universally appreciated, culturally embedded and its consumption unhindered by legal restrictions. While they are partial reflections of a far more complex reality, they are modern day versions of a fantasia that stretches back for centuries. During the late Middle Ages a rich tradition in songs, poems, and drama had developed where artists sought to evoke the pleasures of paradise in rich descriptions of culinary pleasures and bucolic scenery (Shivelbusch 1992). This genre withered after the first founding of European overseas colonies when the means for sensory gratification shifted from the fantastical projection onto the next world, to the material reality of the New World. The possibilities of riches from gold, tropical agricultural produce, or the trade in people helped fracture the rigid boundaries of class and allow social mobility through the accumulation of wealth. It also conjured new visions of earthly delight and avenues to pleasure, unimaginable to previous generations. In due course, the Caribbean centered production of pleasure products became the foundation on which the modern, capitalist economy of consumer products was based (Mintz 1985a, Williams 1944). It was from the start accompanied by a vision of the good life that was this-worldly and sensual, and re-formulated in the contemporary presentations of mass tourism. In this particular European discourse the role of the Caribbean is that of object of consumption, but also as a receptacle for particular European fantasies of "otherness" and the good life (Sheller 2004). Important is a release from the primacy of reason and rationality, a more relaxed relationship with the body allowing for physical indulgence, facilitated by the pleasures of sun, sea and sand, and an easing of conventional taboos, particularly around sexuality. European visitors allow themselves to relax and indulge in behavior that at home would be censored or even prosecuted. This involves critically and importantly the smoking of cannabis or ganja for which the region has gained an international reputation, unjust though this may be.

The ready appeal of the notion of the European imaginary compensates for definitional difficulties spanning referent and object when applied to the Caribbean. People in different parts of Europe relate to different parts of the Caribbean often in accordance with national histories and colonial relationships. Language communities continue to distinguish Spanish speaking Cuba and Dominican

Republic, from Francophone Haiti and France *d'outre mar*, the English speaking Caribbean and the territories that are or once were a possession of the Netherlands. The discussion here is restricted to the collection of islands and coastal states once ruled by the United Kingdom and now members of the Commonwealth and the Caribbean Community and Market (CARICOM). While the circulation of goods, people, ideas and habits is recognized, the significance of the English speaking islands in the acculturation, celebration and subsequently the promotion of cannabis / ganja has been crucial and owes much to the particular web of relationships spun at the height of the British Empire.

As successive generations of Caribbean thinkers have argued sugar was the 'favorite child of capitalism' (Ortiz 1944) and the slave based plantation complex the engine that spurred capitalism and the industrial revolution into motion (Williams 1944). During the 18th century sugar production dominated the agriculture of most islands and their economies, giving rise to huge fortunes but also a political reaction against slavery and the slave trade. Led by civil society organizers, clergy and concerned politicians in the UK, it led first to a ban on the trade in slaves, and in 1838 to the abolition of slavery across the British Empire. The day, still celebrated in the Commonwealth Caribbean, witnessed the prompt and quite unanticipated departure of the entire labor force. Once emancipated, Caribbeans of African descent, turned towards farming, fishing and crafts squatting on land not claimed by white land owners or on abandoned plantations. It left the sugar planters with the problems of a serious labor shortage which was met by recruiting indentured laborers from India. During the 1840s, and 50s some 200,000 left the subcontinent for the Caribbean. Contractual terms entered into by each migrant stated that a lifetime of servitude would be rewarded with the title to a small holding of land. Most of these migrants landed in Trinidad, Guyana and Suriname, but contingents were spread all across the islands. Though the circumstances of many were undoubtedly distressing – part of an outward migration that would take Indian farmers to new homes in Africa and across the Pacific as well – it was a very different and orderly movement of people than that which had preceded it during the African slave trade. Most of the new settlers came voluntarily, accompanied by bundles of possessions and in family units. One of the many features of life in India that found its way onto the ships and was transplanted to the Caribbean was cannabis, used for religious ceremony, as a performance enhancer, for comfort and for spiritual insight for centuries (Chopra and Chopra 1957). In Trinidad and Guyana the cultivation and consumption remained confined to the Indian community, which today is close to half of the total population. It has been argued that the community was large enough to be self sufficient and endogamous. In most of the islands, however, the new migrants were too few in number to establish communities and mixed and intermarried with people of African extraction. In Jamaica the introduction of the new herb of ganja coincided with movements of cultural nationalism rejecting claims of white cultural supremacy and political dominance. Ganja, with its powerful psychoactive action, easy and agreeable mode of administration, and none of the connotation of the whip and the shackle that still spoils the taste of rum, had a ready appeal. To islanders robbed of their own history and self knowledge, cannabis presented a tool free from any European association, from which a new identity could be fashioned (Chevannes 2004). To the Jamaican Rastafarian, ganja was a part of the island's non-European history, and to this day offers a clean, natural alternative to Babylon.

Contested cultivars

For the very same reasons ganja found favor among Jamaican nationalists agitating for repatriation to Africa, better working conditions and political independence, it was viewed with alarm by the authorities. Its use as anything other than a medical tincture was unknown in Britain, but in Jamaica, the land owning members of the Assembly were quick to take advantage. At the meeting members agreed that ganja was responsible for insubordination and truculence among laborers (Chevannes 2004).

This inversion of causality became a dominant theme in the run up to independence. Protest against oppressive and unrepresentative government and exploitative working practices could be attributed to the use of a mind altering drug, and be presented as devoid of carrying any substance. Quickly an association arose of anti colonial politics and the use of ganja embraced by many Jamaican nationalists for its symbolic non-European qualities as well as its pleasant effect. It allowed the police to raid establishments where people associated and to arrest outspoken critics of government in the guise of enforcing drug control laws. In response political organizations such as the Youth Black Faith instructed members not to carry ganja to their meetings. "If policeman intervene in our congregations, him couldn't find no other charge" (Chevannes 1994: 157).

The East Indian connection continued well into the 1930s and 40s. East Indian farmers had begun peddling ganja on open markets, but as use spread and became more established with smoking contests, they began setting up herb yards. They soon gained significance as places of affordable recreation, a focus for social life and a locus for political organization (Chevannes 1994: 157). The repressive stance taken by the colonial authorities, with raids and closures of these yards and the arrests of customers, workers and proprietors survived independence in 1962, as successive governments took a strong position against any proposed change in cannabis legislation. According to the most extensive piece of interdisciplinary research conducted into the subject, (Comitas 1975), ganja use formed a critical part of the social nexus, with important ramifications for the economy, social life, individual well being and cultural identity. Critically, the study sought to debunk a prevailing stereotype that cannabis impacted negatively on productivity bound up in "a-motivational syndrome". Research in rural areas showed that farmers found ganja useful in enhancing their productivity and regarded it as an "energizer" (Comitas 1975). A different perspective on poor motivation comes from a study of Jamaican workers attitude concluding that "Jamaican workers are highly de-motivated and dissatisfied; they are deliberately producing well below their potential; they do not believe that management will share the benefits of increased production with them" (Carter 1997: 169). Low levels of trust and poor relations between workers and management are, therefore, one of the main reasons holding back advances in Jamaican productivity, yet ganja provides a convenient alibi in yet another reversal of causality.

In effect the burgeoning demand for ganja allows a host of small farmers, transporters and peddlers to eke out a living in the informal economy, arguably protected from more capital intensive competition by its legal status. While rising prices for bauxite and tourism provided for high economic growth throughout the 60s, the Jamaican economy was hard hit by the downturn of the 1970s. Ganja provided an economic safety net for many, but it also became a key source of income of the increasingly assertive organized crime groups, closely associated with the country's political class in Jamaica's bizarre political culture of clientelism known as "garrison politics" (Stone 1986), an arrangement describing the dependency of parliamentary candidates on their constituency party to ensure the return of a majority vote, for which they are rewarded with contracts and kickback (Figueroa and Figes 2002). With severe constraints on government largesse during the 1970s, constituency organizations turned to other income sources, and became increasingly independent from politicians who could at best offer protection from prosecution (Harriott 2000). This has not resulted in an easing of drug related legislation to facilitate the work of these gangs, only the suspension of the law for the protection of individual gangsters. The reasons for this can be found beyond the northern and southern rims of the Caribbean basin. Just as the Jamaican economy contracted throughout the 1970s, the activities of organized crime groups in Colombia were assuming a new level of notoriety. Within Colombia they were holding the government to ransom, in an extension of the *plumo o plata* policy of offering a choice: a bullet for non compliance, bribes for compliance (Feiling 2009). Internationally, the cartels from Medellin and Cali were extending operations into the Caribbean, with bases in the Bahamas and contacts in each island. While the financial muscle and firepower of these groups was assuming the proportions of an existential threat to Caribbean mini and micro states, the regional super power to the north was intensifying demands for cooperation on drug control (Cope 1998, West India Commission 1992). As any chance of compromising on a more accommodating arrangement with the "drugs nexus" receded after the election of Ronald Reagan and the return of a more assertive US foreign policy in the region leading to military interventions in Grenada, 1983 and Panama, 1989, the Jamaican government was caught in a cycle of escalating violence in its attempt to enforce drug control. Over the last 20 years there have been regular outbreaks of violence, with armed gangs and the security forces fighting pitched battles in the centre of Kingston, and government withdrawing from large section of the inner city. Public order is now largely maintained by the so called "dons" or heads of neighborhood gangs. According to the Jamaican government gang threat assessment survey in 2009 there are now some 268 groups earning money from cannabis, extortion, prostitution, shipping cocaine, contract killings, and international cybercrime. Nothing summarizes the ongoing interrelationship as closely as the initial refusal by the government of Bruce Golding to allow the extradition of Christopher "Dudus" Coke to the US on drug trafficking charges. Dudus was the don of Tivoli Gardens, which happened to be as from 2005 the parliamentary constituency of the Prime Minister and before that of the one time PM and long serving opposition leader Edward Seaga. In the early months of 2010 the Jamaican government found itself on the horn of a dilemma over the removal of Dudus who came into post in 1992 after the death of his father, the leader of the notorious "Shower Posse" – so called because they showered their some 1,000 or so victims with bullets – in a mysterious jailhouse fire. The gangster controls the electoral machine in the parliamentary seat of the head of government. He is privy to many secrets and private arrangements of leading members of government, an intimacy that finds expression in the regular appearance of leading politicians in the funeral corteges of the most notorious gangsters. Moreover, the actual extradition could spark riots, as followed the death of Lester Coke, with the toll of eight lives, and destabilize an already volatile neighborhood. The case exemplifies the political difficulty of a government that has no control over, and little by way of legitimacy, in sections of the capital, and is beholden to organized crime groups. It can neither cut its connection, nor, given the pressure from international partners. When Bruce Golding finally decided to accede to the US extradition request and ordered the arrest of Dudus Coke, parts of Kingston rose up in arms. For five days security forces and armed gangs battled it out in the different parts of Kingston. By the end, just under a hundred people had been killed, there were many more injuries and some 500 young men were rounded up and held in the national stadium. The economy of the tourism dependant island was severely affected and the reputation of the government in shreds, while Dudus Coke remained at large for many weeks. It was widely rumoured that the 'don' was planning to trade in information on leading politicians in return for a lighter sentence. For that reason there were doubts whether his safety could be guaranteed if he were apprehended by the Jamaican Constabulary. It was speculated that he was hoping to trade in information on leading politicians in Jamaica and beyond for a lighter sentence. For the same reasons his safety could not be guaranteed if apprehended by the Jamaican Constabulary.

The result is an ongoing spiral of violent crime that left Jamaica with a tally of 1,672 homicides in 2009 (Caricom News Network 2009), the highest in its history and one of the highest relative to population in the world.

Smoke filled symbol

In Jamaica, but even more so in other parts of the English speaking Caribbean, then, cannabis remains a contested symbol. To many it is closely associated with the violence and gang culture that has blighted large parts of Kingston as well as Port of Spain and Castries. Positions on the benefits and drawbacks of ganja are isomorphs of other forms of social delineations, and have been famously equated with a longstanding Caribbean opposition of Respectability and Reputation. The pursuit for respect is imbued in the educational system (over stretched but full of examples of good practice), the church and the corridors of government, the largest employer in most Caribbean countries. To those with poor educational attainments, alternative religious associations and working on the land, as casual laborers or in the informal economy the objective is to gain a reputation (Littlewood 1988). Opinions on ganja are divided, with most in the latter group varying from enthusiastic support to at best neutral indifference, while the former will start with indifference and range to prohibition. Frequent anomalies cross the boundaries, and in Jamaica at least, there is little support for either the resort to incarceration for cannabis offenders or chemical spraying for the eradication of plants. Manual eradication was used to clear 307,530 hectares of marijuana in 2004, 303,961 hectares in 2005 and 291,515 hectares in 2006 (MEM 2007). There has been little effect on availability or price.

While positions on the benefits of cannabis are divided, Jamaicans are pretty united in their stand that the metaphor of war is quite unjustified.

The attitude is far less sanguine with regard to cocaine, and particularly towards crack. There are pockets of consumption all over the islands, particularly the city, but they remain small, underground and subject to social stigma (Day 2004). Caribbean cocaine presents a double paradox. On the one hand it remains as readily available as it was some fifteen years ago, when the United Nations Office on Drugs and Crime organized an international conference of regional and partner government to launch the multi stranded Barbados Plan of Action. Hundreds of millions of dollars later, there have been sharp increases in the overall prison population and homicide rates, but cocaine remains widely available and cheap. But this availability, as well as the continuing involvement of a myriad of handlers, boatmen, bagmen, lookouts, security, packers, storers, couriers and so on, has in no way raised its social acceptability. Objections are easily defined by folk notions that distinguish between a synthetic drug like cocaine and a natural herb, like ganja. There is a Manichean opposition at work, where cocaine (including crack) represents all that is wicked, evil, and Babylon, while ganja captures goodness, nature and Africa, with many proponents quite unaware of ganja's Indian origins. The legal prohibition of so benign and beneficial a substance is seen as just one more indicator of the moral corruption of the political system (Broad and Feinberg 1995). Conversely cocaine, invented and consumed mainly by Americans and Europeans, is seen as leaving a trail of detrimental consequences in its wake. Many families have suffered crack related property crime or witnessed the addiction of one of their members. In the open spaces of cities across the region homeless crack addicts are washing cars during the night, where women offer sexual services to feed their habit at night.

There is no doubt that social opprobrium comes at the end of a cycle that kicks off with a celebration of cocaine's peachy pleasures (Hamid 1990) and promise of riches.

In the mid 2000s Suriname, on the fringes of the political Caribbean[1] was opened as a trafficking route into Europe. Invariably some of the cocaine destined for transshipment spilled over into local markets. Paramaribo, a city divided according to class and race, soon had its first crack houses. In one of the poorest neighborhoods inhabited by descendants of former slaves, there are no signs of economic activity, and the large presence of adults during all hours of the day suggests that few are commuting to more prosperous parts for work. The only compound with activity is the crack house, a large double storied, wooden house surrounded by a perimeter fence. On the ground floor rocks of crack are traded for the equivalent of three dollars, while the upper floor doubles up as a flop house. The women working there appear withdrawn, the customers of the ground floor establishment furtive, in the oppressive, listless atmosphere of self destruction and decay. Yet the owner, a young man in a bright red t-shirt, is amiable and effusive in welcoming the church outreach group into his compound. He mobilizes his staff, customers and hangers on to join in the prayer meeting. Next we have the bizarre situation of church elder and neighborhood crack house owner and pimp holding hands in prayer, calling for Jesus to deliver the wretched souls from their addiction.

At work here is the innocence of isolated communities and the celebration of economic success. The attraction of the drugs economy is that it is so easy to enter, and that the skills required are relatively easy to master, as long as it aligns with cultural mores (Bourgois 1995) and the entrant is willing to break the law (Matrix 2007). But the economic opportunities of crack cocaine are outweighed by social censure that sets in within a short period of time. The confluence of medical, social and economic problems for habitual users of this fast acting, short lasting drug has given social backing to the politics of prohibition.

The impact of drug control on society, culture and environment

In the popular discourse on mind-altering substances throughout the Commonwealth Caribbean then, cannabis and cocaine are entirely different entities treated equally by the law. The equivalence is a legal fiction, unsupported by scientific evidence, with no resonance in folkloric taxonomies and cultural experiences, and no political support. International donors entered into the drug control fray for fear of cocaine shipments, not to curtail local cannabis production. Yet the determination, agreed during the mid 1990s in a series of international conferences, to get on top of the 'drug menace' has resulted in the sharpening of legislation, the prioritization of drug offences and an upgrading of law enforcement capabilities. Increases in arrests,

1 Suriname receives international development assistance from the EU under regional programs for the Caribbean and is member of various Caribbean organizations. But in contrast to neighboring Guyana the Surinamese have little affinity with their Caribbean partners. They speak Suritong, not English and prefer bird keeping and fireworks to cricket.

convictions, and prison populations soon followed. Prison overcrowding, accelerated re-offending and the absorption of petty offenders into criminal networks sparked an increase in offending across the region (Singh 2004). Yet comprehensive solutions as suggested by the Jamaican Ganja Commission with the de-penalization of ganja possession ran into US opposition.

Caribbean countries, therefore face an extraordinary challenge, where they are pushed by international partners into a continuously expanding war on drugs, with high costs in terms of physical resources and the strain on governance, at the same time as the use of cannabis is approaching normalization and ganja cultivation and sales are becoming a life line for a battered informal sector. The consequences of this inability to develop a regional response become apparent by the example of St. Vincent, the largest producer of cannabis in the English speaking Caribbean after Jamaica. The difference being that St. Vincent has a population of merely 215,000, and did not start producing cannabis until the 1970s. Since then the island's economy has been most adversely affected by the progressive erosion of trade preferences for Caribbean bananas. The number of registered banana farmers fell to 2,300 in 2003 (EC 2004), with knock on effects on other parts of the economy and rural communities manifest in unemployment rates of 22% in St. Vincent and the Grenadines in 2001. In contrast to neighboring islands, St. Vincent has a highly underdeveloped tourist industry, leaving cannabis production as one of few options where Vincennian farmers enjoy a competitive advantage (Klein 2004b, NERA 2004).

Marijuana production now provides a livelihood for a significant number of farmers, and the main source of revenue for many rural households, supporting family units and entire communities. In the late 1990s, loosely organized ganja farmers emerged to become a factor in national politics (Klein 2004b). According to the US State Department St Vincent is not only the largest producer but also the source of much of the marijuana used in the Eastern Caribbean (INCSR 2006). The government is caught in between the demands of international partners for the enforcement of drug control agreements, and the increasingly assertive constituency

Table 2.1 Tourist arrivals in selected islands

Destination	Tourist Arrivals Jan-Dec 2006	Population
Antigua and Barbuda	253,669	85,000
Barbados	562,558	294,000
British Virgin Islands	356,271	23,000
Martinique	502,053	399,000
St. Lucia	302,510	165,000
St. Maarten / Martin	467,804	33,000
St.Vincent and Grenadines	97,432	120,000

Source: Caribbean Tourism Organization, 2007

Table 2.2 Drug related crimes in St. Vincent

Drug trafficking	2002	2003	2004
Convictions	335	393	107

Source: Mutual Evaluation Mechanism Country Report St. Vincent, CICAD/OAS

of cannabis cultivators and consumers. The costs include a rising prison population of 367 in 2006 (312 per 100,000) (ICPS 2010), overcrowding, criminalization and recidivism, as well as placing heavy demands on the 789 strong police force. It also threatens to erode public support for the law, and to undermine the perception of good governance. In rural areas the policy has marginalized entire communities, by de-legitimizing their means of livelihood.

Yet under pressure from international partners and neighbors, the Vincennian government concedes to participate in regular eradication exercises. Troops from the Regional Security System, the military apparatus of the Organization of Eastern Caribbean States, with US logistical support attack the cannabis farms on the slopes of Mt. Soufriere, the centre of cannabis production. There is no resistance, farmers are usually tipped off days in advance, the date often falls just after the harvest, and troops from around the region enjoy the opportunity to train (Bowling 2010). But the ecological consequences are listed by a Vincennian journalist: Cannabis farmers are pushed deeper into the forest, clearing new land where they can avoid detection under cover of the trees. The consequence has been the rapid deforestation of the island. As a result "our rivers and streams are muddy, full of silt from the removal of valuable top soil when rain comes. In the dry season, the flows are extremely low. Some streams no longer flow, several springs have disappeared. Our coral reefs/ fish nurseries and coastal protection barriers are being stifled by silt eroded from de-vegetated land" (Cottle 2002).

Conclusion

Caribbean countries are trapped in a policy matrix that mandates the prohibition of a substance that is locally grown and enjoys a substantial local market, and is symbolically tied in with media of expression and as a marker of identity. Governments in Jamaica, St. Vincent, Trinidad, Dominica and St. Lucia have long eased up all serious efforts at controlling consumption and are struggling in finding the right response to cultivation. The damage to the environment will erode the long term viability of economies based on tourism and / or agriculture, while the social consequences of increasing persecution are unsustainable levels of crime. One of the key problems is that where drug control is concerned national sovereignty has been pooled, preventing individual countries from designing their own responses. This model, forged at the beginning of the last century is in urgent need of an overhaul, to allow for the formulation of cannabis control suited to countries and their individual needs. One such option would be the Caricom Cannabis protocol to determine the production, distribution and consumption within the English speaking Caribbean, and possibly a quota of exports for overseas markets.

The rationale of the CARICOM Cannabis Protocol is to separate the cannabis and cocaine markets and effect a differential in the way the authorities are dealing with the two substances. The overarching policy principle is taken from the 2002 CARICOM resolution that drugs are a medical, as well as a criminal justice issue, and developed into the pursuit of harm reduction as the primary policy objective. Current policies, as exemplified by the rampages in Kingston, Jamaica in late May 2010, inflict more damage than the actual drugs themselves. In recognition of the inability of governments to impose prohibition by decree, a regulatory approach should be taken. Taking the recommendations of the Jamaican Ganja Commission as a point of departure, the protocol opens with the de-penalization of all cannabis possession, thereby removing a significant burden from Caribbean criminal justice systems (police, courts and prisons) and immediately easing relations between the authorities and the community. The next clauses are aimed to regulate consumption – in private homes and designated places, trade – in designated areas, and production. Cannabis production for commercial purposes, say more than five plants, is restricted to a farming cooperative. The protocol is based on the understanding that most cannabis farmers are strictly that – farmers, often pushed into illegality because legitimate forms of gaining a livelihood have been closed off due to deteriorating terms of trade.

The Caribbean Cannabis Protocol has to be framed by strictures on export and marketing to avoid collision with external partners and stay within the terms of reference of drug control treaties. In all likelihood, some form of accommodation with the current control regime will have to be found, but the price for inertia, is that Caribbean countries are sucked into the vortex of violence that has destabilized Mexico and Colombia. Given the vibrancy of civic institutions in the English speaking Caribbean, often referred to as an chain of democracy, where fundamental democratic freedoms such as the independence of the courts, a free and critical press, and regime change by the ballot box prevail, there is a ready opportunity to build on solid foundations, and possibly pave the way for changes further ashore.

List of references

Armenta, A., Jelsma, M., Metall, P., Blickman, T. and Montanes,V. 2003. *Forward Operating Locations in Latin America.* Amsterdam: Transnational Institute.

Bagley, W.M. and Walker, W.O. 1994. *Drug Trafficking in the Americas.* New Brunswick: Transaction Publishers.

Bayer, I. 2009. *Development of the Convention on Psychotropic Substances 1971.* Unpublished paper Expert seminar on the classification of controlled substances, Transnational Institute, Amsterdam, 10/12/2009.

Beruff, J.R. and Cordero, G. 2005. The Caribbean: The "Third Border" and the War on Drugs, in *Drugs and Democracy in Latin America – The Impact of US Policy,* edited by C.A. Youngers and E. Rosin. Boulder, Colorado: Lynne River Publishers Inc, 15-60.

Bethel, T.A. 2002. Caribbean Narcotics Trafficking: What is to be Done? *The Defence Institute of Security Assistance Management Journal,* 24(3), 80-90.

Bourgois, P. 1995. *In Search of Respect: selling crack in El Barrio.* Cambridge: Cambridge University Press.

Bowling, B. 2010. *Policing The Caribbean. Transnational Security Cooperation in Practice.* Oxford: Oxford University Press.

Bryan, A. 2002. Transnational Organized Crime in the Caribbean: The International Relations Context, in *Caribbean Survival and the Global Challenge,* edited by R. Ramsaran. Kingston, Jamaica: Ian Randle Publishers, 65-82.

Broad, K. and Feinberg, B. 1995. Perceptions of Ganja and Cocaine in Urban Jamaica. *Journal of Psychoactive Drugs,* 27(3), 261-76.

Caricom News Network 2009. *Jamaica opposition alarmed at 2009 crime statistics worst ever* [Online: Caricom News Network]. Available at: http://csmenetwork.com [accessed: 23 February 2010].

Carter, K. 1997. *Why workers won't work. The worker in a developing economy. A case study of Jamaica.* London: Macmillan.

Chevannes, B. 2004. Criminalizing Cultural Practice. The Case of Ganja in Jamaica, in *Caribbean Drugs: From Criminalization to Harm Reduction,* edited by A. Klein, M. Day and A. Harriott. London: Zed, 67-81.

Chevannes, B. 1994. *Rastafari: Roots and Ideology.* New York: Syracuse University Press.

Chopra, I.C. and Chopra R.N. 1957. The Use of the Cannabis Drugs in India. *Bulletin of Narcotics,* 1, 4-29.

Comitas, L. 1975. The Social Nexus of Ganja in Jamaica, in *Cannabis and Culture,* edited by V. Rubin. The Hague: Mouton Press.

Cope, J. 1998. A United States View of Strategic Balance in the Americas, in *Regional Perspectives on Strategic Balance and Confidence Building Measures in the Americas,* edited by J.S. Tulchin and F. Aravena. Stanford, California: Woodrow Wilson Centre, 60-75.

Cottle, Junios Spirit 2002. *Poverty, Marijuana and Deforestation.* Vincennian Press: Kingstown, St. Vincent.

Day, M. 2004. What is the Hook? Diary of Drop in Centre or Rehabilitation before Abstinence, in *Caribbean Drugs: From Criminalization to Harm Reduction,* edited by A. Klein, M. Day and A. Harriott. London: Zed, 155-171.

European Commission 2004. *Working briefs on the SFA program in Dominica, St. Lucia and St. Vincent and the Grenadines.* Bridgetown, Barbados: EC Delegation.

Feiling, T. 2009. *The Candy Machine: How cocaine took over the world.* London: Penguin.

Figueroa, M. and Figes, A. 2002. Homogenous Voting, Electoral Manipulation and the 'Garrison' Process in Post-Independence Jamaica, *Commonwealth & Comparative Politics*, 40, 81-108.

Griffith, I.L. 2004. *Caribbean Security in the Age of Terror – Challenge and Change.* Kingston, Jamaica: Ian Randle Publishers.

Griffith, I.L. 2002. Caribbean Security in the Age of Terror – Challenge of Intrusion and Governance, in *Governance in the Age of Globalization – Caribbean Perspectives,* edited by K.O. Hall and D. Ben. Kingston, Jamaica: Ian Randle Publishers, 383-415.

Griffith, I.L. 1997. *Drugs and Security in the Caribbean – Sovereignty Under Siege.* Pennsylvania: Pennsylvania State University.

Griffith, I.L. 1993. *The Quest for Security in the Caribbean – Problems and Promises in Subordinate States.* Armonk, New York: M.E Sharpe.

Hamid, A. 1990. The political economy of crack related violence. *Contemporary Drug Problems*, 17(10), 31-78.

Harriott, A. 2000. *Police and Crime in Jamaica.* Kingston, Jamaica: University of the West Indies Press.

HAC 2010. *The Cocaine Trade* [Online: Home Affairs Committee, London: Houses of Parliament, House of Commons]. Available at: http://www.publications.parliament.uk [accessed: 20 May 2010].

ICPS 2010. *World Prison Brief.* London: King's College. [Online: International Centre for Prison Studies]. Available at : http://www.kcl.ac.uk/depsta/law/research/icps/worldbrief/ [accessed: 16 August 2009].

International Narcotics Control Strategy Report 2006. *The Caribbean.* Washington, D.C.: U.S. State Department.

Klein, A. 2001. Between the Death Penalty and Decriminalization: New Directions for Drug Control in the Commonwealth Caribbean. *New West India Guide,* 75(3-4), 193-228.

Klein, A. 2004a. The Search for a New Policy Framework: From the Barbados Plan of Action to the Ganja Commission, in *Caribbean Drugs: From Criminalization to Harm Reduction,* edited by A. Klein, M. Day and A. Harriott. London: Zed, 9-64.

Klein, A. 2004b. The Ganja Industry and Alternative Development in St. Vincent and the Grenadines, in *Caribbean Drugs: From Criminalization to Harm Reduction,* edited by A. Klein, M. Day and A. Harriott. London: Zed, 224-244.

Littlewood, R. 1988. Vice to Madness: The Semantics of Naturalistic and Personalistic Understanding in Trinidadian Local Medicine. *Social Science and Medicine,* 27(2), 129-48.

Matrix Knowledge Group 2007. *The Illicit Drug Trade in the United Kingdom.* London: Matrix Knowledge Group. [Online: Home Office] Available at: http://rds.homeoffice.gov.uk/rds/pdfs07/rdsolr2007.pdf [accessed: 16 August 2008].

MEM 2004. *St. Vincent and the Grenadines. Evaluation of progress in drug control 2003-2004.* [Online: CICAD, Organisation of American States]. Available at: http://www.cicad.oas.org/MEM/ENG/Reports/Progress_2003-2004/St%20Vincent%20and%20the%20Grenadines%20-%20ENG.pdf [accessed: 12 May 2010].

MEM 2007. *Jamaica. Evaluation of Progress in Drug Control 2005-2006.* [Online: CICAD, Organisation of American States] Available at: http://www.cicad.oas.org/MEM/ENG/Reports/Fourth%20Round%20Full/Jamaica%20-%20Fourth%20Round%20-%20ENG.pdf. [accessed:14 May 2010].

Meyer, M., Youngers, C. and Bewley-Taylor, D. 2007. *At a Crossroads: Drug Trafficking, Violence and the Mexican State.* Washington Office on Latin America (WOLA)-Beckley Foundation Drug Policy Programme, Briefing Paper 13.

Mintz, S.W. 1985a. *Sweetness and Power: The Place of Sugar in Modern History.* New York: Viking.

Mintz, S.W. 1985b. From Plantations to Peasantries in the Caribbean, in *Caribbean Contours,* edited by S.W. Mintz and S. Price. Baltimore: The Johns Hopkins University Press, 127–53.

NERA Consulting 2004. *Addressing the Impact of Preference Erosion in Bananas on Caribbean Countries.* [On-line: Caribbean Trade Reference Center]. Available at: http://ctrc.sice.oas.org/trc/Articles/DFID,%20bananas.pdf. [accessed: 2 November 2009].

Ortiz, F. 1944. *Cuban Counterpoint: Tobacco and Sugar.* Durham: Durham University Press.

Schivelbusch, W. 1992. *Tastes of Paradise: A social history of spices, stimulants and intoxicants.* New York: Pantheon.

Sheller, M. 2004. *Consuming the Caribbean.* London: Routledge.

Sherrat, A. 1995. Introduction: Peculiar Substances, in *Consuming Habits: drugs in history and anthropology,* edited by J. Goodman, P. Lovejoy and A. Sherrat. London: Routledge, 1-11.

Shulgin, A. 1991. *Pihkal: A Chemical Love Story.* Berkeley: Transform Press,

Singh, W. 2004. Drugs and the Prison System: Impact of Legislative Changes on the Prison Crisis in the Commonwealth Caribbean Region, in *Caribbean Drugs: From Criminalization to Harm Reduction,* edited by A. Klein, M. Day and A. Harriott. London: Zed, 101-19.

SOCA 2008. *UK Threat Assessment.* London: Serious Organised Crime Agency.

Stone, C. 1986. *Class, Race and Democracy in Jamaica.* New York: Praeger.

UNODC and World Bank 2007. *Crime, Violence, and Development: Trends, Costs, and Policy Options in the Caribbean. A Joint Report by the United Nations Office on Drugs and Crime and the Latin America and the Caribbean Region of the World Bank.* Vienna: UNODC.

Vargas, R. 2005. Drugs and Armed Conflict in Colombia, in *Trouble in the Triangle: Opium and Conflict in Burma,* edited by M. Jelsma, T. Kramer and P. Verves. London: Silkworm Books, 193-224.

West India Commission 1992. *Time for Action: A Report of the West India Commission.* Bridgetown, Barbados: Black Rock.

Williams, E. 1944. *Capitalism and Slavery.* London: Andre Deutsch.

Youngers, C. and Rosin E. 2005. *Drugs and Democracy in Latin America: The Impact of U.S. Policy*. Boulder: Lynne Reinner Publishers.

Zirnite, P. 1997. *Reluctant Recruits: The US Military and the War on Drugs*. Washington: Washington Office on Latin America.

Chapter 3
Cannabis Cultivation Practices in the Moroccan Rif

Kenza Afsahi

The Rif is one of the regions in the world where cannabis has been grown using traditional methods for several centuries. Since the 1960s, cannabis cultivation has increased to meet European demand, mobilizing thousands of rural workers as well as generating income and employment in a region suffering from underdevelopment and social marginalization.

This chapter aims to explain the specific nature of cannabis cultivation in the Rif region, while providing the widest possible overview of this agricultural economy.[1] We will see in the first part how the cannabis cultivation industry developed and grew in scale from the 1960s onward. These successive expansions produced several cultivation areas. We will also see how this family-based cultivation is organized, from the sowing stage to transformation of the cannabis into resin. We will complete our investigation by examining how the tasks are shared within the family unit, the use of outside labor, working the land and the use of fertilizers, transformation of herbal cannabis into resin, the quality of Moroccan cannabis and its levels of THC (Tetrahydrocannabinol). Finally, we will see what benefits cannabis brings to the local economy and individuals, as well as the numerous social, economic, and environmental restrictions associated with this activity, which make the situation very complex when it comes to implementing lasting solutions in terms of development.

1 The data used here comes from a doctoral dissertation on cannabis producers (Afsahi 2009). The empirical research is based on qualitative data collection methods: interviews, observations, and focus groups collected through various means between 2002 and 2007. A final field observation was carried out in 2010. The field observation also included quantitative data collected while working with UNODC (United Nations Office on Drugs and Crime) in 2003 and 2004. This data concerns areas of cannabis cultivation, the use of fertilizers and outside labor, the crop calendar, the different yields of rain-fed and irrigated cultivation, areas cultivated with other crops and their yields, revenue from cannabis and other agricultural and non-agricultural activities, and THC levels. The first database from 2003 covers a considerable range, including data for around 2000 farmers spread across five provinces in the Rif. 2003 is a key year when cannabis cultivation seems to have peaked, before declining over the following years.

The growth of cannabis cultivation in Morocco[2]

Originally cultivated in small quantities and consumed using traditional methods, Moroccan cannabis was not initially produced to satisfy the international market. Its origins in Morocco can be traced back to between the seventh and fifteenth century in the wake of one of the many Arab invasions which affected the north of Africa (Lugan 2000). Its cultivation started to develop from the sixteenth century in an area of the Rif region covering some 40 km^2 at Ketama in the province of Al Hoceima, and to some extent at Bab Berred in the province of Chefchaouen. These areas are now considered to be the traditional cultivation region. It is only from the end of the eighteenth century that the Rif became the main producing region (Bellakhdar 1997). Before that time, cannabis had been grown all over Morocco in private gardens, allotments and orchards – but never on a large scale. Cultivation was not restricted to this northern region; evidence of *kif* cultivation has also been traced to the oases in the south of the country, where it was exported to Sudan. At the end of the nineteenth century, Mohammed Ben Tayeb, the dervish that Auguste Moulièras tasked with exploring the Rif, noticed that three tribes were cultivating cannabis: the Beni Bou Nsar, the Beni Seddate, and the Ketama. At the time, *kif* from the Rif was known throughout the country (Moulièras 1895). In 1890, the sultan Moulay Hassan (1873-1894) drew up strict laws to limit its trade, authorizing, however, five *douars*[3] of the original tribes to cultivate *kif*, thus starting a tradition that has continued up to the present day.

The consumption of cannabis became part of the people's daily life. Men would consume it in its chopped form (*kif*) mixed with tobacco and inhaled using a pipe called a *sebsi*. The women would prepare cakes that were very popular during festivals and would use it as a cosmetic or medicinal product (Afsahi 2002).

Protectorates, both French and Spanish, have contributed on several occasions to the development of cannabis cultivation. Since independence in 1956 cultivation has been forbidden throughout Morocco – except in the traditional cultivation area where it has been tolerated in order to mitigate the conflicts inherited, in particular, from the Rif War. Despite being illegal since independence, cannabis cultivation slowly expanded to new tribes, then to new villages in new cultivation areas. During the 1950s, cannabis cultivation, concentrated until then in a restricted area, spread to other tribes. By 1960, there were 12 tribes involved (Zaim 1997).

At that time, the Rif represented an important demographic center, and its population had long been struggling in its own environment (lack of water, lack of land, etc.). Illegal activities, such as the smuggling or cultivation of cannabis, were already enabling the population to survive and develop.

---

2 This part is a brief summary of a piece of work produced using documents and archives, providing a better understanding of the history of cannabis in Morocco. The interviews and observations carried out with producers also helped to paint the historical background (Afsahi 2009).

3 Villages.

An important turning point occurred in the 1970s, where rural workers in the traditional producing regions were taught by Western travelers – mostly groups of hippies fascinated with the Moroccan culture (and inspired by musicians such as the Rolling Stones) – the techniques to turn kif into hashish (Borg 1970). The traditional cultivation area was still isolated, but rural workers started to meet a growing demand in Europe for hashish, and increased their income. This was the start of the "industrialization of *kif*" in the Rif.

During the 1980s and 1990s, the European demand for hashish grew further still. The drug culture was born, and a growing market was established for hashish in Europe and for marihuana in the United States. There was an explosive growth in demand encouraging more cultivation in both active and potential producing countries (Moreno 1997). At the same time, Morocco was experiencing an economic crisis due to its growing external debt and successive poor harvests (Anegay 2001). As cannabis cultivation was still tolerated, structures were put in place for Moroccan trade networks. European users started to source their hashish from Morocco rather than Afghanistan and Lebanon, with Morocco benefiting from the state of war prevailing in these two countries (Clarke 1998). Rural workers slowly increased their cultivation areas: the cultivation region grew from 5,000 to 10,000 hectares during the 1980s, 50,000 hectares in 1994, and 70,000 hectares in 1998 (Anegay 2001).

In 2003, cultivation was taking place in the five provinces of Chefchaouen, Al-Hoceima, Taounate, Larache, and Tétouan across an area totaling 134,000 hectares. In 2003 and 2004, the area being cultivated reached 134,000 hectares and 120,500 hectares respectively. The production of raw cannabis was estimated at 109,000 tons in 2003 and 98,000 tons in 2004; the figures for the production of resin were 3,073 tons in 2003, and 2,763 tons in 2004.[4] During these two years, the province of Chefchaouen alone was cultivating more than half of the total area, and even though a 10% drop in land area was observed between 2003 and 2004,[5] crop production increased by 13% in Chefchaouen (UNODC 2003, 2005).

In 2003, several cultivation areas co-existed: the traditional region, the birthplace of cannabis cultivation in the Rif, and "the new cultivation areas" where cultivation was introduced in the 1980s and 1990s. These different zones created several cultivation areas where techniques were not assimilated in the same way. Ketama remains the "training" village as the one sharing its knowledge with the other communities through seasonal migration. In addition, access to land and water has created a division between small-time farmers cultivating on "*bour*" (rain-fed) plots and those cultivating in large irrigated valleys.

Up to now, cannabis has helped stabilize the economic situation of the population in the region. But whether this leads to further expansion of the industry now depends on government policy. Between 2004 and 2005, cannabis cultivation

4 1,270 kg of raw cannabis was yielded for each hectare of irrigated land and 750 kg for each hectare of "*bour*" (rainfed) land (UNODC 2003).

5 Drop in particular in the province of Al Hoceima due to an earthquake in 2004.

dropped by 40% to 72,500 ha (UNODC 2006) (see figure 3.1). Two factors explain this drop. First, it was a very poor crop year in which a drought reduced the number of irrigated plots. Second, awareness campaigns were encouraging farmers to stop cultivating cannabis, and numerous eradication operations were conducted, especially in the provinces of Larache and Taounate.

In 2006, certain producers in Ketama mentioned that the price of raw cannabis reached 100 DH, thus regaining the price it had before the expansion of cultivation areas in recent years. In 2009, the Moroccan government estimated that there were up to 60,000 hectares of cultivated land and anticipated another drop in 2010 to 50,000 hectares.

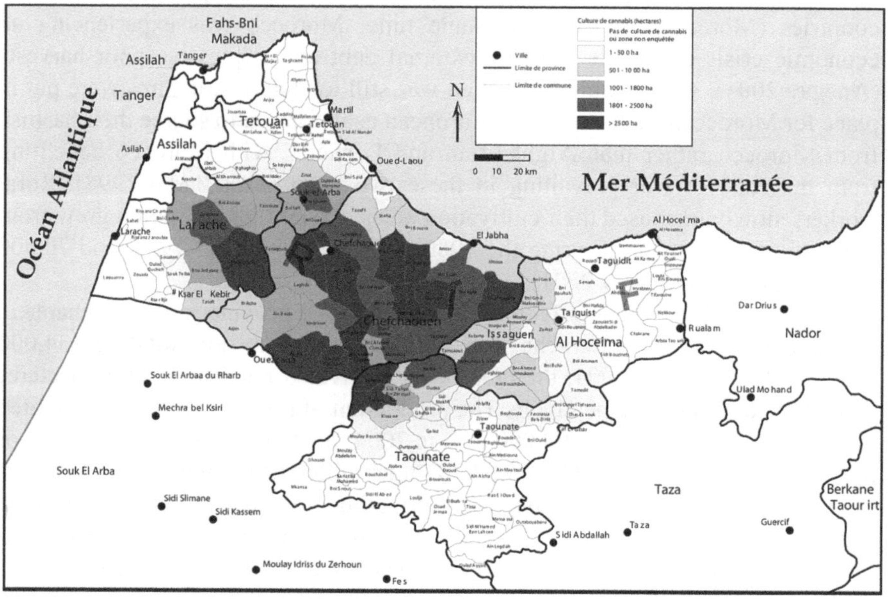

Figure 3.1 Cannabis cultivation in the provinces of Northern Morocco in 2004 (per community)

Organization of family-unit cannabis operations: cultivation, transformation, commercialization[6]

Domestic cultivation and the market economy

Although cannabis is cultivated in different areas depending on geographic (relief and elevation of terrain; presence or absence of water for irrigation) and social (contribution of men and women, mastering of knowledge, risk taking) factors,

6 The description of cultivation stages described in this part is derived from observations made during fieldwork.

organization of this practice remains the prerogative of families, where men, women, and children all play a role. The family work unit is responsible for all cultivation operations (plowing, hoeing, threshing, protecting crops against theft, harvesting) with tasks being shared out according to expertise. Once the men have mastered the knowledge, they teach the women, who become a real support for both the actual cultivation and anything connected to it, such as the preparation of meals for outside labor. The children are also involved in different farming activities, which enables the adults to relieve themselves of certain tasks that are not linked to cannabis. Thus, from the age of seven, when they are not at school, children are tasked with looking after the goats. Young girls are given the job of collecting wood, weeding the cereal plots, separating the cannabis, and transporting the fertilizer.

We distinguish between two types of family farming in the cultivation of cannabis: a) families where the work is done only by members of the family itself; and b) families where paid workers are employed to strengthen the development of the business. We also distinguish between family operations close to domestic economies, mainly located in the traditional cultivation region, and those that move closer to market economies, mainly located in the new cultivation areas.

In the traditional cannabis area, cultivation forms part of the "domestic economy", i.e. the whole family unit must be involved in cultivation-related tasks. The use of outside labor is less prevalent here than in the new cultivation areas. Overall, cannabis is a cash crop whose value is closely linked to the market.

Cannabis cultivation has brought a new division of labor within the family unit. Just like in a small enterprise, each person participates according to their abilities. The men, who manage the family assets, often provide the land and financial capital necessary to buy the crop inputs (fertilizers and plant disease control products), and pay the farm workers when they are necessary. Other members of the family help by looking after the crops. In addition, cannabis cultivation often leads to generation-specific specialization: the older generations are responsible for managing and monitoring the traditional agricultural activities (cereals, animal husbandry, legumes, olive trees, almond trees, etc.), while the young take care of the new cash crop: cannabis.

Women and the accumulation of tasks[7]

Though the drug trade puts men at centre stage in the Rif area, women are highly involved in the cultivation of cannabis. Although their participation differs according to the *douar* they belong to, the environment (availability of land, water, terrain), the family structure (size and composition of the household), and the

7 This part is a summary of work carried out on the role of women in the cultivation of cannabis in the Rif, based on the analysis of 13 interviews carried out in 2003, 30 focus groups in 2004, and observations made throughout the fieldwork.

economic conditions of the household (existence of other resources or activities that generate income), women are allocated tasks that they have gained and mastered knowledge of – mainly weeding and harvesting. However, in some villages, they are involved in virtually all stages of cultivation. Thus, in certain fishing villages on the Mediterranean coast, where the men are off fishing for several days in a row, they have taken on full responsibility for cultivating cannabis and are even involved in selling it.

Most often, however, the men (who are responsible for teaching the women) exclude women from "technical" operations such as irrigation, enriching the soil, plant disease control treatments, and the transformation of cannabis into resin. Several reasons can explain this stigmatization of women at these stages of the cultivation: the low labor requirements, the lack of confidence that the men place in the women, and the risk incurred. These three reasons come together especially when it comes to transforming the cannabis into hashish and selling it, which also falls under communication with buyers/outsiders – an activity exclusively reserved for men in this still very traditional society.

Overall, the knowledge of the women has evolved, particularly in the *douars* where cannabis has been present since the 1990s. In the cultivation stages, where the women do not participate directly, they bring food to the men in the fields. It is the women who also look after the outside labor, as well as regular domestic tasks, which are substantial. Besides cultivation-related work, the women take care of safeguarding the crops; feeding, watering, and milking the animals; supplying water and wood; foraging; household jobs (which is essentially the preparation of meals – a major job when it comes to feeding farm workers); cleaning the home; educating the children, and; going to the market.

Cannabis cultivation and THC

Cannabis is an annual herbaceous plant whose characteristics (appearance, THC level) depend on the conditions (diversity of soil, relief, climate-sun, wind, rain, etc.- diversity in the duration and cycles of seasons, knowledge, cultivation practices) in which they develop. Variation in growing conditions also impacts yields (quality and quantity harvested).

According to Clarke (2004), we still have little information on how *kif* was traditionally produced. Due to the industrial production of hashish for export, the cannabis cultivated has undergone selective reproduction in order to obtain a variety of resinous hashish that resembles Lebanese and *hindu kush* varieties: large leaves, short growing cycle, highly resinous. According to Clarke (2004), varieties of Moroccan cannabis are probably related to *cannabis indica*. Field observations carried out at Bab Berred and Kétama in 2004 and 2010, with rural workers who have been cultivating cannabis for several decades and who are highly involved in trafficking it, have revealed that they had combined two varieties of cannabis: a Moroccan variety and a Pakistani variety, which gives a slightly more golden color to the resin.

Moroccan cannabis and its cultivation possess unique characteristics linked to the climate, landscape, and knowledge of the farmers in the Rif. This knowledge is transferred from generation to generation in the traditional cultivation region, and it is imparted to other areas through outside labor, when farm workers make their seasonal migrations. Over time, producers in non-traditional cultivation areas have also helped developing new cultivation regions. The variety of characteristics in these areas and the disparity in knowledge had an impact on the cannabis THC level and its quality.

The UNODC survey conducted in 2004 (UNODC 2005) relied on a sampling strategy that took five criteria into account: 1) areas at high, medium, or low altitudes; 2) irrigated or rain-fed plots; 3) climate-related factors; 4) the use of fertilizers and pesticides; and 5) processing of the plants. Samples were collected from 30 plots in the three provinces Al Hoceima, Chefchaouen, and Larache, and concerned freshly grown plants that had arrived at maturity, and then been dried and reduced into powder before being transformed into blocks. The results corroborated data contained in literature on cannabis: the tops of the female plants have higher levels of THC (from 1.1% to 7.1 %, average of 2.7%) than the leaves (from 0.2 to 2.6%, average of 1.2%). The level of THC increased from cannabis plants that were still growing (from 0.1% to 1.5%) to dried female plants. It increased again once the plants have been dried and transformed into resin (5.5% to 11.3%, average of 8.3%). The three samples of dried cannabis plants from the province of Larache contained the lowest levels of THC at less than 1%. Samples from the province of Al Hoceima contained relatively high THC levels at more than 3% in the four plots studied. As for the the province of Chefchaouen, samples had intermediate THC levels between 1 and 3%. Powders collected from the plots in the region of Al Hoceima (average THC level of 8.4%) are comparable to those taken from the region of Chefchaouen (average level of 8%). Transformation of the plant is accompanied by a sharp increase in the concentration of THC, probably due to the enrichment of the powder with flowering tops and cannabis plant resin.

The stages of cannabis cultivation

The various cultivation stages come with a considerable cost, particularly for those who take the decision to cultivate cannabis for the first time. The practice of irrigation is rare with just 20% of producers being able to irrigate their land. These are generally those who own vast plantations close to a river or a dam. Few producers are able to dig wells or install irrigation systems in the mountains. Terraced crops in the traditional region are a good alternative as they do not waste water and they allow plants to avoid growing in stagnant water.

Producers must invest on several levels: intensive labor to prepare the soil, the purchase of fertilizers and plant disease control treatments, paying for the involvement of outside labor, as well as the digging of wells, installation of irrigation pumps, marking out of furrows, and for any work requiring hired specialists.

Cannabis cultivation takes place in six stages: sowing, cleaning, harvesting, drying, transformation, and commercialization. Cannabis, whether cultivated on *bour*[8] or irrigated plots, and depending on the agro-climatic zone (altitude, watershed, rain), has a cultivation cycle of 5 to 6 months. Nearly a month after sowing, the farmers carry out plowing twice over to prepare the soils. This operation is carried out using a tractor, loaned at around 300 DH per hour. The seeds are collected during the previous harvests or bought locally for the price of 1000 to 1500 DH per ton. Generally, sowing takes place between mid-February and mid-March. In certain cases, the farmers can stagger the sowing periods so as to maximize the labor available when it comes to harvest.

Care is given throughout the development of the plants. "Cleaning" consists of weeding and separating. Weeding removes all the weeds that prevent cannabis from growing properly. Separation consists of dividing up the male and female plants. This stage is not done in the same way by all farmers. In fact, some farmers believe that the pollen of the male plants strengthens the female plants and do not remove the male plants until later on.

The harvest takes place when the female plants reach maturity; that is, between July and September, depending on the cultivation process. Cannabis grown through rain-fed cultivation is sown and harvested earlier than cannabis grown through irrigation.

Drying takes place on the rooftops of the houses or inside the terraces in July and August, generally out of sight. This stage lasts for approximately one month. The cannabis plants are then arranged in bunches. In rare instances, drying takes place on the stem before harvest. After drying, the plants are stored in a shed or in a room reserved for them.

From plant to drug: transformation and commercialization

Using the dried raw cannabis, the producers make cannabis powder (*chira*) which is then pressed and heated to form the cannabis resin: a dark brown solid paste, called hashish on the market.

Transformation of the cannabis plant into resin, or hashish, is usually carried out using the beating method. It only requires basic means: some tools, cellophane paper, cloth, wooden batons, and a bowl. The bowl is covered with a dark cloth, often black, stretched as much as possible using a baton to create a sieve. The bunches of *kif* are placed on the sieve and covered with clear plastic so that nothing is lost. The next stage is "*nfid*", which consists of hitting the bunches, still covered with plastic, using a thick, short baton. The result is a mass of dried leaves on the sieve, which is put back under the plastic, surrounded by a rubber band, which pressurizes the *kif* leaves. Then, the *kif* is beaten with two long, thin batons for half an hour. The rubber band is removed, and then the plastic followed by the sieve, so that the *kif* powder that has passed through can be collected. The powder is poured

8 Rain-fed cultivation.

into a packet so that none is lost. The worker also rubs off any powder residue on his hands so that it also goes into the packet of powder. The powder is then compressed so that it is as compacted as possible. The whole lot is rubbed on a coarse surface such as denim. This is how the top quality hashish called *Zero Zero* is obtained. The same beating operation, carried out once, twice, or three times, is also used to produce hashish of lower quality.

The fourth stage is the preparation of the paste "*al brissa*" using the powder. This step also has low technical requirements; a single compression machine is required, which gives the resin a flattened, rectangular form, a bar weighing 150 or 250 grams. Generally, it is the most experienced workers who carry out this stage as it poses the greatest risk to its successful commercialization. During this step, the workers must – in addition to having the required experience and competence – gain the trust of the employer, which is clearly reserved for natives of the region. The latter earn exceptional pay for this activity, between 200 and 500 DH per day.

The farmers can extract 2.82 kilos of resin from 100 kilos of dried raw cannabis, (UNODC 2005). In the older production areas, most producers prefer to sell their produce in the transformed state as they have the relevant knowledge, while in the new production areas, the producers call on outside labor to carry out the transformation process on site. This is how more than 90% of producers operate, compared with 10% who say they sell their cannabis in the form of raw bouquets (*mechmoum)* for reasons associated with financial difficulties, insufficient production, or because they do not have the required knowledge.

The commercialization is carried out in the village or nearby in discreet locations (forests, off-the-beaten tracks, sheds, etc.). Commercialization remains the stage that holds the most risk and is not mastered by all farmers. The cannabis market is thus characterized by strong competition between numerous farmers and a reduced concentration of buyers who master the negotiation of trafficking networks and trade routes. The buyers can sometimes exercise pressure on the farmers to lower their prices, using rumors of possible eradications or arrests, thus forcing the farmers to sell their goods at a loss.

Cannabis: its benefits and restrictions

Cannabis and its benefits to the local economy

The economic importance of this cannabis cultivation is firstly measured by the number of people who make a living out of it. In 2003 and 2004, it is estimated that some 800,000 rural inhabitants were involved; the equivalent of 96,600 family farming units. It is also important to add to this number all the farm workers from outside the Rif or from areas where cannabis is not tolerated by the authorities, and who work for the landowners for periods of 2 to 6 months. Cannabis has therefore played an important role in regulating employment in the Rif region, especially for young rural inhabitants. Poverty makes them leave areas with little land and water or *douars* subjected to repeated checks, and they emigrate to *douars* looking for extra labor. Cannabis cultivation, which makes the best of unproductive and even non-irrigated land, enables parts of the population to establish a permanent residence in the Rif.

Overall, cannabis has improved the quality of life of rural farmers. In the new cultivation areas, the populations have mainly invested income earned from cannabis into improving their housing conditions, which up to then had been considered terrible. The architectural landscape of certain *douars* has therefore changed. The richest inhabitants have invested in town houses. Cannabis also allows some people to invest their revenues in the legal regional economy. Since the 1980s, the cannabis market has therefore facilitated the purchase and rearing of cattle in the Oued Laou valleys. In particular, the development of dairy livestock has made up for the drop in revenue experienced during those years when cannabis was prohibited. In the coastal Mediterranean region inhabited by the Ghomara, revenue from cannabis has modernized fishing through the purchase of motors and nets. For some years now, there has been an increase in the number of offers of employment in this sector. One of the consequences of this development is that, with the men doing the fishing, the women are more involved in commercialization of the cannabis and now have their own purchasing power.

Finally, in terms of rural development, revenue from cannabis has also enabled the *douars* to modernize their equipment, dig wells to irrigate the fields, obtain irrigation pumps, and to employ outside labor. The economic importance is also measured by the increase in revenue that enables access to consumption of perishable goods, with access to the souk (open-air market), access to credit, etc.

Despite the pressure that buyers place on farmers to lower their prices, and despite repressive activities by the authorities (production is sometimes eradicated, or the produce is simply not sold), cannabis remains economically beneficial to rural inhabitants. In 2003, it is estimated that a hectare of cannabis had a return of 8 to 10 times the investment when cultivated in rain-fed plots, and 12 to 16 times when cultivated in irrigated plots. This explains a) why cultivators have abandoned traditional legal crops in favor of cannabis, and b) why they favor irrigated cultivation.

Sold on average at 50 DH per kilo in its raw form, it can reach 100 DH during the best years and 20 DH during the worst. Despite fluctuations in price and other uncertainties, cannabis is bringing reasonable returns to farmers, with average annual revenues estimated at 38,900 DH in 2005[9] for a family unit of 8 to 9 people (UNODC 2006).

9 This is an increase of 30% which can be explained by the increase in the price of cannabis between 2004 and 2005. Due to the reduction in available land area, the price of raw cannabis rose from 25 DH per kilo to 50 DH, while the price of resin increased from 1,400 DH to 4,000 DH per kilo. In 2003, cannabis would have yielded 41,000 DH per family. It is important to put these revenues into perspective, given the revaluations of the

However, while cannabis allows farmers to increase their revenue in the short term, income for the following years is unpredictable, both because of the droughts affecting the Moroccan countryside, and because of eradication activities.

Cannabis and its benefits to the individual

The evidence would therefore lead one to believe that the high returns made on cannabis cultivation are the main motivation behind his activity. Moreover, cannabis, in addition to increasing the income of rural inhabitants, allows them to gain access to credit. Through deforestation, it even gives certain people access to land.

However, other motivations also become apparent, motivations linked to the emergence of a new Rif society close to the market economy. For example, a competitive spirit has developed between rural folks, between neighbors of the same village, or individuals of two neighboring villages. This competitive spirit, encouraged by the development of communication channels and by the growth of individualism, has given young people the opportunity to succeed and to make a living from drugs which, according to several testimonies, gives them a greater return than the traditional agricultural systems mastered by their parents. For young people, earning a living from drugs has allowed them, to some extent, to free themselves from a patriarchal society, family pressure, and certain traditional customs. The other well-known advantage concerns the women who, through their high level of involvement in the cultivation of cannabis, have gained recognition in certain villages. This is mainly demonstrated by the fact that they receive income, gain access to places that until then had only been reserved for men, make their own decisions, and obtain luxury items, such as jewelry.

Cannabis and its restrictions

At the same time that the expansion of the cannabis industry stabilized a whole population on the margins of economic development, it is now a) threatening the ecological balance of the region, b) reducing traditional crop practices at the corresponding proportion, and c) changing social and family ties. The Rif is a region with limited resources, and its ecological balance is being weakened by considerable demographic growth, droughts (during some years), and deforestation due to the expansion of areas cultivated for cannabis. In the large valleys where cannabis is cultivated, we are witnessing intensive single-crop farming which is taking place to the detriment of cereal crops, olive trees, and livestock farming. Running along these same valleys are *wadis* where farmers are secretly pumping

revenues carried out during the UNODC surveys. By way of comparison, the revenue from cannabis per person was around 4,900 DH in 2003 and 3,600 DH in 2004, and the GDP per person in 2004 for the whole of the country was 14,843 DH. This puts the farmer's revenue from cannabis into perspective (according to UNODC 2003, 2005, 2006).

out water resources, thus reducing the supply to dams. The best yields come from irrigated land, thus most producers are looking for flat land with means of irrigation, while producers cultivating on rain-fed plots are at the mercy of low yields, especially during droughts.

Moreover, the intensive cultivation of cannabis has strongly depleted the soils. These plots of land, already weakened by erosion, are damaged by mass use of fertilizers, and this practice is accelerating impoverishment of the soils further still (contrary to what the producers claim). All farmers who cultivate cannabis use fertilizers to increase yields. Cannabis plots receive up to 4 times the amount of fertilizer than plots of cereals, plots for which the farmers use fertilizers in a reasonable manner, given the quality of the soils and the expected yield.

While at the start of the twentieth century tribes were making substantial returns on cannabis cultivation, the populations still possessed a considerable knowledge of traditional agricultural crops, arboriculture (fig, almond, and olive trees), and grapes which produced a renowned wine (Basset et al. 1926), and this despite the barren soils of the region. Now, however, traditional crop practices are being lost as the young are recruited into cannabis cultivation. Thus, the transformation of the agrarian landscape from traditional self-subsistence cultivation to single-crop farming of cannabis has increased the deficit of food products in the region. Today, food products sold at the markets come from other parts of the kingdom, or from smuggling.

The women, who represent a considerable proportion of the labor used to cultivate cannabis, tend to lose their knowledge of farming and crafts (pottery, embroidery), because the production of cannabis takes up a large amount of time, and makes an average return 10 times that of legal crops. In certain *douars* of Chefchaouen, the cannabis market is causing the rearing of goats to disappear. This is done directly, as the shepherds prefer cannabis cultivation as it provides a greater income; but also indirectly, as cannabis cultivation without a rotation of crops means the loss of *hioual*[10], which causes a reduction in the amount of forage available for the herds of goats. Finally, deforestation disturbs the normal course taken by the herds.

With this new lifestyle, we are witnessing a loss of social and family ties, and solidarity; the purchase of consumables, such as cars, domestic electrical appliances, women's jewelry, etc. has become a priority. The female workforce is slowly being replaced by seasonal workers. Schooling is not a priority in the villages that cultivate cannabis, where children and young people are involved in cultivation early on. Finally, conflicts, which used to be moderated and managed by a patriarchal system, are increasing between neighbors that have now become competitors. Property disputes caused by cannabis cultivation have occurred on a recurring basis and people have been making accusations to the authorities about their neighbors.

10 Fallow and rotation of crops on the same plot of land from one year to the next.

Conclusion

There is no doubt that cannabis cultivation has influenced the structure of Rif's society by providing subsidies to the population and increasing their quality of life. This is the case for thousands of families as well as outside labor, whether from within or outside the Rif. The women play an invisible but fundamental role throughout the domestic economy (cannabis and other farming/domestic activities). The children are by their parents' side, also getting involved in the various stages of cultivation, which poses a problem when cannabis cultivation becomes a better financial security for the future than schooling could ever be.

However, the new cultivation areas are now threatened by numerous eradication activities, and the expansion trend, at its peak in 2003, is on the decline. Ever since the scale of the cannabis phenomenon in Morocco was revealed in 2003 with the publication of the first official investigation by UNODC and the Moroccan government, the fight against the expansion of cultivation has translated into fierce eradication, particularly in the province of Larache. This was a shock for the inhabitants who were not prepared for life after eradication.

Cannabis revenue has allowed increased access to credit. The producers in the new production regions, particularly in the valleys of Larache or the *douars* of Taounate, are experiencing financial difficulties which are gradually being felt as the reserves are depleted. They have been forced to abandon the standard of living they had in the golden age of cannabis.

Finally, the outside laborers, who were benefiting from 3 to 6 months of work annually, could find themselves in a more precarious economic situation than they are in now, especially those from the poorest *douars* in the Rif and even elsewhere in the kingdom. In the same manner, the rural exodus, which had been contained in the Rif thanks to the cultivation of cannabis, could significantly grow, with the economic crisis having an impact on urban areas. An increase in illegal immigration to Europe remains a possibility.

It therefore seems important that the problems linked to cannabis cultivation are handled with care and without undue haste. In Morocco, the production of cannabis was not born from a particular conflict situation; however removing too quickly what constitutes, by far, the main economy of the Rif undoubtedly presents major risks of socio-economic destabilization of the region if development aid is not heavily invested. The complexity of the Rif's context, in economic, social, and ecological terms means, that the matter must be handled with development in mind. The challenge posed by cannabis in the Rif is that of lasting economic development in one of the poorest regions of the country, whose socio-economic stability is threatened not only by the possibility of cannabis cultivation being brutally eliminated, but also by the now inevitable unbalancing of a production system that is increasingly threatened by exponential demographic growth and ecological disturbance.

For some years now, in particular since the publication of the reports by UNODC, the Moroccan government seems to be taking into account the social and economic breakdown being felt in the northern region. Parallel to the eradication activities, a certain number of basic infrastructure development projects (roads, schools, hospitals) have been put into motion, while other larger-scale projects such as TangerMed or the port of Al Hoceima can have a positive impact on the economy of the northern region. It remains to be seen whether these initiatives will have an impact in the mid and long term on the population living in the area enclosed by the Rif mountains, and if the cultivation of cannabis will survive, and in which form: on a small scale for home consumption as was the tradition, or at a tolerable level in a controlled, restricted zone.

List of references

Afsahi, K. 2009. *Les producteurs de cannabis dans le Rif – Maroc : Étude d'une activité économique à risque* [Cannabis producers in the Rif - Morocco: Study of an economic activity at risk]. Lille: University of Lille 1, Sciences and technologies, Graduate school of economic and social sciences, development and management, Faculty of economic and social sciences (UMR–CNRS 8019).

Afsahi, K. 2002. *La culture du Kif dans le Rif, facteur de changement social* [The cultivation of *kif* in the Rif, a factor of social change]. Master's thesis. Lille: University of Lille 1.

Anegay, K. 2001. *Projet "Introduction et développement des cultures alternatives dans le Rif marocain (phase II)"* [Project: "Introduction and development of alternative crops in the Moroccan Rif (phase II)"], project financed by the European Community. Kingdom of Morocco – Prime Minister – APDN, Rabat 15.

Basset, H. et al. 1926. Kief and Jebala. *Bulletin de l'Enseignement public du Maroc* [Public education bulletin of Morocco], No. 71, Edition E. Larose.

Bellakhdar, J. 1997. *La pharmacopée marocaine traditionnelle Médecine arabe ancienne et savoirs populaires* [The traditional Moroccan pharmacopoeia: Ancient Arabic medicine and popular knowledge]. Paris: Ibis Press.

Borg, G. 1970. *Le voyage à la drogue* [The road to drugs]. Paris: Editions du Seuil.

Clarke, R.C. 1998. *Hashish.* Los Angeles, CA: Red Eye Press.

Clarke, R.C. 2004. *La botanique du cannabis* [The botany of cannabis]. Paris: Editions du Lézard.

Lugan, B. 2000. *Histoire du Maroc* [History of Morocco]. Paris: Edition Perrin.

Moreno, P. 1997. *Estudio del cultivo de cannabis sativa en el rif marroqui : sus consecuencias socioeconomicas para la región* [Study of *Cannabis sativa* cultivation in the Moroccan Rif: its socio-economic consequences for the region]. PhD thesis. Valencia: Polytechnic University of Valencia, Higher Technical School of Agronomists, Department of Economics and Social Sciences.

Moulièras, A. 1895. *Le Maroc inconnu* [Unknown Morocco]. First Part: Exploration of the Rif. Oran: Imprimerie Fouque.

UNODC (United Nations Office on Drugs and Crime) 2003. *Maroc. Enquête sur le cannabis 2003* [Morocco: survey on cannabis 2003]. Vienna: UNODC.

UNODC (United Nations Office on Drugs and Crime) 2005. *Maroc. Enquête sur le cannabis 2004* [Morocco: survey on cannabis 2004]. Vienna: UNODC.

UNODC (United Nations Office on Drugs and Crime) 2006. *Maroc. Enquête sur le cannabis* [Morocco: survey on cannabis] – Preliminary report. Vienna: UNODC.

Zaim, F. 1997. Le Maroc Méditerranéen, l'ultime frontière [Mediterranean Morocco: the final frontier], in *Les Zones défavorisées méditerranéennes : études sur le développement dans les territoires ruraux marginalizes* [Disadvantaged

Mediterranean areas: studies on development within marginalized rural territories]. Paris: Editions L'Harmattan, Editions Toubkal, 309-27.

PART II
Growing in the Developed World

Chapter 4

Medical Marijuana – Exploring the Concept in Relation to Small Scale Cannabis Growers in Denmark[1]

Helle Vibeke Dahl and Vibeke Asmussen Frank

Introduction

Although the term "medical marijuana" is a recent development, the medical use of cannabis has been found throughout history in various cultures all over the world. This chapter intends to illustrate how therapeutic qualities of cannabis continue to play a role by providing an analysis of Danish cannabis growers, who are experienced with recreational use, but whose current cultivation is mainly or partially motivated by their efforts to manage pain and illnesses of various sorts. We emphasize that we do not intend to prove or disprove the medical effectiveness of cannabis, but to provide insight into the therapeutic aspect of its use.

This chapter forms part of a larger study on domestic cannabis cultivation in Denmark designed to explore current trends and themes relating to cultivation, distribution and consumption in the political context of prohibition.[2] The study follows the tradition of ethnographic drug research by applying a user perspective to make clear the understandings and points of views of those under investigation (Agar 1985, Asmussen and Jöhncke 2004, Dahl 2004). In modern cannabis research literature the user oriented approach is relatively sparsely represented and has mainly been applied to uncover recreational aspects of use (Becker 1967, Golub 2006, Hammersley and Leon 2006, Osborne and Fogel 2008). There is also little research available on users' perspectives and subjective experiences with cannabis that is being used for medical reasons (Coomber et al. 2003, Ogborne et al. 2000, Swift et al. 2005, Chapkiss and Webb 2008). The user perspective in this research

1 We express our gratitude to The Scandinavian Research Council for Criminology (NSfK) for supporting this study by a grant.

2 In Denmark, possession of illegal drugs, including cannabis is penalized; maximum sentences for drug offences have recently been raised, and preventive control measures of various sorts enhanced (Frank 2008). With an official license, hemp of low THC content can be cultivated for industrial purposes (textiles, animal feed, etc.) but is otherwise illegal for any personal purpose or use, although buying and selling of hemp seeds and special equipment for in-door growing is legitimate.

parallels that of medical anthropology's distinctions between patients' experience of illness as a meaning-centered model as opposed to physicians' biomedical approach to disease as an alteration in biological structure and functioning. The biomedical approach is detached from subjective, psychosocial and cultural matters (Kleinman 1988, Good 1994, Mattingly 1998).

The chapter is divided in two parts. The first provides an outline of the history of medical use of cannabis with specific references to the Danish context. The second part covers the medical reasons and conditions under which cannabis is grown and used.

Early history of cannabis as a medical agent

Ten years ago, the medical use of cannabis was an almost completely unknown practice in Denmark. Today most people will have at least heard of it from media coverage and public debates. This recent interest in the therapeutic potential of cannabis has prompted us to outline the medical history of cannabis, and the changes in its medical and legal status.

As documented in several bibliographies and comprehensive reviews, cannabis has for millennia served as a euphoriant and a medical agent for a multitude of health complaints, ailments and conditions (e.g., Mikuriya 1972, Abel 1980, Aldrich 1997, Grinspoon and Bakalar 1997, Russo 2001, Earleywine 2002, Fankhauser 2008). The year 1840 marks the beginning of European medicine's study of cannabis when physicians began to call attention to the symptomatic and analgesic utility of the drug in the treatment of various illnesses and pains. Experiments with individuals or groups of patients were carried out, including self-experiments and animal experiments as well. Cases were reported systematically and with detailed information about patients' conditions and suffering, medication doses, frequency of ingestion, and physical and psychological effects etc. (Aldrich 1997, Grinspoon and Bakalar 1997, Russo 2001, 2002). Throughout the 19th century, cannabis preparations of various sorts were found to be useful in the treatment of a wide range of common disorders such as cholera, rheumatic diseases, delirium tremens, tetanus, rabies and convulsions as well as asthma and other respiratory ailments, tuberculosis, venereal diseases etc. (ibid., Lindesmith 1966). Physicians documented not only the beneficial effects but also what patients reported as unpleasant and unwanted pharmacological or psychoactive effects. These were characterized as mental discomfort and confusion, dizziness, space and time distortion and feelings of anxiety and fear. This made some abandon the drug as worthless or dangerous while others regarded the side-effects as less serious compared to other medicines or no treatment at all.

The medical use of cannabis in Europe and USA is considered to have peaked in the late 19th century. By the turn of the 20th century, research and medical prescriptions were declining. Various circumstances contributed to this waning medical interest (Grinspoon and Bakalar 1997). First is the inconsistency in the quality and potency of cannabis used for preparations. Secondly, the invention of the hypodermic syringe in the 1850s led to the subsequent provision of soluble drugs by injection. This faster method of pain relief rendered cannabis (not easily administered by injection) increasingly expendable. Thirdly, the marketing of the chemically more stable new synthetic analgesics and drugs such as aspirin and barbiturates reduced the appeal of cannabis. Finally, economic aspects came into play, as hemp producing countries were constrained in their exports by increased import taxes. A prime example of this is the passing of the Marijuana Tax Act in 1937 that effectively limited marijuana's medical usage in the United States due to heavy taxation and the imposition of strict restrictions on physicians' prescriptions.[3] In 1941, cannabis was removed from the U.S. Pharmacopoeia and National Formulary (Earleywine 2002).

In Denmark and the whole of Scandinavia, knowledge about the therapeutic usage of cannabis-based drugs is scarce. What is certain is that through the 1800s and early 1900s, various cannabis containing extracts and tinctures were available from pharmacies. At the start of the 20th century, Danish newspapers and magazines promoted *Maltos Cannabis*, attested by medical doctors to be "an excellent lunch drink, especially for children and young people" and "a health medicine that has been employed with great success against pulmonary diseases, anemia, gastric catarrh, scrofula, neurasthenia, asthenia and emaciation." The advertisement featured the international prize, awarded to the product during the World Exhibition of Antwerp in 1894. Apparently, it was available from all pharmacies and bigger groceries in Denmark and Norway (Ludvigsen 2002).[4] In Sweden, *Cannabitropin* was used against whooping cough and *Cannabisol* against depression until the 1950s.[5] Various cannabis compounds were still being marketed and used during the first half of the 20th century. The use of cannabis was eventually prohibited in countries which signed the Single Convention on Narcotic Drugs of 1961 and as late as 1964, a

---

3 The US Marijuana Tax Act of 1937 was a culmination of a campaign organized by the Federal Bureau of Narcotics under Harry Anslinger in which the public was led to believe that marihuana was addictive, a toxic and destructive agent capable of provoking psychosis and mental deterioration and a 'killer drug' that triggered crimes of violence and sexual excess (Becker 1966, in: Solomon 1966; Musto 1973; Grinspoon and Balakar 1997). This image of marijuana was transferred to Denmark even before recreational use became known and uncritically passed on in medical scientific books (Møller 1946: 289-308).

4 The Great Nordic Encyclopedia from 1917 has a small chapter on hemp (Cannabis Sativa/Indica) focused on the importance of its fibres for the production of strong textiles and ropes, and only briefly mentions that it had 'earlier, to some extent been used in medicine as an analgesic'. In Gyldendal's Lexicon from 1937 medical use is not mentioned at all, but a specific reference to "Hashi'sh" mentions that it was 'used in mediaeval times to intoxicate those whom you wanted to commit murder'.

5 http://www.medicinskmarijuana.com/fakta.html

factory in Southern Denmark was ordered to discontinue the manufacture of a liniment containing cannabis extracts to treat clavus[6] (Thygesen 1967).

The recent history of cannabis as a medical agent

Due to both prohibition and the increased availability of synthetic drugs, interest in the therapeutic properties of cannabis was gradually replaced by increased attention on its recreational use.

The therapeutic possibilities of cannabis have been overshadowed by its current status as a prohibited drug, its reputation as a drug of abuse, a gateway drug and widespread worries of risks and harmful effects to physical and psychological health (Chapkis and Webb 2008, Earleywine 2002). Despite international agreements on narcotic restrictions to suppress medical use and cultivation for medical purposes, research into the therapeutic utility of cannabis never ceased completely. Clinical trials with both organic cannabis and synthetic cannabinoids have been continuously performed, but within highly limited terms (ibid.).

Since 1996, several US states have passed legislation endorsing herbal cannabis for medical purposes. More recently, Canada and some European countries (UK, Spain, Switzerland, Italy and Austria) have allowed cultivation for research into therapeutic utility and/or stretched the ban by decriminalizing cannabis for certain medical conditions and symptoms. For instance in 2003, Holland allowed access to cannabis products through medical prescription (Fankhauser 2008).

Since the mid-1980s, some of the active substances in cannabis have been produced synthetically as dronabinol. Available in the form of a pill under the trade name *Marinol*, it was approved for the treatment of nausea and vomiting in cancer chemotherapy patients in USA in 1985, and for AIDS patients suffering from weight reduction syndrome in 1992. Today, more than twenty cannabis-derived pharmaceutical compounds are undergoing safety trials and pending approval in the US (Chapkis and Webb 2008). Also, several European countries have permitted prescription of *Marinol* for particular therapeutic purposes (EMCDDA 2002). In addition to synthetic products, the British company, GW Pharmaceuticals has developed a medicine based on botanical cannabis extracts. Marketed as *Sativex*, the liquid is to be administered by a mouth spray to relieve symptoms of multiple sclerosis and for the treatment of severe neuropathic-related cancer pain. Since 2007, this product has been available in Canada on prescription (Chapkis and Webb 2008). However, the lack of clinical evidence of the safety and efficacy of both the synthetic and natural based cannabis compounds have prevented the approval of cannabis in many countries. In Norway, for instance, no cannabis related products are allowed.[7]

6 Clavus is a hard thickening of the skin (especially on the top or sides of the toes) caused by the pressure of ill-fitting shoes.

7 See e.g. www.helsedirektoratet.no, official website of the Norwegian Directorate of Health. This is a specialist directorate and an administrative body under the Ministry of

In Denmark, *Marinol* was outlawed by the Danish Medicines Agency until 2003, when the Danish Parliament – in response to the advocacy of patients' associations – passed a bill releasing *Marinol* on restricted terms (that is, where conventional medicine has proven to be ineffective) to patients suffering from multiple sclerosis, cancer and AIDS (The Danish Health Board 2009, Riis 2003).

As in many other countries the arguments for and against cannabis prohibition are much debated, but so far the medical aspects of cannabis have not received much attention from the Danish public and media. Recent violent clashes between rival dealers in the city of Copenhagen made local politicians propose regulation and legal access to cannabis via public medical practitioners. The idea was immediately dismissed by the spokesman of the Danish Medical Association who claimed that medical doctors had no intentions of acting mediators for an illegal drug "known to cause psychosis" (Krogsgård 2009).

Debates about cannabis as a medical agent are not restricted to political, professional and scientific circles, but have extended to the World Wide Web. On the internet, cannabis users' and growers' forums present the opportunity to share experiences and advice, release testimonies of effects from therapeutic use, inform about new research etc.[8]

Contrary to European patients in the 19th century, who were prescribed cannabis for medical conditions by physicians and who ingested the drug or extracts of the drug orally, contemporary users tend to be experienced or former recreational users who administer the drug by smoking. The following analysis aims to contribute to the ongoing debates about cannabis use in general and as a self-medicating strategy in particular.

Medical marijuana: users' perspectives and experiences

This second part of the chapter examines contemporary understanding and knowledge of the therapeutic properties of cannabis from the perspective of current users. The analysis is based on data provided by volunteer interviewees recruited via a web-survey. The questionnaire was designed to obtain information about trends and themes relating to home growing, distribution and consumption in Denmark.[9]

Health and Care Services and the Ministry of Labour and Social Inclusion of Norway.

8 For instance http://www.drugs-forum.com, http://www.cannabis.net, http://www.humanhemp-health.ca, and the Danish site http://www.psychedelia.dk.

9 The web survey was accessible during the latter half of 2008. 565 persons, including 401 current growers (91 % male, 9 % female) representing a population of predominantly well-educated, well-integrated small scale and non-profit home growers, responded to the online questionnaire (for findings and details on the survey sample see Hakkarainen et al. 2011). Respondents willing to take part in personal interviewing were invited to provide contact information. Participants in qualitative interviewing were informed about the study and its exploratory goals. Confidentiality and anonymity was guaranteed by verbal

The subjects of the study include 19 growers who declared their use to be wholly or partly conditioned by health problems. We wanted to examine whether there was a medical reason for their use and what the outcomes of their experiences were.

The 19 informants, four of them women, were between 25-71 years. The majority held conventional jobs, two were studying, three had been granted disability pensions and one had retired. All had started cannabis smoking as teenagers and perceived themselves as experienced recreational users. Their former and current recreational use pattern varied individually, that is from rarely to regular or daily use in a controlled manner, to periodic excessive and in a few instances self-perceived problematic use. Quite a few had stopped using for several years, mostly after starting a family or a work career, but had resumed it for pleasure or, in a single instance, specifically for medical reasons.

The informants' growing careers spanned 4 to 30 years. 12 were growing outdoor only, 5 grew indoor and 2 "both-and". Most grew between 5-10 plants; a few up to 20 plants and one had around 40 outdoor plants. Except for two who only started growing after their disability had occurred, growing was a strategy for supplying recreational use before medical problems became a motivational factor. Homegrown cultivation allowed easy and stable access to preferred strains of cannabis while staying away from the criminal market and avoiding the attention of the authorities. At the time of interviewing, most were by and large self sufficient, though a few would at times supply their own harvest from other home-growers, alternatively from hashish dealers.

The informants were using cannabis as self-medication in relation to a broad range of health conditions and ailments. All of them reported to suffer from medical and in several cases chronic conditions that had been diagnosed by doctors, and almost all were in regular contact with physicians and specialists from the public health system.

The following section covers issues relating to narratives on medical conditions and symptoms, patterns of medical cannabis use and the perceived effects of that use.

How and why did medical use become an issue?

Interviewees referred either to specific incidences or medical disorders and discomforts as the reason for starting using cannabis therapeutically. However, some described medical usage as a sliding scale from recreational use when they realized its positive contribution to their well-being. Apart from an elderly man

---

consent. No reward was paid. Each interview lasted between 1-2 ½ hours. All interviews were transcribed, processed and coded with the aid of NVivo 8. A total of 42 qualitative interviews were performed, of these 14 grew exclusively for recreational purposes, while 28 included medical purposes as well. We have chosen to focus explicitly on 19 informants who defined their use or part of their use as medical.

who found his homegrown pot to be more effective in relieving the discomforts of nausea and low energy accompanying cancer chemotherapy than the medications he was given, the informants represented two equal groups. One group emphasized the potential of cannabis as a painkiller, the other pointed exclusively to the mind calming and soothing effects in relation to psychological discomforts. In the following, users' own accounts about self-medication with reference to pain related conditions and mental distress will be presented separately.

Cannabis as a painkiller

The group who claimed that their use of cannabis was primarily aimed at pain relief referred to experiences with treating physical and neurological symptoms from acute or temporary conditions such as headache, migraine and post operative pains to chronic nerve injuries and pains caused by back, neck and whiplash injuries, ruptured discs, degenerative arthritis in knees and shoulders, and various forms of sclerosis.

Most within this category had a daily use of cannabis; a few had periods of more intensive use alternating with days or weeks with no medical use, or they used cannabis therapeutically only in acute situations to prevent or alleviate pain. Among the latter were two women who reported marked relief when using cannabis against (pre)menstrual symptoms and abdominal pains and accompanying back- and headache.[10] One usually smoked a joint when pains arose, which gave an almost instant relief; the other used an extract for drinking, which did not work immediately, but to her experience it had longer lasting effects. Both women expressed great satisfaction with the use of this "natural" drug, as alternative to the synthetic drugs and opioids which they previously used.

Only two, both of them men in their forties, claimed their current use of cannabis to be solely medical with the purpose of pain relief. One had not used the drug since his teenage years, when ten years later he contracted serious injuries on his neck and spinal cord after a car accident. After the accident, he resorted to cannabis use.

10 The therapeutic effects of cannabis for 'female diseases, conditions and troubles' have been extensively demonstrated by Russo (2002). In his review Russo (2002) documents that hemp seeds, cannabis leaf juice and other cannabis preparations and mixtures since ancient history and to our times have served as valuable remedies for women with (pre)menstrual disorders, pains and cramps and in relation to basic gynaecological and obstetric matters for thousands of years. Referring to anecdotal experiences as well to more systematic studies, Russo provides comprehensive support of the therapeutic properties of cannabis alleviating nausea and vomiting of pregnancy – also where other remedies have failed; in shortening and reducing birth pain; in promoting uterine contraction in tedious labors without any anaesthetic effects and unpleasant consequences, and in suppressing and preventing haemorrhage after labor.

> After the accident I was prescribed loads of pills. As time went by I got afraid as to whether my stomach and bowls could stand it (…) I'd heard from somewhere that cannabis worked against pains, so around four years ago I gave it a try. Since then I have reduced my use of pills from 40 to 3-4 a day and my pains are no longer as strong (…). In addition to my injuries I got posttraumatic stress which makes my muscles tighten up, but when you smoke you automatically keep your stress level low (…) I smoke from morning till evening, every single day. [male, 42 years]

The other man who declared his current use of cannabis to be for the sole purpose of medical pain relief, was a former heavy user, whose use took new meanings and forms after breaking his back in a work accident.

> Today I use as occasion requires, before the accident it was abuse (…). On top of it all, I had a nasty case of a ruptured disc and ended up being prescribed loads of analgesics. I became dull and apathetic, which gave my family a hard time (…) so I stopped smoking overnight. Despite lots of morphine my back pains grew worse, I only slept little and was being difficult to my entourage ... Earlier I used to dismiss the talk about cannabis for pain treatment as an excuse for smoking, but I got hold of some good hashish, made a joint and then: "Pop!" Five minutes all these dreadful pains blurred and vanished. I tried again a couple of times when the symptoms emerged and realized that it really worked ... Now I'm back in my old job and may once in a while take Panodil [a mild analgesic] and I don't need more than one, maybe two joints a day, primarily in the evenings. [male, 44 years]

Medical use of cannabis for the purpose of pain relief takes various forms as illustrated by the narratives above. They also indicate essential themes that recur in almost all accounts. One is that cannabis is represented as a qualified or superior alternative to conventional medicine. Another is that it is an effective substitute for prescribed opioid-containing analgesics. The properties of and effects from cannabis are constantly being compared to those of prescribed analgesics, or rather to what are perceived as the unpleasant side-effects of opioids. The unsatisfactory effects of conventional drugs such as dizziness, nausea and feelings of weakness and indolence are explained in more detail by participants with chronic pains from fractures and injuries:

> When I smoke I am almost without pain, I am fully clearheaded and I have more appetite than when I take all those morphines. [male, 32 years]

> The difference is that now I can sleep, and I function much better in my daily life. Before, I had no energy, and no appetite. I was bad-tempered and sulky all the time. [male, 37 years]

> My "grow" works much better than those painkillers; it is cheaper and it has a milder impact compared to morphine, which leaves me ineffective and tired and with a stomach that doesn't work and also makes me feel like I'm another person, more distant as if I am not present here and now. I do not experience these things when using my own pot. [female, 47 years]

These examples illustrate another recurring theme that points to changes in the interviewees' original stated purpose of self-medication with cannabis for pain related reasons towards self-medication against side effects produced by other medical agents. The therapeutic effects of cannabis include mood-relieving, muscle relaxing and sedating as well as energizing and appetite stimulating. Thus, in the process of experienced improvement of life quality and daily functioning, the pains seem to become secondary or at least more manageable with the aid of cannabis.

Sclerosis patients in this sample and elsewhere (Earleywine 2002, Grinspoon and Bakalar 1997) explain that cannabis soothes and to some extent prevents pains from muscular tensions and contractions. One participant diagnosed with sclerosis also described his medical use as a means to relieve pain, but as it turned out from his explanations, the pains to be relieved were primarily caused by the medicine he was prescribed to take twice a week. In addition to this, he found cannabis useful for sleeping and managing the spasms connected to his condition, making his situation and daily life tasks more manageable:

> The medicine I take produces insane side effects such as fever cramps and muscle pains. Therefore I always smoke right after and usually also the day after, and it works completely like an anesthetic (…) I usually smoke a joint before going to bed because it makes me sleep better or rather I do sleep (…) It may sound strange to you, but if I smoke a joint it also helps me control and coordinate my motor movements so I can handle the dish-washing. [male, 31 years]

The respondents tend to emphasize that their use of cannabis as pain relief affects a broader range of crucial life aspects more positively than conventional medicine.

Cannabis and mental disorders

The group who described their medical use as a way to handle neuropsychiatric and psychological disorders and emotional distress primarily mentioned that it helped them to suppress, reduce and/or manage depression/depressive symptoms, anxiety, panic attacks and Attention Deficit Hyperactivity Disorder (ADHD). All had used cannabis, some of them intensively and in addition to cannabis some had also used other illegal drugs for longer periods of their life.

Among the latter were two men in their twenties. Both had a troubled past in the school system; for both, a recent diagnosis of ADHD led them to experience the adverse effects of prescribed Ritalin. Thus, they turned to self-medication with home-grown cannabis. One of them said :

> My father, who is actually a doctor, caught me smoking when I was 17, and wanted to know what I was up to. I explained how it put my mind and thoughts at rest and helped me concentrate, all of which he rejected (…) Ritalin made me passive, my spirits went low, I felt disinclined, lost my curiosity. It was loathsome.(…) Realizing why you smoke puts you in the position where you can take decisions instead of groping in the dark ... Today I smoke daily without bad conscience and it has changed my life radically. I've resumed my education and get good grades, but I feel madly aggrieved that I'm criminalized by the State whose only alternative is prescribing me a drug similar to amphetamine. [male, 26 years]

For other respondents, recreational use has been reinterpreted as medical use to ease social anxiety and address periodically recurring depressions. Certain life circumstances causing emotional distress may also trigger a change in purpose of use and use patterns. For a thirty year old man, the attempts to manage a prolonged period of work related stress with cannabis ended in a serious depression for which he was admitted to a psychiatric hospital. He did acknowledge that the increased use of cannabis to find rest and to sleep may have deteriorated his judgment in trying to keep up to the demands from his job thereby pushing himself further into depression than necessary. He however, turned against the purely medical treatment he had received because of the negative effects of this treatment. He also felt negative about the unresponsive attitude of the medical staff regarding cannabis as a medical aid.

> At the psychiatric ward, I was heavily sedated and told to refrain from cannabis because "it is the root of all evil" as they claimed (…) I soon found out that many patients smoked when they had the chance, and it actually helped them in enduring their hospital stay (…).The pharmaceuticals didn't do me any good, and after being discharged, I've stopped taking them and stick to my home-grown, which I've told them. But my confidence in doctors has diminished because of the way they reject cannabis. [male, 28 years]

Those with a history of anxiety, mood and hyperactivity disorders were all experienced cannabis users when they initiated treatment with psychopharmacological medicine. In their experience, cannabis was perceived to alleviate the symptoms of their disorders more satisfactorily and with less unpleasant side-effects than their former use of prescribed drugs.

Positive qualities and negative effects of medical cannabis use

The properties most frequently mentioned by the participants as helpful and relieving were the analgesic, sedative and sleep-inducing effects, all of which concur with effects described in historical as well as more recent medical cannabis literature. In fact, only a minority of the participants explicitly mentioned negative effects. A few referred to former or current problems with short-term memory, while some mentioned social withdrawal and inactivity and others reported having to adjust their usage to find an adequate functional level. At the time of the interview, two were struggling to reduce or (re)gain control of their cannabis use, which had become "too much of a habit", or as a middle aged man explicated: "Although it has a positive effect on your disease, you must be careful not to lose sight of what is symptom relief and what is escapism." However, from the users' perspective, the greatest drawbacks of cannabis for self-medication were: that cannabis users are criminalized by society and that medical professionals were noncommittal or unsupportive (see Hakkarainen et al. 2011 for further discussion).

Defining medical cannabis

In any drug discussion, it can be difficult to draw a definite line between therapeutic and recreational uses. Besides a sharply divided public opinion, both sides claim "scientific evidence" to support their views (Mack and Joy 2001, Joy et al. 2002). According to Chapkis and Webb (2008) opponents of cannabis tend to dismiss users' experiences as anecdotal and biased. They openly accuse medical cannabis users and their advocates of being mere "druggies" defending their access to joints.

Users are against heavy odds in terms of policy, public morality, scientific proof, and the law. Or in other words, up against more dominant rationalities that appear insensitive to subjective experiences and arguments.

In this study, the ones who had told doctors and other medical specialists about their use were met with reactions ranging from absolute rejection and warnings to tacit but incurious acceptance. They were acutely aware that cannabis growing and use placed them on the wrong side of the law, and they typically kept it a secret to non-using relatives, colleagues and employers. At the same time, they resented this secrecy and what, from their perspective, presents itself as double standards regarding the illegality of cannabis as opposed to alcohol and tobacco on the one hand, and conventional and synthetically manufactured medicine as opposed to natural herbal medicine on the other.

When asked to define the term and use of medical cannabis, interviewees qualify the medical use of cannabis in terms of its relieving effect more than the pleasure effects that are secondary if not altogether unimportant and avoidable.

> Medical, that's what I call it now, because right after smoking I go straight to bed. I no longer go for the nice sensations. [male, 38 years]

> I've experimented with how much I exactly need to ease the pains without getting intoxicated. And I think I've found the balance where I get the bodily relief and still maintain a normal relationship with other people. [male, 59 years]

Another few reported that when using cannabis for medical reasons, cannabis no longer produced the same high as before: "It stopped working like that. It's actually quite remarkable and I can't come up with any good explanation." Some more jokingly remarked that "the high" is an unavoidable side-effect that you may just as well enjoy. But for the majority of the participants, the psychoactive effects are interpreted as essential for easing or distracting the attention from discomforts and pains:

> It helps me sleep. I'm not without pains, though, but it makes me accept the pains better, it makes me ignore them to some extent, and that's what makes it all the more tolerable. [female, 53 years]

> Well, the high is surely part of it, you can't really avoid it. It makes your mind relax, and it spreads to your body and loosen up the tensions and you can breathe freely again. [female, 47 years]

> When I suffer really badly and I smoke, I've had that theory that it makes the ache increase right where the pains are centered, and… it's not easy to explain, but you're so focused on the pains and at the same time you seem to forget them, because your thoughts get sidetracked. [male, 59 years]

Participants agree that medical cannabis has therapeutic but not curative properties: "It removes the symptoms of your disease, and that's medicinal, isn't it," as one stated. On the other hand, the individual narratives show that effects are interpreted variously depending on former experiences with the drug, the purpose of use, expectations and setting, all of which go beyond purely chemical induced effects:

> You can't just pick one type of cannabis and claim "this is medical cannabis", because it depends just as much on how you use it, where and in which situations. There may be types that have the same effect on 100 persons in the exact same way, but whether cannabis is medical is up to each of them to decide…[male, 26 years]

> You can't label cannabis as medical. What counts is why and how you use it. [male, 36 years]

These rather conclusive statements echo well-known theories of drug use, such as Becker (1967) and Zinberg's (1984) analyses, in which they demonstrate that drug-induced experiences are not to be seen as automatic consequences of pharmacology, but as products of knowledge and learning, that is socialization and interpretations of the effects.

Conclusion

There are two purposes to the medicinal use of cannabis. One is to relieve physical pains, and the other to alleviate their psycho-emotional state. In the former, users pick up hearsay from media or social networks and try out cannabis to manage acute or chronic pain. In the latter, users have described their medical usage as a sliding scale from recreational use upon realizing the positive contribution of cannabis to their mood and daily functioning. While reasons for use may be different, the similarities between the use patterns of both groups are too glaring to be overlooked. All are experienced recreational users, and all have shifted to the use of cannabis due to the ill effects of conventional medicine, although many continued to use also for pleasure. Thus, as we have shown in this chapter, cannabis serves as substitute to conventional medicine, not only because of its perceived superior effects but also its use is adopted as a strategy to minimize the risk of dependency, especially in relation to prescribed opioids, stimulants, sedatives, and anti-depressants. Another indication of the action taken is the task and activities related to home growing, which after redefining their use as at least partially therapeutic became more urgent to uphold in order to ensure stable access to organically raised plants, but also to avoid the criminal market. Finally, we noted some obvious differences among the participants in terms of consumption patterns and preferences of cannabis type, strength and effects. Whilst there was a general agreement that *Cannabis indica* strains were better suited for therapeutic purposes than *Cannabis sativa*, which on the other hand was preferred by many for social and recreational use, participants employing cannabis as self-medication reported the daily use and preference for the more potent types of cannabis, including indoor grown skunk.

Anecdotal evidence on the use of cannabis for treating a broad range of medical disorders have, in line with the present study, shown positive effects with regard to pain relief, mood-disorders and improvements in health and life quality (Grinspoon and Bakalar 1997, Ogborne et al. 2000, Russo 2001, 2002, Coomber et al. 2003, Swift et al. 2005, Chapkiss and Webb 2008). However, cannabis for medical use continues to be a highly controversial issue, politically and medically. As a classified psychoactive and illegal drug, cannabis has become a political football, both in the international and national arena. This has not only prevented the performance of clinical trials required for medications as evidence of safety and efficiency, but of equal importance is that it has blocked a more pragmatic and an open-minded approach in finding relief and improving quality of life with the aid of cannabis.

The present chapter has presented and identified similarities and varieties in the meanings that study participants ascribe to illness, medical treatment and experiences with the therapeutic efficiency of cannabis. The fact that the study sample is small, that all interviewees were experienced recreational users before medical use became an issue, and that most of them still used also for the sake of pleasure may evoke criticism for producing a biased picture. On the other hand it can be argued that employing the user perspective to this specific group provides qualitative insight and perspectives into ongoing debates on illegal drug use in general and on detailed knowledge about self-medicated use of cannabis in particular.

List of references

Abel, E.L. 1980. *Marihuana: The First Twelve Thousand Years*. [Online: DRCnet Online Library of Drug Policy]. Available at: http://www.druglibrary.org/Schaffer/hemp/history/ first12000/6.htm [accessed: 5 December 2009].

Agar, M. 1985. Folks and professionals: Different models for the interpretation of drug use. *International Journal of Drug Addiction,* 20(1), 173-182.

Aldrich, M. 1997. History of Therapeutic cannabis, in *Cannabis in Medical Practice. A legal, historical and pharmacological overview of the therapeutic use of marijuana*, edited by L.M. Mathre. Jefferson, NC: McFarland, 35-55.

Asmussen, V. and Jöhncke, S. 2004. Indledning – perspektiver på brugere [Introduction – perspectives on users], in *Brugerperspektiver – fra stofmisbrug til socialpolitik?* [User perspectives – from drug abuse to social policy?], edited by V. Asmussen and S. Jöhncke. Aarhus: Aarhus University Press, 9-38.

Becker, H.S. 1967. History, culture and subjective experience: an exploration of the social bases of drug-induced experiences. *Journal of Health and Social Behavior*, 8(3), 163-176.

Becker, H.S. 1966. Marihuana: A sociological overview, in *The Marihuana Papers,* edited by D. Solomon. New York: The Bobs-Merrill Company, 33-65.

Chapkis, W. and Webb, R.J. 2008. *Dying to Get High: Marijuana as Medicine.* New York: New York University Press.

Coomber, R., Oliver, M. and Morris, C. 2003. Using cannabis therapeutically in the UK: A qualitative analysis. *Journal of Drug Issues*, 2, 325-356.

Dahl, H.V. 2004. Ilde hørt? Den larmende tavshed om etnografisk rusmiddelforskning [Unwelcome messages? The deafening silence on ethnographic drug research], in *Brugerperspektiver. Fra stofmisbrug til socialpolitik* [User perspectives. From drug misuse to social policy], edited by V. Asmussen and S. Jöhncke. Aarhus: Aarhus University Press, 39-71.

Danish Health Board 2009. *Notat, Sundhedsstyrelsen* [Information note, Danish Health Board]. Available at: http://www.ft.dk/samling/20081/beslutningsforslag/b131/bilag/1/671079.pdf [accessed: 2 March 2010].

Earleywine, M. 2002. *Understanding Marijuana: A New Look at the Scientific Evidence*. Oxford: Oxford University Press.

EMCDDA 2002. *Medicinal cannabis and derivatives. A legal analysis of the options, their limitations, and current practice in the EU* – EMCDDA-ELDD [Online: European Monitoring Centre for Drugs and Drug Addiction]. Available at: http://eldd.emcdda.europa.eu/attachements.cfm/att_5739_EN_Medical_cannabis_FINAL.pdf [accessed: 2 March 2010].

Fankhauser, M. 2008. Cannabis as medicine in Europe in the 19th century, in *A cannabis reader: global issues and local experiences. Perspectives on cannabis controversies, treatment and regulation in Europe,* edited by S.R. Sznitman, B. Olsson and R. Room. Monograph Series 8, Volume 1. Lisbon: European Monitoring Centre for Drugs and Drug Addiction, 3-16.

Frank, V.A. 2008. Danish drug policy – shifting from liberalism to repression. *Drugs and Alcohol Today*, 8(2), 26-33.

Golub, A., (ed.) 2006. *The cultural/subcultural contexts of marijuana use at the turn of the twenty-first century*. New York: Haworth Press.

Good, B.J. 1994. *Medicine, Rationality, and Experience: an anthropological perspective.* Cambridge: Cambridge University Press.

Grinspoon, L. and Bakalar, J.B. 1997. *Marihuana, the forbidden medicine*. New Haven: Yale University Press.

Hakkarainen, P., Frank, V.A., Perälä, J. and Dahl, H.V. (2011). Small-scale cannabis growers in Denmark and Finland. *European Addiction Research*, vol. 17(3), 119-128).

Hammersley, R. and Leon, V. 2006. Patterns of cannabis use and positive and negative experiences of use. *Addiction, Research and Theory*, 14(4), 189-205.

Joy, J.E., Watson, S.J. and Benson, J.A. 2002. Marijuana and Medicine: Assessing the Science Base, in *Drugs in America: A Documentary History*, edited by D.F. Musto. New York: New York University Press.

Kleinman, A. 1988. *The Illness Narratives. Suffering, healing and the human condition*. New York: Basic Books.

Krogsgård, N. 2009. *Læger vil ikke ordinere hash* [Doctors refuse to prescribe hashish]. *Berlingske* [Online, 12 March]. Available at: http://www.berlingske.dk/koebenhavn/laeger-vil-ikke-ordinere-hash [accessed: 5 December 2009].

Lindesmith, A.R. 1966. Introduction, in *The Marihuana Papers*, edited by D. Solomon. New York: The Bobs-Merrill Company, xxiii-xvi.

Ludvigsen, J. 2002. Malt og hamp til børn og svagelige [Malt and cannabis for kids and weakly persons]. *Bryggeriet Her*. Herning: Aage Damsgård.ApS. Juli, 1-2.

Mack, A. and Joy, J.E. 2001. *Marijuana as medicine? The science beyond the controversy*. Washington DC: National Academy Press.

Mattingly, C. 1998. *Healing dramas and clinical plots. The narrative structure of experience.* Cambridge: Cambridge University Press.

Mikuriya, T.H. 1972. *Marijuana Medical Papers: 1839- 1972*. [Online: MediComp Press]. Available at: http://www.mikuriya.com/mmp.html [accessed: 5 December 2009].

Musto, D.F. 1973. *The American Disease. Origins of Narcotic Control*. London: Yale University Press.

Møller, K.O. 1946. *Stimulanser* [Stimulants]. Copenhagen: Gyldendalske Boghandel, Nordisk Forlag.

Ogborne, G., Smart, R.G., Weber, T. and Birchmore-Timney, C. 2000. Who is using cannabis and why: an exploratory study. *Journal of Psychoactive Drugs*, 32(4), 435-443.

Osborne, G. and Fogel, C. 2008. Understanding the Motivations for Recreational Marijuana Use among Adult Canadians. *Substance Use and Misuse*, 43(3-4), 539-572.

Riis, L. 2003. Fra hash til medicin [From hashish to medicine]. *Farmaci*, 8, 24-25.

Russo, E. 2001. Hemp for Headache: An In-Depth Historical and Scientific Review of Cannabis in Migraine Treatment. *Journal of Cannabis Therapeutics*, 1(2), 1-72.

Russo, E. 2002. Cannabis Treatment in Obstetrics and Gynecology: A Historical Review, in *Women and Cannabis: Medicine, Science, and Sociology*, edited by E. Russo. New York: The Haworth Press.

Russo, E., (ed.) 2002. *Women and Cannabis: Medicine, Science, and Sociology*. New York: The Haworth Press.

Swift, W., Gates, P. and Dillon, P. 2005. Survey of Australians using cannabis for medical purposes. *Harm Reduction Journal*, 2,18-27.

Thygesen, E. 1967. *Er marihuana skadelig?* [Is Marihuana dangerous?]. Copenhagen: Stig Vendelkjærs Forlag.

Zinberg, N.E. 1984. *Drug, Set, and Setting. The Basis for Controlled Intoxicant Use*. New Haven: Yale University Press.

Chapter 5

With a little Help from my Friends – Justifications of Small-Scale Cannabis Growers[1]

Pekka Hakkarainen and Jussi Perälä

Introduction

Drug markets and drug distribution are usually discussed from the point of view of importation when the drug is assumed to originate from outside the consuming country. We call this "the import paradigm" of drug policy discourse. However, increased domestic cannabis cultivation puts this assumption in a new context. The importance of border control as the major frontline of the drugs war diminishes when an enemy is already inside the borders. But what kind of enemy are we speaking about? In many cases, domestic cannabis cultivators are people who only engage in small-scale growing and harvesting mainly for their personal use or sharing with friends (e.g., Potter 2010, Decorte 2010a). As argued by European studies recently conducted in Belgium (Decorte 2008), the Netherlands (Wouters 2008) and the UK (Potter 2008, 2009), the cannabis market becomes less hierarchical and less populated by criminal organizations when the market share of homegrown cannabis rises. Consequently, the trend of substituting imported product in illicit drug markets with product grown by the users themselves introduces new issues to consider in the long-running debate on cannabis. At the same time, this trend amplifies the conflict between cannabis users and drug control policies that are based on established ways of thinking. When cannabis is the most widely used illicit drug, studying domestic cannabis cultivation and cultivators is of a high social and political relevance.

In this chapter we will study the cannabis issue with a focus on the moral justifications for small-scale cannabis cultivation. We are interested in how cannabis growers argue in favor of their growing activity, and what kinds of rhetorical worlds they use when trying to address and convince their audience. We will show that when growers talk about small-scale cannabis cultivation, they

1 We express our gratitude to The Scandinavian Research Council for Criminology (NSfK) for supporting this study with a grant. We also are grateful to Mette I. Snertingdal and the Finnish drug research seminar (the "Seula") for their useful comments on an earlier version of this chapter.

see it as a special kind of moral economy that regulates their relationships to drug markets and toward society at large. As a theoretical standpoint for the analysis, we use a theory presented by Luc Boltanski and Laurent Thevenot in their book *On Justification – Economies of Worth* (2006). Our empirical data is from a study we are conducting on cannabis growing in Finland.

In Finland, the cannabis available in the drug market has traditionally been imported hash. The share of marihuana in the market has been nearly nonexistent and it has likewise been imported. One of the cornerstones of Finnish drug policy rests on the import paradigm. For example, the central drug strategy paper in Finland states that "the important strategic goal in preventing drug supply is to keep Finland as much of a low-level and risky market area as possible for international drug trafficking" (Drug strategy 1997: 3). However, during the last years, domestic cannabis cultivation has also increased in Finland (Hakkarainen, Kainulainen and Perälä 2008). In the 1980s, the police confiscated only some tens of plants annually and in the 1990s no more than a few hundred plants per year. Since 2001, the police have confiscated several thousands of plants annually. For example, in 2007 the police found 1,400 plantations, from which they confiscated 7,600 plants. In most of the plantations, the number of plants was between 5 and 15. In 2008, the number of confiscated plants rose to 14,000 (Perälä 2009). It is obvious that this development seriously challenges the sustainability of current policy, which is based on the assumption that drugs come from foreign sources. We will provide an overview of the local debate on cannabis by briefly outlining the Finnish cannabis policy and social attitudes toward cannabis in public opinion and the media. By analyzing the moral justifications of small-scale growers, we can specify the challenges domestic cannabis cultivation poses for drug policy. Even though our analysis deals with local data on Finland, we believe that at least in some respects it may also have more general, even global, significance.

Data

From June 2008 to the end of the year 38 qualitative face-to-face interviews with cannabis growers were conducted. These interviews constitute the principal data used in this article. As background material for establishing the local context, we use criminal statistics, a sample of media coverage on the subject (N=34) sourced from *Helsingin Sanomat*, the biggest newspaper in Finland, and some other newspapers from 2006 to the spring of 2010, and a web survey conducted among Finnish growers (N=1,298) in the spring of 2009.

To recruit people for the study, a call for interviews was advertised on the Finnish Internet site on cannabis cultivation (www.hamppu.net). Since the forum had over 7,000 registered users, it opened up good possibilities for recruitment. The anonymity of interviewees was guaranteed. Since cannabis growing seems to be a male-dominated activity, only two females volunteered to be interviewed. The age of the interviewees varied between 18–58 years. As seen in Table 5.1, the

Table 5.1 Description of the interviewees

Gender			**Social position**		
Age group	Males	Females	Employed	Students	Unemployed
< 20 y	2	-	-	2	-
20–24	7	-	1	5	1
25–29	16	1	10	6	1
30–34	7	-	5	1	1
35–	4	1	5	-	-
	36	2	21	14	3

interviewees were a group of socially well-integrated people and mostly comprised young adults. Most of them were working or studying, and only three of them were unemployed at the time. Slightly over half of them were married (N=8) or living together with somebody (N=12) whereas 18 of the interviewees were living alone. One fourth of the interviewees had children. The interviews were collected from five different areas all over Finland.

The interviewees were small-scale growers typically running an indoor plantation of one to ten plants at a time, which is the most usual practice in Finland (Hakkarainen et al. 2011). The maximum size of plantation reported was some 40-50 plants cultivated outdoors, with a total harvest of three kilograms of dry bud at a time. The interviewees ranged from beginners growing their first crop to experienced growers who had already tried different plantation sites, several types of technical solutions, varied strains of cannabis plants or crossbreeding their own variety. The interviews were recorded and they lasted from 1.5 hours to over 3 hours. The growers were asked to describe their motivations, tell about their experiences and practices of growing, and evaluate their relationships to other people, authorities and drug policy. The interviewer was one of the authors (Jussi Perälä).

It is interesting to note that in the interviews, growers often justified their participation in the study by stating that they believed the study may bring their views to the eyes of the public and thus have a balancing effect in public discussion. In general, they liked to support their views by citing scientific literature, especially with regards to the effects of cannabis. In a way, they saw science as their ally, and consequently, their positive attitude toward the study might be summarized by the title of a well-known Beatles song, "*With a Little Help from My Friends*". This attitude perhaps encouraged them to patiently explain their experiences, practices and opinions to the researcher. Those with an indoor growing site were even willing to present it to the researcher and some of them showed photos of their previous plantations or harvests. All in all, we think that we got data that is very well suited to the aims of the study.

Theoretical perspective

Drug crime is one of the most condemnable types of crime in modern culture, and people arrested, accused or sentenced for such crimes are heavily labeled and stigmatized by society (Christie and Bruun 2003). Although globally there is much variation in attitudes toward cannabis, its cultivation is forbidden and controlled by international narcotics conventions and international law. Cannabis cultivation is thereby deemed a punishable offence by national legislation worldwide. However, in some countries, producing a small number of cannabis plants for personal use may only result in a civil penalty (see Lenton, this volume).

How do the small-scale cannabis growers handle this conflict with the law? In criminological literature, perspectives for an answer to this question have been opened by the theory of techniques of neutralization (Sykes and Matza 1957). However, even if you can easily find techniques like "The Denial of Injury" and "The Condemnation of Condemners" used in the talk of cannabis growers, we see this as problematic. In fact, small-scale cannabis growers do not fit very well to the basic assumptions of neutralization theory, which state that the offenders have internalized mainstream values, agree that breaking the law is wrong and therefore have to perform a kind of self-talk to reduce feelings of shame and guilt (see Snertingdal 2010). On the contrary, cannabis growers challenge the overpowering dominance of mainstream values, and in a way they can be seen to be looking for a new solution in the middle ground between mainstream society and the criminal underworld. Thus, as we will later see, the core issue in small-scale cannabis growers' relationship to society has more to do with claiming the right to full citizenship rather than excusing or explaining criminal acts. This leads us to widen our perspective toward a more general theory of moral justification.

Instead of one universal moral system, Boltanski and Thevenot (2006), drawing on their readings of classic works of political philosophy by authors such as Hobbes, Rousseau, Saint-Simon and Adam Smith, argue that there are six different and generally shared worlds for moral justifications by which people in dispute can try to resolve their differences and arrive at a common understanding. These worlds are defined as six self-sufficient regimes of justification, and they provide general criteria for arguing and negotiating an agreement. Each of these six worlds carries a certain form of worth, and there are specific types of conventions imbedded in each of these worlds by which the common good can be reached. Following Boltanski and Thevenot, the contents of these six worlds can be summarized by sets of concepts describing values, norms or institutions characterizing the special domain of a certain regime.

1. *The inspired world* is defined by concepts like inspiration, enrichment, love, passion, happiness, creation, discovery, imagination and artistic;

2. *The domestic world* includes things like family, home, reproduction, generations, tradition, trustworthiness, honesty, habits, naturalness, respect, responsibility, conventions, principles, good manners and proper behavior;
3. *The world of fame* is created by the reality of public opinion, others, dignity, media, public image and being recognized;
4. *The civic world* contains citizenship, civil rights, participation, membership, unity, state, policy and politics, legislation, law and order, rules, courts and the judicial system;
5. *The industrial world* is defined by efficiency, performance, the future, functionality, work, energy, professionalism, expertise, reshaping the environment, progress, control and instrumental action;
6. *The market world* is characterized by competition, value, money, profit, winning, opportunism, business, salesmen, clients, buyers, millionaires, wealth and luxury.

Even if Boltanski and Thevenot aim at a general social theory, their model can offer fruitful tools for the analysis of different kinds of conflicts and disagreements at various levels of social interaction and policy (see e.g. Latour 2003). The task of a researcher is to analyze how people in dispute construct and justify their arguments and mutual relationships. Regimes of justification open up six different options to argue for a stand on a topic. Next we will apply this model in analyzing the local dispute around cannabis growing in Finland. First we will briefly outline the dominant views on cannabis growing/use in Finnish society. This outline will provide a context for the arguments of the growers.

Dominating views in the local dispute

Cannabis cultivation in all its forms is forbidden in Finland. According to the Finnish Penal Code (180/1992, Chapter 50:1):

> A person who unlawfully produces or attempts to produce a narcotic substance or cultivates opium poppy, coca or cannabis for use as a narcotic substance or the raw material for a narcotic substance, shall be sentenced for a narcotic offence to a fine or to imprisonment for at most two years.

In other words, even growing one or two plants is defined as a punishable act in the legislation. In practice, sowing and planting have been interpreted as cultivation, and consequently, the acquisition of seeds and suitable equipment for growing has been seen as an attempt to produce cannabis. All cannabis cultivation cases are dealt with in court. Furthermore, a person may be charged in court not only for cultivating a narcotic substance but also for possessing, using or obtaining such a substance. The most common consequence for small-scale cultivation (for own use) is a day-fine, but production on a larger scale with intent to distribute may lead to imprisonment. In general, drug control policy follows a restrictive line and even the use of cannabis is criminalized and punishable by sanctions (Kainulainen 2009). Thus, in the civic world, a cannabis grower is simply defined as *a lawbreaker and a criminal.*

Juha Partanen (2002) has described Finnish public attitudes toward drugs as "narco-phobic". Indeed, in a general population survey in 2006 (Hakkarainen and Metso 2007), only one in ten of the respondents were of the opinion that people should have the right to use cannabis. Interestingly, a slightly bigger share of the respondents (16%) agreed that people should not be punished for growing cannabis. Considering public opinion and formal policy together, it can be said that acceptance of cannabis use and growing is very limited in Finnish society. In the world of fame, the image of a cannabis grower resembles the general picture of *a dope fiend.*

Along with the trend of increasing domestic cultivation of cannabis, the media is showing greater interest in the subject. In the media, the main source of knowledge has been the police, who have claimed that in practice homegrown cannabis is rarely meant for own use only, but for selling and dealing too. In fact, they have argued that along with a growing demand for domestic cannabis, professional criminals have become interested in investing in its production.[2] Thus, in the market world, a cannabis grower is characterized as *a drug dealer* possibly participating in a business run by professional criminals and organized crime. Newspaper articles based on medical expertise have reminded readers that cannabis use includes many potential dangers and harms that are especially prevalent in homegrown cannabis due to the exceptionally high content of THC.[3] Instead of serving to enrich the personal potentialities valued in the inspired world, cannabis is said to drive the user into *passivity* in his or her life. As cannabis users are typically seen as young people, they are also considered to pose *a threat* to the domestic world of family life. In the general population survey in 2006, only five percent of respondents were of the opinion that regular use of cannabis does not involve any risk (Hakkarainen and Metso 2007). Use of cannabis is also seen as a risk for *low performance and efficiency* in the industrial world, and an overwhelming majority of citizens (90%) accept drug testing in schools and work places (ibid.).

Justifications for small-scale growing

Because of the ruling attitude toward cannabis, growers are in constant conflict with society. The question is how do cannabis growers respond to this? Do they accept

2 Kannabiksen viljely Helsingissä on tullut ulos vaatekomeroista [Cannabis cultivation has come out of the closet in Helsinki], Helsingin Sanomat, 13 April 2008; Moni kiinni jääneistä sastamalaisista nuorista kasvatti kannabista myyntiin [Many of the young people caught by the police in Sastamala were growing cannabis for sale],Turun Sanomat, 23 June 2009.

3 Vai vaaratonta? [Harmless?], *Turun Sanomat*, 26 April 2009.

being labeled as a criminal? How do they construct their identity and on what basis? Justifications also include an opportunity for a critique that can be based on the values and principles of a certain regime of justification (Boltanski and Thevenot 2006). As can be seen in the interviews, growers justify their actions and make efforts to negotiate an agreement for the common good by using all those six regimes.

The frame of *the inspired world,* defined by words like creation, enrichment and passion, is very easily found in the justifications of the growers. They are real enthusiasts for their growing activity. They are interested in all new information about seeds, growing technology and best practices they can get from books, journals, Internet sites or more experienced growers. Some of them have even read all the material available. They are constantly improving their growing systems and sites (e.g. with timers, ventilators, temperature and humidity regulating devices), and some of them run them using very advanced technology and techniques. Most growers have employed different strains of cannabis, and some of them have tried both indoor and outdoor cultivation. Growing is fun and you can choose your strains based on your own preferences, they emphasize. Their greatest sources of inspiration are breeding trials, cross-breeding and cloning of their own strains.

> How to get the highest possible THC content (...) One good tip is that one week before harvest you poke a nail through the plant's roots. Somehow the plant foresees that it's going to die and it makes one final push. When it does so, more visible crystal resin forms. There's a notable difference in crystal resin if you torture the plants the last week before harvest and keep them in the dark for three days compared to if you don't. These tips are half based on my own growing experience and half based on what I've heard from other growers. [Male, 26 years, student]

Fanciful talk about a plant consciously responding to a grower's actions shows a great imaginary and almost personal relationship between the plant and the grower. Indeed, growers seek an agreement in the inspired world by presenting their growing activity as a beloved hobby that they are passionate about. In fact, the talk of cannabis growers closely resembles the way women who love flowers speak about gardening, but it is worth noting that these cannabis growers are mostly male. That said, the interviewees typically compared cannabis growing to other, more masculine hobbies like hang-gliding, fixing cars and wine tasting. By drawing an analogy between cannabis growing and some socially legitimate hobbies, they are rhetorically questioning the stigmatizing labels and crackdown measures directed toward them by society.

> This is my hobby. While others go hang-gliding or do something else as a hobby, this is mine. [Male, 29 years, cohabiting, has higher schooling and a steady job]

When it comes to *the domestic world* of home and family life, there is a clear division of labor and responsibility, as the growers are usually men. Their wives, cohabiting partners or girlfriends do not necessarily accept their growing activity, but they may allow it. One of the interviewees said that because of his wife's strict attitude against cannabis, he does not use his homegrown at home. However, in some families, the wives may take part in the consumption of the yield and in some cases the spouses grow it together. Whether their parents and other relatives know about growing varies case by case, but mostly they are kept unaware. However, it may be easier to tell parents about growing marihuana for medical purposes – and also gain their acceptance – than to reveal that one is growing it for recreational use.

> We both grow cannabis and basically we have our own places for growing and in practice I take care of my own plants and then I help my husband with the nutrients and so on (…) My surplus goes to my husband and my motive is to produce for both of us (…) My husband's parents know and for them it's very okay. I haven't told my own family or my kin. [Female, 25 years, university student, married, husband has Multiple Sclerosis and he uses and grows cannabis for medical purposes]

Of course, the situation at home is simpler if the grower is single and lives alone. However, some singles told that they hide their cannabis use and home growing from their girlfriends, at least at the beginning of the relationship. In any case, when a person is growing cannabis in an apartment, he is usually forced to be careful about whom he invites to his home. To sum up, even if growing cannabis in apartments and homes may restrict their family life in some respects, the interviewees tend to present themselves as honest, respectful and responsible citizens who follow the general conventions of proper behavior. Actually, in the regime of the domestic world, they criticize society for its ruling attitude toward cannabis, which disturbs their home and family life, making it impossible for them to lead a normal life in every aspect.

The world of fame, constructed by public opinion and media images, is experienced as being very problematic and unfair by the growers. Images of cannabis users in "narco-phobic" public opinion are closely combined with the image of drug users in general in Finland. No clear distinction is made between cannabis and other drugs, except among the younger generations (Hakkarainen 2005). Cannabis growers criticize this heavily. Because of negative public attitudes they are, in a way, doomed to lead a double life and try to keep their "precious hobby" out of sight. This causes problems even in the most private areas of their lives. For example, in addition to choosing whom to admit into their home, they have to be careful with their landlords, janitors and neighbors. In fact, in a few interviews, some mentioned that they even experienced unpleasant and uncontrollable feelings (e.g. panic reactions) because of society's attitudes and the double life they are forced to live all the time. In a culture where heavy alcohol intake and public drunkenness are widely accepted or at least tolerated, cannabis growers with their alternative private habits of pleasure and intoxication find their situation to be highly unfair and unjust. They feel themselves to be ideologically suppressed and consider it a violation of their dignity and recognition.

> Home growers are stigmatized and said to be crazy. All the phone tapping and everything else, all this because of a plant. [Male, 18 years, student]

Because of the criminalization of cannabis in the Penal Code, the good citizenship of cannabis growers is questioned in *the civic world*. Growers, of course, criticize this very heavily. When growing their own herb, they do not consider that they are committing any criminal offence as such. On the contrary, they typically say that they grow their own stuff because they do not want to support illegal markets and organized crime with their money. They also argue that homegrown cannabis is safer to use and thus better for their health than the stuff available in the illegal markets.

> It's wrong that people are punished for actions they are doing to their own body. [Male, 32 years, has vocational training and a regular job]

As they see their own growing activity as a harmless hobby that does not cause any serious damage to anybody else, they view it more as a kind of civil disobedience than a criminal offence. However, most of them are not for the total legalization of drugs. Rather, they want decriminalization, including a reform of the Penal Code, so that growing cannabis in small amounts for personal use would be de-penalized. They argue that regulation based on civil law could be strengthened while the role of the control based on the Penal Code could be reduced. Some of them were even ready to pay some taxes for their harvests.

> I noticed that I would rather use cannabis than alcohol. I didn't want to get involved in any crime and since it's a natural product, I thought why not grow it myself. (…) I'm a regular and decent citizen and I grow cannabis in my closet. [Male, 29 years, married, has good schooling and a steady job]

As said, their life situation and participation as citizens are based on continuously hiding their double life. Consequently, a fear of being uncovered restricts their needs for full membership and unity. When participating in social activism, e.g. in working for a political party or NGO, as some of them do, they feel that they are not able to speak openly for their "own precious cause", cannabis use and growing. Some of them were members of the Finnish Cannabis Association or its local satellites, but as a study conducted among Finnish cannabis activists has shown, only a very few of the activists are able to do anything visible for their cause (Kekoni 2007). On the contrary, they argue that current drug policy is driving them into their own sub-communities. The contradiction between exclusion and inclusion could not be more obvious when one is constructing his identity as a regular citizen!

> I live in an owner-occupied flat, I do a four-hour working day and despite this I complete 60-70 credit units a year at the university. I'm active in one organization (name excluded) and in one political party (name excluded), especially in its youth branch. On the face of it, I would be a really correct Finnish citizen, sort of a damn Spes Patriae prototype,[4] except that sometimes I smoke cannabis, because I don't like to get drunk. [Male, 26 years, university student]

This self-construction of an identity as a regular citizen is very common in their thinking and talking. They wonder if preferring cannabis over alcohol really constitutes sustainable grounds for exclusion and labeling them as deviants. As wanting to be intoxicated is a general human characteristic, the issue is only about the personal choice of an alternative way to get drunk/high, they argue. And for medical growers, the issue is about an alternative way of treatment and medication.

The industrial world as a moral regime is a world of performance, work, productivity and efficiency. In a way, these values are also prevalent among cannabis growers. Even if small-scale home growers are not aiming to build companies or factories, they take a great interest in growing the plants as well as possible. They use sophisticated equipment and arrangements for enhancing their yield and improving the quality of their product. The amount of the yield is a recurring subject in discussions and comparisons among the growers. They say that growing cannabis demands great precision and they are proud of their expertise. In the field of their precious hobby, they demonstrate that they are not at all unfamiliar with the common good defined by the industrial regime of justification. Progress in the amount and quality of the yield is a central driver of their development efforts. In fact, discontent with the quality of the cannabis sold in the drug markets was typically mentioned as a central motivation for starting to grow their own cannabis. Of course, own production was also seen as a solution to overcoming the problems of availability in the local markets.

> Well, the availability of soap bar hash went down and the quality went lower and lower (…) I wouldn't put that same "shoe sole" in my pipe ever again. [Male, 29 years, cohabiting, one child, has a steady job]

Home growers' relations to *the market world* – characterized by concepts like competition, money, profit and business – are contradictory and reserved. From a practical perspective, growers do not want to buy their cannabis from dealers because of the hassle and high prices. The other reason is moral: they do not want to associate with organized crime. Instead, they start breaking the law on their own.

---

4 "Spes Patriae" is a Latin phrase used in Finnish linguistic practice to refer to young people and graduates as the very hope of their fatherland.

> For me it's important not to support organized crime ... As a cooperative we also are able to produce herb clearly below market prices. [Male, 20 years, growing together with two friends]

On the other hand, most of the home growers were not able to resist making some money off it by selling a small part of their output at least occasionally. However, this is not done for the sake of big profits or expanding their business. As they say, the stuff produced mainly stays within the closed circle of the cultivators and their friends.

> I'm always growing about 50 plants, which is a little too much for two men but on the other hand by doing so I can give it away free and a lot to my friends (...) Every time we visit some other grower we offer some for free and don't take any money (...) but sometimes I have sold some of my extra crop for small sums. I mean I offer it for free but if somebody insists on buying some for his personal use and take it home, I sometimes make an exception – but these are exceptions and for good friends only. [Male, 33 years, has a steady job]

When production exceeds personal needs, growers prefer sharing the surplus with friends, gift giving and trade by barter rather than selling. In fact, they make a clear distinction between themselves and those who make a business out of cannabis cultivation. Thus, in the market world these small-scale home growers are negotiating an agreement that is based on the values of traditional barter economy rather than on the values of modern capitalism.

> It's quite common for us to trade crops with each other. My buddies have good crops and I have good crops, so we trade. Can you give me "ten" (10 grams) and I'll give you ten. Or can you lend me "twenty" (20 grams) and I'll give you back twenty when my crop is ready. That's the way it goes, we try to keep the unnecessary money away from it. [Male, 34 years, cohabiting, has three children and a seasonal job]

Conclusion

In the dispute with the law, drug policy and public attitudes, Finnish small-scale cannabis growers justify their activities by trying to negotiate an agreement for a common good by using different moral regimes, namely the inspired world, the domestic world, the world of fame, the civic world, the industrial world and the market world. This shows that home growing as a political and moral issue is not separable from the culture and worth of western civilization. It is not a simple or one-dimensional phenomenon, but rather a new trend that provokes and challenges present drug policy in various respects. For example, images of organized crime and foreign enemies based on the import paradigm are not a very good fit for domestic home growers, who lead quite ordinary lives and argue for their good citizenship and civil rights in their own country.

When justifying cannabis growing, some regimes have a more central position than others. First of all, the issue seems to concern the right to have full citizenship. As the growers say, they do not see cannabis growing as a real crime ("*mala per se*"), but rather as a personal choice of intoxication or medication that is defined as an offence ("*mala prohibita*") by the moral majority. In their argumentation, they strongly question this definition as an unjust policy that results in social and political exclusion. As a contrast to the label of a delinquent, many of them prefer to emphasize their self-understanding and identity as regular citizens. This argumentation based on the civic world was supported by their arguments in terms of the domestic world, the world of fame and the world of inspiration. As the information about the general social background of the interviewees indicates, their lives are very comparable to those of average ordinary people in Finland; they have families, children and jobs, take part in study programs, etc. However, they felt that they were forced to hide their cannabis preferences in most of their social circumstances. They were doomed to lead a double life, they complained. Furthermore, by defining cannabis growing as their beloved hobby and paralleling it with some socially legitimate hobbies, they challenged the strict dividing lines between different ways of getting inspired, enriched and passionate.

Another very central regime of justification was the market world. As repeated in several interviews, the most important issue in home growing is whether the harvest goes for own use or for sale. The interviewees told that they were mostly growing for themselves, and when they have a surplus from the harvest, they share it with friends and acquaintances or exchange with other small-scale growers. Some sales activity was also reported but it was not for large sums of money or with profit in mind. Actually, in the market world, the growers were negotiating an agreement based firstly on self-sufficiency and secondly on the values of barter economy rather than on the values of the modern market economy. In addition, growers were pleading that by growing their own stuff they were able to avoid contacts with illicit drug markets and organized crime. The meaning of this was ideologically emphasized, but there was also a more practical aspect connected to the industrial world: expertise in home growing and suitable technology for small-scale production was seen as a solution to the problems of availability and quality of cannabis in the illicit drug markets. All in all, they are speaking in favor of a policy reform (e.g. decriminalization) that would normalize their civil rights and citizenship by redefining the position of small-scale cannabis growing somewhere in the middle ground (e.g. under the civil law) between the mainstream society and the criminal underworld.

Is this argumentation presented by the Finnish growers only a local phenomenon? As shown in this book, cannabis growing is a contentious issue worldwide. Of course, some details of the debate may vary from country to country, but in general, the basic lines of the circumstances based on legislation, drug policy and public opinion may be quite similar. In this context, it is not surprising that similarities in the themes of discussion among small-scale growers can be found in different countries. For example, themes such as the quality and availability of cannabis, inspiration and enthusiasm for growing, technological improvements of growing, ideological vs. commercial growing, medical growing, avoiding the illegal circuit, fear and stress about getting caught and rebuked by relatives, taking precautions in social relationships, and criticism of policy have also been found in studies made in the UK and Belgium (Potter 2008, 2010, Decorte 2008, 2010b). However, because small-scale cannabis cultivation has not been studied much (Decorte 2010), it is not possible to make a more detailed comparison. Nevertheless, it can be hypothesized that both global and local features in justifications for cannabis cultivation can be found among small-scale growers in different countries. Global features may be found in general circumstances created by the international law and cooperation in law enforcement, globalized media images and the development of an international subculture of cannabis growing. Local features, on the other hand, might be connected to the toughness of national drug policy and public attitudes toward cannabis, or to other special characteristics of the national culture.

List of references

Boltanski, L. and Thevenot, L. 2006. *On Justification – Economies of Worth*. Princeton: Princeton University Press.

Christie, N. and Bruun, K. 2003. *Den gode fiende* [The good enemy]. 3rd edition. Oslo: Universitetslaget.

Decorte, T. 2008. Domestic cannabis cultivation in Belgium: on (un)intended effects of drug policy on the cannabis market, in *Cannabis in Europe: Dynamics in Perception, Policy and Markets*, edited by D. Korf. Lengerich: Pabst, 69–86.

Decorte, T. 2010. Small scale domestic cannabis cultivation: an anonymous web survey among 659 cannabis cultivators in Belgium. *Contemporary Drug Problems,* 37 (Summer 2010), 341-70.

Decorte, T. 2010b. The case for small-scale domestic cannabis cultivation. *International Journal of Drug Policy*, 21 (4), 271–275.

Drug Strategy 1997 Report by the Finnish Drug Policy Committee, An English summary. Helsinki: Ministry of Social Affairs and Health, Committee Report 1997.

Hakkarainen, P. 2005. Drug use as a generational phenomenon, in *Research on Drugs and Drug Policy from a European Perspective*, edited by L. Kraus and D. Korf. Lengerich: Pabst, 48–61.

Hakkarainen, P. and Metso, L. 2007. Huumekysymyksen muuttunut ongelmakuva: vuoden 2006 huumekyselyn tulokset [Changed picture of the drug problem: results from the drug survey in 2006]. *Yhteiskuntapolitiikka*, 72(5), 541–552.

Hakkarainen, P., Kainulainen, H. and Perälä, J. 2008. Measuring the cannabis market in Finland – A consumption-based estimate. *Contemporary Drug Problems*, 35(2–3), 321–45.

Hakkarainen, P., Asmussen Frank V., Perälä, J. and Dahl, H. 2011. Small-scale cannabis growers in Denmark and Finland, *European Addiction Research,* 17, 119-128.

Kainulainen, H. 2009. *Huumeiden käyttäjien rikosoikeudellinen kontrolli* [Criminal Control of Drug Users]. Helsinki: National Research Institute of Legal Policy, Research Reports No. 245.

Kekoni, T. 2007. *Kannabiksen käyttö, yhteiskunnallinen reagointi ja siihen vastaaminen: Kannabisaktivistien näkökulma* [The Use of Cannabis, Societal Reaction and Responses to it: The Perspective of Cannabis Activists]. Tampere: Acta Universitatis Tamperensis.

Latour, B. 2003. Moderni vai ekologinen [To modernize or ecologize]? in *Luonnon politiikka* [Politics of Nature], edited by Y. Haila and V. Lähde. Tampere: Vastapaino, 70–103.

Partanen, J. 2002. Huumeet maailmalla ja Suomessa [Drugs in Finland and worldwide], in *Huumeiden käyttäjä hyvinvointivaltiossa* [The drug user and the welfare state], edited by O. Kaukonen and P. Hakkarainen. Helsinki: Gaudeamus, 13–37.

Perälä, J. 2009. Cannabis markets, in *Finland – Drug Situation 2009*, edited by S. Rönkä and A. Virtanen. [National Institute for Health and Welfare]. Available at: www.thl.fi/thl-client/pdfs/9bf86f3e-9b30-48a1-bc56-b32981cf0575. [accessed: 27 May 2010].

Potter, G. 2010. *Weed, Need and Greed: A study of domestic cannabis cultivation.* London: Free Association Books.

Potter, G. 2008. The growth of cannabis cultivation: explanations for import substitution in the UK, in *Cannabis in Europe: Dynamics in Perception, Policy and Markets*, edited by D. Korf. Lengerich: Pabst, 87–105.

Potter, G. 2009. Exploring retail-level drug distribution: Social supply, "real" dealers and the user/dealer interface, in *Old and New Policies, Theories, Research Methods and Drug Users Across Europe*, edited by Z. Demetrovics et al. Lengerich: Pabst, 51–74.

Snertingdal, M.I. 2010. *The Co-constitution of Heroin Crime: Narratives of Smugglers and Dealers Meet the Judicial Practices*. Oslo: University of Oslo, Department of Sociology and Human Geography.

Sykes, G. and Matza, D. 1957. Techniques of neutralization: A theory of delinquency. *American Sociological Review*, 22, 664–70.

Wouters, M. 2008. Controlling cannabis cultivation in the Netherlands, in *Cannabis in Europe: Dynamics in Perception, Policy and Markets*, edited by D. Korf. Lengerich: Pabst, 51–68.

Chapter 6

'Stories', 'Facts' and 'Myths'. Perceptions of Domestic Cultivators on Potency and Quality of Cannabis[1]

Tom Decorte

Introduction

It is often suggested that local cultivation of cannabis plants used to be a rare phenomenon and mostly the work of 'amateurs' to meet their own needs in a cheap way, but that it has evolved into a (very) professional enterprise since the late eighties. The majority of empirical studies on cannabis cultivation relate to commercially oriented, large-scale ('industrial') growers, and/or are based on police data (e.g. Weisheit 1992, Plecas et al. 2005, Bouchard 2007, Spapens et al. 2007, Wouters et al. 2007, Hafley and Tewksbury 1995, Walker et al. 1998). Furthermore, indoor cultivation of cannabis is often associated with higher THC-levels, as a reflection of genetic factors (selected seed varieties and cultivation of female plants), environmental factors (the *sinsemilla* cultivation technique and seed production) and freshness (local production sites are closer to the consumer and storage degradation of THC is avoided) (King et al. 2004). Almost simultaneous with the claims that domestic cannabis cultivation and criminal organizations are closely linked, comments in the media, and by policy makers and drug warriors regarding a large increase in the potency of cannabis have raised concerns that the currently available drug is much stronger than in the past. However, the health and psychological effects and risks of cannabis with high THC concentrations are not well understood (Pijlman et al. 2005, Potter et al. 2008). Furthermore, claims on cannabis adulterated with lead, aluminum and glass have been widely reported in the popular media. Both claims (on stronger cannabis and contaminated or adulterated cannabis) have played an important role in recent debates about proposed changes to legal penalties for cannabis use. However, they require critical analysis.

---

1 The author would like to thank Craig Reinarman, Martin Bouchard and Gary Potter for their helpful comments and discussions that contributed to the development of this chapter. In addition the author thanks Pascal Tuteleers for his enthusiastic participation in the collection of data among Belgian cannabis growers.

Between January 2006 and December 2007 we conducted a study of small-scale home cultivation in Belgium. The study consisted of face-to-face interviews with 89 cannabis cultivators and an anonymous web survey among 659 cannabis cultivators. The aim of our study was to recruit as many (small scale) cannabis growers as possible, and to establish a picture as refined as possible of their profiles and backgrounds, motives and experiences, cultivation careers and strategies, as well as their know-how and ideas concerning the cultivation of cannabis. Apart from other findings we report elsewhere (Decorte and Tuteleers 2007, Decorte 2008), a theme which often re-occurred in our growers' narratives was their preoccupation with the strength and the quality of the cannabis they grow in comparison with the cannabis they buy elsewhere. This raised several questions that are still largely unanswered. One important question concerns the reasons why domestic growers choose home growing over buying their cannabis through other supply channels, and related to this: does (the perception of) the strength and the quality of the cannabis on the market stimulate more users to grow their own marihuana? Furthermore, is there a match between 'objective' data on potency and quality of cannabis reported in official studies and the scientific literature, and 'subjective' perceptions of users/growers, and if so, how strong is this match?

In this chapter we first present some findings related to grower's perceptions on potency and quality of cannabis, drawn from our own study of small-scale home cultivators in Belgium (Decorte and Tuteleers 2007). Then we try to assess these perceptions of Belgian growers by examining official data and peer reviewed publications on THC potency, auto-titration mechanisms, and adulteration and contamination of cannabis. On the basis of these data, we explore possible links between (perceptions of) quality and potency of cannabis and policy strategies. We do no more than suggest some hypotheses. A rigorous test of these possible explanations is beyond the scope of this chapter.

The Belgian study on small scale cultivators: a short note on design and methodology

Between 31 March 2005 and 31 August 2006 we interviewed 89 cannabis cultivators through snowball sampling. We used 'privileged access interviewers' to look for experienced cannabis growers in their own social environments, and to interview them –after having been trained intensively – with a semi-structured questionnaire. This questionnaire contained 122 questions on 13 topics: initial growing experiences, patterns of cultivation over time, quitting cultivation, size and destination of their most recent yield, information sources for growing and learning how to grow, rewards and advantages of growing, threats, failures and disadvantages of growing, use of cannabis and other substances, supply channels for cannabis, selling cannabis and other drugs, social networks, experiences with law enforcement, opinions on cannabis policy, and socio-demographic profiles of growers. Interviewers were instructed not to recruit potential participants through official agencies (police, penitentiary institutions…) or treatment facilities. Neither the interviewers nor the participants were paid for their participation in the study. Participants had to reside in Flanders or Brussels, and had to have grown cannabis successfully at least once. Minors and participants who were not growing at the time of the interview (or who considered themselves to be ex-growers) were not excluded from the study.

Based on this questionnaire and after coding all answers to the open-ended questions, a shorter version (54 structured questions, only in Dutch) was developed for use in an anonymous web survey, linked to the website of the Institute for Social Drug Research (ISD) where it could be completed on-line. The attention of potential participants was drawn to the internet survey both through online and offline invitations (Mann and Stewart 2000), including a press release and calls for participation posted on several specialized internet sites, discussion forums (including www.cannabis-belgië.com and www.cannaclopedia.be) and in *Highlife*, a well-known magazine for cultivators of cannabis. 659 questionnaires proved to be sufficiently usable (i.e. more than one third of the questions were answered).

Using a web survey to study a sensitive topic such as cannabis cultivation is a useful avenue to obtain data, but it also presents a number of methodological problems and limitations, such as coverage errors (associated with the degree of internet penetration) (Dillman 2000) and 'volunteer effects' (self-selection of the respondents) (Eysenbach and Wyatt 2002). Both samples in our study were recruited with non-random and non-probabilistic techniques, and thus certainly not truly representative for the total population of Belgian growers. It was impossible to determine the degree and the importance of bias in our sample (Coomber 1997), but both samples remain useful for developing hypotheses and for performing qualitative analyses (Schonlau et al. 2002).

Clearly, we recruited more small-scale than large-scale cultivators. Among the growers we interviewed personally, more than one in four (27%) did not grow more than 5 plants, and more than 70% never grew more than 20 plants at the same time. In the web survey sample, two out of three participants did not grow more than five plants, more than three out of four respondents had a plantation of maximum ten plants. The number of plants cultivated on average during one single harvest, amounted to maximum 8.47 plants (the median was 4).

The average age of the participants in the face-to-face interviews was 30.1 years (range: 17-70), the average age of the web survey participants was 28.5 years (range: 16-60). The majority of them were male: 93.3% in the face-to-face interviews, and 88.5% in the web survey sample.

In both samples, the proportion of outdoor cultivators was remarkably high: 52.0% in the sample interviewed face-to-face, and 53.2% in the web survey sample. Of those who did grow indoors, hardly anyone used a hydroponic culture system (barely 2.2% of the growers we interviewed face-to-face and 3.5% of the web survey sample).

In most cases, the whole yield (or the major part) of home-grown cannabis was intended for personal consumption, and for sharing with family and friends.

Approximately half of the growers we interviewed personally (55.5%) claimed they never sold any home-grown cannabis. The majority of the web survey participants (68.0%) claimed they never sold any home-grown cannabis. Those who did sell only did so when the harvest exceeded their personal needs, and usually to a small number of people (5 to 6) they knew intimately.

Perceptions of cannabis potency and quality: "grower stories"

There is usually more than one reason for starting to grow cannabis, but our study showed that financial benefit (cheaper marihuana), curiosity (checking out if it is really that easy), and the pleasure of growing ('green fingers') are the most important reasons. In our face-to-face interviews, 21 growers (23.6%) refer to the potency of cannabis sold in the Dutch coffee shops. These respondents consider the coffee shops as "too commercial". Too often, they sell 'bad cannabis': too strong, 'too worked up'. Some participants call this cannabis 'crash weed', to indicate the too high THC content of the product, which makes the user sleepy and not 'high' or 'stoned'.

> I am independent: by growing it myself I determine how strong the weed will be. [male grower, 31 years]

A similar picture arose from the web survey: a considerable number of growers started cultivating cannabis because they were not satisfied with the potency of the marihuana sold in Dutch coffee shops. For 47.3% of these participants the argument that home-grown cannabis is healthier ('more organic') was a (very) important motive to start cultivating. Not only is this desire for 'organic weed' an important motive to start growing, some growers try to refine their cultivation techniques for the same reason.

> The commercial cultivation was too much focused on as much crystals as possible, and I wanted a more easy weed, I wanted a more natural weed. [male grower, 29 years]

Most experimental growers do not consciously select a specific variety (such as White Widow, Jack Herer, etc…). But when home growers do consciously select a variety, they are interested in (among other aspects such as the potential yield, the growing speed, etc.) achieving a 'higher quality' product:

> Weed you grow yourself, is better than weed from the coffee shops, like 'Jack Herer'. You get a much nicer high from own weed. Weed from the coffee shops is too much 'boosted', not natural anymore, it is too strong. [male grower, 39 years]

Most of the cultivators we recruited in both samples claimed their own cannabis was milder than the marihuana bought elsewhere (e.g. in Dutch coffee shops)

Table 6.1 Perceived strength of home-grown cannabis versus cannabis bought elsewhere, in two samples

Cannabis I grow is...	Web survey		Interviews	
	N [*]	Valid %	N	%
Stronger than the cannabis I buy elsewhere	45	9.1	9	11.4
As strong as the cannabis I buy elsewhere	143	28.8	19	24.1
Milder than the cannabis I buy elsewhere	308	62.1	51	64.6
Total	496	100.0	79	100.0
I do not wish to answer this question	4			
I don't know exactly	42		10	
Missing	117			
Total	659		89	

[*] Total number of valid answers: 496 (75.3% of the web survey participants); total number of *missing values*: 163 (24.7% of the participants).

(see table 6.1). One in ten claims their home-grown cannabis is stronger than the cannabis they buy elsewhere.

From the face-to-face interviews with growers we know that most growers have no (exact) idea of the average THC-percentage in the cannabis they grow. The few growers who do claim they know compare their home-grown cannabis with marihuana they have bought elsewhere (e.g. in coffee shops) and state they felt more or less 'high' or 'stoned'. Or they rely on the number of 'crystals' on the tops and leafs: '*my hands were sticky from those crystals when I was cutting them*', '*you can*

Table 6.2 Perceived strength of home-grown cannabis and perceived impact on personal consumption, in the snowball sample (N=89)

My home-grown cannabis is...	**Impact on personal consumption**			
	N	**Made me use less**	**No impact on my consumption pattern**	**Made me use more**
stronger than the cannabis I buy elsewhere	9	5 (55.6%)	4 (44.4%)	-
as strong as the cannabis I buy elsewhere	19	-	19 (100.0%)	-
milder than the cannabis I buy elsewhere	51	6 (11.8%)	28 (54.9%)	17 (33.3%)
Total	79			
Missing/don't know	10			
Total	**89**			

see it from the white color on the plant and from the little brown hairs that arise on the tops'. Comments by friends who shared a smoke from their yield also helped these growers to judge the THC content of their home-grown cannabis. The THC content of cannabis from Dutch coffee shops was usually estimated at around 15%. This then was used as a comparator to estimate the THC content of their own cannabis. One grower for example assumed cannabis from Dutch coffee shops contained 30 to 40% THC, and therefore estimated the THC percentage in his home-grown cannabis at 10 to 15%. Only one participant 'knew' the exact THC content, because it was mentioned on the packaging, when he bought seeds via the internet.

Table 6.3 Perceived strength of home-grown cannabis and perceived impact on personal consumption, in the web survey sample (N=659) [*]

My home-grown cannabis is...	**Impact on personal consumption**			
	N	**Made me use less**	**No impact on my consumption pattern**	**Made me use more**
stronger than the cannabis I buy elsewhere	45	20 (44.4%)	22 (48.9%)	3 (6.7%)
as strong as the cannabis I buy elsewhere	143	-	143 (100.0%)	-
milder than the cannabis I buy elsewhere	308	23 (7.5%)	224 (72.7%)	61 (19.8%)
Total	**496**	**100.0**		
I do not wish to answer this question	*4*			
I don't know exactly	*42*			
Missing	*117*			
Total	**659**			

[*] Total number of valid answers: 496 (75.3% of the web survey participants); total number of *missing values*: 163 (24.7% of the participants).

Furthermore, heedful of William Isaac Thomas's theorem that 'if men define situations as real, they are real in their consequences', the idea that home growers *perceive* their marihuana to be milder may have important consequences for their personal patterns of consumption.

Tables 6.2 and 6.3 show that among those growers who claim their home-grown cannabis is stronger than the cannabis they buy elsewhere, almost all claim this did not have an impact on their personal pattern of consumption, or made them use less. Among those growers who claim their home-grown cannabis is milder than the cannabis they buy elsewhere, a majority state it did not have an impact on their personal pattern of consumption. In the snowball sample, 33.3% of them claimed it made them use more, and in the web survey sample 19.8% of them claimed they used more cannabis, because of this difference in strength. This raises interesting questions, related to the self-titration hypothesis, which we will discuss in the next section.

Next to our respondents' stories and statements on the potency (THC content) of the cannabis they grow (and as different from the cannabis they buy or used to buy elsewhere), a reoccurring theme in their narratives is related to the 'quality' of cannabis. Cannabis sold elsewhere (e.g. in the Dutch coffee shops) is 'bad' because it is seen as 'chemical bullshit'. For 45.1% of the web survey participants the superior quality and flavor of home-grown cannabis was a (very) important advantage of growing your own.

> Especially because I get stoned myself from my own weed and I know what I am smoking. It is not sprayed flock! [female grower, 29 years]

> I can determine myself what happens with my produce: no genetic engineering. I am against an economic mentality and I am opposed to pesticides. I compare growing cannabis to growing tomatoes: your own produce tastes best and it has more quality. [male grower, 33 years]

Although they are not looking for monetary gain, many home growers start using 'professional' equipment (artificial lighting, organic and nutritious substances, fertilizers), both to enhance their yield and to improve the quality of their marihuana. When growers give each other advice and tips, they often emphasize 'organic' growing strategies ('just let nature do its thing!') to keep their cannabis free from mould, bacteria, heavy metals and insecticides. As with other consumer goods, quality is also dependent on the appearance, the taste and the smell (Maalsté and Panhuysen 2007). Through careful plant breeding, cannabis growers often seek to develop a set of effects in the same way that winemakers breed grapes to produce a particular flavor or bouquet in wine (Weisheit 1992: 56). Personal preferences in consumers play a role too. It is similar to perceptions on the quality of wine: some prefer a Bordeaux, others swear by a 'rioja' (Maalsté and Panhuysen 2007).

Although cannabis is less likely to be adulterated than illicit drugs which are available in powder or tablet form (heroin, cocaine, amphetamines and ecstasy), many of our respondents believe cannabis is likely to have been contaminated with pesticides and other substances to enhance yield during cultivation. This perception is particularly linked to indoor grown cannabis, and to cannabis sold in the Dutch coffee shops. For this reason, some grow cannabis outdoor, because they consider it more organic and to have received less chemical treatment than indoor grown cannabis. Others state they started growing their own cannabis (indoor and/or outdoor) to be able to exclude contamination.

The growers' preoccupation with the strength and the quality of the cannabis they grow in comparison with the cannabis they buy elsewhere is a theme which often re-occurs in their narratives. Most of these growers' stories seemed to be based on a binary opposition: there is 'bad' cannabis ('too strong' and 'adulterated' or 'dirty'), produced by commercially oriented growers, and amongst others sold in Dutch coffee shops; and there is 'good' cannabis you grow yourself: 'mild', 'natural' and 'pure'. The commercial growers are said to boost their cannabis to make money and they care not how they produce it nor of the consequences of their actions to those who buy cannabis.

Cannabis potency: the "facts"

But is there a match between these 'subjective' perceptions of users/growers and the 'objective' data on potency and quality of cannabis reported in official studies and the scientific literature? In many European countries, the U.S. and Australia, a number of commentators in the drug field have claimed that the THC content of cannabis products has increased up to 10, 20 or even 30 times over the past two decades (for quotations on these claims, see e.g. Hall and Swift 2000, Reinarman 2009). These claims have been widely and uncritically reported in the popular media, and have also been used to explain an apparent increase in the adverse health and psychological effects of cannabis use among young people who are regular users of the drug (Hall and Swift 2000). However, others have critically analyzed these claims and the available evidence supporting them, and concluded that the 'facts' are less alarming than they have sometimes been presented (King et al. 2004). These claims far exceed the smaller increases in potency reported in U.S. Government and European Union studies (Reinarman 2009) and in the scientific literature (Earlywine 2002).

In Van Tichelt's study of THC levels in 'Belgian' cannabis, cannabis samples seized in 2003 and 2004 were analyzed. It appeared that in 2003 the average THC level was 13.6% in marijuana and 15.2% in hash; in 2004 this average was 13.2% in marijuana and 14% in hash (Van Tichelt et al. 2005). The study did not make a distinction between imported cannabis products and locally produced products. As this was the first ever analysis of its kind in Belgium, its results cannot be compared with any previous year. In the neighboring country, the Netherlands, THC content of cannabis products is monitored in more detail and over a longer period. These data are relevant to our findings on growers' perceptions presented above, as Dutch coffee shops are a very important source of supply for many Belgian cannabis consumers. The annual monitoring of the concentration of THC in cannabis preparations sold in Dutch coffee shops since 1999 did show important differences between THC levels in Dutch home-grown marijuana and in imported marijuana. Percentages of THC in imported marijuana remained unchanged (Pijlman et al. 2005). Weed from plants cultivated in the Netherlands, 'Dutch weed', is two to three times stronger than weed imported from abroad (in 2004 for example 20.4% versus 7.0%, Pijlman et al. 2005). The increase in potency of Dutch marijuana compared to imported weed started in the nineties (it went from 8.6% in 1999/2000 to 20.4% in 2003/2004), but now seems to have reached its top: average THC percentage of Dutch marijuana lowered again to 17.5% in 2005/2006 (Niesink et al. 2006).

Similar increases in average THC content were observed in the United Kingdom (Potter et al. 2008), and in North America, but in Australia and New Zealand the picture is less clear (King et al. 2004). The increased THC content has been attributed to the cultivation of particular cannabis strains, including hybrids of the *Cannabis sativa* plant such as 'skunk' or 'nederwiet', and the use of hydroponic growing methods, with artificial control of 'daylight' length, propagation of female cuttings and prevention of fertilization (Hall and Swift 2000, King et al. 2004). Others have argued that 'law enforcement pressures have pushed cannabis growers indoors and thus towards high-intensity technologies of production' (Reinarman 2009: 33, see also Bouchard 2007). An ironic consequence of drug control might then be that 'by means of such indoor technology, growers produce fewer but more potent plants, which both reduces their risk of arrest and maximizes profit per-plant' (Reinarman 2009: 33). The increased THC content of herbal cannabis produced by indoor methods is also a consequence of freshness: production sites are close to the consumer and storage degradation of THC is thus avoided (King et al. 2004).

The information on THC levels in cannabis needs to be assessed with caution. Data on potency trends over 5 or 10 years are available only from a few countries. In some of these the test sample sizes are low or unknown. Questions exist in terms of how representative the data are: whereas the samples in the Dutch monitoring study are obtained twice a year from Dutch coffee shops (Pijlman et al. 2005), samples in other studies elsewhere are mostly derived from police and customs seizures (ElSohly et al. 2000). Moreover, how representative are seizures of the overall illicit market? In addition, for a number of methodological reasons, both the reliability and comparability of data from different forensic laboratories is questionable (King et al. 2004). Claims that cannabis in the US available in the late eighties was much stronger than that available in the seventies ('a new, stronger and more dangerous drug', were countered by Mikuriya and Aldrich (1988) with the argument that samples from the middle 1970s were not representative of cannabis consumed at that time and that the samples from the 1970s under-estimated THC potency because they were not properly stored, allowing their THC content to degrade.

Exaggeration and variation aside, several authors report that in addition to the regular varieties of cannabis which have always been sold, there now are some more potent strains available in the Dutch coffee shops than once was the case (Pijlman et al. 2005, Reinarman 2009). Niesink et al. (2006) also argue that the number of coffee shops that sell Dutch hash products is still small, and that the number of coffee shops that (still) sell imported weed, is decreasing. If this trend is to continue the next years, it would mean that the supply of 'softer' (imported) cannabis products would shrink, while the supply of 'stronger' (locally produced) cannabis products would remain stable or even increase.

An important question to address is whether the availability of a more potent form of cannabis is in itself an issue. Public health consequences of cannabis consumption probably is not a simple function of the strength of the cannabis consumed (it is not the case with alcohol either). At population level, research suggests that it is the total quantity of cannabis consumed that is important rather than the concentrations in which it is sold. And increased THC potency may have little or no adverse health effects when users are able to adjust or 'titrate' their dose to achieve the desired state of intoxication (Zimmer and Morgan 1997, Mikuriya and Aldrich 1988). Research on whether cannabis users are able to titrate their dose of THC by modifying the amount of smoke they inhale is scarce and not univocal. In controlled residential laboratory settings, some studies suggest cannabis users are able to titrate (Perez-Reyes et al. 1982, Heishmann et al. 1989), while other studies report that cannabis users have limited or no ability to titrate their dose of THC (Matthias et al. 1997, Wu et al. 1988, Chait 1989, Kelly et al. 1997). Most of these laboratory studies worked with small samples of participants, and have used only two or three (Chait and Burke 1994) potencies, and usually fairly low doses, as compared to potencies of cannabis sold on the street (between 0.5% and 3.5%) (Chait and Burke 1994, Kelly et al. 1994, Kelly et al. 1997, Kirk et al. 1998, Wachtel et al. 2002). Furthermore, these experimental studies suggested that many other set and social context factors were important, such as the age of onset of use, frequency of use and the user's experience, the user's expectancies (Kirk et al. 1998), the route of ingestion and the individual smoking technique (joints versus the use of a water pipe) (Hall and Swift 2000), the price of different cannabis products (Haney et al. 1997, King et al. 2004), etc.

Studies that were conducted in non-laboratory ('natural') settings, seem to suggest that most users have a particular level of altered consciousness they regard as preferable and that they tend to adjust their intake to the potency of the drug (Korf et al. 2007). Similar to our findings presented above, Reinarman et al. (2004) found that most users use less than usual when they encounter more potent cannabis. A number of researchers have argued that users of stronger varieties inhale less smoke (smaller volumes or 'puffs') to get high, which would clearly be a health benefit from more potent cannabis (Zimmer and Morgan 1997, Matthias et al. 1997, Heischman et al. 1989). Mikuriya and Aldrich (1988) convincingly argue that highly potent cannabis has a long history of recreational use and that calling it a 'new drug' is misleading. They also suggest that although new cannabis may be more potent the practice of *auto-titration*, or the self-regulation of doses, means that users are not necessarily becoming more intoxicated (Mikuriya and Aldrich 1988). Korf also found the extent of self-titration varied with type of cannabis user and stage of career. Younger users proportionally use more often and more cannabis with higher THC levels, whereas more experienced blowers regulate their use by using less and less risky (Korf et al. 2007). This is consistent with claims made by owners of Dutch coffee shops, who say the strongest cannabis varieties are especially popular among younger, experimental blowers, while older and more experienced blowers avoid these varieties and prefer softer cannabis (Van Scharen 2007).

Cannabis adulteration and contamination: the "facts"

There are only a few peer reviewed studies which discuss adulteration of cannabis in Europe. In Germany in 2008 there was a report of 29 patients admitted to hospital in the Leipzig area for lead poisoning as consequence of smoking adulterated cannabis (Busse et al. 2008). Analysis of cannabis samples revealed the drug had been adulterated with lead to increase the drug weight by approximately one tenth. An anonymous screening program undertaken after the source of lead poisoning was confirmed screened 145 individuals, of which 95 had blood lead levels which required treatment.

In Rome forensic analysis of a seizure of 80 cannabis plants grown indoors and a grey-white powder, also found at the scene, confirmed the presence of naphthalene (which is commonly used as a pesticide) (Fucci 2003).

In 2006 the Scientific Institute of Public Health in Belgium issued an 'early warning message' which stated that several cannabis users from France, Belgium and the Netherlands reported adulteration of their cannabis with other substances. Some mentioned crystalline particles, others mentioned white powder on the flower buds. Some users felt ill (adverse effects such as head ache, poor sight...) but the early warning stated no clinical evidence was found to show a relation between the crystals or the white powder and the adverse effects experienced by these users. Analyses of different samples of this 'suspect' cannabis showed no other psychoactive substances than THC. Neither sand nor grounded glass were found in these samples.

In 2007 the Department of Health in the UK issued three health alerts about herbal (skunk) cannabis contaminated with microscopic glass particles. In the May 2007 alert it was stated that approximately 5% to 10% of herbal cannabis seizures forensically examined were contaminated with glass, and in September 2009 the alert stated that there had been 151 cases in the UK and Ireland in the previous year. In Belgium, the Scientific Institute of Public Health issued another 'early warning' that same year, which mentioned two cases of serious breathing difficulties in France, probably due to the adulteration of cannabis with microscopic glass particles (0.02 to 0.3 mm). In the March 2007 alert it was stated that one similar case was detected in Belgium. According to this alert, cannabis users often claim their cannabis is adulterated with sand, bulb glass or glass wool, but none of these were found in laboratory analyses.

Verweij et al. (2000) analyzed samples of cannabis in the Netherlands and found that all seven samples tested positive for mould cultures, with six or seven testing positive for *penicillium* species. In the national drug report of the Netherlands for 2006 there was mention of further research conducted at the University of Leiden which confirmed the presence of bacteria and fungus in cannabis being sold in Dutch coffee shops (Van Laar et al. 2007).

There is almost no research conducted on and around the adulteration or contamination of cannabis beyond the narrow and limited focus of the forensic science community. It is therefore impossible to formulate reliable answers to questions such as: how often is cannabis adulterated, or contaminated? If it is, does this happen accidently or purposively? And if so, why do some cannabis producers, distributors or sellers adulterate their product?

Discussion

The data from our study on small scale cannabis growers in Belgium suggest that a considerable number of growers believe 'commercial' cannabis is 'too worked up'. Moreover, many cannabis users and growers believe that during cultivation the plants are typically sprayed with pesticides and other cultivation chemicals, particularly those grown indoors under hydroponic conditions. Simultaneously, most of the cultivators we recruited in our study claimed their own cannabis was *milder* than the marihuana bought elsewhere (e.g. in Dutch coffee shops), and the *superior quality and flavor* of home-grown cannabis is perceived as a (very) important advantage of growing your own.

To verify whether this binary opposition in the narratives of our growers ('dirty' and 'strong' cannabis, produced by commercially oriented growers, and amongst others sold in Dutch coffee shops versus 'mild cannabis of superior quality, grown by yourself') reflects with biological and economical realities, we would need studies that compare laboratory analyses of potency and quality of representative samples of home-grown cannabis with, for example, cannabis sold in Dutch coffee shops.

Claims that the potency of cannabis products have increased spectacularly, made by a number of commentators and reported widely in the media, far exceed the smaller increases in potency reported in official studies and in the scientific literature. Similarly, cases of cannabis adulterated with lead and glass or contaminated with pesticides or bacteria do occur, but the attention that the media give to these rare cases of adulterated or unusually potent cannabis, can create a false impression, both among the general population and among cannabis users, that these levels of potency and these adulteration practices are typical of the cannabis products consumed in a given country. When looking at the available evidence supporting them, the facts of this matter, as weak as they may be, seem less alarming than they have sometimes been presented (King et al. 2004).

However, from a qualitative point of view, both the current images of the 'typical' cannabis grower (that are, arguably, the linchpins on how the cannabis market is thought to work) and the considerable consensus among respondents on this issue and the coherence of their stories are important. With the emergence of domestic cannabis cultivation, the 'commercial cannabis producer' took centre stage and the potency and quality of locally produced cannabis became the focus of media, political and public concern. The notion that cannabis nowadays is a 'new' drug, much stronger than in the past, and full of impurities and adulterants likely to lead to adverse effects and serious harm, is a common one. There is hardly a source of authoritative or public information that does not subscribe to it and/or propagate it. However, those who have critically analyzed these claims and the available evidence supporting them, concluded that the 'claims' far exceed the 'facts', as they are reported in the scientific literature.

Users, it seems, have incorporated the repeated assertions on potency and quality in the media or via politicians or police, as 'facts'. Not only does this raise concerns about potency and quality of cannabis among users, it also seems to help them explain problems they experience as a consequence of their use. It is common for drug users, even experienced ones, whose 'high' is in some way different to previous experiences (particularly where there is some unwanted physical consequence: stomach ache, sweating, nausea, etc), to blame the negative experience on the unexpectedly high potency of cannabis, or contamination with bacteria or pesticides. These beliefs might prove useful as a political football for pretty much anyone concerned with the 'drug problem', regardless of perspective. In his book *Pusher myths*, Coomber (2006) argued that such notions (like 'high potency cannabis' and 'dirty cannabis') are commonly conceived of as widespread by drug field experts and workers, by the police, politicians, the general public, users and even dealers and producers themselves. They are convenient ideas for almost everyone, both for those who call for total prohibition of cannabis, as for those from a harm reduction- or legalization-perspective.

Another important question we want to raise here is how (perceptions of) 'potency' and 'quality' relate to trends in the cannabis market, and to cannabis policies. In a comparative study of cannabis users in Amsterdam and San Francisco, Reinarman found that preferences with regard to potency differed sharply by city. Amsterdam respondents were significantly more likely to prefer mild or moderate strength cannabis whilst San Francisco respondents were more likely to prefer stronger varieties. In an attempt to explain these differences in potency preferences, Reinarman (2009) suggested more intensive drug law enforcement (as observed in San Francisco) might push the market toward a preference for more potent forms of cannabis. 'When supplies are not always reliable in either quality or quantity, more users are likely to feel they can never be certain of adequate potency and thus more often opt for the stronger varieties [...] In Amsterdam, three decades of *de facto* decriminalization have fostered a stable and translucent retail cannabis market in which users are reliably able to buy cannabis of the potency they prefer. These market characteristics may militate against uncertainty and allow users to reach more precisely the level of high they desire' (Reinarman 2009: 34).

Whether or not Reinarman's hypothesis could also apply to Belgian cannabis users – in other words whether more intensive law enforcement in Belgium has pushed the Belgian market toward a preference for more potent forms of cannabis – is impossible to assess with our data. Here we do no more than suggest a hypothesis having to do with a growing dissatisfaction with the average potency and quality of 'Dutch' weed among Belgian cannabis users.

Although the retail of cannabis in Dutch coffee shops is tolerated (decriminalized), the production of cannabis and the supply of these coffee shops is not regulated. Maalsté published 18 interviews with large-scale cultivators and other entrepreneurs in the Dutch commercial cannabis sector (Maalsté and Panhuysen 2007). These commercially oriented growers testify about the increasingly criminal character of the cannabis trade (threats, possession of weapons, rip-offs and snitching) and claim that the old-school, 'idealistic' cultivators and small scale growers were pushed out of the market by the intensified repressive approach pursued by the Dutch government, and replaced by more commercially oriented players who calculate the penalty as a professional hazard. These growers are not always interested in quality and in knowledge about the possibilities of the plant, but they are more interested in strong weed varieties and the financial profit that they can generate. According to some growers, this leads to a scantier supply of varieties, questionable quality, pernicious practices and higher prices (Maalsté and Panhuysen 2007). Under such circumstances, users are less able to buy cannabis of the potency and quality they prefer.

Our growers' narratives might reflect the construction of user lore on quality of cannabis, based on personal experiences and stories from other users and/or growers. Together with the dominant discourse on extremely high THC-percentages in Dutch marihuana (and the psychological dangers related to them), these elements may help explain why many (Belgian and Dutch) users became dissatisfied with the strength and the quality of the cannabis they used to buy in Dutch coffee shops, and decided to start growing their own cannabis, in search of a better (i.e. 'milder', 'healthier' and 'more organic') product. As their distrust in corporate growers and the way they conduct their business increases, users become more interested in growing their own product. As such, it may be seen as an attempt to gain more control over the strength and quality of cannabis, by consumers who demand a good quality product and who have lost confidence in the product sold elsewhere (see also Potter 2010).

As we stated earlier, the aim of this chapter was to do no more than suggest some hypotheses. A rigorous test of these possible explanations is beyond the scope of this chapter, but the elements presented above make clear that a number of important research questions remain unanswered. A range of academic research suggests that there is sufficient individual variation in types of cannabis growers and cannabis production, but little, if anything, is known about the exact market share and role of these different types of cannabis producers. Some studies (Decorte and Tuteleers 2007, Potter 2010,) seem to suggest the market significance of small-scale, independent or 'ideological' cultivation should not be underestimated, but this market segment is still under-researched. To what extent has the number of non-commercially oriented cultivators increased or decreased, and what explanations can be found for these trends? Furthermore, there are major differences in the organization of cannabis markets between continents, and these may have different consequences in terms of quality and potency of cannabis products. Moreover, both the legal framework and applied law enforcement strategies have their own (un)intended effects on different types of cannabis growers, on cultivation techniques, and on the potency and quality of locally produced cannabis, etc. And finally, the *perceptions* and *ideas* of growers around quality and potency of the cannabis they grow or buy elsewhere may have important consequences for their personal patterns of consumption, and are worth studying in more depth.

List of references

Bouchard, M. 2007. A capture-recapture model to estimate the size of criminal populations and the risks of detection in a marijuana cultivation industry. *Journal of Quantitative Criminology,* 23, 221-41.

Bovenkerk, F. and Hogewind, W.I.M. 2002. *Hennepteelt in Nederland: het probleem van de criminaliteit en haar bestrijding* [Cannabis cultivation in the Netherlands: the problem of criminality and law enforcement]. Utrecht: Willem Pompe Instituut voor Strafwetenschappen.

Busse, F., Omidi, L., Timper, K., Leichtle, A., Windgassen, M., Kluge, E. and Sturnvoll, M. 2008. Lead poisoning due to adulterated marijuana. *New England Journal of Medicine*, 358(15), 1641-2.

Chait, L.D. and Burke, K.A. 1994. Preference for high- versus low-potency marihuana. *Pharmacology, Biochemistry and Behaviour,* 49(3), 643-7.

Chait, L.D. 1989. Delta-9-tetrahydrocannabinol content and human marijuana self-administration. *Psychopharmacology* (Berl.), 98(1), 51-5.

Coomber, R. 1997. Using the Internet for Survey Research. *Sociological Research Online* [Online], 2(2). Available at: www.socresonline.org.uk/2/2/2.html [accessed: 4 April 2010].

Coomber, R. 2006. *Pusher Myths: Re-Situating the Drug Dealer*. London: Free Association Books.

Decorte, T. 2007. Characteristics of the cannabis market in Belgium, in *Drugs in society: European perspectives,* edited by J. Fountain and D.J. Korf. Oxford/ New York: Radcliffe Publishing, 28-38.

Decorte, T. 2008. Domestic marihuana cultivation in Belgium: on (un)intended effects of drug policy on the cannabis market, in *Cannabis in Europe: dynamics in perception, policy and markets*, edited by D.J. Korf. Lengerich, Pabst Science Publishers, 69-86.

Decorte, T. 2010. Small scale domestic cannabis cultivation: an anonymous web survey among 659 cannabis cultivators in Belgium. *Contemporary Drug Problems,* 37 (Summer 2010), 341-70.

Decorte, T. and Tuteleers, P. 2007. *Cannabisteelt in Vlaanderen. Patronen en motieven van 748 telers* [Cannabis cultivation in Flanders (Belgium). Patterns and motives among 748 growers]. Leuven, Voorburg: Acco.

Dillman, D.A. 2000. *Mail and internet surveys: the tailored design method.* London: Wiley.

Earleywine, M. 2002. *Understanding marijuana: a new look at the scientific evidence*. New York: Oxford University Press.

El Sohly, M.A., Ross, S.A., Mehmedic, Z., Arafat, R., Yi, B. and Banahan B.F. 2000. Potency trends of delta9-THC and other cannabinoids in confiscated marijuana from 1980-1997. *Journal of Forensic Science,* 45, 24-30.

Eysenbach, G. and Wyatt, J. 2002. Using the internet for surveys and health research. *Journal of Medical Internet research,* 4(2), 13.

Fucci, N. 2003. Growing cannabis with naphthalene in Rome. *Forensic Science International*, 138(1), 91-93.

Hafley, S.R. and Tewksbury, R. 1995. The rural Kentucky marijuana industry: organization and community involvement. *Deviant Behaviors*, 16, 201-21.

Hall, W. and Swift, W. 2000. The THC content of cannabis in Australia: evidence and implications. *Australian and New Zealand Journal of Public Health*, 24(5), 503-8.

Haney, M., Comer, S.D., Ward, A.S., Foltin, R.W. and Fischman, M.W. 1997. Factors influencing marihuana self-administration by humans. *Behavioural Pharmacology*, 8(2/3), 101-112.

Heishman, S.J., Stitzer, M.L. and Yingling, J.E. 1989. Effects of tetrahydrocannabinol content on marijuana smoking behavior, subjective reports, and performance. *Pharmacology, Biochemistry and Behaviour*, 34(1), 173-9.

Kelly, T.H., Foltin, R.W., Emurian, C.S. and Fischman, M.W. 1997. Are choice and self-administration of marijuana related to delta9-THC content? *Experimental and Clinical Psychopharmacology*, 5(1), 74-82.

Kelly, T.H., Foltin, R.W., Emurian, C.S. and Fischman, M.W. 1994. Effects of delta9-tetrahydrocannabinol on marijuana smoking, dose choice, and verbal report of drug liking. *Journal of the Experimental Analysis of Behavior*, 61, 203-11.

King, L.A., Carpentier, C. and Griffiths, P. 2004. *An overview of cannabis potency in Europe*. Insights no. 6. Lisbon: European Monitoring Centre for Drugs and Drug Addiction (EMCDDA).

Kirk J.M., Doty, P. and de Wit, H. 1998. Effects of expectancies on subjective responses to oral delta-9-tetrahydrocannabinol. *Pharmacology, Biochemistry and Behavior,* 59(2), 287-93.

Korf, D.J., Benschop, A. and Wouters, M. 2007. Differential responses to cannabis potency: a typology of users based on self-reported consumption behavior. *International Journal of Drug Policy*, 18, 168-76.

Maalsté, N. and Panhuysen, M. 2007. *Polderwiet. Een veelzijdig en onthullend beeld van de wietteelt in Nederland* [Dutch marihuana. A miscellaneous and unveiling image of marihuana cultivation in the Netherlands]. Baarn: De Fontein.

Mann, C. and Stewart, F. 2000. *Internet communication and qualitative research: a handbook for researching online*. London: Sage.

Matthias, P., Tashkin, D.P., Marques-Magallanes, J.A., Wilkins, J.N. et al. (1997), Effects of varying marijuana potency on deposition of tar and D9-THC in the lung during smoking. *Pharmacology, Biochemistry and Behavior*, 58, 1145-50.

Mikuriya, T.H. and Aldrich, M.R. 1988. Cannabis 1988. Old drug, new dangers. The potency question. *Journal of Psychoactive Drugs*, 20(1), 47-55.

Niesink, R., Rigter, S., Hoek, J. and Goldschmidt, H., 2006. *THC-concentraties in wiet, nederwiet en hasj in Nederlandse coffeeshops (2005-2006)* [THC-concentrations in marihuana, Dutch marihuana and hash in Dutch coffee shops (2005-2006)]. Utrecht: Trimbos Institute.

Perez-Reyes, M., DiGiuseppi, S., Davis, K.H., Schnidler, V.H. and Cook, C.E. 1982. Comparison of effects of marihuana cigarettes of different potencies. *Clinical Pharmacology and Therapeutics*, 31, 617-24.

Pijlman, F.T.A., Rigter, S.M., Hoek, J., Goldschmidt, J. and Niesink, R.J.M. 2005. Strong increase in total delta-THC in cannabis preparations sold in Dutch coffee shops. *Addiction Biology*, 10, 171-80.

Plecas, D., Malm, A. and Kinney, B. 2005. *Marihuana growing operations in British Columbia revisited 1997-2003*. Abbotsford, Dept. of Criminology and Criminal Justice – University College of The Fraser Valley.

Potter, G. 2010. *Weed, Need and Greed: A study of domestic cannabis cultivation*. London: Free Association Books.

Potter, D.J., Clark, P. and Brown, M.B. 2008. Potency of delta-9-THC and other cannabinoids in cannabis in England in 2005: implications for psycho-activity and pharmacology. *Journal of Forensic Sciences*, 53(1), 90-4.

Reinarman, C. 2009. Cannabis policies and user practices: market separation, price, potency, and accessibility in Amsterdam and San Francisco. *International Journal of Drug Policy*, 20, 28-37.

Reinarman, C., Cohen, P. and Kaal, H. 2004. The limited relevance of drug policy: Cannabis in Amsterdam and San Francisco. *American Journal of Public Health*, 94, 836-842.

Schonlau, M., Fricker, R.D. and Elliott, M.N. 2002. *Conducting research via E-mail and the web*. Santa Monica: Rand.

Spapens, T., van de Bunt, H. and Rastovac, L. 2007. *De wereld achter de wietteelt* [The world behind cannabis cultivation]. Den Haag: Boom Juridische Uitgevers.

Van Laar, M.W., Cruts, A.A.N., Verdurmen, J.E.E., van Ooyen-Houben, M.M.J. and Meijer, R.F. 2007. *The Netherlands National Drug Monitor, Annual report 2006*. Utrecht: Trimbos Institute.

Van Scharen, H. 2007. Te straffe wiet? [Too strong weed?]. *Knack*, 25 april 2007, 99.

Van Tichelt, K., Canfyn, M., Govaerts, C., Lenaerts, K., Piette, V. and Parmentier, F. 2005. *Δ^9-THC-concentraties in cannabis in 2003 en 2004* [Δ^9-THC-concentrations in cannabis in 2003 and 2004]. Brussels: Wetenschappelijk Instituut Volksgezondheid.

Verweij, P.E., Kerremans, J.J., Voss, A. and Meis, J.F.G.M. 2000. Fungal contamination of tobacco and marijuana. *Journal of the American Medical Association*, 284(22), 2875.

Wachtel, S.R., El Sohly, M.A., Ross, S.A. and de Wit, H. 2002. A comparison of the subjective effects of delta 9 tetrahydrocannabinol and marijuana in humans. *Psychopharmacology*, 161, 331-9.

Walker, L., Cocklin, C. and Blunden, G. 1998. *Cannabis highs and lows: sustaining and dislocating rural communities in Northland*. Department of Geography, University of Auckland.

Weisheit, R.A. 1992. *Domestic marijuana. A neglected industry*. New York: Greenwood Press.

Wilkins, C. and Casswell, S. 2003. Organized crime in marijuana cultivation in New Zealand: an economic analysis. *Contemporary Drug Problems,* 30, 757-77.

Wouters, M., Korf, D.J. and Kroeske, B. 2007. *Harde aanpak, hete zomer. Een onderzoek naar de ontmanteling van hennepkwekerijen in Nederland* [Tough policy, hot summer. A study of dismantling of cannabis plantations in the Netherlands]. Amsterdam: Rozenberg Publishers.

Wu, T., Tashkin, D.P., Rose, J.E. and Djahed, B. 1988. Influence on marijuana potency and amount of cigarette consumed on marihuana smoking pattern. *Journal of Psychoactive drugs*, 20(1), 43-6.

Zimmer, L. and Morgan, J. 1997. *Marijuana myths, marijuana facts: a review of the scientific evidence*. New York: The Lindesmith Center.

Chapter 7
Professionals or Amateurs? Revisiting the Notion of Professional Crime in the Context of Cannabis Cultivation[1]

Martin Bouchard and Holly Nguyen

Introduction

Professional crime is an elusive concept, perhaps as much as the offenders who are considered to be "professional criminals". The malaise with professional crime is analogous to the difficulty scholars have with the concept of organized crime. At times, the notion of professional crime is used to represent activities and the way they are conducted. At other times, it embodies a subculture of its own, a criminal milieu for elites where only a selected few are invited to join – the professional criminals. Edwin Sutherland's initial formulation of the concept of the professional criminal embodies all aspects: a subculture of serious and skilled offenders, who not only interact for various reasons outside of criminal purposes but also take pride in their craft.

But do professional criminals still exist, and if they do, how should they be defined? The question is important because a look into the past 75 years of research since Sutherland published *The Professional Thief* does not offer a clear answer. The majority of scholars who searched for a contemporary version of Sutherland's professional thief fell short (see Hobbs 1997, Tremblay 2010). The impression is that if he was active today, Sutherland's professional thief himself would have a hard time living up to his own early 20th century professional standards. Professional criminals are both elusive and in need of a contemporary definition. We argue that the general failure in locating contemporary professional criminals reflects the difficulty in a) finding suitable approaches to gain access to professional criminals (the research design problem); b) establishing a relatively objective standard to evaluate offenders and their "degree of professionalism" (the

1 The authors would like to thank Tom Decorte, Pekka Hakkarainen and the group present at the Copenhagen meeting of the Global Cannabis Cultivation Consortium for the useful comments made on an earlier version of this chapter. Eric Beauregard, Jon Caulkins, Karine Descormiers, Gary Potter, Dirk Korf, Owen Gallupe, and Pierre Tremblay also made useful suggestions.

problem of the dependent variable); c) properly defining the parameters within which the contemporary underworld operates (the historical context problem).[2]

Fortunately, some clarification can be found by drawing on recent research on criminal careers. More specifically, research on criminal achievement showed that successful and professional offenders can be found in general inmate populations if researchers focus on standard rational choice criteria such as relative impunity, as well as efficiency in earning substantial money from crime (Morselli and Tremblay 2004, Tremblay and Morselli 2000). Standard research designs may thus provide access to such elite populations, to the extent that offenders are evaluated on standard criteria. As to whether a distinct subculture of professionals is still present – and if so, what that subculture might look like – remains an unresolved issue. Hobbs (1997) offers an important contribution in redefining the contemporary underworld and its less romantic, more entrepreneurial nature.[3] According to him, money, more than honor, defines the contemporary underworld. At the same time, Hobbs also concludes that "Nobody is excluded from participation in contemporary serious crime" (Hobbs 1997: 70). In other words, there would be no real alcove for the professional, no barriers to entry into the underworld because such an underworld does not exist.

While we agree that over time, many of the noble features of the subculture of professionals have disappeared, we contend that barriers to entry to a different kind of underworld still prevail. For example, research on the social structure of drug trafficking and organized crime showed that the safest and most lucrative crime opportunities are still restricted to a limited pool of offenders who have a) access to the key contacts necessary to import and distribute large quantities, and b) the required level of competence to successfully undertake high stakes criminal ventures (Bouchard 2007, Caulkins et al. 2009, Desroches 2005, Morselli 2001, 2009, Tremblay, Bouchard and Petit 2009). Similar conclusions were drawn in criminal achievement research, even when examining more diverse samples of offenders involved in both predatory and market crimes (Bouchard and Nguyen 2010, Kleemans and de Poot 2008, McCarthy and Hagan 2001, Morselli and Tremblay 2004, Morselli et al. 2006). In other words, both criminal and social capital act as natural barriers to entry into the parts of the underworld where contemporary professional criminals are likely to be found.

The first objective of this chapter is to propose a classification of offenders that takes these clarifications into account. The classification will be introduced in the next section. The second objective is to illustrate what might constitute a career as a "professional" in the context of cannabis cultivation. Drawing from interviews

---

2 The reader will find an extensive development of some of these points in a recent book Pierre Tremblay (2010) devoted to the contemporary legacy of Sutherland's ideas in criminology entitled "Le Delinquant Ideal" ("The Ultimate Criminal").

3 "What had formerly manifested as locally organized applications of extortion, and craft based larcenies, have now mutated into entrepreneurial activities which should be regarded as indigenous renditions of global markets" (Hobbs, 1997: 69).

conducted with cannabis growers in Montreal and Vancouver, we compare the trajectories of two growers whose careers flirted with the world of professionals.

Searching for suitable professional criminals

What are the appropriate criteria to define professional criminals? The idea of know-how, and skills is invariably tied to the notion of professionals. Professionals embody the highest standards of skills: they are experts, the best in their field. This is the image we have, for example, when we think of professional athletes. The idea of skills is also present in most work on professional crime (e.g. Hobbs 1997, Sutherland 1937), and is difficult to avoid as an essential criteria for our classification. Proficiency in a specific criminal activity, however, is not a sufficient condition to be considered a professional. The concept of "professional" is also embedded the notion of "profession", something that implies a commitment to the activity as a full-time occupation, a way of making a living. Commitment is the second essential criteria for our classification. The importance of both skills and commitment to professional crime is especially salient in the context of cannabis cultivation: many participants are accomplished growers of the plant, but opt to grow a small quantity of cannabis that will simply cover their own consumption (Decorte 2008, Potter and Dann 2005). Taken together, these two criteria produce the classification presented in figure 7.1 below.

		Skill level	
		High	Low
Commitment level	High	Professionals	Average career criminals
	Low	Pro-Ams	Amateurs

Figure 7.1 Classification scheme of of professional criminals

According to this classification, professional criminals are individuals who are both highly skilled and show a high level of commitment to the activity. Individuals who score low on both criteria are amateurs. An amateur can be anyone who is just dabbling in cultivation, without real success. Also important are offenders who do not neatly fit into the usual professional/amateur dichotomy. First, we find what we call the average career criminals, offenders who are poorly skilled but who are nonetheless committed to a life of crime. These offenders are the bread and butter of the criminal justice system and of general theories of crime (e.g. Gottfredson and Hirshi 1990). In the context of the cannabis cultivation industry, these are the growers attracted to the potential to make money but never realized that cultivation would be so much work or would require a learning curve. Such offenders were found in past research in samples of incarcerated adult growers (Weisheit 1992).

Second, we find the "pro-ams": skilled offenders who do not make a living out of crime. The pro-am concept is increasingly used in a variety of domains to refer to those individuals who set professional standards for an activity in which they are not committed to full-time (Leadbetter 2004). Anyone familiar with the literature on cannabis cultivation will recognize that the majority of growers interviewed in recent studies (Decorte 2008, Hough et al. 2003, Potter and Dann 2005) can be considered pro-ams. Pro-ams are interested in the intangible rewards from cultivation (Weisheit 1991); they are passionate and knowledgeable about the plant, its appearance, its taste, and its physiological effects. They are not amateurs but connoisseurs; not professionals but aficionados. Even if cultivation can be time consuming for pro-ams, it is not a full-time occupation, and never a means of living.

Before we turn to our cases studies, four comments are in order. First, the classification shows ideal types – there is variation within each category, and individuals can move from one category to another over time. Previous work indicates that many growers start small and perfect their skills before making a larger financial and time commitment by increasing the size of their operations (Weisheit 1992). Second, our classification does not include the notion of subculture. In theory, nothing prevents a skilled and committed grower from being considered a professional, for example, without also being a member of a specific subculture of professionals. In practice, however, many of those growers are likely to be part of some kind of cultivation-specific professional milieu, as shall be illustrated below. Third, this classification does not offer clear guidance on the measurement of key concepts. While commitment level might be operationalized as the amount of time spent in the activity in comparison to a standard reference point, the concept of skills is more difficult to evaluate. Outcome measures such as plant (or lamp) yield, attrition rate (proportion of plants harvested), and criminal earnings should be considered. The amount of money earned from crime is a necessary, though not a sufficient condition to be considered a professional. It is possible for some average career criminals to earn large sums despite low skills; but all professional criminals should be high earners.

Finally and most importantly, our two key characteristics (commitment and skill level) can be applied to a specific activity (e.g. cannabis cultivation) and can be used more generally (e.g. professional criminal). This feature of our classification avoids confusion with prior use of the terms. For example, one can be a "professional criminal" involved in the cultivation industry (i.e. someone who would have cultivation-specific skills) without being a "professional grower" (e.g. an investor with no cultivation specific skills). In other words, professional growers may not be considered professional criminals in the broader sense of the term, and vice-versa.

Fieldwork and sample

The two cases that will be used to illustrate part of the classification are taken from two separate sets of interviews. First, nine male respondents were interviewed in Montreal and Quebec City in 2005-2006 (Table 7.1). Growers were recruited in a variety of informal ways, in the snowball sampling tradition. A few key contacts were known to the researcher, and provided access to others. Interviews were conducted in cafés or pubs in Quebec city (N = 2) and in Montreal (N = 7). Marc, the subject of a detailed case study below, was introduced through a colleague working as a social counsellor. She had Marc as part of her case load. Information was gathered on many topics, including details on the dynamics of their career in cannabis cultivation, and a variety of issues including the social and economic world of cannabis cultivation. Two of our respondents can be classified as amateurs, two started as amateurs but finished their careers as professionals, but the majority of respondents were pro-ams. Apart from Leon who was a trimmer for large sites, professionals were the only ones involved in sites over 100 plants. Their careers in cultivation (7 and 12 years) also proved to be significantly longer than others (from 1 to 6 years).

Table 7.1 Characteristics of the Montreal/Quebec sample of growers

Name	Gender	Age	Role(s)	Classification	Career length	Location/ technique	Most typical size (number of plants)
Marc	Male	26	Manager	Amateur to professional	12 years (94-05)	Indoor/ Hydro	1800 plants
Quasi-modo	Male	33	Co-owner	Amateur to professional	7 years (98-04)	Out+Indoor/ Soil+ Hydro	80 plants (Max: 400 plants)
Daniel	Male	33	Owner	Pro-Am	3 years (94-96)	Indoor/ Hydro	20 plants
Fabien	Male	28	Co-Owner	Pro-Am	4 years (02-05)	Out+Indoor/ Soil	20 plants (Max: 75 plants)
Max	Male	25	Co-Owner	Pro-Am	3 years (03-05)	Indoor/ Soil	20 plants
Frank	Male	23	Co-Owner	Pro-Am	6 years (98-03)	Outdoor/ Soil	20 plants
Leon	Male	25	Labourer	Amateur	2 years (00-01)	Indoor/ Hydro	220 plants
Paul	Male	21	Owner	Pro-Am	3 years (03-05)	Indoor/ Soil	3 plants
Roger	Male	23	Owner	Amateur	1 year (2004)	Indoor/ Soil	1 plant

All four of the participants in the second set of interviews are Vietnamese: two male and two female who reside in the lower mainland of British Columbia (Table 7.2). This group was chosen because the Vietnamese population has been identified as key players in Vancouver's cultivation industry (Malm et al. 2008), and are a suitable comparison group for the Caucasian growers met in Montreal. Common cultural background with the researcher gave access to the first respondent, who introduced her to others. Information was gathered on a number of issues including entry into the industry, learning experiences and the dynamics of the Vietnamese industry. The roles for each of the participants differed. One participant worked as a labourer for only two harvests whereas another participant worked as a carpenter, setting up new grow-ops, and eventually becoming a co-owner. The average time spent in the industry was 4 years and the size of the sites greatly varied, from a site in an urban apartment with 56 plants, to multiple barns located on countryside farms with 585 plants. The average age of three of the participants was 55 and one participant (Mai) was in her early 30s. She is the object of our second case study below because her career offered a detailed account of a grower who did not succeed in becoming a professional, despite full-time commitment to the activity. For the most part, the participants started as laborers and after learning the ropes, became site owners themselves.

Table 7.2 Characteristics of the Vancouver sample of growers

Name	Gender	Age	Role (s)	Classification	Career length	Location/ technique	Typical size (number of plants)
Teresa	Female	51	Labourer	Amateur	1 year (2001)	Indoor/ Soil	150 plants
Dat	Male	55	Carpenter/ Labourer	Average career grower	4 years (03-07)	Indoor/ Soil	270 plants (Max: 585 plants)
Mai	Female	33	Labourer to owner	Average career grower	5 years (02-06)	Indoor/ Soil	80 plants Max: 184 plants
Tom	Male	58	Electrician/ owner	Professional (?)	n/a	Indoor/ Soil	n/a

Tom is the only participant who refused to provide personal details about his own involvement. This interview is nonetheless interesting because he revealed that, in the Vietnamese culture, participation in cultivation remains quite secretive, as knowledge of a site brings on would-be thieves and that is why cannabis cultivation is something that people do with their family members. He also discussed how the cannabis industry is now only 20% of what it used to be in the Vietnamese community. He described the early days of the industry as a contagion effect. Many viewed cultivation as an opportunity to make a living and the illegality of it was just a consequence. Very similar circumstances were described by Silverstone and Savage (2010) in their recent study of Vietnamese cannabis growers in the United Kingdom.

Results

Case study 1: Marc's development into a professional grower

At the time of the interview, Marc was 26 years old and living in a halfway house. Only four months before the interview he received a 23 month sentence for cannabis cultivation. Even though it was his first conviction, Marc had been involved in the industry ever since he set up his first grow-op in his closet at the age of 13. The peak of his career occurred right before his arrest, when he was in charge of a large hydroponic cultivation site of over 2,000 plants.

There are two key processes in Marc's career that are important to describe: a) how he became a grower so early in adolescence, and b) how he developed into a professional grower later in his career. In each case, Marc relied on rich cultivation-oriented social capital – key contacts who acted as mentors through different phases of his career. We distinguish between two types of mentors: 1) social mentors, who introduced Marc to a new milieu and 2) technical mentors, who provided support to improve his skills as a grower. As shall be seen below, this social opportunity structure (Cloward, 1959; Kleemans and de Poot 2008) was essential in Marc's successful development into a professional grower.

Differential association in the family environment

To become a cannabis grower, one needs to associate with others who are already in the industry. In order to understand how a 13 year old is able to grow 3 plants at home, one needs to look no further than his family environment. When asked about his first production, Marc mentions his family and how he was attracted to the milieu very naturally.

> Ever since I was born, my mom had been smoking, my dad was smoking, I did not see anything wrong with it, I was like absorbed into the milieu. When I was 12 my brother was growing at home... one or two plants, and it gave me the motivation to grow. My mom is a horticulturist, she loves plants and she thought (cannabis) was a beautiful plant, it's a very nice plant after all. So at 13 I started to grow three plants in my closet. At the time, I was not even smoking that much. It was only for the thrill of growing a plant.

Interestingly, it was not his mother or brother who acted as a first mentor, but it was Roger, a friend of his father's who owned a large cultivation site:

> At 13 I started and when I was younger, we sometimes visited a friend of my dad who was growing. It was the first time that I saw a large site and it really sparked my interest in growing it myself... I asked him how I could start my own and he gave me a basic recipe that you can buy at Home Depot.

As his technical mentor, Roger taught Marc everything he needed to know about starting a cultivation site. His mother was crucial, instead, as a social mentor – granting him the permission to grow in his bedroom. At 13 years old, Marc relied on both types of mentors to become a cannabis grower.

Figure 7.2 illustrates Marc's social environment when he started growing cannabis at 13 years old. Full lines indicate technical mentors (actively contributed to his site), and dotted lines indicate indirect technical mentors (passive contribution to his start-up operation). While Roger provided most of the technical guidance, it was Marc's friend Bob who gave him his first cuttings, and who provided complementary advice. Even though both were well versed in the art of cultivation, Marc's brother only got involved later and his mother simply tolerated his grow op, without being involved herself. Figure 7.2 makes it easy to understand why Marc started growing cannabis. His motivations were not based on money, but on pleasure. In fact, Marc was merely imitating what he saw around him – he wanted to belong. It is only later that other motivations, such as financial incentives, became more central to his involvement.

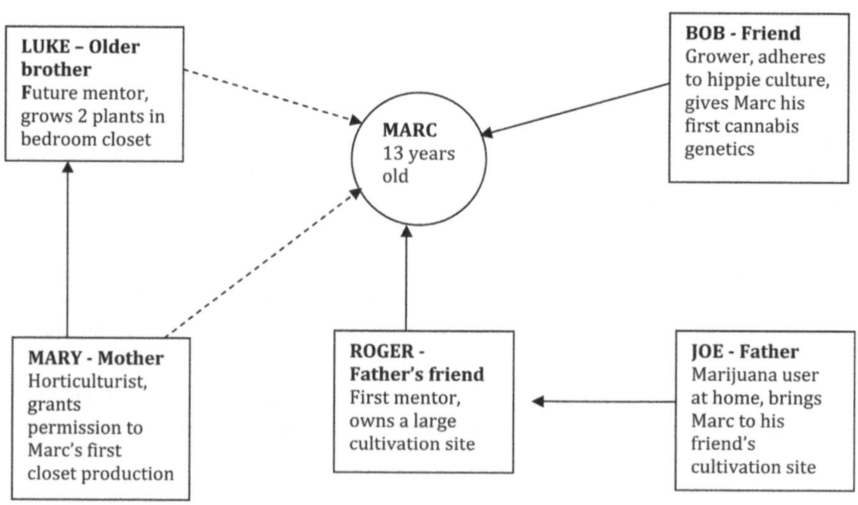

Figure 7.2 Marc's network when he started growing at 13 years old

Skills development and social opportunity structure

Marc stopped his closet production when the smell became too strong for visitors not to notice what was occurring in the brothers' respective bedrooms. He later resumed his involvement in cultivation when he left his parent's house and rented an apartment. He was 18 years old at the time, and volunteered to grow cuttings in his closet for his friends who were interested in outdoor cultivation. Marc learned the technique from his brother Luke (dotted line, Figure 7.2), who himself learned from their mother (full line from Mary to Luke, Figure 7.2) who, as a horticulturist, was extremely knowledgeable about growing (any) plants. Moving to his own apartment and learning how to grow cuttings marks a transition in Marc's career that will later lead to his big break into the world of professionals. This process of increasing commitment into the cannabis cultivation industry and parallel disengagement from the legitimate economy is illustrated in Figure 7.3 below.

After finishing high school, Marc continued to perfect his growing techniques but employment in the legitimate sector left him little time for growing. Soon after graduation, Marc met his second social mentor, his roommate's friend who became very much interested in Marc's cultivation know-how in general and his skills with cuttings in particular. Marc described this encounter as his true entry into the milieu:

> That's when I really entered the milieu. I was working as a cuttings delivery man. It was my roommate's friend who hired me. We talked a little... he saw that I knew what I was talking about and that I was a reliable guy and all. He asked me to start doing deliveries. As we were talking, he realized that we had common acquaintances, that he was working with a friend of mine. He trusted me right away.

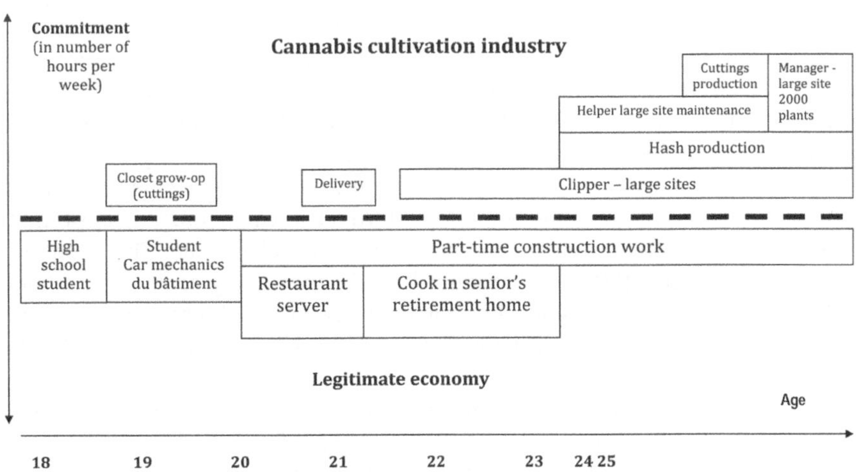

Figure 7.3 Marc's career in the cultivaiton industry

Marc received between 300 and 1,000 cuttings at his apartment, and had to deliver them the same day. He was also transporting money from one location to the next, ending up at his boss' place with the money. Marc encountered difficult situations which he was able to diffuse and find solutions to. His boss was not willing to help but ironically, it is this very type of situation that enabled him to meet his third social mentor, who gave him a promotion:

> Sometimes there were 'fucks'. Some cuttings were dead and they wanted new ones. But my boss did not want to help, he was saying 'deal with this shit yourself'. I was feeling bad because I was the one who had the contact to go and get the money, and I was in front of the guy buying them. The guy buying saw me make phone calls, trying to find solutions, and he saw that I was serious, that I was reliable. Even if I was being played on my side, I was not hiding from it, he saw that I was honest. Then he offered me a job as a clipper on his cultivation sites, and I started to do that.

Marc was 21 when he started clipping in large cultivation sites (Figure 7.3). That job was not enough to make a living so he continued working in legitimate jobs. Marc was a good and expeditious clipper; he was reliable, knowledgeable about the plant, and these qualities were noticed by his boss. After one year, he received a promotion: helper for the maintenance of a large cultivation site (there would always be between 1,200 and 2,000 plants). At first, Marc took care of the plants and of the equipment, fed, cleaned and cured the plants when needed, switched the water, etc. Given the time commitment that this job required and the better pay it provided (he earned $ 100/pound produced), he decided to quit his job in a retirement home and left the legitimate economy almost entirely (Figure 7.3).

Behind the scenes, Marc benefited from the advice of his third and last technical mentor, a friend who owned a horticulture equipment shop. Interestingly, the development of this relationship coincided with Marc's increasing responsibilities on the site. His hours were steadily increasing, and he was even asked to give his own advice and ideas to help improve the performance of the grow op. Thus, when the person in charge left, Marc became the natural replacement to manage the entire site himself. With the help of his third technical mentor, he showed that he could handle the management and maintenance of a large site. This promotion increased his pay to $400/pound produced. At the time, the greenhouse contained 70 lamps (1,000 watts), making his potential revenue $28,000 every 3 months (based on a ratio of 1 pound per lamp, a conventional ratio for growers in Quebec [Bouchard 2008]).

Marc never made such an amount. First, because there were always problems (spiders, humidity levels) with the site that would hinder performance, something not uncommon for cultivation sites in general (Bouchard 2008). His best result was 55 pounds for a single harvest ($22,000). Second, because he was soon arrested. After 6 months as manager of the site and a second smaller harvest, the police showed up at the site, a triplex where he was also living:

> I was returning home from the grocery store and they were already busting the place. I knew what was going on but decided to come in anyway. All of my stuff was upstairs, the lease was under my name, my dog was there... I hid some money and some pot that I had on myself in my car and I saw that door was completely gone. There was six of them. They arrested me, they were undercover, they told me I was charged for production of illicit drugs, we know about the grow-op downstairs. My career, that was the end of it! (laughs)

Marc's story illustrates the importance of a social opportunity structure (Cloward, 1959; Kleemans and de Poot 2008) in getting access to the world of professional growers. Skills are essential, but skills alone are not sufficient: one needs a platform to demonstrate these skills, and the opportunity to build trust with significant others (Burt 1992, Lin 2001). Ironically, it is when Marc is able to make all of these conditions converge and gets accepted into the milieu that he becomes highly exposed to detection. His successful entry into the world of professionals did not make him a professional "criminal" (he was at lowest level possible in that world), but merely a professional "grower".

Case study 2: Mai's failed ascent into professional cannabis cultivation

Our second case study describes a very different trajectory. Mai, 34 years old at the time of the interview, spent five years in the Vietnamese cannabis cultivation industry in Vancouver from 2002-2006. During her short time as a grower, Mai was involved in 10 different houses with a total of 16 co-offenders. She received money from a dozen harvests, for a modest total of $137,000 for her 5 years of full-time involvement. Although she earned a mean of $27,000 annually, 50% of her total income came in her last year of involvement. Her trajectory from one house/project to another is illustrated in Figure 7.4 below.

Mai's career is very different than Marc's. Mai was never exposed to the industry until she was offered the opportunity in her mid 20s. She also lacked any appreciation or love for the plant itself and was only drawn to growing for the opportunity to make money. While size is a major difference (80 plants vs. 2,000 plants), Mai's first cultivation opportunity was similar in nature to the one Marc obtained at the end of his career, when he was hired to help with the maintenance of the large site (Figure 7.3). In other words, Mai made a horizontal entry into the milieu, while Marc had for long been developing his skills as a grower before he caught his break.

Her rapid ascent may explain some of the difficulty she had with becoming successful in the milieu. Her lack of skills and contacts in the milieu limited her options and led to her involvement in risky ventures and disappointing harvests, including several where she received no money at all. Mai had no real mentors, neither social nor technical. Consider how she started in the industry: She began working as hired help, looking after the physical site making it appear occupied, but had little interaction with the plants themselves. She did not know anything

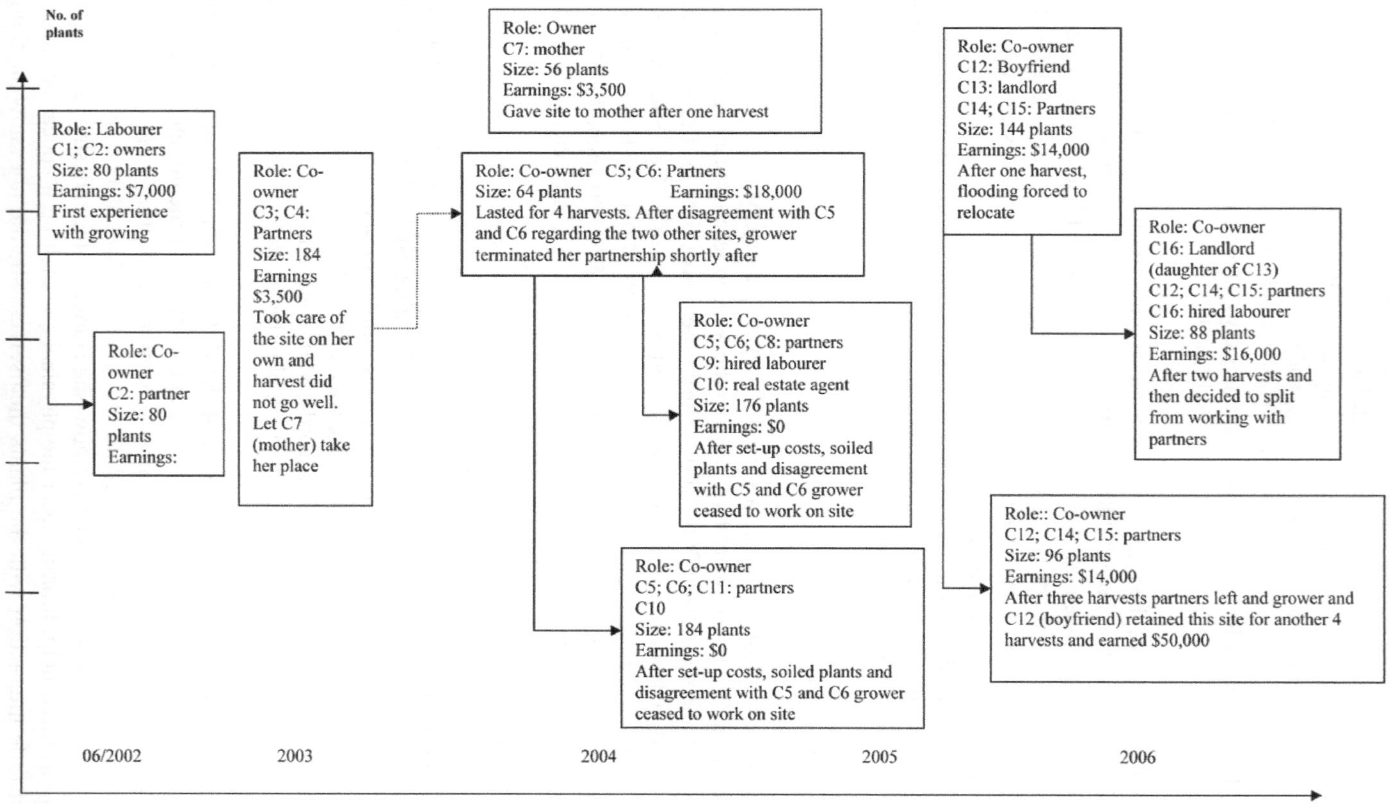

Figure 7.4 Mai's career in the Vietnamese cannabis cultivation industry

about cultivation and had to learn from scratch. While common ethnicity helped build trust and gave her the initial opportunity, her partners made sure to keep her dependent on them:

> *Mai*: Yes, they taught me how to harvest. But when they were feeding the plants, they tried to hide their secrets from me. They didn't tell what type of food they put in the plants.
>
> *Interviewer*: Why do you think they hid it from you?
>
> *Mai*: Because some people don't want you to know everything and then you'll always be dependent on them. When you learn then you'll get better and start your own site.

The position itself was risky. The two partners (C1 and C2) needed someone to live in the house because it had just been robbed and they wanted to have someone stay there during the nights. As it happens, a few months into it, robbers came to the house again (but they ended up being chased away by neighbours).

Mai was unable to really make it on her own. She lacked the contacts to distribute large amounts of cannabis in the market. She also had trouble finding suitable houses for growing (the ones she found had previously been visited by robbers/police), and lacked the skills to produce successful harvests consistently. In 2004, for example, she became involved in larger operations of 176 and 184 plants, but failed to generate any income (Figure 7.4). Entire harvests were spoiled due to buying wrong strains of cannabis and irregular watering. Partnerships with older, more experienced growers also proved challenging for Mai. Not only did she feel animosity towards the unfair division of labor, her share of the profits was always less than she expected.

Her best days as a grower came in the last 18 months of her involvement. Mai met her boyfriend (C12) and they started a grow house together with two other partners (C14 and C15). This dynamic was more favourable to an equal division of labour. Each partner brought with them the contacts they made over their short careers, which enabled them to pool resources to sell their harvests. Their experiences together were not, however, without mishaps: a flood, spoiled crops, and forced evacuations occurred. Finally, Mai and her boyfriend retained one of the sites for four more harvests but because of dropping wholesale cannabis prices they ultimately retired from cannabis cultivation. Mai's career in the Vietnamese cannabis cultivation industry is not unique. In fact, it is rather characteristic of many individuals who are enticed by the potential of earning big money and where access to equipment and tutelage are plentiful. Despite having some of the right ingredients to become a professional, including full time commitment to the craft, Mai was not particularly skilled or successful. In her own words, "I didn't have a good time growing; I didn't seem to make money out of it."

Discussion and conclusion

This chapter had two main objectives. First, to propose a classification of offenders that could not only accommodate the notions of "professional" and "amateur" criminals, but also provide meaningful categories of offenders for everyone falling in between these two extremes. We showed that by focusing on two key characteristics – skill and commitment level – we could derive four types of offenders: professionals (skilled and committed), average career criminals (committed but unskilled), pro-ams (skilled but uncommitted), and amateurs (unskilled and uncommitted). The proposed classification is activity-specific (professional growers are not necessarily professional criminals – e.g. Marc) but can also be used to represent offenders more generally.

The second objective was to illustrate what might constitute a career as a "professional" in the context of cannabis cultivation. Although lack of space prevented us from a full demonstration, our 13 respondents could be classified into one of the four categories.[4] Because of our interest in the world of professionals, we proceeded to show in some detail the career trajectory that led two of our respondents to be within reach of actually becoming professional growers. The two case studies illustrated the importance of a social opportunity structure to succeed as a professional grower. While Marc had a head start early in adolescence where he could learn the ropes alongside a number of social and technical mentors, Mai had no such background when she entered the industry. She had to slowly learn by making her way through many trials and errors until she found some stability in her fifth and last year of involvement. Ironically, while Marc's skills allowed him to enter a world where the stakes were much higher, he also had little control over his destiny. He was a professional grower working for a professional criminal. Accordingly, he was the one who took the fall when the large indoor site he was running was detected by the police.

This reminds us of the difference between professional growers and professional criminals who may simply invest in cultivation ventures, without being skilled growers themselves. The classification proposed in this chapter allows for such special cases. The obvious next step is to apply our ideas in other contexts, and to other types of crimes. The operationalization of skill level, for example, is facilitated through in-depth interviews with participants in a specific activity (e.g. burglars, bank robbers, street dealers, drug smugglers). The work of Wright and Decker (1996) or Steffensmeier (1986) are good examples of this. We are confident that the classification can be applied to the context of most criminal careers and activities. Although the diversity of crime involvement in most offenders' criminal careers may not appear suitable to the notion of professionalization, recent studies

4 The careers of pure amateurs are much less complex, and illustrating it would have taken too much space for the purpose of this study. As for the pro-ams, we invite the readers to consult the very rich accounts described in Gary Potter's ethnographic work in the United Kingdom (Potter 2010, Potter and Dann 2005).

showed that over the life course, offenders go through many periods of high specialization in one activity (McGloin et al. 2007). Offenders may demonstrate variation in skills and commitment in any one of these activities. Such patterns would be captured by the proposed classification.

Not discussed in the context of this chapter is the high prevalence of pro-ams in our sample (5/13 – not counting Marc who was a pro-am for most of his career). A review of the past typologies of growers found a similarly high prevalence of growers who were sometimes highly skilled but never transformed those skills into a full-time occupation (Decorte 2008, Hough et al. 2003, Potter and Dann 2005, Weisheit 1991). The classification has also been developed to accommodate such growers – labeling them as either professionals or amateurs would be unsatisfactory. The pro-am concept more appropriately captures this category of growers, as it does in a variety of other (legal) contexts (Leadbetter 2004).[5]

Finally, the proposed classification offers an additional conceptual tool that helps avoid labeling individuals who engage in criminal behavior involving a group of skilled offenders as automatically belonging to "organized crime". Hafley and Tewksbury (1995) concluded their interesting study of the marijuana cultivation industry in Kentucky with the idea that the growers they met in rural Kentucky were "organized crime". Upon careful examination of their results, one could safely say that most of the growers they met merely created their own subculture of professional growers within a rural cannabis cultivation industry. The distinction may be important as the organized crime label carries important criminal justice consequences, despite the absence of consensus on what organized crime might be.

---

5 To be sure, the notion of pro-am is not meant to replace the grower typologies of these authors. We simply argue that under a more general offender classification, these growers would be found in the pro-am category.

List of references

Bouchard, M. 2007. A capture-recapture model to estimate the size of criminal populations and the risks of detection in a marijuana cultivation industry. *Journal of Quantitative Criminology*, 23, 221-41.

Bouchard, M. 2008. Towards a realistic method to estimate the size of cannabis cultivation industry in developed countries. *Contemporary Drug Problems*, 35, 291-320.

Bouchard, M. and Nguyen, H. 2010. Is it who you know, or how many that counts? Criminal networks and cost avoidance in a sample of young offenders. *Justice Quarterly*, 27, 130-58.

Burt, R.S. 1992. *Structural Holes: The Social Structure of Competition*. Cambridge, MA: Harvard University Press.

Caulkins, J. 2009. How illegal drugs enter an island country: insights from interviews with incarcerated smugglers. *Global Crime*, 10, 66-93.

Cloward, R.A. 1959. Illegitimate means, anomie, and deviant behaviour. *American Sociological Review*, 24, 164-76.

Decorte, T. 2008. Domestic cannabis cultivation in Belgium: The unintended effects of the national drug policy on the cannabis market, in *Cannabis in Europe: Dynamics in Perception, Policy and Markets*, edited by D.J. Korf. Lengerich: Pabst Science Publishers, 69-86.

Desroches, F.J. 2005. *The Crime That Pays: Drug Trafficking and Organized Crime in Canada*. Toronto: Canadian Scholar's Press Inc.

Hafley, S.R. and Tewksbury, R. 1995. The rural Kentucky marijuana industry: Organization and Community Involvement. *Deviant Behavior*, 16, 201-21.

Hobbs, R. 1997. Professional crime: Change, continuity and the enduring myth of the underworld. *Sociology*, 31, 57-72.

Kleemans, E. and de Poot, C. 2008. Criminal careers in organized crime and social opportunity structure. *European Journal of Criminology*, 5, 69-98.

Lin, N. 2001. *Social Capital: A Theory of Social Structure and Action*. Cambridge: Cambridge University Press.

Malm, A., Kinney, B. and Pollard, N. 2008. Social Network and Distance Correlates of Criminal Associates Involved in Illicit Drug Production. *Security Journal*, 21, 77-94.

McCarthy, B. and Hagan, J. 2001. When crime pays: Capital, competence, and criminal success. *Social Forces*, 79(3), 1035-59.

McGloin, J., Sullivan, C., Piquero, A. and Pratt, T. 2007. Local life circumstances and offending specialization/versatility: Comparing opportunity and propensity models. *Journal of Research in Crime and Delinquency*, 44, 321-46.

Morselli, C. 2001. Structuring Mr. Nice: Entrepreneurial opportunities and brokerage positioning in the cannabis trade. *Crime, Law, and Social Change*, 35, 203-244.

Morselli, C. 2009. *Inside criminal networks*. New York: Springer.

Morselli, C. and Tremblay, P. 2004. Criminal achievement, offender networks and the benefits of low self-control. *Criminology*, 42(3), 773-804.

Morselli, C., Tremblay, P. and McCarthy, B. 2006. Mentors and criminal achievement. *Criminology*, 44(1), 17-43.

Potter, G. 2010. *Weed, Need and Greed: A study of domestic cannabis cultivation.* London: Free Association Books.

Potter, G. and Dann, S.L. 2005. Urban crop circles: Urban cannabis growers in the north of England, in *Cocktails and Dreams: Perspectives on Drug and Alcohol Use,* edited by W.R. Palacios. Upper Saddle River, New Jersey: Pearson Prentice Hall, 89-109.

Silverstone, D. and Savage, S. 2010. Farmers, factories, and funds: organized crime and illicit drug cultivation within the British Vietnamese community. *Global Crime*, 11, 16-33.

Steffensmeier, D. 1986. *The Fence: In the Shadow of Two worlds*. Totowa, N.J.: Rowman and Littlefield.

Sutherland, E. 1937. *The professional thief.* Chicago: University of Chicago Press.

Tremblay, P. 2010. Le Delinquant Ideal [The Ultimate Criminal]. Montreal: Liber.

Tremblay, P. and Morselli, C. 2000. Patterns in criminal achievement: Wilson and Abrahamse revisited. *Criminology*, 38(2), 633-659.

Tremblay, P., Bouchard, M. and Petit, S. 2009. The size and influence of a criminal organization: a criminal achievement perspective. *Global Crime*, 10(1/2), 24-40.

Weisheit, R.A. 1991. The intangible rewards from crime: The case of domestic marijuana cultivation. *Crime and Delinquency*, 37(4), 506-527.

Weisheit, R.A. 1992. *Domestic Marijuana: A Neglected Industry*. Westport: Greenwood Press.

Wright, R. and Decker, S. 1996. *Burglars on the Job*. Boston: Northeastern University Press.

Chapter 8
Co-offending Networks in Cannabis Cultivation

Aili Malm, Rebecca Nash and Samuel Vickovic

Introduction

Cannabis cultivation is rarely a lone venture. Not only do cultivators co-offend to grow the plants, they often work with suppliers, distributors, sellers, and others along the commodity chain to get their product to market. Working in groups could be termed a necessity for both indoor and outdoor mid- to large-scale cannabis growers. Indoor operations routinely use hydroponic equipment that requires regular maintenance and electricity by-passes to avoid detection. Outdoor operations are usually located in remote, inaccessible areas, so people are needed for transportation, surveillance, and cultivation. In both cases, the plants themselves need extensive care and attention if the cultivators expect to produce high-yield crops. Once the crops have been harvested, it is common for mid- to large-scale growers to sell on the domestic market and export to other countries. Both of these markets require cooperation with several individuals along the cannabis supply chain (Malm and Bichler, in press). Simply put, cannabis cultivation usually requires co-offending behavior.

While the occurrence of co-offending in cannabis cultivation has been substantiated through empirical research (Plecas, Malm, and Kinney 2005), the shape, composition, and structure of these co-offending relationships have not been examined in any depth. Waring (2002) emphasizes the importance of this type of examination stating that identifying different co-offending forms with specific markets/crimes aids our understanding of the nature of co-offending relationships. Set in the context of British Columbia, Canada, we investigate co-offending in all cannabis cultivation cases coming to the attention of the police from 1997 – 2003. From this data, multi-year co-offending networks are built using an individual-level focus. The shape, composition, and structure (redundancy) of these networks are examined. We then discuss the advantages (including increased trust) and disadvantages (including lack of innovation, knowledge, opportunities, and referrals) of redundant criminal networks for cannabis cultivators.

Co-offending networks in cannabis cultivation

At the outset of this chapter, it is important to differentiate between co-offending network and criminal network (for a more complete discussion of these concepts see Warr 2002, and Waring 2002). A co-offending network is defined as two or more individuals involved in a criminal act together (Felson 2003, Reiss 1988, Reiss and Farrington 1991). Co-offenders function in order to provide each other with information and assistance in order to carry out criminal acts. They also provide positive reinforcement of one another's criminal tendencies. Most studies define co-offenders as individuals linked to the same crime by law enforcement. This is an especially important distinction when researching cannabis cultivation given that some instrumental actors are not considered co-offenders in the eyes of law enforcement. Criminal network is a more inclusive term. Criminal networks include co-offenders; however, they also include kinship, formal organization, and legitimate relationships (Malm, Bichler, and Van de Walle 2010). The focus of this chapter is co-offending networks in cannabis cultivation.

Past studies of co-offending focus on juvenile delinquents primarily because co-offending tends to decline (McGloin et al. 2008) and co-offending groups tend to get smaller (Reiss 1988) with age. Reiss (1988) states that most co-offending groups are unstable and the relationships are short-lived. Reiss and Farrington (1991) also found that co-offenders have many different partners, and are unlikely to commit crimes with the same individuals over time. McGloin et al. (2008) found some stability in co-offending relationships for frequent offenders, but in general, delinquents do not tend to reuse co-offenders. Since cannabis cultivation is predominately carried out by older individuals (Plecas, Malm, and Kinney 2005), it is possible that co-offending networks will display different patterns than juvenile offending. There are other factors specific to this crime that could differentiate co-offending network patterns from those seen in previous research.

Cannabis cultivation takes some organization, and requires skill in order to yield any plants (Bouchard 2007). It is generally separated into three methods: indoor, indoor hydroponic, and outdoor. There are also different motives for cultivating: personal use, small-scale distribution, and large-scale distribution. Both the cultivation method and motive could potentially affect co-offending network dynamics (Bouchard 2008).

When discussing co-offending network structure in relation to cannabis cultivation it is important to understand that this crime requires knowledge and skill. Networks could benefit from having a highly specialized network of co-offenders who always work together, but at the same time, they could benefit from the sharing of information between cultivation networks. In this chapter we explore whether the complexity of cannabis cultivation affects the stability of co-offending networks, due to the fact that it requires organization and special skills. The next section of this chapter discusses co-offending networks and the social network concepts of redundancy and composition.

Network redundancy

Network redundancy refers to the overlap among individuals in one's co-offending network. A person whose network consists of connections that are all linked to each other has high redundancy, while individuals who have few connections are in non-redundant networks (McGloin and Piquero 2010). Redundant networks are also termed *closed networks*. Redundancy is measured using the statistic of network density. Dense/redundant networks facilitate trust, common identities, and constrain the behavior of their members; at the same time density limits the opportunity to associate with individuals outside the network (Haynie 2001).

There is a long-standing debate in the social capital research on the benefits of closed, redundant networks. Coleman (1990) theorizes that network closure is a source of social capital for two reasons. First, direct connections improve communications, and second, network closure makes it easier for individuals to trust one another. On the other side, Burt (1992) and Granovetter (1985) argue that social capital is held by people in brokerage positions. Brokers are individuals who connect individuals who otherwise would not be connected. They have a competitive advantage because they control the flow of information between individuals. However, Granovetter (1985) also states that the threat of sanctions, common in co-offending relationships, makes it more likely for trust to build between people with mutual friends (closed networks).

Morselli and Tremblay (2004) interviewed 284 inmates in Quebec, Canada and asked them about criminal earnings and criminal networks. They found that network redundancy has a direct impact on criminal earnings – a less redundant network leads to higher criminal earnings. They hypothesized that this relationship was due to information and commodity diffusion. The idea of diffusion, which is the spread of ideas, attitudes, practices, traits, and information, is relevant to redundancy in co-offending networks (Rogers 1995). For instance, Conway and McCord studied adult co-offenders and found that nonviolent offenders who co-offend with violent offenders tend to use violence in the future (2002). In contrast, low density slows or prevents the spread of information (Coleman 1964).

McGloin and Piquero (2010) studied the co-offending networks of 218 juvenile delinquents in Philadelphia. They found that redundant co-offender networks are related to offender specialization in group crimes, but not in crimes overall. They assert that non-redundant co-offending networks potentially have access to an array of criminal norms, skills, and knowledge, which may translate into a versatile offending profile. Offenders within a redundant network will have relatively constrained exposure structuring a more specialized offending profile.

Network composition

Homophily and homogeneity are two ways of measuring individual (egocentric) network composition. The homophily principle states that similarity breeds connection. Homophily affects all different types of relationships and it results in people's personal networks being socially, behaviorally, and interpersonally homogenous (McPherson, Smith-Lovin and Cook 2001). Ethnic homophily creates the strongest separation in personal networks, followed by age and gender (McPherson, Smith-Lovin and Cook 2001). While homogenous groups are more cohesive, dependent, and insulated from outside opinions than diverse groups

(Jenssen and Greve 2002, Surowiecki 2004), homophily also limits information and commodity diffusion (McPherson, Smith-Lovin and Cook 2001).

Current study

Using data drawn from police files in British Columbia, Canada, this study explores the composition and structure of co-offending networks specific to the crime of cannabis cultivation. This presents an opportunity to compare results from previous research on general co-offending networks with networks built from co-offending activity in a specific type of crime – a crime that is also group-oriented and requires specialized knowledge. Theoretically, the unique factors related to cannabis cultivation should yield different results than the existing research conducted primarily on delinquents or general offending, concerning co-offending network shape, structure, and composition. Specifically, it is hypothesized that:

H_1 Cannabis cultivators engaging in another cultivation operation will re-use co-offenders more than criminals who engage in a variety of different types of crimes, and this will be exhibited in more "closed" network shapes. "Closed" network shapes are defined as networks where all co-offenders are re-used in every cannabis cultivation offence conducted by the individual. This follows from research showing that more specialized offending results in higher co-offender stability than diverse offending histories (McGloin and Piquero 2010). This hypothesis is also shaped from diffusion literature (Conway and McCord 2002, Rogers 1995).

H_2 Cannabis co-offending networks will be more redundant than general offending networks. This is drawn from research showing that specialized offending is related to higher redundancy (McGloin and Piquero 2010, Morselli and Tremblay 2004), and that it is easier to build trust, common identities, and behavioral control over members in redundant networks (Coleman 1990, Granovetter 1985, Haynie 2001).

H_3 Co-offending networks in cannabis cultivation will exhibit homophily and homogeneity in terms of ethnicity, age, and gender (Jenssen and Greve 2002, McPherson, Smith-Lovin and Cook 2001, Surowiecki 2004).

Method

Data source

Data for this project were collected through a review of every cannabis cultivation police file occurring between 1997 and 2003 from all law enforcement jurisdictions in the province of British Columbia, Canada. Researchers visited 120 police departments and performed file reviews. Information collected relevant to this chapter include data about the suspect, the nature of the police investigation, the size and type of the growing operation, the amount of marijuana seized, and the presence of various cultivation equipment.[1]

Over 25,000 incidents of cannabis cultivation were reviewed. The dataset includes small, medium, and large scale operations. 34 percent of the operations were small scale, with less than 50 plants. 47 percent were medium scale – 50 to 299 plants. 19 percent were large-scale operations of over 300 plants. The number of incidents increased each year from 1997 through 2000, and then leveled off between 2000 and 2003. The vast majority of these cases involved indoor operations (81percent) and their size and sophistication appear to be increasing. The police case files indicate that cannabis was seized in both live plant and dried form. The average number of plants seized per indoor growing operation over the seven year period is 180, with the average increasing each year. The average quantity of harvested marijuana seized has tripled since 1997 in both indoor and outdoor operations. Another variable that measures the increasing sophistication of growing operations is the use of special high voltage light bulbs. The average number of special lights seized per growing operation is relatively high (14) and has consistently increased over the seven-year study period. Sophisticated indoor operations require large amounts of electricity. In a few cases, special electric generators are used, while in others, particularly in small to medium size operations, electricity is consumed and paid for, but the operation is frequently moved to avoid detection. Operators often attempt to avoid detection as a result of their high consumption of electricity by stealing the electricity or by "diverting it", tampering with the meter, or by-passing it altogether. According to available information on file, the percentage of indoor marijuana growing operations involving the theft of electricity remained relatively stable over the seven years (20 percent).

The file review identified a total of 15,588 suspects involved in cannabis cultivation. Seventy-seven percent of all suspects were male, two percent of all the suspects identified were under the age of 18, and the average age of suspects was 35 years old. From 1997 through 1999, the most frequently occurring ethnicity reported in the suspect data is Caucasian, although the percent of Vietnamese suspects has increased from two percent in 1997 to 36 percent in 2003. Other minority groups have increased from four percent in 1997 to ten percent in 2003, many of these from Mainland China. Seventy-four percent of all known suspects were born in Canada, with Vietnam being the second most common country of origin. Very few foreign born suspects were from the United States or Europe. For the purpose of this research, the ethnicity specified in the police file was used as the study variable. While nine ethnicities were identified, the groups were collapsed to white, Asian, and other.

The criminal record of each suspect was checked to determine if he or she had a record of prior criminal convictions. For approximately 20 percent of these suspects, it was not possible to determine previous criminal history due to incomplete or unmatchable file information. The suspects typically had

---

1 For a full description of this dataset, see Plecas, Malm and Kinney (2005).

a substantial criminal history, with 47 percent of all suspects having prior criminal convictions (57 percent had drug offences and 41 percent a history of violent offences). The percentage of suspects with a criminal record was lower for suspects of Vietnamese origin (28 percent) than for all other suspects (53 percent). A possible reason for this may be that many Vietnamese suspects are recent immigrants. In addition, the number of suspects involved in previous drug offences, particularly cannabis production, has increased since 2000, suggesting that many of the suspects are setting up another grow operation after they are initially caught.

As mentioned at the beginning of this chapter, cannabis cultivation is rarely a lone venture. 9,484 of the 15,588 suspects involved in cannabis cultivation (61 percent) had at least one incident of co-offending during the seven-year study period. Due to the fact that this research defines co-offenders as suspects linked to the same cultivation site by law enforcement, this is most likely an underestimation of the incidence of co-offending. Figure 8.1 is a *sociogram* of networks based on all co-offending in this dataset. The sociogram shows one large cluster of 21 components. The principal component (the largest component of connected co-offenders) represents 31 percent of the sample.
Also mentioned earlier in this chapter, working in groups could be necessary for both indoor and outdoor mid- to large-scale cannabis growers. Table 8.1 illustrates how the number of co-offenders is likely to increase as the size of the cultivation operation increases.

In order to examine the stability of co-offending over time, we further refine this dataset down to a subset of 651 individuals who have at least two cannabis cultivation charges and at least one co-offender in each case.

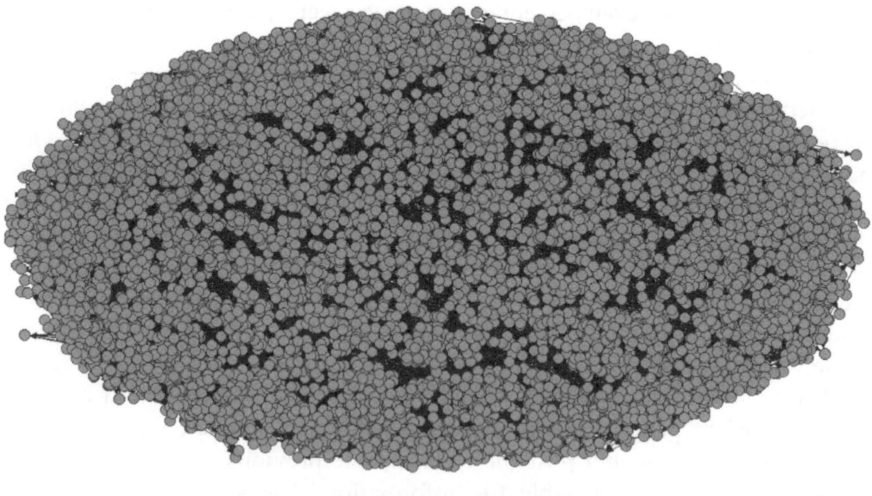

Figure 8.1 Co-offending sociogram (N=9,484)

Table 8.1 Average number of plants seized by number of co-offenders

Number of co-offenders	0	1	2	3	4	5+
Average number of plants seized	149	166	216	258	292	429

Network shape and redundancy

Since this chapter explores the shape, redundancy, and composition of individual co-offending networks, the egocentric approach to network analysis was chosen over the whole network approach (Wasserman and Faust 1994). While the whole network approach captures all links within a population of interest, egocentric networks focus on a single actor and define all of the individuals they are tied to and the links between these associates.
Co-offending networks were created for each of the 651 cannabis cultivators

Table 8.2 Descriptives for 651 cannabis cultivators included in study

	Mean	Standard Deviation	Minimum	Maximum
% White	56.50	--	--	--
% Asian	40.70	--	--	--
% Other	2.80	--	--	--
% Male	71.60	--	--	--
Age	34.28	9.79	15	84
# of cultivation Incidents	3.2	.34	2	5
Density	77	.19	.27	1.00
# of unique co-offenders	3.34	2.29	1	18

who committed at least two co-offenses in the study period (1997-2003). Each egonet was formed using co-offending ties between cannabis cultivators in a binary, symmetric (non-directional) adjacency matrix. A symmetrical (non-directional) link simply means that when person A co-offends with person B, person B is also co-offending with person A. The value of each matrix cell ranged between zero (no co-offending between individuals) and one (co-offending present). Each associate affiliated with the ego had a cell value of one. Table 8.2 provides descriptive information for the sample.

UCInet 6.0 (Borgatti, Everett and Freeman 2006) was used to determine the shape, composition, and structure of each co-offending network.

This study uses the technique set out by McGloin and Piquero (2010) to construct cumulative co-offending networks. All incidents of cannabis cultivation involving one or more co-offender over the study period are included in each subject's co-offending network. For example, if ego A and two co-offenders were caught for cannabis cultivation in 1997, and then ego A and one different co-offender were caught in 2000, the two incidents would be combined along with any co-offences between individuals to form ego A's cumulative cannabis cultivation co-offending network. The process is illustrated in Figure 8.2. We used density to determine the redundancy of cannabis cultivation co-offending networks. Density is measured by dividing the number of observed ties by the number of possible ties multiplied by 100.

Network composition

Two measures were used to determine the composition of cannabis cultivator co-offending networks. The first variable measures homophily/heterophily. Homophily/heterophily determines whether egos interact with others like themselves (in this case we are considering ethnicity and age) using the formula $\frac{E-I}{E+I}$ $\frac{E-I}{E+I}$, where E is the number of ties to co-offenders of a different ethnicity and I is the number of ties to co-offenders of the same ethnicity/age. The second variable measures homogeneity of the ego's co-offenders – are the co-offenders alike? Homogeneity/heterogeneity is calculated using the Hirschman-Herfinadahl index (HHI) which is defined as the sum of the squares of shared members across groups and calculated using the formula $H = \Sigma_{i=1}\left(\frac{G_i}{G}\right)^2$ $H = \Sigma_{i=1}\left(\frac{G_i}{G}\right)^2$, where G is the number of co-offenders in the co-offending network. HHI values range between 0 and 1, with values near zero corresponding to heterogeneous co-offending networks and values approaching one indicating homogenous networks.

Results

Network shape and redundancy

Following the methodology set out in McGloin and Piquero (2010), we describe the variety of network shapes present in cannabis cultivation co-offending (Figure 8.3). A total of 101 cultivators were dyads, meaning that they co-offended with the same person for each offence. The next four types of co-offending networks represent variations on the dyad where co-offenders are re-used in every crime – closed triad, closed quad, closed five, and closed six. A total of 88, 44, 12 and one individual(s) fit each of these shapes, respectively. The density in each of these types is always equal to one.

The next group includes 108 individuals who fit the open triad shape. Open triads occur when the ego co-offends with two separate co-offenders and the accomplices have not co-offended with one another. Regardless of how many

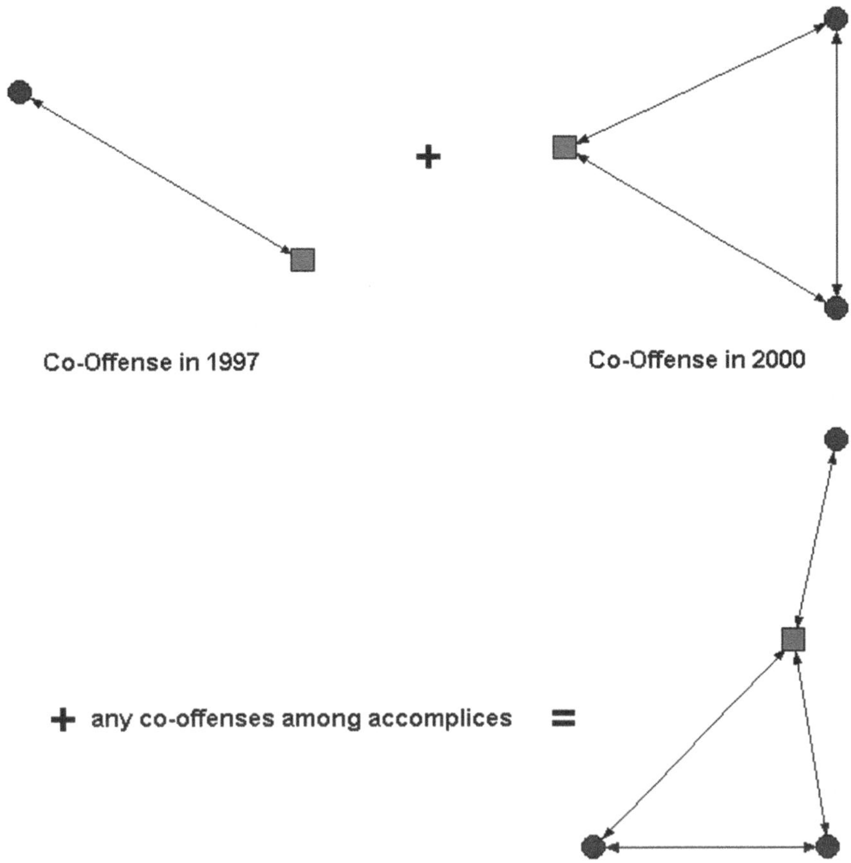

Figure 8.2 Steps in Constructing Egocentric Co-offending Network

times the ego and each accomplice co-offend, the density in these networks will always equal .67. There are also three individuals who illustrate the open quad shape. These cultivators have three separate co-offenders who have never worked with one another. The density of the open-quad type is always .50.

The final three types of cannabis cultivation co-offending network shapes have variable densities. Three individuals illustrate the common pair type. In this type, an ego has one person whom they always co-offend with – the common pair. The rest of the network is made up of co-offenders whom the common pair co-offend with, but the accomplices (or accomplice groups) don't co-offend with one another. The densities range from .67 to .73. The next 152 subjects have a kite-shaped network. In kite networks, the ego has a dyad that forms the "tail" of the kite, and a larger group that all co-offend with one another. Kite densities range from .38 to .88. The last 137 individuals belong to the heterogeneous category. As

Table 8.3 Cannabis co-offending network shape by average number of plants seized

Shape of network		Average number of plants seized
CLOSED	Dyad	229
	Closed Triad	234
	Closed Quad	465
	Closed Five	323
	Closed Six	412
OPEN	Open Triad	191
	Open Quad	166
MIX	Kite	292
	Heterogenous	362
	Common Pair	148

stated in McGloin and Piquero (2010), this type represents too much variation to characterize as one shape. The densities in this group range from .27 to 1.0.

In order to ascertain whether different network shapes are associated with different patterns of cultivation, network shape and number of plants seized were compared. Table 8.3 shows that closed and heterogeneous network shapes are more likely to occur in large growing operations. Individuals with open co-offending networks tend to have the smallest operations.

Network composition

The EI index of homophily for ethnicity is-.78. This indicates that accomplices of cannabis cultivators have a strong tendency to choose co-offenders of the same ethnicity. The HHI for ethnicity is .72, suggesting that cannabis cultivators tend to co-offend with others of the same ethnicity. The EI index of homophily for age is-.30. This indicates that cannabis cultivators have a weak tendency to choose co-offenders of a similar age. The HHI for age is .56, suggesting that accomplices of cannabis cultivators tend to co-offend with others of various age ranges. Finally, the EI index for gender is .24, showing that cannabis cultivators work with both genders. Similarly, the HHI for gender is .65, showing that accomplices co-offend with both genders as well.

Discussion

In an effort to better understand the phenomenon of co-offending, criminological researchers have started to use social network analysis to study personal co-offending networks (McGloin and Piquero 2010, Morselli and Tremblay 2004). In this chapter, we test previous findings that co-offender networks specializing in a specific type of crime will be structurally different from networks of co-offenders committing different types of crime (McGloin and Piquero 2010). Further, this research represents the first exploration into co-offending patterns in cannabis cultivation.

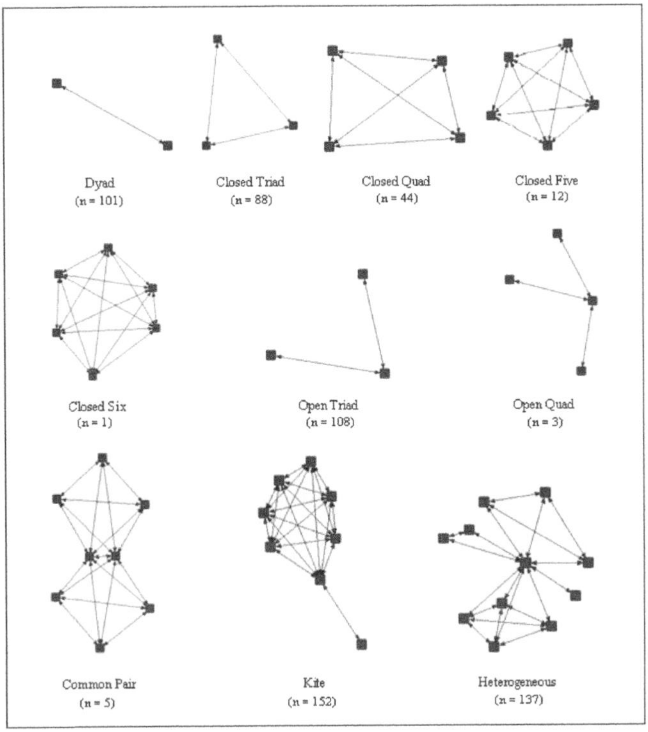

Figure 8.3 Types of Egocentric Co-offending Networks

In order to test hypotheses one and two, the results of this study must be compared to results from research conducted on general co-offending networks. Hypothesis one states that cannabis cultivators engaging in another cultivation operation will re-use co-offenders more than criminals who engage in a variety of different types of crimes, and this will be exhibited in more "closed" network shapes. "Closed" network shapes are defined as networks where all co-offenders are re-used in every cannabis cultivation offence conducted by the individual. The network shapes defined in McGloin and Piquero's (2010) study of juvenile co-offending provided the template for this research; however, four additional shapes were seen in our data: closed five, closed six, open quad, and common pair. The star shape, seen in juvenile co-offending, was not seen in cannabis cultivation. Table 8.4 shows that "closed" networks comprise over 40 percent of the networks in cannabis cultivation, while they only represent four percent of the juvenile co-

Table 8.4 Comparison of cannabis co-offending network shape

Shape of network		Cannabis co-offending (N=651)	Juvenile co-offending (n=218) (McGloin and Piquero, 2010)
CLOSED	Dyad	16.4%	2.2%
	Closed Triad	14.3%	.9%
	Closed Quad	7.2%	.9%
	Closed Five	2.0%	--
	Closed Six	.2%	--
OPEN	Star	--	3.7%
	Open Triad	17.6%	11.5%
	Open Quad	.5%	--
MIX	Kite	24.7%	15.6%
	Heterogeneous	21.0%	65.1%
	Common Pair	.8%	--

offending networks. One might theorize that this difference is due to the reduced number of co-offences for the specialized population (3.2 vs. 4.2); however, the average reduction of one co-offence cannot completely account for the tenfold increase in closed networks in the cannabis cultivation data. While the proportion of open networks is similar for both groups, mixed networks are far more prevalent in general juvenile co-offending. This might be due to the many different types of crimes included in juvenile co-offending networks; each type of crime could involve a different set of co-offenders resulting in a heterogeneous network shape. The average number of unique co-offenders in the McGloin and Piquero article is also far higher (7.45) than our data (3.34), supporting the findings of previous research that co-offending group size decreases with age (Haynie 2001, McGloin and Piquero 2010, Reiss 1988).

Hypothesis two asserts that cannabis co-offending networks will be more redundant than general delinquent co-offending networks. This is supported by the average density for cannabis cultivation of .77 and the average density for delinquent co-offending of .52. These results are expected due to the nature of cannabis cultivation.

In crimes such as cannabis cultivation, trust among co-offenders is very important. Von Lampe and Johansen (2004) define trust in co-offending situations as co-offenders not violating agreements regarding the crime, not violating expectations of considerate behavior, and protecting the secrecy of the crime. They also state that trust based on direct connections is stronger than trust based on indirect connections. It then stands to reason that redundant co-offending networks will have greater levels of trust than non-redundant networks.

The theories of Coleman (1990) and Granovetter (1985) also help explain why closed networks are more common in cannabis cultivation than general delinquent co-offending. The threat of sanction is more concerning to cannabis cultivators because their primary motivation is financial and they are more likely to engage in cost-benefit decision-making than juvenile delinquents. These works can also help explain the finding that closed networks are more likely to occur with large-scale cannabis cultivators.

The time involved in cannabis cultivation could also help explain why cannabis cultivation may require co-offenders and why these co-offending networks may be redundant. Most crimes happen as discrete events in a very short time period. Cannabis cultivation, however, takes several months during which time the grower is at constant risk of arrest or theft of the plants. This means that, especially for larger operations, growers may need help, but they want to be sure the help can be trusted for long periods of time.

The redundancy and stability of cannabis cultivation co-offending networks provides counter-evidence to the contention that criminal organizations and co-offending arrangements involved in serious crimes are always changing and highly impermanent (Dorn, Levi and King 2005, Edwards and Levi 2008). Rather, such ever-changing relationships and instability may be the result of offenders switching crime types or roles in illicit markets rather than an inherent statement about the nature of criminal organizations and co-offending. Future research should focus on the temporal stability of co-offending networks in other crimes common to criminal enterprise groups. Further, future research should also examine individual co-offending networks incorporating data on changing roles within illicit markets.

In answering the previous two hypotheses, this study considers how co-offender networks differ based on offender versatility. It is important to reiterate that for the purpose of this research, the authors operationalize cannabis cultivation co-offending networks by only including co-offenders who were involved in cannabis cultivation, rather than all of the co-offenders across the career of the ego. In other words, this study considers specialized group offending rather than offender specialists. Approximately half (47 percent) of the sample in this research engaged in crimes other than cannabis cultivation during their criminal career, but including these crimes in the co-offender networks was outside of the scope of this research. Future research should consider whether growers who specialize in cannabis cultivation throughout their criminal careers co-offend with other specialists, and whether their network structure differs from generalists who co-offend with specialists.

The results of this research offer mixed support for hypothesis three. Co-offending networks in cannabis cultivation exhibit homophily and homogeneity for ethnicity, but, we see evidence of heterophily and heterogeneity in the age and gender composition of cannabis cultivation networks. This lends support to the contention that ethnic ties are stronger than age or gender bonds (McPherson, Smith-Lovin and Cook 2001). These results must be contextualized within the British Columbia setting and the ever-increasing proportion of Vietnamese involved in cannabis cultivation. Bouchard and Nguyen (this volume) suggest that in the Vietnamese culture, growing marijuana is something that you do with your family to make a living and illegality is just a necessary consequence. The authors also state that secrecy and trust are especially important among Vietnamese cultivators, and common language and familial bonds are seen as traits that facilitate these types of bonds.

The primary limitation facing this study concerns its use of *known* cannabis cultivation. Reliance on data generated by police reports may produce gaps in the co-offending network, and definitional biases associated with organizational directives can artificially distort the nature of the networks' structure. As with most social network analyses of criminal behavior, the networks examined here are likely to be incomplete and contain blurred boundaries. Successful, highly organized cultivators will likely avoid police detection and never appear in a police-based dataset. These findings may also have been distorted by law enforcement directives and initiatives. For instance, the police may focus more attention on individuals once they are "known" cannabis cultivators; therefore, biasing the data.

Another limitation concerns the comparison between this research and the results of McGloin and Piquero (2010). Since McGloin and Piquero are dealing with juveniles and this study deals with adults, it is not possible to completely disentangle the extent to which differences between the two studies are the result of substantial differences in the ages of their subjects or are the result of the unique features of cannabis cultivation. Future research should focus on comparing co-offending networks from different types of crimes.

Conclusion

To close, this chapter provides insight into the frequency, shape, composition, and structure of co-offending relationships in cannabis cultivation. In their 2010 article, McGloin and Piquero challenge criminologists to pay more attention to co-offending network structures in specific crimes, stating that co-offending can be extremely varied and with variation comes the potential to shed light on specific crime patterns. This study shows that the majority of cannabis cultivation is carried out by more than one individual, and that group offending is even more likely as the growing operation increases in size. We also show that cannabis cultivation co-offending networks are more likely to be redundant than general juvenile co-offending networks. The results support the argument that redundant networks are more likely to be found in situations where trust is important and the threat of sanction is ever-looming (Coleman 1990, Granovetter 1985, Von Lampe and Johansen 2004).

These findings support adopting law enforcement policies targeting co-offenders and offender networks. Police departments should consider instituting patrols and task forces that focus specifically on co-offending and criminal organizations, especially for crimes where co-offending is common, such as cannabis cultivation. Generally, departments should ensure that information about co-offending is maintained and accurate. Too often, files are closed after a single arrest has been made.

In their study of criminal enterprise structure along the illicit drug supply chain, Malm and Bichler (in press) argue that significant variation occurs at each niche within the drug market and warn that characterizing the network structure of the market as a whole is misleading. We strongly support this statement. By creating co-offending networks based exclusively on activity within one market niche – production – we find strong evidence of stable and long-lasting partnerships. If an individual were to stop cultivating cannabis and start distributing marijuana and cocaine (this change in roles in fairly common in criminal enterprise), their co-offenders are also likely to change. Based on the results presented in this chapter, future research should focus on crime-, or role-specific analysis of criminal networks.

List of references

Borgatti, S.P., Everett, M.G. and Freeman, L.C. 2006. *UCINET 2.0 for Windows: Software for Social Network Analysis.* Harvard: Analytic Technologies.

Bouchard, M. 2007. A capture-recapture model to estimate the size of criminal populations and the risks of detection in a marijuana cultivation industry. *Journal of Quantitative Criminology*, 23, 221-241.

Bouchard, M. 2008. Towards a realistic method to estimate cannabis production in industrialized countries. *Contemporary Drug Problems,* Summer/Fall, 291-320.

Burt, R. 1992. *Structural Holes: The Social Structure of Competition.* Cambridge, MA: Cambridge University Press.

Coleman, J.S. 1964. *Introduction to mathematical sociology.* Glencoe, Illinois: Free Press.

Coleman, J.S. 1990. *Foundations of Social Theory*. Cambridge, MA: Cambridge University Press.

Conway, K. and McCord, J. 2002. A longitudinal examination of the relationship between co-offending with violent accomplices and violent crime. *Aggressive Behavior,* 28, 97-108.

Dorn, N., Levi, M. and King, L. 2005. *Literature Review on Upper-Level Drug Trafficking.* [Online: Home Office]. Available at: http://www.homeoffice.gov.uk/rds/pdfs05/rdsolr2205.pdf [accessed: 10 January 2009].

Edwards, A. and Levi, M. 2008. Researching the organization of serious crimes. *Criminology and Criminal Justice*, 8, 363-388.

Felson, M. 2003. The process of co-offending. *Crime Prevention Studies,* 16, 149-167.

Granovetter, M. 1985. Economic and social structure: the problem of embeddedness. *American Journal of Sociology*, 91, 481-510.

Haynie, D.L. 2001. Delinquent peers revisited: Does network structure matter? *The American Journal of Sociology,* 106(4), 1013-1057.

Jenssen, J. and Greve, A. 2002. Does the degree of redundancy in social networks influence the success of business start-ups? *International Journal of Entrepreneurial Business and Research*, 8, 254-267.

Malm, A.E., Bichler, G. and Van De Walle, S. 2010. Comparing the ties that bind criminal networks: Is blood thicker than water? *Security Journal,* 23, 52-74.

Malm, A.E. and Bichler, G. Networks of Collaborating Criminals: Assessing the Structural Vulnerability of Drug Markets. *Journal of Research in Crime and Delinquency*, in press.

McGloin, J.M. and Piquero, A.R. 2010. On the relationship between co-offending network redundancy and offending versatility. *Journal of Research in Crime and Delinquency*, 47(1), 63-90.

McGloin, J.M., Sullivan, C.J., Piquero, A.R. and Bacon, S. 2008. Investigating the stability of co-offending among a sample of youthful offender. *Criminology,* 46(1), 155-188.

Morselli, C. and Tremblay, P. 2004. Criminal achievement, offender networks and the benefits of low self control. *Criminology*, 42, 773-804.

McPherson, M., Smith-Lovin, L. and Cook, J.L. 2001. Birds of a feather: Homophily in Social Networks. *Annual Review of Sociology*, 27, 415-444.

Plecas, D., Malm, A.E. and Kinney, B. 2005. *Marihuana growing operations in British Columbia 1997- 2003*. Abbotsford, British Columbia: University of the Fraser Valley.

Reiss, A.J. 1988. *Co-offending and criminal careers*. Chicago, IL: University of Chicago Press.

Reiss, A.J. and Farrington, D.P. 1991. Advancing knowledge about co-offending: Results from a prospective longitudinal survey of London males. *Journal of Criminal Law and Criminology,* 83, 360-395.

Rogers, E.M. 1995. *Diffusion of innovations.* 4th edition. New York, NY: Free Press.

Surowiecki, J. 2004. *The Wisdom of Crowds: Why the Many are Smarter Than the Few and How Collective Wisdom Shapes Business, Economies, Societies and Nations*. New York, NY: Doubleday.

Von Lampe, K. and Johansen, P. 2004. Organized crime and trust: On the conceptualization and empirical relevance of trust in the context of criminal networks. *Global Crime*, 6, 159-184.

Waring, E. 2002. Co-offending as a form of social organization, in *Crime and Social Organization*, edited by E. Waring and D. Weisburd. New Brunswick, NJ: Transaction Publishers, 31-48.

Warr, M. 2002. *Companions in Crime: The Social Aspects of Criminal Conduct.* New York, NY: Cambridge University Press.

Wasserman, S. and Faust, K. 1994. *Social network analysis: Methods and applications*. Cambridge, MA: Cambridge University Press.

Chapter 9
Cannabis Cultivation in the United States

Ralph A. Weisheit

Introduction

The cultivation of cannabis in the United States is hardly a new phenomenon. As early as 1918 guards at San Quentin were trained to spot cannabis plants among other plants cultivated by inmates in the prison garden. Although *cultivation* was not an issue in wider society, cannabis *use* in the U.S. was a public concern in the early 1900s, leading to the 1937 Cannabis Tax Act, a federal law criminalizing cannabis. In those early years cannabis use was primarily limited to artists, musicians, and Mexican immigrants. In the 1960s cannabis use became more mainstream. Although there was widespread public awareness of cannabis use, cannabis cultivation remained out of public awareness until the 1980s. The reasons for the lack of awareness of marijuana cultivation are unclear, but perhaps it is because for much of the 60s and 70s cannabis from Mexico, grown in large fields and harvested by machine, was relatively inexpensive and easy to obtain. Beginning in the late 1960s, the U.S. government made a concerted effort to end the movement of cannabis from Mexico. First, in 1969 Operation Intercept attempted to stop the flow of cannabis from Mexico by intensively searching vehicles and people coming to the U.S. from Mexico. This operation ended after only 21 days, but did cause spot shortages of cannabis in the U.S. (Gooberman 1974). Second, in 1975 the U.S. government worked with Mexican officials to spray the herbicide *paraquat* on Mexican cannabis fields. One effect of this eradication effort was to make U.S. consumers wary of contaminated Mexican cannabis. Spot shortages combined with concerns about tainted cannabis made domestic cultivation an appealing option, one helped by the ease with which the plant could be grown (Weisheit 1992).

In 1982 the Drug Enforcement Administration (DEA), the federal government agency responsible for enforcing drug laws, ventured its first estimate of the size of the domestic cannabis crop, an estimate it would then compare with the amount reportedly seized in that year. It was assumed that seizures probably represented only 10 to 20 percent of the actual crop, but when official counts were concluded, *38 percent more marijuana had been seized than authorities had thought existed* (DEA 1982). It was also estimated that somewhere between 25 and 50 percent of the cannabis consumed in the United States had been grown there (National Drug Enforcement Policy Board 1986). This was a remarkable demonstration of the extent to which the problem had been largely invisible and it prompted more systematic data collection by the federal government and made available to the public. Official awareness of cannabis cultivation continued to expand during the 1980s so that by the end of the decade authorities had seized cultivated plants in each of the 50 states. There were credible estimates that in the mid-1980s there were between 1 and 2 million recreational cannabis growers and as many as 250,000 commercial growers (National Drug Enforcement Policy Board 1986). Even by conservative estimates the value of domestically grown cannabis in the late 1980s was $32 billion, more than double that of the most valuable legitimate crop, corn (Weisheit 1992).

Despite the number of people involved and the cash value of domestic cannabis, cannabis growers had not only escaped the attention of authorities, but of researchers. The 1980s and 1990s saw an explosion of research on illicit drugs, including domestic drug dealing and the international trafficking in drugs. Largely missing from this research was the study of domestic cannabis cultivation. Researchers and authorities knew more about networks moving cannabis from Mexico, South America, and Southeast Asia than they did about production in their own back yard. That would change somewhat in the 1990s, but compared with research on other drug markets domestic cannabis cultivation remains understudied. This chapter will briefly summarize some of the research from the 1990s and provide an update on what is currently known about cannabis cultivation in the United States. First, however, it is instructive to consider cannabis use patterns in the United States.

Cannabis use in the United States

Cannabis is by far the most commonly used illicit drug in the United States. An estimated 15.2 million people, or 6.1 percent of the U.S. population, are reported to have used the drug in the past month and 3.6 million people reported to have been using the drug on a daily basis (Substance Abuse and Mental Health Services Administration 2004, 2008).

The percentage of Americans using cannabis hasn't changed much over time, but the potency of cannabis consumed in the U.S. has increased substantially. THC is the primary mind-altering ingredient in cannabis and the percent of THC in cannabis is a major indicator of its potency. In 1976, tested samples of cannabis contained an average of only .9% THC. By 2009 the percent of THC in tested samples of cannabis had risen to 8.49% (National Center for Natural Products Research 2009). In the 1970s domestic cannabis tended to be more potent than imported, but by the 2000s, the situation was reversed. In 2008 the potency of imported cannabis was about double that of domestically grown (10.05% THC vs. 4.80%). Some have suggested that because of handling and storage methods, measures of THC in the 1970s tended to underestimate the potency of cannabis seized by authorities (McLaren et al. 2008). While this may be an issue for overall reported levels of potency, it should be less an issue for the comparison of domestic and imported marijuana, as both would have been subject to the same measurement error.

Types of growers: the late 1980s

Beginning in 1988 I undertook a study in which commercial cannabis growers were interviewed about their motivations and experiences (Weisheit 1992). From the interviews with growers and with officials attempting to arrest growers, three general types of grower were identified. First, were the so-called *hustlers*. These individuals were motivated by money. Their operations were large and designed to maximize profits. For them cannabis represented a product and any ideological commitment to a cannabis subculture was purely coincidental. Hustlers often engaged in other legitimate businesses, all with the goal of making as much money as possible. This category of grower was the smallest in terms of numbers of participants, but because their operations were large the volume of cannabis they produced was substantial.

Second, in size and number of participants were *pragmatists*. These growers were also interested in money, but for more practical reasons and not as a goal in itself. For pragmatists, growing cannabis was a way to overcome a financial hardship. Some were losing their farms, others had lost their jobs, others had low paying jobs, while others had medical bills they could not pay. Some were involved in the cannabis culture and some were not, but most had hopes of eventually leaving the cultivation business, or at least commercial cultivation, after their immediate financial crisis had passed.

Finally, the third and largest category of cannabis grower also tended to have the smallest operations. These so-called *communal growers* grew primarily for personal consumption and to share with friends. When they sold their product it was mainly to acquaintances and had as much to do with granting favors as it did with making a profit. They often sold their finished product for below the going market rate and nearly always had a commitment to the larger pro-cannabis culture. Many became fascinated with the process of growing and enjoyed experimenting with new varieties of cannabis and with new growing techniques (Weisheit 1991).

Growers in the late 1980s were almost always U.S. citizens, often living in rural areas where their operations more easily escaped detection. Growers in this period also tended to be long-term residents of their communities. As will be discussed below, by the 2000s things were changing: (a) the amount of cannabis grown in the U.S. continued to expand, (b) there were changes in the broader social context in which cannabis was viewed, (c) new groups were engaging in domestic cannabis cultivation, and (d) cultivation operations took on new forms. Understanding current trends in domestic cannabis cultivation requires understanding the changing social context in which cannabis cultivation has taken place.

The social context of contemporary cannabis cultivation

In the United States cannabis has long been an illegal substance to which there have been mixed reactions. Sometimes it is portrayed as a sinister drug that serves as a stepping stone into increasingly harder drugs, while at other times it is portrayed as less harmful than alcohol, or even as beneficial (Eddy 2009). The stance of the federal government has decidedly favored viewing cannabis as a dangerous drug to be suppressed by public information campaigns warning of its dangers, and by criminal sanctions against those undeterred by such warnings.

Over time a series of factors that, taken together created a new environment in which cannabis cultivation would spread. The federal government has remained steadfast in its opposition to cannabis, but as a result of these events states and localities gradually softened their stance toward the drug. These events included:

(1) The spread of cocaine and then methamphetamine drew public attention and police efforts away from cannabis. By comparison cannabis seemed less a threat to the social order. By 2007 parents reported they were more worried about their teen driving drunk, shoplifting, or having sex than they were worried about their teens using cannabis (CASA 2007). Annual surveys of students in the 8th, 10th, and 12th grades found that between 1992 and 2009 there was a decline in the perceived harm from regular cannabis use (Monitoring the Future 2009).

(2) Debates about the medicinal value of cannabis intensified. Under U.S. law, the Drug Enforcement Administration (DEA) is the agency responsible for deciding whether cannabis will be made available for use as a medicine. The agency has resolutely refused to lift federal restrictions, even denying requests for research to determine if and for which conditions cannabis is an effective medicine. Under federal law there is no distinction between medicinal use and recreational use of cannabis and the federal penalties for cultivating cannabis can be harsh. "Growing marijuana is considered *manufacturing* a controlled substance, a felony. A single plant can bring an individual up to five years in federal prison and up to a $250,000 fine for a first offense." (Eddy 2009)

However, the U.S. operates under a bifurcated system of drug laws in which federal laws and the laws of individual states are relatively independent. Thus, while possessing cannabis for medical purposes remains a federal crime for which the individual may be fully prosecuted, individual states are at liberty to allow cultivation, possession, and use of cannabis for medicinal purposes. This is important because some 99 percent of cannabis arrests in the United States are made at the state level (Marijuana Policy Project 2008).

In 1996 voters in the state of California approved Proposition 215, making California the first state to legalize the medicinal use of cannabis with a doctor's prescription. Proposition 215 also allowed approved medicinal cannabis users to cultivate plants for personal use. One by one other states have followed suit. By the beginning of 2010 a total of 14 of the 50 states had enacted legislation allowing for medical cannabis use (Table 9.1). In addition, momentum was favoring the passage of medical cannabis legislation in the nation's capital, Washington, D.C.

Table 9.1 Laws Favoring Medicinal Cannabis by State

State	Date of Legislation	State	Date of Legislation
California	1996	Hawaii	2000
Alaska	1998	Maryland	2003
Oregon	1998	Vermont	2004
Washington	1998	Montana	2004
Maine	1999	Rhode Island	2006
Colorado	2000	New Mexico	2007
Nevada	2000	New Jersey	2010

Sources: Marijuana Policy Project 2008, Kocieniewski 2010.

(Craig 2010). The New Jersey statute is particularly interesting because it explicitly states that state and local police are not required to assist federal authorities in the enforcement of federal laws.

The growing interest in medical cannabis has led to activities that would have been unthinkable just 25 years ago. In Colorado 50 medical cannabis growers from around the country compete for the "Western Slope Cannabis Crown," based on the potency of their cultivated cannabis. The event also includes a "People's Choice" award in which attendees can vote for their favorite (Sackariason 2010). In California, a mega-store described as the "Walmart of weed" provides all the equipment and technical assistance needed to cultivate medical cannabis (Kuruvila 2010). Around the country schools have had to decide how to deal with students who bring legally prescribed medical cannabis to school (Knickerbocker 2010), while in Michigan, Med Grow Cannabis College has a curriculum designed to provide "Professional training for the medical cannabis industry (Lewin 2009)." All of these events reflect a very different mindset about cannabis, a mindset no longer limited to viewing cannabis use as "Reefer Madness."

In November 2009, the federal government's firm position against medical cannabis was dealt another blow when the American Medical Association urged the federal government to allow research on medical cannabis, to allow for the development of cannabis-based medicines, and to allow for the development of alternative systems for delivering the drug (Hoeffel 2009). In addition, for the first time the federal government softened its stance on medical cannabis when the Justice Department announced that the DEA would no longer arrest medical cannabis users and suppliers for so long as they followed state laws. Cannabis growers whose behavior fell outside of state law would still be aggressively pursued (The Associated Press 2009).

Unfortunately, the issue of compassionate use of cannabis has been used (some might say hijacked) by both those seeking to make cannabis freely available as a recreational drug and by those seeking to ban any use of the drug (Eddy 2009). Whatever the motives on either side of the issue, the spread of legislation allowing medical cannabis has undercut federal government messages that the drug is of no medical value (Drug Enforcement Administration 2006). Further, as individual states enact legislation favoring medical cannabis it becomes easier for other states to pass similar legislation.

These state laws have a direct impact on cultivation. Each state, with the exception of New Jersey "... allows patients to grow, possess and use medical cannabis if approved by a medical doctor. Patients may also be assisted by a caregiver, who is authorized to help the patient grow, acquire, or consume medical cannabis (Marijuana Policy Project 2008: 6)." While states generally place limits on the amount that can be grown, the laws have the effect of encouraging people to learn about cannabis cultivation. This knowledge transfers directly to the cultivation of cannabis for recreational use, because the same types of plants can be used for both recreational and medicinal use, and because for each type of use potency matters.

(3) A weak U.S. economy in the late 2000s provided strong economic incentives to cultivate cannabis. While research in the early 1990s showed that many cannabis growers became involved in response to job loss, unexpected medical expenses, or the pending foreclosure on their property (Weisheit 1992), a similar pattern appears to have happened during the 2000s. During the early 2000s it was estimated that the cash value of domestically cultivated cannabis was about $36 billion, more than 50 percent greater than corn, the next most valuable cash crop (Gettman 2006). This same report concluded that cannabis was one of the top three cash crops in 30 of the 50 states. Further, these estimates were based on figures from the early to mid-2000s, before the sharp economic downturn of the late 2000s, when economic pressure to cultivate would be much greater. Some in law enforcement believe the downturn in the U.S. economy in the late 2000s has pushed more people into cultivating cannabis (Alford 2009).

"Pocketing a street value of up to $2,000 per plant, a successful grower can quickly rise in local prominence – new trucks and boats popping up in poor areas are often a sign of successful cultivators, police say (Jonsson 2009)." Especially in east Tennessee, Kentucky, and West Virginia, tough economic times may be motivating descendents of moonshiners to take the high risk and put spades in the earth.

Tough economic times have also led to an increase in calls to allow another kind of cultivation, in which the cannabis plant is used for industrial applications rather than for its medicinal or mind altering properties. A push by farmers to allow for the cultivation of hemp may have undercut the image of cannabis as dangerous, just as medical cannabis initiatives may have done. Hemp is the industrial version of cannabis, useful in a wide range of products from paint thinner to paper, to cloth. It is essentially the same plant as that used for intoxication, but with minimal levels of THC, rendering it useless as a recreational drug. In 1992 a nonprofit organization, the Hemp Industries Association, was formed to promote hemp as an agricultural product. Since then, farmers seeking to expand their crop options have become increasingly vocal in their support for hemp as an agricultural product. In one case a 51-year-old farmer who raised garbonzo beans joined another farmer, a

Republican state legislator from North Dakota, in obtaining a state permit to grow hemp. However, the DEA refused to recognize the permit and the farmer, along with five others was arrested when he protested the DEA's position by planting hemp in the lawn of DEA headquarters (MacPherson 2009). These same farmers had unsuccessfully requested that the federal court force the DEA to recognize the North Dakota state law legalizing hemp as an agricultural product (Slevin 2007).

(4) In the 1980s and early 1990s there were no reports of domestic cannabis cultivation operations conducted by international organizations. Things changed in the late 2000s when reports emerged that Asian and Mexican drug trafficking organizations (DTOs) were running large-scale grow operations in the United States. Asian DTOs focused their attention on large-scale indoor operations in several states, including Ohio, Colorado, Georgia, Texas, and California (National Drug Intelligence Center 2009). The general pattern was to use the weak housing market to buy suburban homes with minimal credit checks and few questions asked. The homes were often expensive, in the $500,000 to $600,000 range. Carpets were removed, there was little or no furniture, windows were covered and tens of thousands of dollars worth of lights, hydroponics, and growing equipment were installed. In some cases wall were removed to add more growing space (DEA 2008, Barboza and Pierson 2007).

Mexican DTOs have been moving Mexican cannabis cultivation sites closer to the U.S. border and are increasingly setting up operations within the U.S., particularly on public lands. These operations have been uncovered in a number of states, though they are more common in the West where there are simply more public lands and where there is a large Mexican immigrant population. The operations tend to be large. In one operation 25,000 plants were found, while another had 30,000 plants (Saillant 2009, DEA 2007).

Thus, several social changes have occurred that have brought about a shift in domestic cannabis cultivation. Our attention now turns to what is known about trends in the extent to which cannabis is cultivated within the U.S.

Cannabis cultivation expands in the 2000s

As an illicit activity, and one that is remarkably easy to undertake, it is impossible to know precisely how much illicit cannabis is cultivated in the United States or how many people are engaged in cultivation. Absent any precise measure, it is possible to have a rough gauge of the problem from official seizure data, recognizing that such data are the product of both the amount of cultivation and state resources allocated to finding and eradicating cultivated cannabis. With this limitation in mind, data from the Drug Enforcement Administration's Domestic Cannabis Eradication/Suppression Program are available from its inception in 1982 through 2009 (DEA 1982 through 1993, Pastore and Maguire 2010). As Figure 9.1 shows, the number of cultivated cannabis plants seized in the U.S. increased until 1992, after which it declined until the late 1990s, and then gradually rose until 2004. Beginning in 2004, seizures rose dramatically so that by 2009 more than 10 million cultivated plants were reportedly seized, the largest number ever reported and more than triple the number seized just five years earlier.

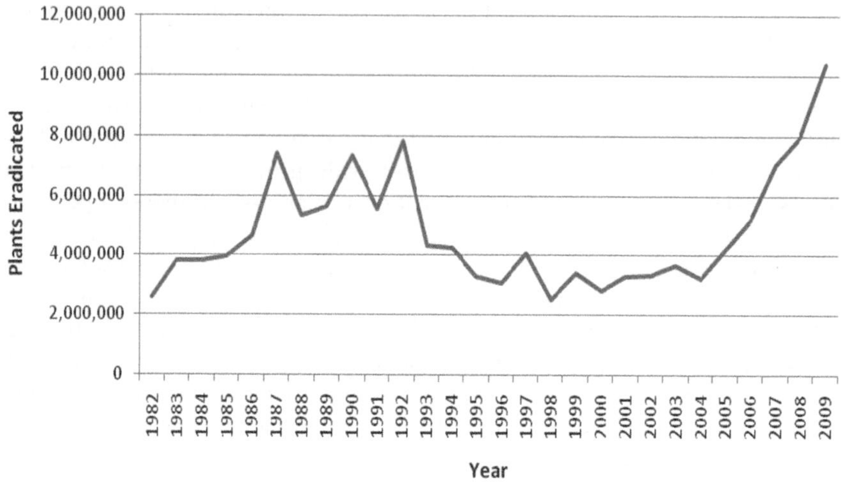

Figure 9.1 Number of Cannabis Plants Seized and Eradicated

Source: U.S. Drug Enforcement Administration

This increase in production in the mid to late 2000s was not evenly distributed across the 50 states. While there were seizures in all 50 states, the bulk of these plants (more than two-thirds) were seized from one state, California. California presents a unique illustration of how factors that encourage production have all come together in one state.

Cannabis cultivation in California

For a variety of reasons, California provides a good natural laboratory in which to study the issue of cannabis cultivation in the U.S. The factors that might lead to increased cultivation can be clearly seen in the state and California has historically served as a bellwether for other social changes in the country as a whole. As one business publication put it, "when things happen in California, they're picked up and embraced throughout the country (Cadrain 2007)."

As Figure 9.2 shows, much of the increase in domestic cannabis cultivation, as measured by seized plants, during the 2000s can be accounted for by dramatic increases in seizures in California. In 2000, California accounted for 29 percent of all seized cultivated cannabis plants in the U.S., but by 2009 the state accounted

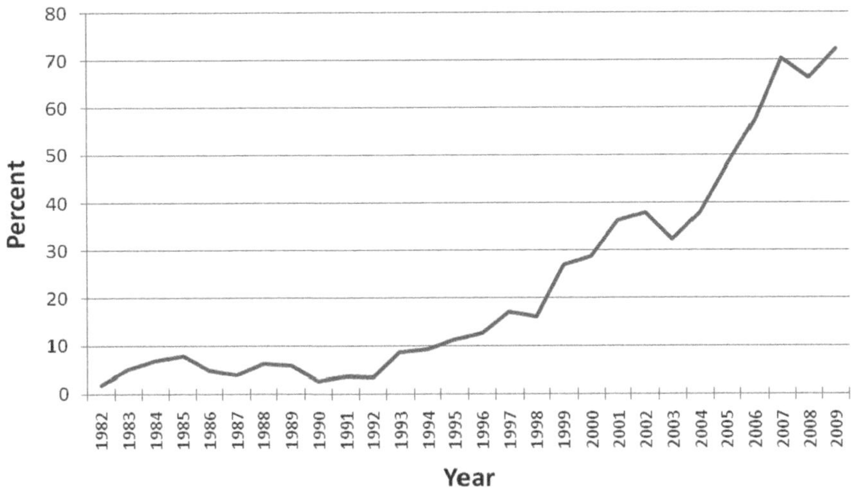

Figure 9.2 Cannabis Plants Seized in California as a Percent of all Seized Plants

Source: U.S. Drug Enforcement Administration

for 72 percent of seized cultivated plants. Before discussing more specific aspects of cannabis cultivation in California, it is useful to provide a broader context by describing some general characteristics of the state.

The general setting California is the third largest state in the United States, covering 423,967 square kilometers, making it larger than Germany (357,000 sq km) but smaller than Spain (505,000 sq km). The state's southern border is shared with Mexico, a major supplier of imported cannabis. Geographically California is a land of extremes. It includes the highest point among the 48 contiguous states – Mount Whitney at 4,419 meters above sea level, as well as the lowest point among the 48 contiguous states – Death Valley at 86 meters below sea level.

With about 37 million people, California is by far the most populous state in the United States and has a population just under that of Spain (41 million). The state is 1,239 km long (north-south) and 402 km wide, with most cannabis cultivation taking place in the northern, less populous half of the state. The northern half of the state includes mountains, valleys, and plateaus and in general has limited summer rainfall, making it necessary to irrigate cultivated outdoor plants. In 1979 California and Hawaii became the first two states in which the DEA undertook cannabis eradication efforts (Gettman 2006).

Medical cannabis California was the first state to legalize medical cannabis, and there is no state in which the medical cannabis statute is more vague. In California there are no legal restrictions on the types of ailments for which the drug may be prescribed. Consequently, it is possible to obtain medical cannabis for just about any discomfort one might feel. The near absence of restrictions on the conditions for which cannabis can be prescribed has invited abuse and some have suggested this has led to the *de facto* legalization of cannabis for recreational purposes. In the city of Los Angeles alone there may be as many as 1,000 dispensaries (Moore 2009) and at least three local magazines devoted specifically to medical cannabis (Appleford 2010). In early 2008 Los Angeles was the site of the unveiling of medical cannabis vending machines (National Public Radio 2008). Following passage of the voter initiative, the legislature sought to limit the number of plants that may be possessed for medical purposes to six mature plants or 12 immature plants. However, the California Supreme Court struck down any limits as an unconstitutional amendment to the voter initiative (Hoeffel 2010).

A weak economy The economy of California has struggled for decades, brought on in part by voter initiatives that make it difficult to raise taxes, while other voter initiatives mandate increased state spending. By the end of the 2000s the state's deficit had reached crisis proportions. One response to the budget crisis has been a call for legalizing and taxing cannabis intended for recreational use. The Republican governor has publicly stated that he is open to discussion of the issue and a survey of the public found that 56 percent of voters in the state supported legalization (McKinley 2009). In early 2010, when the state's budget deficit was expected to exceed $60 billion, "the state Assembly's public safety committee approved a bill ... to tax and regulate cannabis in a manner similar to alcohol (Wood 2010)." By some estimates legalization would bring as much as $1.4 billion a year into state coffers, though it is impossible to know how much revenue would be raised (McKinley 2009). However, one study suggests that if cannabis were legalized in California the pre-tax retail price would drop by as much as 80 percent, which in turn would have an impact on tax revenue (Kilmer et al. 2010).

Foreign drug gangs California has also seen the influence of Mexican and Asian drug trafficking organizations on domestic cannabis cultivation. The two groups operate very differently. In general, Mexican drug trafficking organizations (DTOs) are responsible for large outdoor growing operations located primarily in the northern half of the state (Alford 2009). In contrast, Asian DTOS have been responsible for large and elaborate indoor cannabis grow operations.

Authorities have identified a number of indoor cultivation operations in California, many of which are operated by Asian DTOs (Winton 2008). Nationally, 53 percent of cannabis plants cultivated indoors were found in California (National Drug Intelligence Center 2008). These operations are typically in well-to-do suburban neighborhoods. In 1991, the first year in which the DEA separated their counts of indoor and outdoor cultivated plants, there were 303 indoor grow operations found in California yielding nearly 46,000 plants. By 2008 there were 748 indoor grow operations found, yielding nearly 183,000 plants.

In addition to indoor grow operations, California has a proliferation of outdoor cultivation operations run by Mexican DTOs. About 36 percent of California's population is Hispanic, and of those 41 percent are foreign born and 83 percent are of Mexican origin (Pew Hispanic Center, no date). This, combined with the state's close physical proximity to Mexico has facilitated the movement of Mexican DTOs into California.

California has an extensive network of federal and state public lands and these lands are favored locations for large cannabis grow operations run by Mexican DTOs and worked by immigrant labor. Federal land alone covers some 15.2 million acres, or nearly 15% of the state's land area (Bureau of Land Management 2010). Authorities estimate that the number of cannabis plants eradicated in California national forests accounts for "an average of 83 percent of all plants eradicated from all U.S. national forests between 2004 and 2008" (National Drug Intelligence Center 2009). In 2008 alone about 2.5 million plants were seized from national forests in California.

The way ahead

Since 1982, when the DEA first publicly recognized that cannabis cultivation was an issue in the United States, the landscape of domestic cannabis cultivation has changed considerably. The social environment in which cultivation occurs and the patterns of cultivation have changed substantially. While cannabis continues to be cultivated in every state, the center of production has shifted from the Midwest farmland in the 1980s to California in the West.

The hustlers, pragmatists, and communal growers of the 1980s still exist, but new groups have added to the ranks of each. The native-born hustler whose large-scale operations were nearly always outdoors, still exist. Now, however, there are also hustlers from Asian DTOs operating sophisticated indoor grow operations. There are also hustlers from Mexican DTOs operating large scale outdoor operations. The pragmatists of the 1980s, who cultivated cannabis to get them through tough economic times still exist. Now, however, there are also farmers pressuring lawmakers to allow (low THC) hemp as a cash crop, to ease their economic pain. The communal growers of the 1980s still exist. Now, however, communal growers focused on cannabis as a recreational drug have been joined by those wishing to raise cannabis for medical purposes. In practice it has become difficult to make a clear distinction between the two groups.

Predicting trends in the production and use of any drug is like predicting fashion trends, a difficult task at best. It appears the mood of the country is shifting toward a softer approach to cannabis and cannabis cultivation. But it is likely this softer approach will hit its limits well before there is full legalization. There are several reasons why this might be true.

First, it seems unlikely that federal or state authorities will completely abandon legal control of cannabis. Tremendous resources flow into the war on drugs and agencies are unlikely to easily give up control of those resources. In 2008, there were 1,702,537 arrests for illicit drugs in the United States. There were more arrests for illicit drugs than for any other offense, and about half of those arrests were for cannabis (Federal Bureau of Investigation 2009). Cannabis is only one part of the war on drugs, but an important part.

Further, there is no evidence that the public would support full legalization. In addition to the country's historic fondness for prohibition, citizens are increasingly placing limits on access to tobacco, are drawn to organic foods, and are requiring restaurants to include calorie counts on their menus. In such an environment it is almost certain that substantial legal restrictions on cannabis will continue, albeit with some moderation of legal penalties.

A more likely scenario is that state and federal officials will continue efforts to take out large-scale growing operations and arrest those involved, while turning a blind eye to small-scale operations – something known as selective enforcement. It is also possible that small operations will be formally exempt from criminal penalties. Under this approach authorities would serve something comparable to an anti-trust function, minimizing violence and official corruption that might accompany very large and very lucrative operations.

Second, while the U.S. is likely to retain legal sanctions against cannabis, it is likely to expand access to medical marijuana. Despite efforts by the Drug Enforcement Administration to block research on medical cannabis, there is evidence to support the use of cannabis for glaucoma, nausea from chemotherapy, loss of appetite, and pain (Earleywine 2002). Some of these afflictions are more likely to strike senior citizens, a group that typically has a very high voter turnout. This group is also of a generation that was likely to have tried marijuana in their youth. As the population ages, senior citizens will become an increasingly influential proportion of the electorate, putting pressure on lawmakers to allow cannabis for medical purposes.

The move to allow compassionate medical cannabis use represents a major policy shift, but the consequences of this shift are yet unknown. California was the first state to allow medical cannabis use and the statute's vague wording has led to criticisms that the law has been misused by those seeking cannabis for recreational purposes. What is missing in California and in states with more restrictive statutes is an objective study of the social costs and benefits of allowing medical cannabis use. Variations in the extent to which state laws restrict access to medical cannabis provide a natural laboratory for studying the issue and would provide useful information for policy makers.

These thoughts about future enforcement patterns and access to medical marijuana are, of course, speculation. Whatever the future holds, it is difficult to imagine a scenario in which the country turns back the clock and cannabis is once again viewed as an "evil weed" whose use turns otherwise healthy sane individuals into victims of "reefer madness."

List of references

Alford, R. 2009. Growth industry: Recession blamed as marijuana farming increases from California to Appalachia. *Los Angeles Times* [Online, 10 September]. Available at: http://www.latimes.com/news/nationworld/nation/wire/sns-ap-us-meltdown-marijuana,0,1361790.story [accessed: 10 September 2009].

Appleford, S. 2010. Weed mags sprout across Los Angeles: Publications reap windfall from pot ads. *L.A. Weekly* [Online, 21 January]. Available at: http://www.la-weekly.com/content/printVersion/833117 [accessed: 21 January 2010].

The Associated Press 2009. Justice Department memo rules on medical marijuana. *The Los Angeles Times* [Online, 19 October]. Available at: http://www.la-times.com/news/nationworld/nation/la-na-medical-marijuana19-2009oct19,0,5561435.story [accessed: 19 October 2009].

Barboza, T. and Pierson, D. 2007. For pot growers, suburbia is fertile ground. *Los Angeles Times* [Online, 30 March]. Available at http://www.latimes.com/-news/local/la-me-pot30mar30,0,7623921.story?coll=la-home-headlines [accessed: 30 March 2007].

Bureau of Land Management 2010. *U.S. Bureau of Land Management in California – Take It Outside*. Available at: http://www.blm.gov/ca/st/en.html [accessed: 2 February 2010].

Cadrain, D. 2007. California, the bellwether: Progressive employment laws and court decisions from the Golden State often influence state laws and company policies in the rest of the nation. *AllBusiness.com*. Available at: http://www.all-business.com/legal/legal-services-litigation/5505185-1.html [accessed: 1 February 2010].

CASA 2007. *National Survey of American Attitudes on Substance Abuse XII: Teens and Parents*. The National Center on Addiction and Substance Abuse. New York, NY: Columbia University.

Craig, T. 2010. D.C. Council bill proposes up to 5 medical marijuana dispensaries. *The Washington Post* [Online, 19 January]. Available at: http://www.washington-post.com/wpdyn/content/article/2010/01/19/AR2014299151.html [accessed: 21 January 2010].

Drug Enforcement Administration 1982. *Domestic Marijuana Eradication/Suppression Program, 1982*. Washington, D.C.: U.S. Department of Justice.

Drug Enforcement Administration 1983. *Domestic Marijuana Eradication/Suppression Program, 1983*. Washington, D.C.: U.S. Department of Justice.

Drug Enforcement Administration 1984. *Domestic Marijuana Eradication/Suppression Program, 1984*. Washington, D.C.: U.S. Department of Justice.

Drug Enforcement Administration 1985. *Domestic Marijuana Eradication/Suppression Program, 1985*. Washington, D.C.: U.S. Department of Justice.

Drug Enforcement Administration 1986. *Domestic Marijuana Eradication/Suppression Program, 1986*. Washington, D.C.: U.S. Department of Justice.

Drug Enforcement Administration 1987. *Domestic Marijuana Eradication/Suppression Program, 1987*. Washington, D.C.: U.S. Department of Justice.

Drug Enforcement Administration 1988. *Domestic Marijuana Eradication/Suppression Program, 1988*. Washington, D.C.: U.S. Department of Justice.

Drug Enforcement Administration 1989. *Domestic Marijuana Eradication/Suppression Program, 1989*. Washington, D.C.: U.S. Department of Justice.

Drug Enforcement Administration 1990. *Domestic Marijuana Eradication/Suppression Program, 1990*. Washington, D.C.: U.S. Department of Justice.

Drug Enforcement Administration 1991. *Domestic Marijuana Eradication/Suppression Program, 1991*. Washington, D.C.: U.S. Department of Justice.

Drug Enforcement Administration 1992. *Domestic Marijuana Eradication/Suppression Program, 1992*. Washington, D.C.: U.S. Department of Justice.

Drug Enforcement Administration 1993. *Domestic Marijuana Eradication/Suppression Program, 1993*. Washington, D.C.: U.S. Department of Justice.

Drug Enforcement Administration 2006. *The DEA Position on Marijuana*. Available at: http://www.justice.gov/dea/marijuana_position.html [accessed: 5 June 2010].

Drug Enforcement Administration 2007. DEA announces marijuana bust in Tonto National Forest. *News Release*. Available at: http://www.usdoj.gov/-dea/pubs/states/newsrel/phnx110107p.html [accessed: 10 September 2009].

Drug Enforcement Administration 2008. DEA foils indoor marijuana grow operation. *News Release*. Available at: http://www.usdoj.gov/dea/pubs/states/-newsrel/la072208p.html [accessed: 30 July 2008].

Earleywine, M. 2002. *Understanding Marijuana: A New Look at the Scientific Evidence*. New York: Oxford University Press.

Eddy, M. 2009. *Medical Marijuana: Review and Analysis of Federal and State Policies*. Report Number RL33211. Washington, D.C.: Congressional Research Service.

Federal Bureau of Investigation 2009. *Crime in the United States, 2008*. Available at: http://www.fbi.gov/ucr/cius2008/index.html [accessed: 7 June 2010].

Gettman, J. 2006. Marijuana production in the United States, 2006. *The Bulletin of Cannabis Reform* [Online], December, 1-28. Available at: http://www.drugscience.org/Archive/bcr2/MJCropReport_2006.pdf [accessed: 30 July 2009].

Gooberman, L.A. 1974. *Operation Intercept: The Multiple Consequences of Public Policy*. New York: Pergamon Press.

Hoeffel, J. 2009. Medical marijuana gets a boost from major doctors group. *Los Angeles Times* [Online, 11 November]. Available at: http://www.latimes.com/news/nationworld/nation/la-na-marijuana-ama112009nov11,0,3003312.story [accessed: 11 November 2009].

Hoeffel, J. 2010. California Supreme Court strikes down limits on medical marijuana possession. *The Los Angeles Times* [Online, 21 January]. Available at: http://latimesblogs.latimes.com/lanow/2010/01/california-supreme-court-strikes-down-limits-on-how-much-medical-marijuana-a-patient-can-possess.html [accessed: 21 January 2010].

Jonsson, P. 2007. Marigolds make way for marijuana in suburbs. *The Christian Science Monitor* [Online, 5 March]. Available at: http://www.csmonitor.com/2007/0305/p01s02-ussc.html [accessed: 5 March 2007].

Jonsson, P. 2009. A surge in marijuana farming this year may be due to unemployment as well as growing demand for the drug. *The Christian Science Monitor* [Online, 10 September]. Available at: http://www.csmonitor.com/2009/0910/p02s04-usgn.html [accessed: 11 September 2009].

Kilmer, B., Caulkins, J.P., Pacula, R.L., MacCoun, R.J. and Reuter, P.H. 2010. *Altered State? Assessing How Marijuana Legalization in California Could Influence Marijuana Consumption and Public Budgets*. Santa Monica, CA: RAND Corporation.

Knickerbocker, B. 2010. Marijuana in the classroom? Sometimes it's legal. *The Christian Science Monitor* [Online, 23 January]. Available at: http://www.csmonitor.com/layout/set/print/content/view/print/275534 [accessed: 25 January 2010].

Kocieniewski, D. 2010. New Jersey vote backs marijuana for severly ill. *The New York Times* [Online, 11 January]. Available at: http://www.nytimes.com/2010/01/12/-nyregion/12marijuana.html?sq=New%20Jersey%20medical%20marijuana&st=cse&scp=1&pagewanted=print [accessed: 16 August 2010].

Kuruvila, M. 2010. IGrow: Walmart of weed opens in Oakland. *The San Francisco Chronicle* [Online, 28 January]. Available at: http://sfgate.com/cgi-bin/article.cgi?f=/c/a/2010/01/28/BA4T1BOGCV.DTL [accessed: 28 January 2010].

Lewin, T. 2009. At this school, it's marijuana in every class. *The New York Times* [Online, 29 November]. Available at: http://www.nytimes.com/2009/11/29/-education/29marijuana.html?scp=3&sq=School+marijuana&st=nyt [accessed: 29 November 2009].

MacPherson, J. 2009. Protesting farmers arrested while trying to plant hemp at DEA headquarters in Virginia. *The Chicago Tribune* [Online, 14 October]. Available at: http://www.chicagotribune.com/business/sns-ap-us-farm-scene-hemp-protest,0,2136756.story [accessed: 18 October 2009].

Marijuana Policy Project 2008. *State-by-State Medical Marijuana Laws*, Washington, D.C.: Marijuana Policy Project.

McKinley, J. 2009. Push to legalize marijuana gains ground in California. *The New York Times* [Online, 28 October]. Available at: http://www.nytimes.com/2009/-10/28/us/28pot.html?scp=1&sq=Legalize+Marijuana+California&st=nyt [accessed: 28 October 2009].

McLaren, J., Swift, W., Dillon, P. and Allsop, S. 2008. Cannabis potency and contamination: A review of the literature. *Addiction*, 103, 1100-1109.

Monitoring the Future 2009. Teen marijuana use tilts up, while some drugs decline in use. *Press Release*. Available at: http://monitoringthefuture.org/pressreleases/-09drugpr_complete.pdf [accessed: 31 January 2010].

Moore, S. 2009. Los Angeles prepares for clash over marijuana. *The New York Times* [Online, 18 October]. Available at: http://www.nytimes.com/2009/10/18/-us/18enforce.html?scp=1&sq=Los%20Angeles%20Clash%20Marijuana&st=nyt [accessed: 18 October 2009].

National Center for Natural Products Research 2009. *Quarterly Report Potency Monitoring Project, Report 104*. University of Mississippi: University, Mississippi.

National Drug Enforcement Policy Board (NDEPB) 1986. *Analysis of the domestic cannabis problem and the federal response, staff /report*. Cited in Jon Gettman 1987. *Marijuana in American – 1986*. Washington, D.C.: National Organization for the Reform of Marijuana Laws (NORML).

National Drug Intelligence Center 2008. *National Drug Threat Assessment, 2009*. Available at: http://www.justice.gov/ndic/pubs31/31379/index.htm [accessed: 19 October 2009].

National Drug Intelligence Center 2009. *Domestic Cannabis Cultivation Assessment 2009*. Available at: http://www.justice.gov/ndic/pubs37/37035/public.htm [accessed: 26 January 2010].

National Public Radio 2008. Automated marijuana machines unveiled in L.A. [Online, 30 January]. Available at: http://www.npr.org/templates/story/-story.php?storyID=18548099 [accessed: 1 February 2010].

Pastore, A.L. and Maguire, K. (Eds.). 2010. *Sourcebook of Criminal Justice Statistics*. Tables 4.38.2003 through 4.38.2009. Available at: http://www.albany.edu/-sourcebook/tost_4.html#4_e [accessed: 21 October 2009].

Pew Hispanic Center (n.d.). *Demographic profile of Hispanics in California, 2007*. Available at: http://www.pewhispanic.org [accessed: 25 January 2010].

Saillant, C. 2009. Pot farm fire reveals a troubling trend: Drug rings' operation in the state and federal forests are becoming more sophisticated, officials say. *The Los Angeles Times* [Online, 18 August]. Available at: http://www.latimes.com/news/local/la-me-fire19-2009aug19,0,3207658.story [accessed: 20 August 2009].

Sackariason, C. 2010. 'Cannabis crown' coming to Aspen. *Post Independent* (Glenwood Springs, CO). [Online, 23 January]. Available at: http://www.postindepen-dent.com/article/20100123/VALLEYNEWS/100129949&parentprofile=search [accessed: 2 February 2010].

Slevin, P. 2007. Farmers ask federal court to dissociate hemp and pot. *The Washington Post* [Online, 12 November]. Available at: http://www.washingtonpost.com/wp-dyn/content/article/2007/11/12/AR20071112.htm [accessed: 19 October 2009].

Substance Abuse and Mental Health Services Administration 2004. Daily marijuana users. Available at: http://www.oas.samhsa.gov/2k4/dailyMJ/dailyMJ.htm [accessed: 30 January 2010].

Substance Abuse and Mental Health Services Administration 2008. *Results from the 2007 National Survey on Drug Use and Health: National Findings*. Rokcville, MD: Office of Applied Studies.

Weisheit, R.A. 1991. The intangible rewards from crime: The case of domestic marijuana cultivation. *Crime and Delinquency*, 37(4), 506-527.

Weisheit, R.A. 1992. *Domestic marijuana: A neglected industry*. Westport, CT: Greenwood Press.

Winton, R. 2008. 4 arrested in raids on suspected Southland pot operations. *The Los Angeles Times* [Online, 22 July]. Available at: http://www.latimes.com/-news/local/la-me-pot23-2008jul23,0,4394184.story [accessed: 22 July 2008].

Wood, D.B. 2010. California edges toward legalization of pot. *The Christian Science Monitor* [Online, 12 January]. Available at: http://www.csmonitor.com/USA/-Society/2010/0112/California-edges-toward-legalization-of-pot [accessed: 21 January 2010].

Chapter 10
Cannabis Cultivation in Spain – The Case of Cannabis Social Clubs[1]

Xabier Arana and Virginia Montañés Sánchez

Introduction

The objective of this chapter is to provide an overview of the use of cannabis in Spain and its regulation, both criminal and administrative, including the effects this regulation has on people who use or are somehow related to the substance.

One of the characteristics of Spanish legislation in this area is the legal uncertainty. Legally, the consumption of cannabis is not criminally punishable, but is subject to administrative penalties. Similarly, cultivation and possession are considered crimes when they involve trafficking, but not in the case of personal consumption. It is usually the police who initially decide whether a crime has occurred or not. However, there are cases in which the police have reported an incident as a crime and, later, the judicature has ruled that it was not.

Since the 1990s, a section of the cannabis-using population has developed various proposals, both at the theoretical and practical level, aimed at reducing their current legal insecurity. A result of this work has been different collective cannabis plantations and, more recently, the creation and promotion of Cannabis Social Clubs (CSCs). CSCs are concrete proposals for the self-production and distribution of cannabis, born within the cannabis social movement itself, which could become an alternative model of cannabis supply regulation to the one currently existing within the illegal market.

Cannabis use in Spain

The first signs of cannabis use in the Iberian Peninsula date back to the Neolithic period, according to archaeological and paleontological studies cited by Juan Carlos Usó (2005: 23). However, it was from the 10th century onwards that use became widespread among the population, facilitated by the Muslim invasion and the installation of Muslim culture on Spanish territory. Another factor was the use

1 The authors wish to express their gratitude to José Afuera, Martín Barriuso, Fernanda de la Figuera, Joep Oomen, Iker Val and Jenny Rodríguez for their contributions during the development of this chapter.

of this plant among witches in the Middle Ages, which caused the Inquisition to pursue its use in the 12th Century.

Despite this persecution, the use of cannabis in Spain has been documented both in literary and scientific texts. Apparently, until the late 19th century the primary role of cannabis was therapeutic, and the step to recreational use occurred during the occupation, called 'the Protectorate', that the Spanish government exercised over Morocco between 1912 and 1956 (Usó 2005: 27).

After the pacification of the area in the 1930s, the colonial army became the main route of penetration into Spain. When civil war broke out, the use of cannabis was so entrenched in the army that the dictator Francisco Franco came to part-pay wages in cannabis to the Berber soldiers, organising regular supplies from Morocco to the front lines. After Franco's victory, the use of cannabis spread from the Protectorate to the main Spanish cities on the coasts near Africa. At the beginning, this use was limited to the underground world, but over the four decades of the Protectorate cannabis use became common across mainstream society (Usó 2005: 27).

During the 1960s, cannabis use spread to the counter cultural movement. Smoking reefers became a hallmark of both new groups of youngsters belonging to the "rock culture" (Romaní 1999: 89) and many leftists and democrats (Marín 2008: 149). Thus, cannabis became the prohibited substance most used by young people.

This increase in consumption also caused a price increase, which in turn determined that many cannabis users decided to cultivate the plant. Other reasons to grow were the bad quality of the substance bought on the black market, more access to hashish than to marijuana in the black market, the wish of a part of the users to participate in the whole process from growing to using marijuana, the satisfaction derived from self-sufficiency, and the need to avoid risks like crossing borders with the substance. The first plantations were found underground in Barcelona, near the cemetery, and in small home plantings in pots or private gardens. Gradually, the police would discover cannabis plantations, of varying size and importance, all across Spain (Usó 1996: 207).

In 1985 there were between 1,200,000 and 1,800,000 cannabis users in Spain (Usó 2005: 29). Currently, cannabis remains the most used prohibited substance in Spain. According to the household survey of the Spanish Monitoring Centre on Drugs, 27.3% of the Spanish population reported having ever used cannabis in 2007, 10.1% used it in the previous year, 7.1% used it in the last month and 1.5% used it daily during the latter period (DGPNSD 2008: 14).

According to this survey, cannabis use is more widespread among men (13.6% used it the last year) than women (6.5%), and among young people aged 15-34 (18.8%) than among older people (4.0%). The mean age of initiation to drug use among the respondents has remained relatively stable over the period between 1995-2005 at 18.5 years, while some basic indicators of cannabis use (experimentation, use during the last year and during the last 30 days) doubled during this decade, although with a slight decline over the past two years (DGPNSD 2008: 14, Marín 2008: 48).

Analysis of Spanish cannabis related legislation (criminal and administrative): cultivation, consumption, sharing, selling and therapeutic use of cannabis

Since cannabis and its derivatives are included in the Schedules of Narcotic Drugs under International Control, they are regulated both in Spanish criminal and administrative law. Under Article 368 of the Spanish criminal law, those individuals who cultivate, produce, traffic, or *otherwise* promote, encourage or facilitate the illicit use of toxic drugs, narcotics or psychotropic substances, or possess them for such purposes, shall be sentenced from one to three years imprisonment and a fine up to double of the value of the seized drug, in the case of substances that do not cause serious damage to health. (Spanish legislation differentiates between substances that cause serious damage to health and others.) Cannabis and its derivatives are considered by jurisprudence as substances that do not cause serious damage to health (Arana 2005: 127).

Such penalties may be increased depending on the assumptions set out in articles 369[2] and 370[3] of the Criminal Law. However, use and possession for use purposes do not face criminal penalties but administrative ones. Otherwise, some cases included in Article 368 of the Criminal Law (shared use or collective consumption, delivery to users with no potential spread, donations to addicts by family members or close persons of minimum amounts of drugs free of charge for moral reasons or to facilitate their treatment for drug dependency) are not always punished criminally by the jurisprudence given, amongst other reasons, the huge gap between what Criminal Law prohibits and what is considered socially acceptable (Arana and Germán 2004).

In the administrative field, several laws relating to cannabis and its derivatives, and to people using or researching on these substances, coexist under Spanish law. Law No. 17/1967 on Narcotics had the purpose of updating the Spanish legislation to the demands of the 1961 Single Convention. Article 22 specifies that industrial, therapeutic and scientific uses will be permitted. Therefore, any other use would be prohibited.

The Organic Law 1/1992 of 21 February on the Protection of Citizens' Security has been integral in the prosecution of many users – young people in general, for using or possessing cannabis in public places, even if not intended for trafficking. In the preamble of this law, reference is made to drug trafficking as a criminal

2 Under this rule, the penalties will increase one grade and the fine to up to four times the original amount in a number of cases, including cases where the offender is a public servant, a physician, a social worker, or a teacher, where the substances were provided to minors, where the quantities are considered "large" (Marijuana: 10 kgs.; hashish: 2.5 kgs.; hashish oil: 30 grams), where violence was involved, etc.

3 According to Article 370 of the Criminal Code, the penalty will be higher in one or two degrees than that prescribed in Article 368 in many of the same cases discussed above. In addition, a fine up to three times the value of the drugs seized may be imposed.

phenomenon of concern for citizens' security. However, as shown in Figure 10.1, the vast majority of interventions made by the different police forces have not been directed against drugs trafficking, but against people using cannabis.

This Law, currently in force, considers as a *serious order offence*, punishable by administrative sanctions (Arana and Germán, 2005: 56), the following:

- Drugs use in public places, roads, facilities and transports (Art. 25.1).
- The tolerance of illegal consumption or trafficking of toxic drugs, narcotics or psychotropic substances in public facilities or lack of diligence by the owners, managers or officers in order to prevent them (Art. 23).
- The unlawful possession, even if not intended for trafficking, of toxic drugs, narcotics or psychotropic substances (Art. 25.l)

The penalty for such serious offences against public safety can range between 300.5 and 6,010 Euros. Under Article 28.2, the offences listed in Article 25 may be penalized further with the suspension of driving licenses for up to three months, the withdrawal of weapons permits or licenses and, of course, the seizure of the toxic drugs, narcotics or psychotropic substances. The second paragraph of Article 25 foresees the possibility of suspending sanctions "if the offender is referred to treatment for addiction in a duly authorized service or centre in the manner and time determined by regulation". This issue has been widely criticised because the vast majority of those using illegal substances have no need, from a health standpoint, to undergo treatment or detoxification. At the same time, this referral to treatment in order to suspend the administrative sanction has been used to artificially increase the number of people seeking treatment.

Effects of prohibitionist policy on people using cannabis

The effects of the prohibitionist policy on people using cannabis are numerous. These effects include the added risk to health, the possibility of stigmatization and, above all, the legal uncertainty. The lack of access to cannabis compared to the access other people have to alcohol, tobacco or other legal drugs means having to choose between two options: to grow or to go to the black market for self-provision. A number of people choose the first option, though it is not always easy (space requirements, risk of theft, etc.), nor does it guarantee the supply for the whole year. People who resort to the black market do not have any guarantees on the quality of the substance and the adulteration it has undergone.

In a cultural context where there is an ethnocentric conception of drugs and their uses, the mere fact of using a substance different from the conventional ones (alcohol, coffee, tobacco, legal pharmaceutical drugs), especially if the user belongs to one of the most vulnerable sections of society, has serious risks of being marginalised "without further inquiry, to proceed immediately to their widespread discrimination and persecution. Herein lies the pernicious side of the stereotype" (Castillo 1986: 15) and stigmatization.

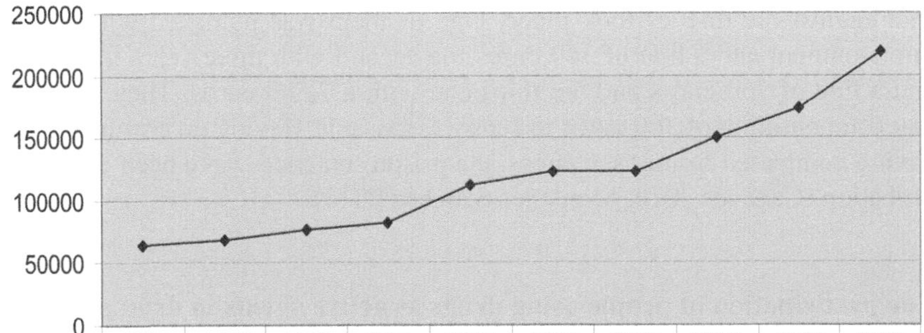

	1997	1998	1999	2000	2001	2002	2003	2004	2005	2006
Serie1	63855	67677	76564	81302	112270	122285	122634	150193	173096	218656

Figure 10.1 Police reports for drug possesion and consumption in public places (1997-2006)

Source: OED 2008: 183

However, what most concerns a large proportion of cannabis users is the legal uncertainty they face. A clear example in the field of administrative penalties for possession and/or consumption, shown in figure 10.1, is the evolution of police reports for drug use and possession in public places from 1997 to 2006. By 2006, the penalties were far beyond three times higher of those imposed in 1997. Although these figures not only collect data relating to cannabis and its derivatives, but all substances included in the international conventions on narcotic drugs and psychotropic substances, most of the cases are related to cannabis derivatives. Of the 218,656 persons reported in 2006, slightly more than 3 out of 4 (77.3%) were reported for having or using cannabis in public places (OED 2008: 182).

For over two decades, one issue of concern for cannabis growers for self-use is the proliferation of thefts carried out in the weeks before the harvest. In many cases, the person going to report the theft ends up being accused of committing a crime against public health (Canavés 2010). Lately, however, there have been cases where, after reporting the robbery to the police, not only has the grower not been accused of a crime against public health, but the thieves have been persecuted by the police and the judiciary (Canavés 2010, Montañés Sánchez 2010).

Thus, in the summer of 2008, Jenny Rodriguez discovered three young men stealing seven marijuana plants grown in the garden of her house. After pushing her out of the way, the youths fled in a car with the stolen plants. She called the local police to report the incident, and since they were near her home, they arrested the men and seized the plants. The police started preliminary inquiries against her for growing marijuana. During the investigation of the case, Jenny stated that she uses marijuana for therapeutic reasons, presenting a medical certificate that records she is a cannabis user. The judge dismissed the case noting no evidence of a crime, since it was a crop for her personal use. On 3 December 2009 the trial against the thieves took place. One of them was punished with two years imprisonment and a fine of 360 euros the second with three years imprisonment and a fine of 360 euros and the third one with a 7,500 euros. They also have to pay compensation of 360 euros to Jenny for assault. Having no criminal record or having completed former sentences, the prison sentences have been commuted to probation (Canavés 2010, Montañés Sánchez 2010).

The participation of people using drugs as active agents in drug policies

Although there were some precedents (Usó 1996: 304, 2009: 52), it is generally considered that the activist movement of people using cannabis in Spain started with the creation of the Association Ramón Santos for Cannabis Studies (ARSEC, in Spanish) in Barcelona in 1991 (Marín 2008: 164).

ARSEC had four key objectives: first, to inform its members on cannabis related issues, from the scientific, medical and legal points of view; second, to study and research on these issues; third, representation and defense of their members given the legislative and jurisprudential gap and ambiguity existing around the use of psychoactive substances whose trade is forbidden by law; and, fourth, monitoring and reporting the activities of any government that could undermine inalienable rights of the person (Usó 1996: 304).

Following the creation of ARSEC, a large number of associations emerged throughout the country. They had similar characteristics and objectives and even, in some cases, similar names: AMEC, SECA, ARSECA, etc. (Barriuso 2003: 103). The figures range from hundred (Barriuso 2005c: 99) to forty associations (Marín 2008: 130). It seems to be impossible to determine the real number, "given the unstable and fleeting nature of many of them" (Barriuso 2005c: 99).

This cannabis mobilization came in parallel with the initiation of an anti-prohibitionist movement, which in 1989 took shape in the Alternative Platform on Drugs, composed of judges, police, politicians, journalists, trade unionists and leaders of related movements. In 1991, the Platform for Legalization presented a manifesto signed by five hundred professionals from the health, education, law, and culture sectors in the Basque Country (Usó 1996: 378). A year later, the Study Group on Criminal Policy, formed by prestigious jurists, published an "Alternative Proposal to the current criminal policy on drugs" (GEPC 1992).

In 1996 a group of these associations formed the State Coalition for the Normalization of Cannabis. The following year, the Coalition launched the campaign "Against the prohibition, I grow"[4], defending the right to self-produce, and proposing collective plantations to support members of ARSEC who were

4 They used the Spanish term "me planto", which means both "I grow" and "I balk".

awaiting sentencing by the Supreme Court for having initiated the first collective plantation in Spain (Barriuso 2005c: 101).

At the same time, the Magazine Cáñamo (Cannabis), dedicated to the culture of cannabis, was launched. This magazine became a turning point in opening the debate on drug prohibition in the media. Created by several members of ARSEC in 1997, Cáñamo has achieved unprecedented levels of circulation and distribution due to the seriousness, independence and rigor of the articles and to the charismatic personality of its director, Gaspar Fraga, who died recently. Later on, other magazines devoted to cannabis culture were born – El Cogollo, Mundo High, Yerba, La María Soft, Spannabis Magazine, Soft Secrets – although Cáñamo remains the magazine of reference for a large number of activists (Barriuso 2005c: 100, 2003: 103; Marin 2008: 160).

Another turning point in the cannabis movement was the creation of Cannabiscafe in 2001.[5] This internet forum serves as a meeting point among the associations working in this area and hosts virtual rooms that they use to meet privately.

Similarly, the emergence of grow shops (stores specializing in cannabis cultivation related products) also gave a boost to cannabis activism. Many of the owners of these first stores were involved in some kind of association (Marín 2008: 384).

In 2002, the State Coalition for the Normalization of Cannabis disappeared and a year later the Federation of Cannabis Associations (FAC) was established, now comprised of 16 associations. The Federation has strengthened its position as the country's landmark organisation concerning cannabis. According to Marín, the creation of the FAC has been "a major step in the development of coalitions and greater action" (Marín 2008: 263). In fact, the FAC plays a key role in defining and developing the cannabis social club model, as well as making it known to the rest of Europe through its involvement with the European Coalition for Just and Effective Drug Policies (ENCOD).

The heterogeneity of cannabis associations, in terms of their composition and approaches, and also their lack of resources and low social impact, has been highlighted (Barriuso 2005c: 99). During 2008 and part of 2009, ENCOD carried out a study on the capacity of drug user organisations to influence policy dialogue. A high percentage of Spanish cannabis organisations participated in this study. The results highlighted their difficulties: little training in political strategy, legal insecurity, social stigma and self-stigma, lack of recognition among authorities, low female presence in the associations and weak implementation of gender mainstreaming (ENCOD 2009).

However, despite this evidence, cannabis associations have achieved a number of successes that have "contributed to a profound social and cultural change around cannabis for psychoactive use" (Barriuso 2005c: 99), contributing to the normalization of cannabis use and serving as a model for organisations in other

5 http://cannabiscafe.net

countries, such as the Belgian club *Trekt Uw Plant,* established in 2006. In 2006, ENCOD took the model of the cannabis clubs as the centerpiece of the campaign *Freedom to Farm.* This international campaign, still running, advocates for the decriminalization of the three prohibited plants: cannabis, opium poppy and coca (ENCOD 2007, Oomen 2007: 72).

Study of the different experiences of collective plantations in Spain and their consequences

The use of cannabis derivatives for self-consumption by users has experienced an interesting development, especially when various uses of this substance have been rooted in a sector of the population. The sources initially employed were going abroad to obtain the substance (mainly Morocco or the Netherlands) or growing cannabis in pots or small plots. Since the 1990s, however, there have been numerous experiments in launching collective cannabis plantations.

The first experience of collective cannabis cultivation began in Catalonia in 1994, following a letter sent by ARSEC to the public prosecutor. They proposed that, since in 1974 the Supreme Court had ruled that the simple drug use is not a crime, growing it for personal use should not be a crime either. The public prosecutor then acknowledged that the cultivation of marijuana in amounts no higher than normal use should not be considered a crime, but he did not dare to state "in the absence of concrete facts" (Barriuso 2003: 104, Usó 2009: 56). However, the police seized the plantation and, although the provincial court acquitted the 4 people responsible for the cultivation, the prosecutor appealed to the Supreme Court. They were condemned in 1997 to four months of jail and a fine of 3,000 euros.

That same year, in the Basque country, the Association *Kalamudia*, drawing on ARSEC's experience, informed the public prosecutor's office and the media that they would establish a collective plantation. It was a success, and a few months later they harvested the crop. Subsequently, *Kalamudia* planted again on two other occasions, in 2000 and 2001, without problems (Usó 2009: 56).

A few years later, a new association was created by former members of *Kalamudia.* Under the name PANNAGH, they continued growing cannabis in a closed circuit only for their members. However, in October 2005, in the context of an investigation into the trafficking of narcotic substances, the municipal police discovered PANNAGH's plantation. A judge ordered the seizure of the plants and the arrest of the landowner and the people present. The gross weight of the plants was 150 kg. After drying and disposal of the non psychoactive parts, the net weight was 17.40 kg. This was the reason why the defense demanded the termination of the proceedings, since it was clear that the plants were destined for self-consumption and not for illegal trade. The judge rejected that request but, after a further appeal by the defense before the provincial court, the court issued an order of dismissal. Following that order, PANNAGH requested the return of the seized plants. The prosecutor opposed but, through a court decision, marijuana was returned to PANNAGH. Members of the association convened a press conference to publicize the return of marijuana seized and to denounce its poor condition (Rodríguez 2007).

Another relevant case, this time with a final verdict by the provincial court of San Sebastian, is the one against the president of GANJAZZ ART CLUB, a club registered in 2002 by former members of *Kalamudia*. As in the case of PANNAGH, the prosecutor presumed there were sufficient grounds to prosecute the president of the Association, Iker Val. However, the court acquitted him claiming they could not conclude that he was involved in the trafficking of illicit drugs. The report by the Health Unit that was the basis for the hypothesis of the indictment was flawed by reports provided by other experts. The court did not assess trafficking because the plantation did not belong to one person but to 25 regular users of the substance, which had agreed to carry out the collective cultivation as was set out in the association' statutes. Moreover, the inspection did not find suitable tools for distribution or any amount of money.

The court took into account the following aspects of the Association and its president:

- GANJAZZ ART CLUB is an officially registered association of cannabis users.
- In its statutes the following are included as objectives of the Association: a) To integrate as members regular users of cannabis that voluntarily request it, b) To report and investigate issues related to cannabis, c) To facilitate means for its members to exercise the rightsgranted to them by law, d) To develop artistic and creative activities, e) To promote social debate related to users' legal and social status, f) Representation and defense given the gaps in legislation and jurisprudence regarding the consumption of substances such as cannabis, g) Monitoring and reporting, when appropriate, the activities of the government that effectively undermine inalienable rights of individuals, h) The promotion of any substance use is not an objective of the association.
- One of the objectives and activities of the program, signed by each partner, is to create a private space or consumption room suitable for members' activities.
- The Association is equipped with internal operating rules. The Board approved an "Agreement of shared and collaborative activity" for 2007 in order to keep out a shared cultivation. The space or land effectively grown would not exceed 1 m^2 and/or a female plant per person.
- The defendant is a regular user of cannabis, has a normalized labor activity and, as chairman of the Association, has participated in numerous activities sponsored by public agencies aimed to give answers to palliative and therapeutic uses of cannabis, prevention, research, education and personal accountability to drug use.

The stay of proceedings in the PANNAGH case and the acquittal in the case of the President of GANJAZZ ART CLUB is a major step forward to the self-supply of cannabis among cannabis users in a closed and non-profit circuit, but they do not set case law, i.e. given a similar situation, another tribunal might issue a different ruling.

Cannabis social clubs: a social response to domestic cultivation of the substance

In 1999, the autonomous government of Andalucía asked the Interuniversity Institute of Criminology of Andalucía for a report analysing the conditions that a premise should conform to dispense cannabis while respecting the Spanish legal framework. The report took two years to be published (Muñoz and Soto 2001), but it had already been released in 1999. That year the Association Ramón Santos for Cannabis Studies of Andalucía (ARSECA) organised a conference in the Faculty of Law, Málaga, on the occasion of their second cannabis contest *"La Bellaflor"*, where one of the authors, Susana Soto, presented the conclusions of the report (Márquez 1999).[6] That report laid the groundwork and established the criteria that have provided the framework for the creation of the cannabis social clubs (Barriuso 2005: 162, 2003: 106).

Cannabis Social Clubs (CSC) are a proposal of self-production and self-distribution of cannabis for the personal use of adults, which are organised in non-profit systems of shared responsibility with the goal of reducing the risks associated with cannabis use and its derivatives, and to prevent possible harms (ENCOD 2007, Ganjazz 2009, FAC 2009).[7]

CSC's are non-profit associations whose members are adult cannabis users, most of whom use it recreationally, although others use cannabis medicinally. People who join the club have to fulfill conditions in order to avoid risks of selling or passing on to third persons or to minors. The CSC members organise a professional, collective cultivation of limited quantities of cannabis to cover the personal needs of their club members and the system is regulated by security and quality checks (Barriuso 2005a: 163, Barriuso 2005b, Barriuso 2007: 72, ENCOD 2009: 223, Oomen 2007: 71).

The first CSC was created in Barcelona, Spain, in 2001 and was followed by others in Catalonia and the Basque Country (Barriuso 2005a: 163). It is very difficult to determine the actual number of clubs and associations with collective plantations currently operating in Spain. In the Federation of Cannabis Associations there are 5 clubs or associations with collective plantation federated, but there are an undetermined number of groups with different legal status operating in

6 Fernanda de la Figuera (personal communication, 15 November, 2009).

7 Iker Val (personal communication,16 November, 2009).

Spain.Numbers range from 22 to 37 depending on the informant.[8] As mentioned above, clubs are also being developed in other European countries like Belgium, Switzerland and the Netherlands (Oomen 2007: 77).

According to their members, this system contributes to the reduction of risks and harms related to cannabis use since "the uncertainty about the quality and possible adulteration of the product purchased on the black market is over. In a production system in closed circuit, the partner/s know the quality of what they consume, to which variety it belongs, how it has been cultivated, and so on. Furthermore, the association can serve as a point of advice and exchange of information, helping to create a new culture of use, which... is essential for true normalization" (Barriuso 2005a: 165). Other advantages mentioned include preventing minors from accessing the substance and avoiding the possibility of the so-called "cannabis tourism" (ENCOD 2009: 223).[9]

In this sense, GANJAZZ ART CLUB, describes its intervention program and activities as a "program for the reduction of risks and harms associated with cannabis" addressed to "users who are unable or unwilling to leave when their consumption becomes problematic, and who don't have access to existing social and health services, since they are mainly oriented to abstinence" (Ganjazz 2009: 2). One of the objectives of the area of services for members is to "reduce the risks and potential harms associated with cannabis use and with the existing misinformation," which includes activities such as an information service, a program of risk reduction in palliative use of cannabis, workshops on responsible use of cannabis and professional legal advice service (Ganjazz 2009: 20).

In November 2009, the first meeting of cannabis clubs was held in Vitoria, Spain. 25 Spanish cannabis organisations met to discuss their legal situation, ethical operating criteria and the proposal to implement a certificate of quality for clubs federated in the FAC (FAC 2009).

Conclusion

Cannabis is the most used illegal substance in Spain, not only by young people but also among adults. As a substance included in the schedules of the international conventions on narcotic drugs and psychotropic substances, in Spain it is regulated both in the field of criminal law and in administrative law.

Cultivation and possession for personal use are not punished. However, under the Organic Law 1/1992 of 21 February on the Protection of Citizens' Security, consumption in public places and possession, even if not intended to traffic, are punished with fines which range from 300.5 to 6,010 Euros. These fines can be waived if the person "is subject" to treatment for addiction, as stated by law. The

8 José Afuera (personal communication, 10 November, 2009); Iker Val (personal communication, 16 November, 2009).

9 Martín Barriuso (personal communication, 20 November, 2009).

vast majority of people fined for possession and/or consumption in public, are related to cannabis (in 2006 more than 3 out of 4 cases).

The current prohibitionist policy has clear negative effects on those using cannabis, because there is an added risk for their own health, stigmatization and, above all, legal uncertainty. Added to these questions there are the thefts that people who grow cannabis for their own use suffer.

Confronting stereotypes of cannabis users as "apathetic", "individualistic" and so on, a sector of them has made an effort to fight hard to assert a different drugs policy, which takes into account the rights and demands of those using drugs.

The so-called cannabis movement, composed of individual users, associations, networks, magazines, books, *grow shops*, etc., has become an important drive to change the stigmatized view of cannabis and those who use it, while proposing alternatives on how to regulate the cannabis market without participating in the black market.

Since the early 1990s, several associations have experimented with self-cultivation for their members. The last two experiences in the Basque Country, with the stay of proceedings in the PANNAGH case and the acquittal in the GANJAZZ ART CLUB case, are important steps towards the self-supply of cannabis among cannabis users in a closed and non-profit circuit, but they do not set any kind of case law so, therefore, with similar facts, another Spanish tribunal may sentence opposite.

Cannabis Social Clubs (CSC) are a model of non-profit self-production and self-distribution of cannabis for personal use of adult people, which are organised in non-profit systems of shared responsibility. This system arises from the associative movement itself, and it can become one of the sources of cannabis supply regulation totally different to the one employed in the illegal market.

List of references

Arana, X. 2005. Cannabis: Normalización y legislación [Cannabis: Normalization and legislation]. *Eguzkilore,* 19, 121-128.

Arana, X. and Germán, I. 2004. *Delimitación del "status" jurídico del ciudadano "consumidor de drogas". Propuesta de Carta de Derechos de los Usuarios de Drogas* [Definition of the legal 'status' of the citizen that uses drugs. Proposal for a Bill of Rights of Drug Users]. Vitoria – Gasteiz: Servicio Central de Publicaciones del Gobierno Vasco.

Arana, X. and Germán, I. 2005. *Documento técnico para un debate social sobre el uso normalizado del cannabis* [Technical paper for a social debate on the normalized use of cannabis]. Vitoria – Gasteiz: Servicio Central de Publicaciones del Gobierno Vasco.

Barriuso, M. 2003. La prohibición de drogas, el tabú moral a la desobediencia civil [The prohibition of drugs, from moral taboo to civil disobedience], in *Globalización y drogas. Políticas sobre drogas, derechos humanos y reducción de riesgos* [Globalization and drugs. Drug policies, human Rights and risk reduction], edited by X. Arana, D. Husak and S. Scheerer. Madrid: Dykinson, 83-117.

Barriuso, M. 2005a. Propuesta de modelo legal para el cannabis en el Estado español [Proposal of a legal model for cannabis in Spain]. *Eguzkilore*, 19, 151-68.

Barriuso, M. 2005b. Adiós al guetto: el discreto encanto de la normalidad [Goodbye to the ghetto: the discreet charm of normality]. *Revista Española de drogodependencias*, 30 (1-2), 206-12.

Barriuso, M. 2005c. Abriendo brechas en el muro: diez años de movimiento cannábico en España [Breaking the wall: ten years of cannabis movement in Spain], in *Cannabis*, edited by Colectivo Interzona. Madrid: Ediciones Amargord, 99-106.

Barriuso, M. 2007. Más allá de las excusas: hacia una regulación legal no prohibicionista para el cannabis [Beyond excuses: towards a legal non prohibitionist regulation of cannabis], in *Hablemos del cannabis. Avances en drogodependencias* [Let's talk about cannabis. Advances in drug addiction], edited by L. Pantoja. Bilbao: Universidad de Deusto, 107-32.

Canavés, M. 2010. Condenados, ladrones de marihuana [Thieves of marihuana Convicted]. *Revista Cáñamo*, 145, 22.

Castillo, J. 1986. La función social del castigo: el caso de la prohibición legal del consumo de "drogas" [The social function of punishment: the case of legal prohibition of "drug" use]. *Revista Española de Investigaciones Sociológicas* [Spanish Journal of Sociological Research], 34, 7-21.

DGPNSD (Delegación del Gobierno para el Plan Nacional sobre Drogas) 2008. *Informe de la encuesta domiciliaria sobre alcohol y drogas en España (EDADES) 2007/08* [Report of the Household Survey on alcohol and drugs in Spain]. Available at: http://www.pnsd.msc.es/Categoria2/observa/pdf/InformeEdades2007-2008.pdf. [accessed: 2 March 2009].

ENCOD 2009. *Use of Drugs and Advocacy*. Vitoria: Servicio Central de Publicaciones del Gobierno Vasco.

ENCOD 2007. *Cannabis Social Clubs. Draft to the Project*. [Online: European Coalition for Just and Effective Drug Policies]. Available at http://www.encod.org/info/test.html [accessed: 9 June 2009].

FAC 2009. *Cómo crear un club social de cannabis* [How to create a cannabis social club]. Madrid: FAC.

Ganjazz 2009. *Programa de intervención y Actividades* [Intervention and Activities Programme]. Donostia: Asociación Ganjazz Art Club. Asociación de Usuarios de Cannabis de Guipúzcoa.

Grupo de Estudio de Política Criminal 1992. *Una alternativa a la actual política criminal sobre drogas* [An alternative to the current criminal drug policy]. Valencia: Tirant lo Blanch.

Marín, I. 2008. *La cultura "cannábica" en España (1991-2007). Análisis socioantropológico de un nuevo tipo de movimiento social* [The cannabis culture in Spain (1991-2007). Socioanthropologic analysis of a new type of social movement], (Phd thesis), Granada: Universidad de Granada. Available at http://hera.ugr.es/tesisugr/17510673.pdf. [accessed: 29 March 2009].

Márquez, H. 1999. La marihuana sale del armario [Marijuana out of the closet]. *El País*, 1 November. Available at : http://www.elpais.com/articulo/andalucia/marihuana/sale/armario/elpepuespand/19991101elpand_21/Tes [accessed: 29 November 2009].

Montañés Sánchez, V. 2010. "Si te consideras un delincuente, no denuncies". Entrevista a Jenny Rodríguez, cultivadora de marihuana ['If you consider yourself a criminal, don't denounce'. Interview with Jenny Rodriguez, marijuana grower]. *Revista Cáñamo*, 147, 60-62.

Muñoz, J. and Soto, S. 2001. El uso terapéutico de cannabis y la creación de establecimientos para su adquisición y consumo [The therapeutic use of cannabis and the creation of facilities for purchase and consumption]. *Revista de Derecho Penal y Criminología*, 7, 49-94.

OED (Observatorio Español sobre Drogas) [Spanish Monitoring centre on Drugs] 2008. *Informe 2007* [Report 2007]. Madrid: Plan Nacional sobre Drogas.

Oomen, J. 2007. Alternativas europeas en políticas de drogas. El papel de los ciudadanos [European alternatives on drug policies. The role of citizens], in *Hablemos del cannabis. Avances en drogodependencias* [Let's talk about cannabis. Advances in drug addiction], edited by L. Pantoja. Bilbao: Universidad de Deusto, 107-132.

Rodríguez, H. 2007. "María" de ida y vuelta [Maria, round trip]. *El Correo Digital* [Online, 26 April]. Available at: http://www.elcorreo.com/vizcaya/-prensa/20070426/gente/maria-vuelta_20070426.html [accessed: 4 June 2010].

Romaní, O. 1999. *Las drogas. Sueños y razones* [The drugs. Dreams and reasons]. Barcelona: Ariel.

Usó, J.C. 1996. *Drogas y cultura de masas (España 1855-1995)* [Drugs and mass culture (Spain 1855-1995)]. Madrid: Taurus.

Usó, J.C. 2005. Historia y evolución del consumo de cannabis en España [History and evolution of cannabis use in Spain], in *Cannabis*, edited by Colectivo Interzona. Madrid: Ediciones Amargord, 23-30.

Usó, J.C. 2009. La represión del cannabis en España. Breve historia de un expolio continuado [The repression of cannabis in Spain. Brief history of a continued plundering]. *Cáñamo*, 144, 50-57.

PART III
Responses to Growing in the Developed World

Chapter 11
Marihuana Behind and Beyond Coffeeshops

Dirk J. Korf

Introduction

Cannabis is an illicit drug in the Netherlands, but marihuana and hashish are openly sold in so-called coffeeshops. In general coffeeshops are café-like places, although some function more as a take-away store where one can buy, but not use cannabis. The import and export of cannabis was introduced into the Opium Act in 1928. Possession, manufacture and sale became criminal offences in 1953. Statutory decriminalization of cannabis took place in 1976. De facto decriminalization, however, set in somewhat earlier, when at a local level authorities in the 1970s began to tolerate so-called "house dealers" in youth centers. Experiments with this approach were formalized in the revised Opium Act of 1976. This law distinguishes between Schedule II substances (mainly cannabis products) and drugs that represent an "unacceptable" risk (such as heroin and, cocaine; Schedule I). Also, the law differentiates on the basis of the nature of the offence. For example, drug use is not an offence, possession of up to 30 grams of cannabis is a misdemeanor, while possession of more than 30 grams is a criminal offence.

Official national Guidelines for Investigation and Prosecution came in force in 1979. According to these guidelines the retail sale of cannabis to consumers is tolerated when the house dealer meets certain criteria, including no hard drugs and no underage clientele. From the late 1970s onwards, hashish and marihuana were sold predominantly in coffeeshops. Although the national government never intended this development, through case law it was decided that coffeeshops were to be tolerated according to the same criteria as house dealers. During the 1980s coffeeshops captured an increasingly larger share of the Dutch retail cannabis market (Jansen 1991).

In the mid 1990s, the focus came to be on curbing the number of coffeeshops. Since then the number of coffeeshops steeply dropped from about 1,500 to 702 in 2007 (Bieleman et al. 2008). Moreover, in 1996 local communities got the opportunity to decide whether or not they would allow coffeeshops. According to the most recent figures, 337 of the 443 municipalities (76%) have decided to not allow coffeeshops at all (Bieleman et al. 2008); consequently, they can close down such locations, even if they do not violate the AHOJ-G criteria.

Coffeeshops sell cannabis to consumers from their "front door", but of course this is only possible when the shops are sufficiently supplied. The supply of coffeeshops is commonly known in the Netherlands as the "back door", even though in reality both suppliers and customers use the same door to enter the coffee shop. The Dutch policy of tolerance does not apply to the back door, but this problem has been ignored for many years. This inconsistency is understandable considering the dilemma that it would not be very difficult for law enforcement to locate and prosecute the suppliers, but by doing so the whole coffeeshop system would be undermined. Nevertheless, in the past years the backdoor issue has gained prominence on the political agenda. This is partially caused by the fact that coffeeshops increasingly sell domestically grown marihuana (instead of imported foreign hashish), and the image has been created of domestic marihuana production being more and more in the hands of criminal organizations.

The main purpose of this chapter is to discuss how and why Dutch law enforcement has strengthened their effort against growing marihuana, and to explore some consequences of and intrinsic conflicts within this new policy. In the next section we describe the role of coffeeshops within the Dutch retail market. We then proceed to consider the national policy towards cannabis cultivation and recent trends in law enforcement, with a discussion of arrests and seizures. Next we explore the dynamics in marihuana supply and discuss some possible effects of criminalization on the marihuana market, particularly price and purity. Finally, we examine some conflicting interests and critically discuss recent developments in Dutch cannabis policy.

Coffeeshops and the cannabis retail market

There are several reasons why not all cannabis users buy their hash or marihuana in coffeeshops. Some are similar to those in countries without coffeeshops, for instance users who grow their own marihuana and those who leave the purchase to others or only smoke for free with others (Reinarman et al. 2004). Other reasons are more specifically associated with coffeeshop policy. Firstly, coffeeshops are not distributed evenly over the Netherlands. About half (51%) of all coffeeshops are located in the five largest communities (> 200,000 citizens), in particular in Amsterdam, while most municipalities with less then 40,000 inhabitants do not have any coffee shop. Secondly, coffeeshops are prohibited from selling cannabis to minors (below 18 years of age).

We investigated these issues in a study on the role of "non-tolerated dealers" – suppliers other than coffeeshops – at cannabis retail market in the Netherlands (Korf et al. 2005, Wouters and Korf 2009). The study was conducted in ten municipalities with more than 40,000 inhabitants, geographically spread throughout the country and different as regards their size and coffeeshop density (number of coffeeshops per 10,000 residents), including two municipalities which did not have any coffee shop at all. Local experts were face-to-face interviewed in all ten communities (4-6 per community; policymakers, police, outreach workers, coffeeshop owners/staff), a survey was made among approximately 800 current cannabis users (recruited in the evening and at night on the street and in entertainment and shopping districts, but not in coffeeshops) and an ethnographic field study was conducted in five communities (mainly observations and informal conversations with users, dealers and other "grass root" experts).

In all ten municipalities there was a non-tolerated cannabis market at the retail level. We distinguished two main categories, i.e. fixed and mobile sale points. The fixed non-tolerated sales points can be divided into home dealers and under-the-counter dealers primarily at clubs or pubs. The mobile non-tolerated sales points can be divided into home delivery after cannabis is ordered by telephone (mobile phone dealers) and street sales in the street and at spots where people hang out (street dealers). In addition, there are home growers, who can be either fixed or mobile dealers. We found that, whether or not municipalities have coffeeshops, the non-tolerated sale of cannabis is widespread. At the retail trade level, the non-tolerated cannabis market was very similar in all the municipalities in the study and it manifests itself in the same sales modes in virtually all the municipalities (Korf et al. 2005).

In the municipalities with coffeeshops, it is estimated that approximately 70% of the local cannabis sales go directly through the coffeeshops. The higher the coffee shop density, the greater was their percentage of the local sales. In municipalities with no coffeeshops or a low coffee shop density, users most frequently buy cannabis somewhere else (as well). The major reasons why non-tolerated cannabis dealers also operate in municipalities with coffeeshops are the geographic distribution of the coffeeshops, and the minimum age they adhere to. It is especially the mobile phone dealers and home dealers who take advantage of the geographic gaps in the cannabis market and are mainly active in districts where coffeeshops are rare or non-existent. For minors, the minimum age at coffeeshops is an important reason to have hashish or marihuana delivered or to buy it on the street or from a home dealer (Wouters and Korf 2009). The latter has been confirmed in school surveys, although they also show that minors often acquire cannabis via older peers and others who have access to coffeeshops (Monshouwer et al. 2008, Nabben et al. 2008).

Marihuana growers and grow shops

At most marihuana cultivation sites in the Netherlands, the plants grow in pots or trays placed under grow lights. Plunger pumps, irrigation systems and other professional or semi-professional equipment are often present as well. Cultivation sites may be found in sheds, warehouses or other commercial buildings, as well as on other types of premises such as private dwellings. Outdoor cultivation also takes place, but on a much lesser scale. Outdoor grows may be camouflaged using other plants like maize, but they may also be planted arbitrarily in the hope they can grow undisturbed until harvest time. Officially, cultivation of five plants or more per person is against the law, but it is often not regarded by police as an actual cultivation site. In such cases, the plants are often seized but no charges are pressed.

Dutch law enforcers frequently employ the terms "small" and "large" cultivation sites. Although the number of plants is commonly the most important criterion for the police to distinguish these, and locations with over 500 plants generally being considered "large" cultivation sites, there is no clear dividing line: technical equipment present at a site is also taken into consideration. The more technically advanced and organized a cultivation site is, the more likely it is to be labeled by law enforcement as professional.

So-called "growshops" occupy an important position within the Dutch marihuana sector. They sell seeds, fertilizers, seedlings and nursery-stock to growers, give advice and sell lamps etc. for large-scale cultivation. Also, there are growshops that take care of the (pre-)financing of growers, buy harvests and sell to intermediates and coffeeshops. The production of seedlings is a fair amount of work, because it requires specific lighting, climate conditions and nutrition, in particular with large numbers of seedlings in "clone rooms". For that reason growers frequently turn to growshops or specialized "seedling farmers" to obtain seedlings.

Law enforcement: clampdown of marihuana cultivation sites

In recent years, Dutch police and justice have increased their actions against the marihuana growers. The control of organized crime in and behind marihuana cultivation was an important argument for intensifying policy. The number of suspects of cannabis possession or trafficking increased between 2002 and 2007 from almost 5,000 to over 7,500, while the number of persons who were also suspected of possessing or trafficking hard drugs doubled, amounting to over 2,500. Taken together this amounted to nearly 11,000 cannabis suspects in 2007. By far the greatest part of these suspects was brought to the Public Prosecutor (close to 10,000 in 2007) and the majority was called to court (almost 6,000 in 2007). (NDM 2010).

A major explanation for the increasing number of arrests in connection with cannabis is the strongly rising number of dismantled marihuana cultivation sites up to approximately 6,000 in 2005 and 2006 (Wouters et al. 2007), even though recently a slight decrease has been reported, with 5,200 dismantled sites in 2007 and 4,700 in 2008 (NDM 2010). We estimated that roughly 2.7 million marihuana plants, clones and seedlings were confiscated during and destroyed after cultivation site dismantling operations in 2005 and about 2.8 million in 2006. Consequently, the average number of plants (including clones and seedlings) was approx. 450 per site. We emphasize that these figure refer to dismantling activities only.

Dynamics in marihuana supply

Formerly a significant importer of hashish, the Netherlands has steadily developed into a major marihuana-producing country (Decorte and Boekhout van Solinge 2006, Jansen 2002). Although this phenomenon of "import substitution" is not typically Dutch, it is very likely that a clampdown in the 1990s on large-scale hashish smuggling (Klerks 2000) has boosted the cultivation of marihuana for the domestic market. Since then, two significant developments have occurred. First, the cannabis market underwent major organizational and structural changes. In the past, a limited number of smuggling rings imported a large share of the hashish, which then found its way from large "offices" via "intermediary offices" to the consumer market (Korf and Verbraeck 1993). This commercial structure has since been overturned, not least as a consequence of infighting, including liquidations, amongst the big players on the hashish market (Leistra 2004). Partly in conjunction with the growing expertise in the cultivation of marihuana, whose quality became increasingly competitive with that of hashish, new players entered the Dutch cannabis market. That resulted in radical changes in cannabis distribution patterns, in terms of both the people involved and the organizational structures. Second, the focus of law enforcement shifted from large-scale cross-border hashish smuggling, which was mainly the remit of customs officials, to the control of clandestine marihuana cultivation on Dutch territory, in which the regional police forces play a crucial role.

In a national survey among approx. 150 cannabis market experts (mostly police or from the coffeeshop sector) conducted in 2007, we inquired whether in the past years they had noticed changes in three areas: the types of cultivation sites, the types of people owning and running them, and the market (Wouters et al. 2007). Respondents were most likely to report shifts in the *types of cultivation sites,* and almost a quarter believed these were major changes. The most characteristic change seemed to involve relocation to different types of premises (fewer sites in private dwellings) or areas (more sites outside urban areas), as well as scale enlargement and technological advances. Half of the respondents believed that changes were occurring in the *marihuana market,* and many of them classified these as major changes. The fewest changes were reported in the *types of growers;* less than 10% believed there were major changes, and the reported changes mostly suggested greater variation. This, in combination with the types of cultivation sites being encountered, led some respondents to speak of a more sinister atmosphere and an increasing involvement by organized crime in marihuana cultivation. Others contradicted this, though, and it may be too hasty to assume criminal involvement simply on the basis of the technical equipment found at cultivation sites. All things considered, we concluded that the dismantling of marihuana cultivation sites, in combination with accompanying measures such as evictions (see section 7), may have triggered some changes such as the relocation of cultivation sites, but that relatively autonomous processes were also at work. Significant among these were technological innovations, most of which were neither specific to marihuana cultivation nor specific to the Netherlands (Wouters et al. 2007).

More recently law enforcement shows a tendency to increasingly emphasize the involvement of criminal organizations in the Dutch marihuana market (*Adviescommissie Drugsbeleid* 2009, Van Laar and Van Ooijen-Houben 2009, Emmett and Boers 2008). This tendency is also clearly reflected in the media.

Spring 2010, for example, newspapers and television reported on the dismantling on several occasions of a sea container hidden under the ground with thousands of marihuana plants, allegedly to reduce the risk of discovery by law enforcement. At the same time media reported on the dismantlement of small cultivation sites, for example a report on 6 March 2010 in the daily newspaper 'Het Parool' about rounding up three sites in Amsterdam: one "large growery" with 160 plants, 12 plants in a bedroom and 24 plants in a student residence (X 2010).

Price and quality

Although not all observers our study mentioned in the previous section reported changes in the marihuana market, many of those who did so spoke of very significant shifts, pointing mainly to the soaring price of "nederwiet" (Dutch weed), particularly in 2006. Data we obtained at the kilogram level from coffee shop owners in the three largest Dutch cities (Amsterdam, Rotterdam and The Hague) indeed confirmed this price rise: from a median price of most often sold "nederwiet" of € 2,600 – € 2,800 in 2004, to € 2,800 – € 3,300 in 2005, and € 3,200 – € 3,600 in 2006. Yet this could not automatically be attributed to the dismantling operations, or at least not entirely. The summer of 2006 was a hot one, and, due to insufficient or failing air conditioning and/or watering systems in indoor cultivation sites, the number of crop failures was relatively high. We detected a mild sense of panic in the marihuana market, and the very rumors of supply shortages may have driven prices even higher. Our impression that the prices had again begun to decline in Spring 2007 led us to doubt whether there was a continuing upward trend (Wouters et al. 2007). From then on, even though coffeeshop owners and marihuana growers in informal conversations confirm price fluctuations as a consequence of seasonal influences (with fluctuations in supply as well as in demand), they consistently report higher prices per kilo than before. Between spring 2009 and spring 2010 the cost price per kilo for the most frequently sold kinds of "nederwiet" was € 3,500 – € 4,000.

This development of cost price per kilo runs quite parallel to the price development in selling price per gram in coffeeshops. Price and THC content of cannabis as sold in coffeeshops in the Netherlands have been systematically monitored by the Trimbos Institute since 1999. THC-concentrations in the most often sold kind of "nederwiet" more than doubled between 1999/2000 and 2003/2004, from an average of 8.6% to 20.4%. In subsequent years, the average concentration stepwise dropped to 15.1% in 2008/2009. Imported hashish showed an increase in THC-concentration from 11%-12% in the first two years to 17%-18% in 2002, and then remained rather stable. Until 2006/2007 THC-concentrations in imported marihuana remained quite stable at around 6%, but increased to 8.4% in 2007/2008 and 9.9% in 2008/2009. Price of "nederwiet" in coffeeshops remained relatively stable between 1999/2000 and 2005/2006, with an annual average of € 6.00 – € 6.40 per gram, and then increased, amounting to € 8.10 in 2008/2009. The retail price of imported hashish fluctuated between 1999/2000 and 2004/2005, but from then on show an upwards trend, up to a maximum of € 8.70 euro in 2008/2009 (Pijlman et al. 2005, Niesink et al. 2005, Niesink et al. 2009).

These show remarkable parallels between imported hash and domestically cultivated marihuana, in THC-concentrations as well as in price. The higher price of "nederwiet" could be a consequence of shortage, but why then did hashish also become more expensive? Apparently, this is not to be attributed to an increased demand for hash, for the preference for hashish or marihuana did not change according to surveys among coffeeshop visitors conducted in Amsterdam in 2001 and 2009 (Benschop et al. 2010). What previous research did show was that a substantial part of the cannabis consuming population was malcontented with the then, in their perception, too high THC-concentrations in "nederwiet" (Korf et al. 2007). Coffeeshops also received complaints from customers. Therefore it is plausible that the decline in THC-concentrations has been a response to consumers' preferences for milder marihuana.

Dynamics in cannabis policy

In recent years, the Dutch government has significantly toughened its policies to control marihuana cultivation (*Adviescommissie Drugsbeleid* 2009, *Cannabisbrief* 2004, Emmett and Boers 2008, *Notitie Integrale Aanpak Hennepteelt* 2006). A nationwide trend emerged of increasingly frequent and vigorous police cooperation with other institutions and with commercial firms. Increasing numbers of organizations were involved in dismantling operations, and cooperation between them was intensified. The dismantlement policy was being formalized under the label "integrative approach". More and more regions have put their cooperative arrangements onto paper, and drawn up contracts to enable exchanges of information and to define responsibilities.

With the exception of acutely dangerous situations that require immediate action, the phenomenon of "harvest days" has spread over many parts of the country. Many police regions mount planned, all-day actions to bust several cultivation sites in sequence. Most regions employ combinations of harvest days and ad hoc raids. Dismantlement has become a structured, streamlined and even routinely conducted campaign; financial interests play an increasingly prominent role. Energy companies, sometimes in conjunction with private dismantling contractors, are the most important partners in the actual dismantling operations. They have a dual function. Because electricity for many marihuana cultivation sites is illegally tapped, it is safer to have professional electricians shut off the power. But the energy companies also have much to gain from closing down as many sites as possible, as the police report enables them to claim large sums in back payments for the stolen electricity. Dismantling firms are popular because they save the police a great deal of money and dirty work. Housing associations are also involved in the dismantling activities, though they are not usually present when a site is raided.

Another development is the confiscation of criminal proceeds under the so-called *Pluk-Ze* legislation. Reportedly, the policy on dismantling marihuana cultivation sites generates a sizeable proportion of the revenues obtained by government under this legislation (which also applies to hard drugs trade and other criminal activities). Grow shops also are increasingly targeted by law enforcement authorities in their campaign against marihuana cultivation and the organizers behind it.

In the implementation of the Dutch national government to control marihuana cultivation, several processes of change may be identified which relate to the actual practice of site dismantling and to the broader public safety policies pursued. They are: commercialization; confiscation of criminal proceeds; the use of anonymous tip-offs; and bureaucratization.

Commercialization

Garland (2001) identifies a new style of management and practice in institutions involved with criminal justice, with a focus on cost-effective management of risks and resources. Under this method, the most costly law enforcement measures are to be reserved for serious types of crime or for criminality thought to be linked to it. Evidently, marihuana cultivation is viewed as one of those serious types of crime. As the Dutch law enforcement authorities increasingly work with performance indicators, and that is now the case with respect to confiscations of criminal proceeds and the imposition of fines. In such circumstances, it is relatively easy to "score points" by raiding marihuana sites.

Dutch police forces engage commercial firms in the dismantling operations. Dismantling firms might be tempted to take over investigative tasks from the police and set out in search of cultivation sites themselves. What is certain, in any case, is that Dutch police work closely with energy companies. In view of the illegally tapped electricity, these have a significant interest in closing down as many sites as possible. After sites have been raided, the companies can use the police reports to claim large sums in back payments from growers that have stolen electricity. What safeguards are in place to keep dismantling firms and energy companies from working together to maximize profits?

Confiscation of criminal proceeds

Since 1993, Dutch courts have been authorized to seize revenues from criminal activities. This also applies to the proceeds of marihuana cultivation. On the basis of the numbers of plants seized and the presumed number of past harvests from a particular site, authorities estimate how much gross revenue the site will have generated. If a grower provides proof of costs incurred for the site, such as potting soil, equipment, wages and energy costs (if paid), these are deducted from the estimate. Wrongfully claimed social benefits as well as dismantling costs, illegally tapped electricity and any other accrued debts (such as the repair of damages to rental properties) must be reimbursed. As each court district has a minimum yearly amount prescribed for confiscations of criminal proceeds, the raids on marihuana sites play an important part in achieving this target.

Anonymous tip-offs

For several years now, Dutch police have been able to act on anonymous tips from the public about criminal or suspicious activities. People can call a toll free telephone number known as *Meld Misdaad Anoniem* ("report crime anonymously", in short: M.). Members of the public are encouraged to phone this number to report activities such as marihuana cultivation in their neighborhood. All tips to this nationwide hotline are first screened on criteria such as whether they contain sufficient information and refer to an existing address. If so, they are transmitted as "usable tips" to the police region that has jurisdiction. In 2005, more than 10,000 M.-tips were received, nearly half of which were drugs-related. By 2009, the number had exceeded 14,000, over half about drugs, predominantly cannabis. As a result, over 240,000 marihuana plants were seized (an average of 4,700 per week).

We can infer from these figures that this police hotline has been very successful in mobilizing the public in its operations against cannabis cultivation. What types of people report suspected marihuana cultivation sites? Since the hotline has a strict policy of not keeping information about callers, it is not feasible to give a profile of the anonymous informers. This leaves us with the question what interests are involved in the tipping. Are the informers simply law-abiding citizens performing their civic duty, or might marihuana growers themselves be using the hotline to obstruct or eliminate their competitors? If so, could these be systematic campaigns by rival criminal organizations? When police follow up such tips, are they inadvertently assisting in the feuds of organized criminals, thereby becoming "partners in crime"?

Street-level bureaucracy

In the policy of dismantling marihuana growing sites, the typical scenario of *street-level bureaucracy* looms large. As Lipsky (1980) observed, centrally formulated policy has to be put into practice at lower levels. Staff on the ground have their own discretionary powers and make their own interpretations of their tasks. The original aim of cracking down on organized crime does not necessarily remain paramount. Moreover, as indicated above, Dutch police forces are increasingly bound by national government to "performance contracts" that specify quantifiable targets for police work; non-achievement of those targets affects police funding. In terms of the dismantling of marihuana cultivation sites, the practice that has emerged might be characterized as predominantly hit-and-run: busting a maximum number of sites with maximum efficiency, that became an easier task with the success of the anonymous tip-offs, irrespective of the potential impact on organized crime.

Four comments need to be added to this observation. First, hit-and-run operations are in some cases consistent with official national-level policy, as when acute situations like fire hazards or flooding come to light. Second, contrary to what might be implied by "hit-and-run", many operations, as already observed, are based on a systematic strategy, evidenced by practices such as staging "harvest days" and hiring dismantling firms. Third, by extension, hit-and-run operations can indeed be effective in fighting organized crime if carried out on a large scale (Van de Bunt and Kleemans 2007). Fourth, the number of cases accompanied by thorough investigation of the organizations behind marihuana cultivation tends to get obscured by the sheer number of dismantling operations. Although most operations are indeed characterized by the hit-and-run approach of swift action, other cases are the objects of longer police investigation. A study by Spapens et al. (2007) has shown convincingly that criminal investigations like these – in particular when targeting organizations involved in export to other countries – yield a wealth of information about the ways marihuana cultivation is organized, and may even enable police to successfully track down and prosecute the organizers behind this type of drug trade. At the same time, such investigations are extremely time-consuming and therefore costly, and budgeting that time and expenditure in advance is far more difficult than is the case for harvest days. Long-term investigations are therefore less compatible with the culture of police performance contracts.

Although thousands of marihuana cultivation sites continue to be dismantled every year in the Netherlands, the tide seems to have turned in the past few years. However, a significant increase can be observed in the number of investigations into cannabis related organized crime (whether in combination with hard drugs or not), from an average of 50 per year in 2000 – 2005, to over 150 per year in 2006 – 2008 (NDM 2010). This indicates a shift of prioritization in the direction of more complex and costly law enforcement operations.

Changing Dutch drug policy: some theoretical reflections

Property offences (e.g. burglary, theft and pick pocketing) are clear examples of "deliver work": victims usually report the crimes themselves. With "get work" the police searche for criminal offences and so to a large degree the police can determine how strong it focuses on such crimes. Drug offences are classical examples of get work, but can tilt in the direction of deliver work with the help of citizens. In recent years this has been especially true for the policy towards cannabis cultivation. Civilians are called on to anonymously report to the police whenever they suspect marihuana production in their neighborhood and this, as was established before, is fruitful.

What has caused law enforcement to strengthen their effort against growing marihuana? While a definite answer cannot be given here, we nonetheless offer a few possible explanations. As was mentioned, a shift occurred when The

Netherlands became more of a producing country (of marijuana) instead of an importer (of hashish). Concerns about criminal organizations being involved with marihuana cultivation were growing (Bovenkerk and Hogewind 2002, Fijnaut and De Ruyver 2008, Spapens et al. 2007). As Dutch-grown weed became stronger, worries about harmful effects of cannabis on public health, especially with regard to young people, increased. In previous years, intensified collaboration between care and repression (the "integral approach") had resulted in a near disappearance of "open drug scenes" of street dealers and hard drug users (Van Laar and Van Ooyen-Houben 2009). Now that the fight against such scenes has largely been accomplished, it very much appears so as if the police seek employment in the fight against marihuana cultivation.

With its fight against marihuana cultivation, Dutch law enforcement intents to make a sign against the normalization of cannabis use (Emmett and Boers 2008). In the drug debate the concept of "normalization" is used in two different ways. On the one hand, the normative definition refers to policy goals. In the 1980s the Dutch government aimed at integration of drug users in society (Van Vliet 1990). On the other hand, in the academic discourse normalization signifies the sociological understanding of developments in (the meaning of) drug use, with drug use being viewed as one of many ways to express personal identity, along with, for example, music, dressing style and gadgets (Parker et al. 1998, Duff 2003). Normalization as a social process appears to occur largely spontaneously and relatively independent of national drug policy. For instance, prevalence of cannabis use in the Netherlands is rather similar to Germany or France (Van Laar and Van Ooyen-Houben 2009), and differences in cannabis use patterns in Amsterdam and San Francisco are almost non-existent (Reinarman et al. 2004).

Does drug policy not make a difference at all? Yes, it does. We have mentioned the strong decline of nuisance caused by addicts and street dealers. However, drug policy appears to have little impact on price and quality of drugs. Despite, or maybe because of the dismantlement of numerous ecstasy labs, the price of ecstasy per pill has dropped immensely: from around € 15 twenty years ago, to around € 5 today. Leaving temporary fluctuations aside, the quality of ecstasy remained quite stable. Concurrently, the price of cocaine dropped from approximately € 100 to € 50 per gram, without a significant decline in quality, even though many thousands of cocaine smugglers were arrested and often also detained in the past decade (Korf 2010). Against this background, the price increase of domestically cultivated marihuana appears as even more striking.

Epilogue

The Netherlands is the only country in Europe that officially allows the sale of cannabis to consumers, via coffeeshops. To supply the product to customers calling at the "front door", the coffeeshops have to stock themselves illegally via the "back door". Although the increasing domestic cultivation of marihuana is not an exclusively Dutch phenomenon, the "back door" policy and the coffeeshops are. In the past decade, cannabis has increasingly been defined as a problem in the Netherlands, not only with regard to the involvement of organized crime in the cultivation of marihuana, but also older issues like cannabis addiction and cannabis psychosis (schizophrenia) are resurfacing in social and political discourse. Such concerns have translated into more repressive strategies against marihuana cultivation. In practice, the Dutch strategy has predominantly resulted in dismantling large numbers of cannabis cultivation sites; to a lesser extent, but increasingly, there are longer-term police investigations into criminal networks and organizers of large-scale marihuana cultivation. The structural and organizational characteristics of the Dutch cannabis market are in a state of flux, due to relatively autonomous processes fuelled by technological innovations, but also in reaction to the policies being pursued by the authorities. The price of marihuana has increased significantly and there are persistent signals, coming also from law enforcement (Emmett and Boers 2008) – as an interpretation of the advanced technological level of growing equipments and presence of "booby traps" at cultivation sites observed by the police, but also based on a study that found an increasing number of killings of marihuana growers and organizers (Spapens et al. 2007) – that more and more criminal organizations are involved in cannabis farming. In addition to hardening of the domestic marihuana sector, displacement to other countries has been reported (Van de Donk et al. 2009).

The involvement of organized crime dominates the political discourse on marihuana cultivation. It has become *bon ton* to state that ideologically motivated growers from the past have disappeared completely. In Spring 2010, Mr. Max Daniel, head of the national Cannabis Task Force, stated in a national television program that small scale cultivation, as it exists in countries like Belgium (see Decorte, this volume) has vanished altogether. Unfortunately, small scale marihuana growers have never been the subject of serious scientific studies in the Netherlands. However, they do exist, as is illustrated by a survey we conducted in 2009 among 266 coffeeshop visitors in Amsterdam – by far the city with the most coffeeshops – and of whom 9% reported to grow marihuana, but only on a small scale that was not enough for self-supply the whole year (Benschop et al. 2010).

Coffeeshops have brought on the Netherlands a unique problem. While selling cannabis at the front door is tolerated, supply (at the back door) remains prohibited. More than likely, the concentration of the vast majority of the cannabis market at around 700 locations affects the organization and structure of the cannabis market in higher echelons. A monopolistic market has not occurred, yet it seems very likely that such a concentrated retail market increases the risk of criminal involvement.

Two options for regulating the supply of coffeeshops keep being debated in the Netherlands: persistent repression of the illegal cultivation of cannabis versus a plea for a next step towards decriminalization by regulating the backdoor problem, allowing the cultivation of marihuana under strict conditions for coffeeshops only. Only the future can tell which direction the Netherlands will choose.

List of references

Adviescommissie Drugsbeleid 2009. *Geen deuren maar daden. Nieuwe accenten in het Nederlands drugsbeleid* [No doors but acts. New emphasis in Dutch drug policy]. Den Haag: Ministeries van VWS, Justitie and BZK.

Benschop, A., Nabben, T. and Korf, D.J. 2010. *Antenne 2009. Trends in alcohol, tabak en drugs bij jonge Amsterdammers* [Antenna 2009. Trends in alcohol, tobacco and drugs among Amsterdam youth]. Amsterdam: Rozenberg Publishers.

Bieleman, B., Beelen, A., Nijkamp, R. and de Bie, E. 2008. *Coffeeshops in Nederland 2007* [Coffeeshops in the Netherlands 2007]. Groningen: Intraval.

Bovenkerk, F. and Hogewind, W.I.M. 2002. *Hennepteelt in Nederland: het probleem van de criminaliteit en haar bestrijding* [Cannabis cultivation in the Netherlands: the problem of crime and the fight against it]. Zeist: Kerkebosch.

Cannabisbrief 2004. *Drugbeleid. Brief ministers over het cannabisbeleid* [Drug policy. Letter from the Ministers on cannabis policy]. TK, vergaderjaar 2003-2004, 24 077, no. 125. The Hague: Sdu.

Decorte, T. and Boekhout van Solinge, T. 2006. Het aanbod van cannabis in Nederland en België [The supply of cannabis in the Netherlands and Belgium]. *Tijdschrift voor Criminologie*, 48(2), 144-54.

Duff, C. 2003. Drugs and youth culture: is Australia experiencing the "normalization" of adolescent drug use? *Journal of Youth Studies*, 6(4), 433-446.

Emmett, I. and Boers, R. 2008. *Het groene goud* [The green gold]. Zoetermeer: KLPD.

Fijnaut, C. and De Ruyver, B. 2008. *Voor een gezamenlijke beheersing van de drugsgerelateerde criminaliteit in de Euregio Maas-Rijn* [Towards a joint management of drug-related crime in the Euregion Maas-Rhine]. Tilburg/Gent: Euregio Maas-Rijn.

Garland, D. 2001. *The culture of control. Crime and social order in contemporary society.* Chicago: University of Chicago Press.

Jansen, A.C.M. 1991. *Cannabis in Amsterdam. A geography of hashish and marihuana.* Muiderberg: Coutinho.

Jansen, A.C.M. 2002. De economie van de cannabissector in beleidsperspectief [The economy of the cannabis sector from a policy perspective]. *Economisch Statistische Berichten*, 87 (4354), 276-78.

Klerks, P.P.M.H. 2000. *Groot in hasj. Theorie en praktijk van de georganiseerde criminaliteit* [Big in hashish. Theory and practice of organized crime]. Alphen aan den Rijn/Antwerpen: Samson/Kluwer Rechtswetenschappen.

Korf, D.J. 2010. *Coke bij de vis. Misdaad en moraal.* [Cocaine in fisherman's villages. Crime and morality]. Amsterdam: Vossiuspers.

Korf, D.J. and Verbraeck, H. 1993. *Dealers en dienders* [Dealers and cops]. Amsterdam: Bonger Institute, University of Amsterdam.

Korf, D.J., Wouters, M., Nabben, T. and van Ginkel, P. 2005. *Cannabis zonder coffeeshop* [Cannabis without coffeeshops]. Amsterdam: Rozenberg Publishers.

Korf, D.J., Benschop, A. and Wouters, M. 2007. Differential responses to cannabis potency: A typology of users based on self-reported consumption behaviour. *The International Journal of Drug Policy*, 18, 168-76.

Leistra, G. 2004. *De vermoorde onschuld. Misdaad in Nederland* [Innocence assassinated. Crime in the Netherlands]. Amsterdam: Balans.

Lipsky, M. 1980. *Street-level bureaucracy. Dilemmas of the individual in public services.* New York: Russell Sage Foundation.

Monshouwer, K., Verdurmen, J., van Dorsselaer, S., Smit, E., Gorter, A. and Vollebergh, W. 2008. *Jeugd en riskant gedrag* 2007 [Youth and risk behaviors 2007]. Utrecht: Trimbos Institute.

Nabben, T., Benschop, A. and Korf, D.J. 2008. *Antenne 2007; Trends in alcohol, tabak en drugs bij jonge Amsterdammers* [Antenna 2007. Trends in alcohol, tobacco and drugs among Amsterdam youth]. Amsterdam: Rozenberg Publishers.

Notitie Integrale Aanpak Hennepteelt 2006. *Drugbeleid.* Brief van de minister van BZK aan de voorzitter van de TK inzake Notitie Integrale aanpak hennepteelt [Drug policy. Letter from the Home Office Minister to the Chair of the Parliament regarding the White Paper on Integrated Approach Cannabis Cultivation]. TK, vergaderjaar 2005-2006, 24 077, no. 184.

NDM 2010. *Nationale Drug Monitor. Jaarbericht 2010* [National Drug Monitor. Annual report 2010]. Utrecht: Trimbos Institute.

Niesink, R.J.M., Rigter, S. and Hoek, J. 2005. *THC-concentraties in wiet, nederwiet en hasj in Nederlandse coffeeshops (2004-2005)* [THC-concentrations in weed, Dutch weed and hashish in Dutch coffeeshops (2004-2005)]. Utrecht: Trimbos Institute.

Niesink, R.J.M., Rigter, S., Hoek, J. and de Boer, N. 2009. *THC-concentraties in wiet, nederwiet en hasj in Nederlandse coffeeshops (2008-2009)* [THC-concentrations in weed, Dutch weed and hashish in Dutch coffeeshops (2008-2009)]. Utrecht: Trimbos Institute.

Parker, H., Aldridge, J. and Measham, F. 1998. *Illegal leisure. The normalization of adolescent recreational drug use.* London: Routledge.

Pijlman, F.T.A., Rigter, S.M., Hoek, J., Goldschmidt, H.M.J. and Niesink, R.J.M. 2005. Strong increased in total delta-THC in cannabis preparations sold in Dutch coffeeshops. *Addiction Biology*, 10(2), 171-80.

Reinarman, C., Cohen, P.D.A. and Kaal, H. 2004. The limited relevance of drug policy: Cannabis in Amsterdam and San Francisco. *American Journal of Public Health*, 94, 836-42.

Spapens, A.C.M., van de Bunt, H.G. and Rastovac, L. 2007. *De wereld achter de wietteelt* [The world behind the cultivation of cannabis]. Den Haag: WODC.

Van de Bunt, H.G. and Kleemans, E.R. 2007. *Georganiseerde criminaliteit in Nederland. Derde rapportage op basis van de Monitor Georganiseerde*

Criminaliteit [Organized crime in the Netherlands. Third report based on the Monitor Organized Crime]. Den Haag: WODC.

Van Laar, M. and van Ooyen-Houben, M. (eds.) 2009. *Evaluatie van het Nederlandse drugsbeleid* [Evaluation of the Dutch drug policy]. Utrecht/Den Haag: Trimbos Institute/WODC.

Van Vliet, H.J. 1990. The uneasy decriminalization: a perspective on Dutch drug policy. *Hofstra Law Review*, 18(3), 717-50.

Wouters, M., Korf, D.J. and Kroeske, B. 2007. *Harde aanpak, hete zomer. Een onderzoek naar de ontmanteling van hennepkwekerijen in Nederland* [Tough policy, hot summer. A study of the dismantling of cannabis cultivation sites in the Netherlands]. Amsterdam: Rozenberg Publishers.

Wouters, M. and Korf, D.J. 2009. Access to licensed cannabis supply and the separation of markets policy in the Netherlands. *Journal of Drug Issues*, 39(3), 627-52.

X 2010. Drie hennepkwekerijen ontdekt en opgerold [Three marijuana cultivation sites discovered and dismantled], *Het Parool*, 6 March, 25.

Chapter 12
Reforming Laws Applying to Domestic Cannabis Production as a Harm Reduction Strategy – a Case Study

Simon Lenton

Introduction

In March 2004 Western Australia became the fourth Australian jurisdiction to implement a *prohibition with civil penalties scheme* for minor cannabis offences when the Cannabis Infringement Notice (CIN) scheme came into effect. Under such schemes, sometimes called "decriminalization", the possession and cultivation of cannabis remains illegal. However, under specified amounts and conditions those apprehended could be eligible for a *civil penalty* such as a fine or infringement notice, rather than a criminal penalty resulting in a criminal record (Room et al. 2010). The record of a criminal conviction can lead to a range of long lasting adverse social impacts including employment and housing problems, further attention from police and so on (Erickson 1980, Lenton, Bennett and Heale 1999, Lenton, Christie et al. 1999). The *civil penalty* schemes can be distinguished from *prohibition with cautioning* schemes that operate for cannabis in the other four non-civil penalty states in Australia. Importantly, in the context of this chapter, these cautioning schemes apply to cannabis possession and smoking implements (for the first, second or third offence), but not to cultivation of cannabis (Room et al. 2010).

This chapter focuses on the implementation' debate and outcome of the CIN scheme as they specifically relate to cannabis cultivation. The background and implementation of the CIN scheme (Lenton 2004, Lenton and Allsop 2010) more generally have been described elsewhere and are not addressed here. Under the CIN scheme possession of not more than 2 non-hydroponic cannabis plants by an adult attracted a penalty of $A200. No more than 2 plants per household could be eligible for an infringement notice. Hydroponic cultivation of cannabis plants was ineligible for an infringement notice but subject to criminal conviction.

The intent of the scheme re cultivation

The main features of the WA CIN scheme enacted in the Cannabis Control Act of 2004 were designed by an eight member Ministerial Working Party on Drug Law

Reform which was established in January 2001 by the Minister of Health who had responsibility for tabling the legislation in Parliament. The author (Lenton) as a drug researcher with experience in research on cannabis, health and the law was one of the working party's members (Lenton 2004, Lenton and Allsop 2010). The issue of including plants in the scheme and the provisions related to these occupied a significant amount of the group's time and energy. The inclusion of plants had been previously endorsed by the Labor Government established Community Drug Summit held in September 2001, and given a mandate by the evidence-based drugs policy platform which the Labor Party brought to the March 2001 election which they won. This stated "We propose a decriminalized regime which would apply to possession of 50 grams of cannabis or less and cultivation of no more than two plants per household" (Australian Labor Party WA Branch 2001). Other major influences on the deliberations regarding plants were what the scheme's overall objectives which, while recognizing that that cannabis like other drugs can cause harm, were to: (i) Not encourage cannabis use, nor patterns of use which may increase harm; (ii) Reduce the adverse social costs of being apprehended for a minor cannabis offence; (iii) Move cannabis supply away from large-scale, criminal, commercial suppliers; and (iv) Free up the police and the courts to deal with more serious crimes (Prior et al. 2002).

Making the cultivation of plants eligible for an infringement notice was a key strategy in attempting to shift the supply side of the cannabis market by moving cannabis supply away from more harmful large-scale, criminal suppliers to less risky small scale and self suppliers. There had been some evidence of the involvement of criminal elements in large-scale cannabis supply in Australia (Sutton and McMillan 2000). Criminal elements had been implicated in the overlap of the Australian cannabis market with that for more harmful drugs and in risks to public safety as a result of use of "booby traps" and other measures to protect crops and avoid detection (Australian Bureau of Criminal Intelligence 1999). Yet the evidence was that self supply was a very small part of the market. For example, a study of WA cannabis users apprehended and convicted for the first time found only 17% reported cultivating their own as their main source of supply and while larger proportions dabbled in cannabis growing most cannabis was supplied from the illicit market (Lenton, Bennett and Heale 1999). Sutton had previously argued that if police and other authorities did not see every incident of "cultivation of cannabis for non-personal use as an activity which must be suppressed", but rather "an opportunity to undermine criminal networks capacity to dominate cannabis markets", then greater separation of cannabis from other drug markets could theoretically be achieved (Sutton 2000: 158).

Consistent with this argument, in relation to the goal of shifting the market the working party's report stated:

> It is clearly desirable that any option seeks, as far as is possible, to separate the supply of cannabis from the supply of other more harmful illicit drugs. The majority of cannabis users do not grow their own cannabis.

> Consequently any legislative system which does not criminalize personal use of cannabis needs to recognize that demand cannot be met entirely by users growing their own cannabis. Accordingly the preferred model recognizes the need for flexibility to be followed in the enforcement of the law regarding activities in relation to those who obtain small quantities of cannabis for personal use.[Source: Prior et al. 2002: 3]

Yet, by the time the Bill was introduced into Parliament the articulation of this goal of the scheme was made less contentious by focusing on where law enforcement should shift its attention to, rather than on "shifting markets" as seen in the Minister's speech introducing the legislation:

> Law enforcement and the criminal justice system should target and heavily penalize those connected or involved in the business of large-scale cannabis supply, those who also supply other prohibited drugs, and those engaging in violence or stand over tactics. [Source: Parliament of Western Australia 2003b]

However, while shifting police activity was a goal of the scheme, it was acknowledged as something which was difficult to monitor and police data systems did not provide detail on the extent to which police had disrupted the activities or organized criminal groups operating in the cannabis market (Drug and Alcohol Office 2007b). As a result, the review of the first 3 years of the scheme concluded that it was not possible to determine the extent to which the WA Police had redirected their activities towards those involved in serious types of cannabis offences (Drug and Alcohol Office 2007b).

Two other features of the CIN scheme related to cannabis cultivation and provided a response against criticisms that the WA Government was going "soft on cannabis" (Editorial – The West Australian 2006, Harvey 2003, Vermeer and Spagnolo 2005). Firstly, the laws applying to cultivation of cannabis for selling and supplying were made tougher. When the CIN Scheme was introduced, the number of plants deeming an individual to be a cannabis supplier was reduced from 25 to 10. Thus under the cannabis law changes for up to 2 non-hydroponic plants (per household) adults could receive an infringement notice, for 1-2 hydroponic plants or 3 to 9 plants (hydroponic or not) a simple criminal conviction applied, and for 10 or more plants there was a presumption of intent to sell or supply, which is an indictable offence.

Secondly, WA police were given powers to regulate the sale and supply of equipment that could be used for the hydroponic cultivation of cannabis A new offence was created of "*Selling or supplying anything that the person knows will be used to cultivate a prohibited plant...by hydroponic means*" and that persons thus convicted could then be prohibited from selling hydroponic equipment for up to 2 years and fined $2,000 and/or face 2 years imprisonment with maximum penalties increasing to $20,000 and 5 years for an indictable offence (WA Misuse of Drugs Act 7a(1)) (Drug and Alcohol Office 2007a). These provisions were enacted because in South Australia there had been claims of links between organized criminal networks and a significant number of hydroponic equipment shops (Government of South Australia 2002) and concerns that some in the hydroponics industry in South Australia were co-coordinating large scale cannabis supply collectives of smaller growers (Prior et al. 2002).

Theoretical issues

The Cannabis Infringement Notice Scheme and other civil penalty schemes are examples of attempts to apply theory of *marginal deterrence* to regulation of cannabis in the community. Marginal deterrence theory is an extension of general deterrence theory (Becker 1968, Schneider and Ervin 1990) which asserts that "undesirable behavior can be curtailed if punishment is sufficiently certain, swift, and severe" (Schneider and Ervin 1990: 585-586). Two subtypes of deterrence effects have been described: (i) *general* deterrence – the prevention of criminal activity by others, and (ii) *specific* deterrence – the dissuasion of law breakers from further offending (Tyler 1990). Marginal deterrence occurs when an individual is "deterred from committing a more harmful act owing to the difference, or margin, between the expected sanction for it and for a less harmful act" (Shavell 1992: 345). It has also been referred to as a "stepladder" rather than a "fortress" approach (Zimring and Hawkins 1973). An example of penalties informed by marginal deterrence theory would be increasing levels of fine for progressively higher speeds over a maximum speed limit for driving. Some drivers will be *absolutely deterred* in that they will never drive above the speed limit, but others, *marginally deterred* may limit their speed so as not to drive more than 10kph over the speed limit to avoid the more severe escalating penalty (Barratt et al. 2005). Consistent with this theory the WA CIN scheme aimed to shape the behavior of cannabis users and growers by providing a reduced penalty (i.e. a civil penalty rather than a criminal charge) if they chose to behave within the levels as laid out in the law, notably possession of not more than 30 grams of cannabis and/or cultivation of not more than 2 non-hydroponic cannabis plants. Data presented below points to the likely impact of the scheme with regards to marginal deterrence.

The application of marginal deterrence principles to applying civil rather than criminal penalties to minor cannabis cultivation and use offences is consistent with a *harm reduction* approach which "refers to policies, programs and practices that aim primarily to reduce the adverse health, social and economic consequences of the use of legal and illegal psychoactive drugs without necessarily reducing drug consumption" (International Harm Reduction Association 2009). Among the principles of harm reduction which have been articulated is the: "avoidance of exacerbating the harm caused by the misuse of drugs … including the unintended harms which may result from the strategy itself" (Lenton and Single 1998: 218). Those who adopt a harm reduction approach would ask: "does the enforcement of the criminal law against non-dependent infrequent users of a drug, primarily as a deterrent, outweigh the negative impacts such as the costs of enforcement, the impact of a criminal record, and the marginalization of large numbers of citizens?" (Lenton and Single 1998: 218).

Practical considerations

Hydroponic versus non-hydroponic

The question of whether both hydroponic and non-hydroponic cultivation of cannabis should be eligible for an infringement notice was an important one for the working party designing the CIN scheme. Previous research had suggested that since at least the late 1990s the WA market was dominated by higher quality / hydroponic cannabis rather than outdoor or "bush" cannabis (Lenton, Bennett and Heale 1999). In WA, the growing of cannabis indoors in soil under lights had not been a widely reported practice so effectively the distinction was between outdoor (bush) and indoor (high quality/potency and probably hydroponic cannabis). A study of "at least weekly" cannabis users interviewed in 2002-2003 (just prior to the CIN scheme coming into effect) found 80% said that the form of cannabis they typically "scored" over the previous 6 months was "hydroponically cultivated cannabis heads", even though 50% preferred to smoke "bush" (outdoor) or non-hydroponic heads (Chanteloup et al. 2005). Additionally, it was anticipated that many cannabis growers would be unwilling to shift from growing hydroponically to non-hydroponically. This was due to the obvious advantages of indoor hydroponic growing methods in terms of concealment (from both law enforcement, potential crop thieves, and potential visitors who would not approve of one's cannabis growing), the higher likelihood of getting a crop to maturity, better per plant yield, the number of crops that can be grown per year and user preference. Furthermore, outdoor cultivation, whilst very viable in WA's Mediterranean climate, was not possible for those who lived in apartments without access to soil.

However, at the same time there was increased media coverage and public awareness of the emerging literature on the adverse health effects of cannabis and in particular the risk of mental health problems (e.g. Arseneault et al. 2002, van Os et al. 2002, Zammitt et al. 2002), which was in turn being linked to potency and to hydroponics. In the media and public discourse on the issue cannabis was seen as "a very different drug" to that which was around when current day parents were smoking the drug as teenagers. Spurious claims that there had been a 30 fold increase in cannabis potency since the early 1980s attributed to hydroponic cultivation methods and cultivation of "skunk" (Hall and Swift 2000) had been reported in the press as responsible for apparent increases in cannabis-related harms, including psychosis, and were central to arguments against proposed cannabis reforms. The evidence on the health effects of cannabis was well known by those on the working party and seizure data and other expert comment pointed to a modest increase in cannabis potency (Hall and Swift 2000). On this basis, and because of the importance of including hydroponic cultivation in the scheme to maximize the market shifting effects, the working party did not exclude hydroponic cultivation from in its final report submitted to the Minister of Health in late March 2002 (Prior et al. 2002). However, after a color photo of the Leader of the Opposition and his Drugs Spokesperson in front of 8 kg of bagged lawn clippings which they claimed represented the amount of cannabis that could be grown in 1 year by two hydroponic plants was published in *The West Australian* newspaper on March 11 2002 (Tickner 2002), the Labor Cabinet decided that those apprehended for hydroponic cultivation would receive a criminal charge, rather than a civil penalty. This was reflected in the *Cannabis Control Bill 2003* which was put before the Parliament. Exclusion of hydroponic cultivation was also consistent with steps being taken in other Australian jurisdictions. For example in 2001 South Australia excluded "artificially enhanced cultivation" from its civil penalty scheme (Drug and Alcohol Office 2007b).

The legal definition of "hydroponic" cultivation

Mindful of the limiting effect that excluding indoor cultivation of cannabis would have on the market shifting goal of the scheme, in advising the drafters of the legislation, the working party sought to use the legal definition of "hydroponic" cultivation to mitigate the possible exclusion of all indoor cultivation from the scheme. Civil penalty schemes in two other jurisdictions had previously addressed the issue, but in different ways. In South Australia "artificially enhanced cultivation" was defined as "*cultivation in a solution comprised wholly or principally of water enriched with nutrients or cultivation involving the application of an artificial source of light or heat*" (Parliament of South Australia 1984), whereas in the Australian Capital Territory, the definition *did not refer to* artificial growing medium thus *"Artificially cultivate means* (to) *hydroponically cultivate or cultivate with the application of an artificial source of light or heat"* (Parliament of the Australian Capital Territory 1989). The Western Australian working party sought to include a definition of "hydroponic cultivation" in the Cannabis Control Bill but were informed by the Parliamentary Council responsible for drafting the Bill, that due to the current convention of not burdening legislation with unnecessary definition, the "usual meaning" of the term was applied. This was to some extent clarified in the Minister's Second Reading Speech which defined hydroponics without reference to use of artificial lighting thus:

> The Bill prevents police officers issuing a CIN under clause 7 where cannabis is being grown hydroponically. This exclusion recognizes the greater yields of hydroponically grown cannabis. Hydroponic cultivation in this context is intended to have its ordinary meaning; that is, cultivation by placing the roots of the plant in a liquid nutrient solution rather than in soil.[Source: Parliament of Western Australia 2003b: 5697]

The working party's intention was that this definition would provide some guidance to the police and the courts such that cannabis plants which were cultivated indoors under artificial lights could be included under the CIN scheme and thus eligible for an infringement notice (rather than a criminal charge) on the condition that their roots were in soil.

Regulation of plant numbers and size

The number of plants eligible for an infringement notice is an important one. Ideally the number of plants would be workable for growers to self supply, while at the same time be seen to be acceptable from a public and political point of view. Theoretical and empirical literature in criminology emphasizes the importance of public attitudes to the law in determining its effectiveness in regulating behavior (Sarat 1977, Silberman 1976). More generally, a "moral commitment" to a particular law has been found to be one of the most powerful predictors of whether people will obey that law (Paternoster and Piquero 1995, Tittle 1977). In a telephone survey of 809 members of the WA public conducted in October 2002 it was found that 59% of respondents believed that growing up to 2 cannabis plants (hydroponic or non hydroponic was not specified) should not be classified as a criminal offence (Fetherston and Lenton 2005).

At the time that the CIN scheme was being designed a number of Australian jurisdictions had reduced the number of plants in the civil penalty schemes. For example, in South Australia the original 10 plant limit, which was set in 1987 well before the emergence of hydroponic cannabis cultivation, was reduced to 3 plants in 1999 due to concerns about larger yields as a result of hydroponics. This was further reduced to 1 plant in 2000, and to 1 non-hydroponic plant in 2001 (Drug and Alcohol Office 2007b). Another reason was that there was credible police evidence that criminal gangs were syndicating cannabis cultivation by aggregating cannabis plants that individuals were growing under the original 10-plant which were then being sold in South Australia and interstate (Sutton and McMillan 2000). In 2004 the ACT government also reduced the number of plants eligible for an infringement notice in that jurisdiction from 5 (either hydro or non-hydro) to 2 non-hydroponic (Drug and Alcohol Office 2007b).

In previous work recommending a civil penalties scheme for the Victorian Government (Lenton et al. 2000), which was never implemented, the number of cultivated plants eligible for an infringement notice was set as:

> 10 growing plants, of which no more than 3 shall be mature (possess flowering heads or be more than 50cm in height)… Height should be measured vertically from the point at which the plant stem emerges from the leveled ground, or growing medium in the case of hydroponics, to the top of the tallest stem. [Source: Lenton et al. 2000: 200]

The justification for this limit was that it would

> provide enforceable levels for police while allowing the grower to have a reasonable number of juvenile plants for crop selection and sexing while also acknowledging that some plants will not survive due to the vagaries of growing …The limit of three plants in head prevents growing more than 3 plants under 50 cm of the shorter varieties, favored by many indoor hydroponic growers, which could otherwise all be in head and therefore contain considerable amounts of heads. [Source: Lenton et al, 2000: 206]

Subsequent to this publication the author was made aware that the height restriction was problematic when applied to hydroponically cultivated plants which can be grown horizontally, in that they are tied down under low mesh to maximize the amount of the plant which is exposed to the overhead lights. A response to this was to apply a radius, rather than a height restriction i.e. being a 50 cm arc from where the stem exits the growing medium. However, although this seemed a workable plant size restriction, the WA police representatives on the Ministerial Working Party for Drug Law Reform which drafted the CIN scheme would not countenance such complexities as plant size, maturity, or flowering status. For police to support the scheme there simply needed to be a limit on the number of plants, no matter the size, and despite discussing the issues re sexing and viability, that number was set at two, with the reductions in plant limits in other jurisdictions providing precedence for that position.

Another restriction on cannabis cultivation employed in the CIN scheme was to apply the two plant limit to households, rather than to individuals. As Swensen (2006) noted, in the South Australian case it had been claimed that organized commercial cultivation of cannabis was occurring under the civil penalty scheme in that state as, because the plant limit applied to individuals rather than households, in multi adult dwellings where a number of adults resided, each person grow up to 10 plants and then these could be easily aggregated for sale.

Dealing with other anomalies in cannabis cultivation

In the deliberations of the working party two other issues regarding growing were given considerable thought. The first of these was the difference between the amount of cannabis that could theoretically be grown on two cannabis plants, and the amount of harvested cannabis (30 grams) eligible for an infringement notice and the second issue was the size, or yield, of a cannabis plant which would be eligible for an expiation notice. Clearly not all cannabis plants are of the same size or contain the same amount of cannabis. Outdoor plants in particular were likely to be larger, while indoor plants although smaller were likely to produce larger weights of female heads (flowering tops) (Bouchard 2007, Gettman 2006). As previously noted De Launey (1996) had found great variability in yield but concluded an average outdoor plant yielded approx 4 ounces (113 grams) and more recent plant yield estimates in North America range from approx 25 grams (indoor) to 200 grams (outdoor) (Bouchard 2007, Gettman 2006) and in the Netherlands 34 grams (indoor) (Toonen, Ribot and Thissen 2006).[1] Even though at the time of drafting the CIN scheme the working party only had access to the De Launey estimate, the more recent figures confirm that 2 mature outdoor cultivated cannabis plants could yield more than 30 grams of dried harvested cannabis. In the end the decision was taken that the central issue was whether the cannabis cultivated (or harvested cannabis possessed) was a reasonable amount for personal use or was likely to be for supply to others and that this decision was best left to the police who, had the option of either issuing an infringement notice, or if they believed the amount of cannabis was more than for personal use, could charge the person with a criminal possession or supply charge and have the courts make a decision. For practical purposes "a plant" for the purpose of determining the plant limit, was a "growing plant" but if that plant was pulled up or harvested it was treated as cannabis and the 30 gram limit was applied. While recognizing the imperfect nature of these decisions in terms of recent harvest, or storage of some cannabis for later use, the plant and weight limits were clear to all, including users, and they could make their decisions based on various risks and benefits. In a practical and political sense this provided a response to the scare tactics of the opponents of the scheme who tried to discredit the plant limit by taking the highest available limits of plant yield (see Tickner 2002).

The media and political debate

The inclusion of cannabis cultivation within the CIN scheme was a major focus of media coverage and political debate from before the implementation of the scheme and beyond (Lenton 2004, Lenton and Allsop 2010). It has been noted above that Liberal opposition's use of the media resulted in hydroponic cultivation being excluded from the scheme. During the parliamentary debate an opposition Member of Parliament claimed that the Bill:

> is about children being stupefied by being allowed to grow cannabis. They will not have to get out of their pajamas or have to work out how to get the money to buy cannabis; they can grow it outside their bedroom window. Before they go to school in the morning, they can just break a bit off and dry it out. [Source: Parliament of Western Australia 2003a]

---

1 Whilst it is not relevant to the regulation of outdoor cannabis cultivation, one potential mechanism for limiting the amount of indoor cannabis grown is to limit the amount of lighting. Light bulbs used in hydroponics are often 400 to 600 watts. The cannabis yield per watt of lighting has been calculated at between 0.5 grams (Bouchard 2007) and 0.99 grams (Toonen et al. 2006).

The West Australian, which took a consistently negative view towards the scheme once it was enacted also focused on the inclusion of plants in the scheme. An editorial on the day the scheme was enacted noted:

> Households could grow two cannabis plants without occupants facing criminal charges. They would face $200 fines and be made to attend drug education classes.
>
> There are inconsistencies in the law because two plants can amount to much more than 30g. So people can be penalized not so much on the basis of how much cannabis they possess as on whether they hold it as a plant or processed form.
>
> In any case it is a fair bet that most responsible adults would think that two plants provide too much cannabis to attract the degree of official tolerance that is now available. People who may have baulked at growing cannabis in their backyards under threat of criminal records are likely now to be emboldened by the softer regime. And those who grow more than they need are likely to make the surpluses available to others....
>
> The critical system is whether the system will result in more cannabis use, particularly among the young... West Australians must be informed about the consequences of this experiment which must be ended if cannabis use increases.
>
> [Source: Editorial – The West Australian 2004]

This last statement is particularly interesting as despite documented evidence that cannabis use was continuing to decline in WA since the scheme's introduction (see below), the press editorial position remained staunchly against it (Lenton and Allsop 2010). Much of the media coverage and political debate reinforced a mistaken view by many that cultivation of cannabis was legal or "allowed" under the CIN scheme. Police also reported that a number of the people they had contact with believed cultivation was now legal and this was thought to be related to the media debate (Sutton and Hawks 2005).

Evidence of impact

Statistics on the WA CIN scheme

There was no indication of an increase in cannabis use due to the introduction of the CIN scheme as its opponents had claimed. The proportion of West Australians 14 years and over that had used cannabis in the previous 12 months fell from

17.5% in 2001, to 13.7% in 2004 (the year the scheme came into effect), and down to 10.8% in 2007 (Australian Institute of Health and Welfare 2002, 2005, 2008). Rates among School children also declined (Miller and Lang 2007). This is not to claim the reduction in cannabis use has been because of the CIN scheme. The changes have occurred Australia-wide and began before the CIN scheme was implemented. Interestingly, despite a decline in public support from 79% of the WA public surveyed believing the scheme as a whole was "a good idea" in 2002, to 66% in 2007 still more than two thirds supported the scheme 3 years after its inception (Fetherston and Lenton 2007).

With regards to cannabis cultivation specifically, while there was a concern among some critics of the CIN scheme that it would result in a vast increase in the amount of cannabis cultivated in Western Australia, there is no evidence that this occurred. In the 3 year period up until the end of March 2007 there were a total of 255 CINs issued for cultivation of cannabis and these comprised 2.7% of the 9,328 CINs issued over this period (Drug and Alcohol Office 2007b). Furthermore, in the eight quarters prior to the operation of the CIN scheme there were on average 183 cannabis cultivation charges per quarter. In the 13 quarters after the CIN scheme came into effect this declined to an average 167 cannabis cultivation charges or CINS per quarter (Drug and Alcohol Office 2007b).

Anticipated impact with regards to marginal deterrence

Research conducted with regular cannabis users, prior to the laws coming into place, (Barratt et al. 2005) suggested that the CIN scheme might produce marginal deterrence effects among the small number of people purchasing or growing outside the limits expiable under the CIN scheme. That is, some people said they would be willing to change their purchasing or growing patterns to fit within the CIN scheme levels, something they would not have done had the criminal penalties scheme been maintained. For example 17 (23%) of the 77 respondents who typically purchased under 15 grams of cannabis said that intended to cease purchasing from the illicit market altogether and switch to growing their own cannabis. Additionally, 5 of 11 respondents who said they had typically grown between 3 and 9 non-hydroponic plants before the scheme came into effect said that they intended to decrease their plant numbers to fit within the scheme. Furthermore, as the CIN scheme reduced the deeming provisions for dealing down from 25 to 10 plants, it was interesting that 3 of the 4 hydroponic growers who were growing over 10 plants intended to reduce this to below 10 when the scheme came into effect (Barratt et al. 2005). On the other hand 16 respondents gave reasons why their growing intentions would not be affected by the CIN scheme, most (n=14) because the law was not seen as relevant to their decisions regarding growing.

Impact on market separation

As has been explained, one of the initial goals of the CIN scheme was to separate the cannabis market from other drugs by making cultivation of 2 non-hydroponic plants an expiable offence. However, existing data suggest impacts on the market were limited. It is possible that the exclusion of hydroponic cannabis from the scheme militated against this. A pre-post telephone survey of the general public (Fetherston and Lenton 2007) found that 25% of those who had used cannabis in the previous 12 months said they had grown at least some of the cannabis they had smoked in the past year, up from 11% in 2002, before the scheme came into effect (Fetherston and Lenton 2007). However, as yet unpublished post change results from the in-depth interview study of regular users suggests that while the scheme may have encouraged some regular users to try growing, there was no evidence that it increased the proportion who grew as a main source of supply.

The fate of the reforms

In 2007, the *Cannabis Control Act (2003)* was subject to a three year legislative review as determined by a clause within it. The review was conducted by a steering group chaired by the Drug and Alcohol Office, which was the Government Department given responsibility for the scheme, and included WA Police as major stakeholders (Drug and Alcohol Office 2007a, 2007b).

The review recommended continuing the CIN scheme, and noted that there was solid evidence that the scheme had been broadly successful at meeting its objective but recommended a number of measures to "enhance its effectiveness" (Drug and Alcohol Office 2007a). Importantly the police considered that "...the scheme was unnecessarily complex, particularly in relation to the growing of non-hydroponic plants [which]... is a barrier to consistent and streamlined implementation" (Drug and Alcohol Office 2007a). As a consequence, cultivation of up to two non-hydroponic plants (included in the original Act) was to be excluded from the scheme under Labor's proposed amendments.

However, in September 2008 the Labor government was replaced by a Liberal and National (conservative) government which has a "tough on drugs and tough on crime" platform and promised to repeal the CCA and reintroduce criminal penalties for growing cannabis. Cautions will apply for first offenders in possession of not more than 10 grams of cannabis or a used smoking implement and who complete a brief Cannabis Intervention Session (Banks 2009, Phillips 2009). At the time of writing these legal changes had passed the WA Parliament but were not expected to come into effect until late 2011.

Conclusions and the implications for policies of cannabis control

What conclusions can be drawn from the CIN scheme experience of trying to regulate cannabis cultivation under a civil penalties model? While the rationale for including plants in the scheme was well intended in terms of trying to separate the cannabis market from that for other drugs and provide cannabis users with a somewhat less penalized method of self supply, it appeared to have negligible impact on the market. This was likely adversely affected by the exclusion of hydroponic cultivation from the scheme, a political decision, which may have undermined marginal deterrence effects. However, it cannot be determined from the existing data on the WA CIN case whether the effect on the market would have been greater had hydroponic cultivation been included. The evidence that does exist suggests that for many users the law may have had only a modest impact, if at all, on their growing decisions and cannabis growing was not feasible or worth the risk for many, particularly when most cannabis is obtained from "friends". Furthermore the goal of the designers of the scheme to have police selectively focus their activity on the most harmful elements of the market, large scale criminal suppliers, rather than small scale user growers, was effectively removed by the political process. It appeared that such a notion was judged not publicly acceptable even by a party with a strong will for cannabis law reform. The low proportion of CINs issued for cultivation, combined with apparent police dissatisfaction with issuing notices for cultivation offences made it an obvious sacrificial lamb for a government wanting to demonstrate it was willing to "toughen up" the cannabis laws in the face of considerable media criticism and attacks from the conservative side of politics, and anxiety about cannabis and mental health effects. This occurred despite declining rates of cannabis use and high levels of public support for the scheme. The notion that excluding cultivation of non-hydroponic cannabis plants from the scheme would send people back to the illicit market dominated by hydroponic cannabis got little traction in the debate. When the Liberal government was elected the fate of the scheme and the civil penalties for cannabis cultivation were sealed.

It is unclear what implications there are from the WA CIN scheme for other attempts to regulate user cultivation of cannabis. Indeed, it may be the case that it is easier to regulate larger scale cannabis cultivation through a government controlled regulated availability model (see Room et al. 2010), than it is to regulate small scale growers under a civil penalty scheme. However, discrepancies between the amount of cannabis eligible for cultivation and that for possession once harvested are likely to be issues in any future civil penalty schemes. Where hydroponic cultivation of cannabis is included it may be that regulation of lights, rather than plants provides the most appropriate regulatory tool. If the experience of the WA CIN case example rings true in other cases then, what is politically expedient or sustainable, rather than what the research literature recommends is likely to influence the shape and detail of any future scheme to regulate cannabis.

List of references

Arseneault, L., Cannon, M., Poulton, R., Murray, R., Caspi, A. and Moffitt, T.E. 2002. Cannabis use in adolescence and risk for adult psychosis: longitudinal prospective study. *British Medical Journal,* 325, 1212-213.

Australian Bureau of Criminal Intelligence 1999. *Australian Illicit Drug Report 1997-98.* Canberra: Commonwealth of Australia.

Australian Institute of Health and Welfare 2002. *2001 National Drug Strategy Household Survey: State and Territory Supplement AIHW cat. no. PHE37* Canberra: AIHW.

Australian Institute of Health and Welfare 2005. *2004 National Drug Strategy Household Survey: State and territory supplement. Drug statistics series. AIHW cat. no. PHE 61* Canberra: AIHW.

Australian Institute of Health and Welfare 2008. *2007 National Drug Strategy Household Survey: State and territory supplement. Drug statistics series no. 21. Cat. no. PHE 102* Canberra: AIHW.

Australian Labor Party WA Branch 2001. *Drugs and crime – breaking the cycle* [Online: Australian Labor Party]. Available at: http://www.wa.alp.org.au/-policy/camp2001/drugs.pdf [accessed: 9 September 2001].

Banks, A. 2009. "Get tough" approach in marijuana legislation. *The West Australian,* 12 October, 6.

Barratt, M., Chanteloup, F., Lenton, S. and Marsh, A. 2005. Cannabis law reform in Western Australia: an opportunity to test theories of marginal deterrence and legitimacy. *Drug and Alcohol Review,* 24(4), 321-30.

Becker, G. 1968. Crime and punishment: An economic approach. *Journal of Political Economy,* 76(2), 169-217.

Bouchard, M. 2007. A Capture–Recapture Model to Estimate the Size of Criminal Populations and the Risks of Detection in a Marijuana Cultivation Industry. *Journal of Quantitative Criminology,* 23, 221-41.

Chanteloup, F., Lenton, S., Fetherston, J. and Barratt, M. 2005. Expected impacts of the Cannabis Infringement Notice Scheme in Western Australia on regular users and their involvement in the cannabis market. *Drug and Alcohol Review,* 24(4), 311-319.

de Launey, C. 1996. The real value of a cannabis plant. Report on a 1995 survey of cannabis crop growers in northern NSW. *Alternative Law Journal,* 21(3), 127-30.

Drug and Alcohol Office 2007a. *Statutory review of Cannabis Control Act 2003. Report to the Minister for Health: Executive summary.* Perth, Western Australia: Drug and Alcohol Office.

Drug and Alcohol Office 2007b. *Statutory Review of Cannabis Control Act 2003. Report to the Minister for Health: Main report.* Perth, Western Australia: Drug and Alcohol Office.

Editorial – The West Australian 2004. Dangers in new laws on cannabis. *The West Australian,* 23 March, 16.

Editorial – The West Australian 2006. Soft cannabis laws must be reviewed. *The West Australian*, 29 June, 18.

Erickson, P. 1980. *Cannabis criminals: the social effects of punishment on drug users*. Toronto: Addiction Research Foundation.

Fetherston, J. and Lenton, S. 2005. Community attitudes towards cannabis law and the proposed Cannabis Infringement Notice Scheme in Western Australia. *Drug and Alcohol Review*, 24(4), 301-309.

Fetherston, J. and Lenton, S. 2007. *A pre-post comparison of the impacts of the Western Australian Cannabis Infringement Notice scheme on public attitudes, knowledge and use*. Perth: National Drug Research Institute, Curtin University of Technology.

Gettman, J. 2006. Marijuana production in the United States. *Bulletin of cannabis reform*. Available at: http://www.drugscience.org/Archive/bcr2/MJCropReport_2006.pdf [accessed: 12 December 2009].

Government of South Australia 2002. *National competition policy review: Proposal to licence hydroponic equipment retailers – Report of the review panel*. Adelaide: South Australian Government.

Hall, W. and Swift, W. 2000. The THC content of cannabis in Australia: evidence and implications. *Australian and New Zealand Journal of Public Health*, 24(5), 503-508.

Harvey, B. 2003. Soft approach has its risks. *The West Australian*, 27 May, 9.

International Harm Reduction Association 2009. *What is Harm Reduction? A position statement from the International Harm Reduction Association*. [Online: International Harm Reduction Association]. Available at: http://www.ihra.net/Assets/2316/1/IHRA_HRStatement.pdf [accessed: 27 May 2010].

Lenton, S. 2004. Pot, politics and the press – Reflections on cannabis law reform in Western Australia. *Drug and Alcohol Review*, 23(2), 223-233.

Lenton, S. and Allsop, S. 2010. A tale of CIN – The Cannabis Infringement Notice Scheme in Western Australia. *Addiction*, 105, 808-816.

Lenton, S., Bennett, M. and Heale, P. 1999. *The social impact of a minor cannabis offence under strict prohibition – the case of Western Australia*. Perth: National Centre for Research into the Prevention of Drug Abuse, Curtin University of Technology.

Lenton, S., Christie, P., Humeniuk, R., Brooks, A., Bennett, M. and Heale, P. 1999. *Infringement versus conviction: The social impact of a minor cannabis offence under a civil penalties system and strict prohibition in two Australian states (monograph No. 36)*. Canberra: Publications Productions Unit, Commonwealth Department of Health and Aged Care, National Drug Strategy.

Lenton, S., Heale, P., Erickson, P., Single, E., Lang, E. and Hawks, D. 2000. *The regulation of cannabis possession, use and supply: A discussion document prepared for the Drugs and Crime Prevention Committee of the Parliament of Victoria. (NDRI Monograph No. 3)*. Perth: National Drug Research Institute, Curtin University of Technology.

Lenton, S. and Single, E. 1998. The definition of harm reduction. *Drug and Alcohol Review,* 17(2), 213-220.

Miller, J. and Lang, A. 2007. *ASSAD Drug Report 2005.* Canberra: TNS Social Research.

Parliament of South Australia, Controlled Substances Act, S. 45A, 45A (1984).

Parliament of the Australian Capital Territory 1989. *Drugs of Dependence Act s.*162(2).

Parliament of Western Australia 2003a. *Parliamentary Debates, Legislative Assembly. Extract from Hansard [ASSEMBLY – Thursday, 10 April 2003] p6650b-6667a (Ms Sue Walker MLA).*

Parliament of Western Australia 2003b. *Parliamentary Debates, Legislative Assembly. Cannabis Control Bill 2003 Second Reading. pp.5694–5698 [Thursday, 20 March 2003] (R.C. Kucera, Minister of Health).*

Paternoster, R. and Piquero, A. 1995. Reconceptualizing deterrence: An empirical test of personal and vicarious experiences. *Journal of Research in Crime and Delinquency,* 32(3), 251-86.

Phillips, Y. 2009. Labor dope law in sights. *The West Australian*, 21 February, 60.

Prior, J., Swensen, G., Migro, J., Tomassini, R., Marshall, A., Lenton, S., et al. 2002. *Implementation of a scheme of prohibition with civil penalties for the personal use of cannabis and other matters – Report of the Working Party on Drug Law Reform to the Minister for Health.* Perth: Drug and Alcohol Office, Health Department of WA. Available at http://www.wa.gov.au/drugwestaus/core.html [accessed: 11 December 2002].

Room, R., Fischer, B., Hall, W., Lenton, S. and Reuter, P. 2010. *Cannabis Policy: Moving Beyond Stalemate*. New York: Oxford University Press.

Sarat, A. 1977. Studying American legal culture: An assessment of survey evidence. *Law and Society Review,* 11, 427-88.

Schneider, A.L. and Ervin, L. 1990. Specific deterrence, rational choice, and decision heuristics: Applications in juvenile justice. *Social Science Quarterly,* 71(3), 584-601.

Shavell, S. 1992. A note on marginal deterrence. *International Review of Law and Economics*, 12, 345-55.

Silberman, M. 1976. Toward a theory of criminal deterrence. *American Sociological Review,* 41, 442-461.

Sutton, A. 2000. Cannabis law and the young adult user: Reflections on South Australia's Cannabis Expiation Notice System. *International Journal of the Sociology of Law,* 28, 147-62.

Sutton, A. and Hawks, D. 2005. The Cannabis Infringement Notice Scheme in Western Australia: A review of policy, police and judicial perspectives. *Drug and Alcohol Review,* 24(4), 331-6.

Sutton, A. and McMillan, E. 2000. Criminal justice perspectives on South Australia's Cannabis Expiation Notice procedures. *Drug and Alcohol Review,* 19(3), 281-6.

Swensen, G. 2006. *Reform of Minor Cannabis Laws in Western Australia, the United Kingdom and New Zealand.* Thesis. Murdoch University.

Tickner, L. 2002. Battle looms over cannabis. *The West Australian,* 11 March, 7.

Tittle, C.R. 1977. Sanction fear and the maintenance of social order. *Social Forces,* 55, 579-96.

Toonen, M., Ribot, S. and Thissen, J. 2006. Yield of illicit indoor cannabis cultivation in the Netherlands. *Journal of Forensic Sciences,* 51(5), 1050-4.

Tyler, T. 1990. *Why people obey the law.* New Haven: Yale University Press.

van Os, J., Bak, M., Hanssen, M., Bijl, R.V., de Graaf, R. and Verdoux, H. 2002. Cannabis use and psychosis: A longitudinal population-based study. *American Journal of Epidemiology,* 156(4), 319-27.

Vermeer, T. and Spagnolo, J. 2005. Fight pot use: PM – Howard slams WA's "soft" law. *The Sunday Times,* 18 December, 3.

Zammitt, S., Allebeck, P., Andreasson, S., Lundberg, I. and Lewis, G. 2002. Self reported cannabis use as a risk factor in Swedish conscripts of 1969: historical cohort study. *British Medical Journal,* 325, 1199-203.

Zimring, F.E. and Hawkins, G.J. 1973. *Deterrence: The legal threat in crime control.* Chicago: University of Chicago Press.

Chapter 13
A Review of Cannabis Properties and Experiments for its Biological Control[1]

Margaret Kalacska, Pablo Arroyo-Mora, Eva Snirer and Rick Parent

Introduction

Information derived from research into the properties of cannabis is available from a variety of sources specific to disciplines such as medicine, genetics, policy, crime analysis and botany. In addition, there is a significant amount of information from popular sources such as books published by growers or cannabis enthusiasts as well as reports from sources such as the United Nations, the US Drug Enforcement Agency, the Bureau for International Narcotics and Law Enforcement Affairs, the National Drug Intelligence Center and the Treasury Board of Canada among others.

Considerable resources are spent each year in Canada to eradicate illicit cannabis grow-ops. The characteristics of the grow-ops such as average size, planting environment, use of deterrents, preference of growth media, among others, varies by region and as such there is no stereotypical "Canadian grow-op". Grow-ops can consist of only a few plants (e.g. less than 10) to a few thousand (Kalacska and Bouchard 2010). In general though, the grow-ops in Canada are smaller than can be found in other countries such as Morocco. Regardless of the number of plants in a grow-op, cannabis has many unique ecological and biological characteristics that make its location and eradication challenging. If cannabis is considered as a 'pest' from an ecological or agricultural perspective, 'biological control' is a theoretical means by which its population could be controlled. In such a context biological control refers to mechanisms such as herbivory, predation and parasitism to reduce the population of the target species, *Cannabis* in this case. Canada does have an important industrial cannabis (i.e. hemp) industry and therefore, any type of controlling agent must be specific to the drug producing

1 The authors would like to thank Martin Bouchard, Tom Decorte and Kenza Afsahi for helpful comments and discussions on the global cannabis cultivation market that contributed to the development of this chapter. In addition the authors thank Uzay Sezen for his participation in the development of the cannabis genetics section, and the Royal Canadian Mountain Police for their assistance in collecting some of the data analyzed. Additionally, two anonymous reviewers provided helpful feedback on an earlier version of the chapter. Financial support was provided by Public Safety Canada.

plants without being detrimental to the hemp industry. A reliable biological control agent for cannabis could become a useful tool for law enforcement to both reduce the population of illicit cannabis with less financial and personnel resources than mechanical destruction of plants and to prevent the use of sites repeatedly by growers. In some cases the growers themselves invest significant resources into the development of grow sites. If those sites become inhospitable to the cannabis plant it would prevent their reuse of the sites and the resources invested into the development of those grow sites.

By summarizing the most relevant information from a variety of sources, the background information is provided to understand the unique responses of this plant to biological control efforts and why it is a very difficult species to eradicate (for illicit grow-ops). Aspects such as the biology, ecology, chemical composition and spectral properties of the cannabis plant are summarized followed by a review of the literature on biological control efforts that have been tested with this species. While biological control can be highly effective for certain species, the results from the literature indicate that such efforts have not been successful with cannabis for a variety of reasons. The main objectives of this chapter therefore, are to introduce the unique characteristics of *Cannabis* as a plant species well as to describe the successes and pitfalls of biological control efforts.

In this chapter we use the term cannabis to refer to all species and strains of the plant (unless otherwise specified). For consistency, it is also used in place of the common term "marijuana" or "marihuana" as is used in some of the sources cited. In addition, the information is meant to be most relevant to plants selected or selectively bred for drug use (i.e. high THC content – see cannabis chemistry section). In Canada the threshold for cannabis plants to be considered "hemp" rather than drug producing plants is less than 0.3% THC in the leaves and flowering parts (Health Canada 2006). We refer to hemp as industrial *Cannabis* in some sections of this chapter.

Cannabis botany, distribution and ecology

The genus *Cannabis* belongs to the family Cannabaceae. Three species of *Cannabis* are generally recognized: *C. sativa*, *C. indica* and *C. ruderalis* (Clarke et al. 2006, Green 2005). Although there is still a controversy regarding the different species and varieties of *Cannabis* (Clarke et al. 2006), for this chapter we focus on the species *Cannabis sativa* L. (common name: marihuana or marijuana) and comment on *C. indica* and *C. ruderalis* because of their use in breeding treatments for selecting desirable traits that can be specific to local environmental conditions or product requirements (Green 2005). *C. sativa* differs morphologically from the other two recognized species of cannabis. At the plant level *C. sativa* is a tall plant averaging 1 to 3 m with long internodes between branches (Green 2005). At the leaf level, leaves of *C. sativa* are pointy without markings and patterns, usually with 6 to 12 blades per leaf. All species of cannabis are dioecious, meaning there are separate male and female plants.

At the flower level male and female cannabis plants are only distinguishable after blooming, although some preliminary genetic work has shown otherwise (see genetics section). Cannabis requires wind for pollination to occur. Differentiating between male and female plants is important because at harvest the female plants contain the levels of THC content desired by the growers.

According to Clarke et al. (2006) cannabis originated either in the valleys of Central Asia or in northern South Asia along the foothills of the Himalayas, but in modern times has a nearly worldwide distribution and can grow naturally without human cultivation. In terms of the different species, pure *C. sativa* is typically found in warmer, lowland climates (Thailand, Mexico and South Africa, for example). *C. indica* likely originated in northern India and C. *ruderalis,* a more recently recognized species, can be found growing naturally in Central Asia (UNODC 2006). Growers refer to "varieties" of cannabis that may be pure plants from any of the species or crosses between the species. Common terms for the varieties are names of the location of origin such as Mexican, Colombian, Hawaiian, Southeast Asian, etc. or creative names such as White Widow and Northern Lights. Nevertheless, each variety shares several similar characteristics.

Cannabis is an annual herb that can reproduce sexually (seed) or through vegetative propagation (cloning). Basic requirements for growth are good light conditions, well-drained soils, sufficient nutrients, and water. Although cannabis can grow in a variety of soil types, it prefers loams rich in nitrogen, with a neutral pH (UNODC 2006). As with many other herbs, after seed germination juvenile plants increase biomass (leaves) with increasing day length (Clarke et al. 2005). This prepares the plants for the next stage of shorter days (less light availability) after the summer solstice. At this point the plants enter the flowering stage and seed development (Campbell and Reece 2005) which varies between 3 to 8 weeks (Clarke et al. 2006). Once seeds develop they can be dispersed naturally or harvested for additional production. In northern latitudes (30 to 60 degrees) seeds are usually planted between March and May, and if the plants are pure *C. sativa*, would produce flowers between September and November, in a six-month growth cycle (UNODC 2006). However, this may not be optimal for most growers. Therefore, generally the plants used are varieties of cannabis that are crossed with *C. indica*. Pure *C. indica* has a much shorter flowering period (Greene 2005). Due to the option of vegetative propagation in cannabis, seeds are not necessary to achieve a full life cycle under controlled conditions (light, soil and water). By prohibiting pollination, growers have been able to produce a new "type" of cannabis product called "*sinsemilla*" (without seeds) with higher THC content than what is derived from pollinated plants (Clarke et al. 2006, UNODC 2006).

One of the most important traits of cannabis is its photoperiod sensitivity. By manipulating the number of hours of sunlight the plants receive, it is possible for the growers to obtain two harvests in certain locations. In addition, cannabis does not require a dark period to complete its photosynthetic cycle (Greene 2005). If plants are exposed to only 12 or 13 hours of sunshine per day, they will be "forced" to flower (Clarke et al. 2006, Greene 2005).

Chemical constituents of cannabis

Cannabis plants contain over 400 compounds, some of which are unique to these plants (Brenneisen 2006, Novak et al. 2001). The specific chemical constitution of cannabis varies and is influenced both by the genetics of the plant (mainly affects the cannabinoids) and their environment (mainly affects the terpenoids) (ElSohly et al. 2006). Environmental effects can be as broad as a continent or as specific as a grow operation. However, cannabis originating from different countries has also been shown to have unique differences in cannabinoids, indicating that the effects are a combination of both genetics and environment (ElSohly et al. 2006).

The unique differences in chemistry have led to the branch of research known as "cannabis profiling" or "cannabis fingerprinting". Following a multivariate analysis of the chemical compounds ElSohly et al. (2006) found that twenty-two of the indicator compounds are terpenes, sixteen are cannabinoids, two are hydrocarbons, two are non-cannabinoid phenols, three are fatty acid esters and one is an aromatic compound.

In a comparison of indoor and outdoor grown plants originating from Jamaica (in natural soil and in pots with commercial potting soil), the chemical constituents of the indoor plants were differentiated without error from both outdoor groups (ElSohly et al. 2006). Differences were also observed between the outdoor groups, even though there was some error. These results indicate that while light and temperature may be the key drivers of chemical composition, soil can also be a factor. In a second experiment involving daughter plants from a variety of origins ElSohly et al. (2006) found that even though genetic relationships do affect the chemical profile of the plants, the environment plays a greater role. They also found that plant age is an important influence on the chemical profile of the cannabis plant.

There are sixty-six cannabinoids that have so far only been found in cannabis plants. "Cannabinoid" refers to a group of organic compounds with the basic C_{21} terpenophenolic structure and are subdivided into ten groups, of which the four main ones are (Brenneisen 2006, Mechoulam et al. 1967):

- Cannabigerol (CBG)
- Cannabichromene (CBC)
- Cannabidiol (CBD)
- Δ^9-Tetrahydrocannabinol (THC)

CBG was the first cannibinoid to be identified and six cannabinoids are part of this class (Brenneisen 2006). CBD compounds are the most prevalent in cannabis plants grown for hemp and are a trade-off with the THC compounds because

CBD are the biosynthetic precursor to THC (UNODC 2006). Nine compounds constitute the THC class. Δ^9-Tetrahydrocannabinol is the main psychoactive compound. The precursory THC acids also classified in this same group are not psychoactive (Brenneisen 2006).

Other classes of compounds include: Δ^8-Tetrahydrocannabinol (Δ^8-THC is similar to Δ^9-THC but is less potent), Cannabicyclol, Cannabielsoin, Cannabinol and Cannabinodiol (their concentrations in the plant depend on the age and storage conditions because they are the oxidation artifacts of THC and CBD), Cannabitriol and Miscellaneous (eleven compounds with unusual structures) (Brenneisen 2006).

The distinctive odour of cannabis plants is due to the terpenoids, the most abundant class of compounds (140 in total) can be found in other plants in different combinations and abundances (Brenneisen 2006, Novak 2001, ElSohly 2002). The main structure of the terpenoids is formed by isoprene units (C_5H_8) that make monoterpenoids (C_{10} skeleton), sesquiterpenoids (C_{15} skeleton), diterpenoids (C_{20} skeleton) or triterpenoids (C_{30} skeleton) (Brenneisen 2006). The yield of terpoenoids depends on the type of cannabis (grown for drug vs hemp), harvest time, pollination, gender, age of plants at harvest, cultivation type (indoor or outdoor), drying and storage conditions (Brenneisen 2006, Mediavilla and Steinemann 1997). The amount of terpenoids decreases with time following harvest. For example Mediavilla and Steinemann (1997) found that freshly harvested outdoor grown cannabis contains on average 10L/ha. The same study found that non-pollinated "*sinsemilla*" cannabis produced 18L/ha versus 8L/ha for pollinated cannabis. The specific breakdown varies between indoor and outdoor grown cannabis (Table 13.1).

Compounds from the THC class of cannabinoids do not contribute significantly to the essential oils of cannabis, even in the varieties of cannabis grown specifically for high THC content, for example, Mediavilla and Steinemann (1997) only found a concentration of 0.08% of THC in the essential oils of drug cannabis. The concentrations of the dominant terpenes determined from a study of five cultivars from Europe, are listed in Table 13.2:

Cannabis also contains a broad range of other compounds: hydrocarbons, Nitrogen-containing compounds, carbohydrates, flavinoids, fatty acids, non-

Table 13.1 Breakdown of terpenoids in outdoor and indoor grown cannabis

Terpenoid	Indoor grown	Outdoor grown
Monoterpenes	92%	48-92%
Sesquiterpenes	7%	5-49%
Others	1%	-

Source: Brenneisen 2006.

Table 13.2 Concentration ranges of dominant terpenoids

Terpene	Concentration
myrcene	21.1-35.0%
A-pinene	7.1-14.6%
A-terpinolene	7-16.6%
trans-caryophyllene	12.2-18.9%
α-humulene	6.1-8.7%

Source: Mediavilla and Steinemann 1997.

cannabinoid phenols, alcohols, aldehydes, esters, ketones, acids, lactones, phytosterols, etc (Brenneisen 2006). The only vitamin found so far is vitamin K (Brenneisen 2006). Cannabis also contains the essential photosynthetic pigments such as chlorophyll (a and b) and accessory pigments such as carotenes and xanthophylls (all of which are of importance in remote sensing applications) (Gamon et al. 1992, Asner 1998, van der Meer 1999). Eighteen elements have also been reported (Na, K, Ca, Mg, Fe, Cu, Mn, Zn, Hg, etc.) (Brenneisen 2006) some of which are common to plants whereas others less so. Increased nitrogen-containing compounds are also of interest to remote sensing (as a means to detect clandestine grow-ops) because of the effect of nitrogen concentration on reflectance (see spectral response section) (Cho and Skidmore 2006). The relative effect of the other compounds unique to cannabis on its spectral response is yet to be determined.

Genetics

Cannabis (family, Cannabaceae) is an ancient cultivated plant with three major species: *C. sativa, C. indica* and *C. ruderalis* (Schultes et al. 1974). Cannabis has two separate sexes (dioecious) determined by the XY sex determination system quite similar to that of humans. Male plants possess the heterogametic (XY) chromosomes while the females bear the homogametic (XX) chromosomes (Moliterni et al. 2004). In psycho-active cultivars, female plants possess the psycho-active compound Δ^9-tetrahydrocannabinol (THC) (ElSholy 2006). The sex of the plant is almost impossible to determine visually until the plant reaches reproductive maturity which occurs in a late stage of plant development, therefore considerable genetic work was necessary to characterize DNA markers associated with the male sex (Moliterni et al. 2004, Sakamoto et al. 1995, Flachowsky et al. 2001, Peil et al. 2003). A large number of genetic markers have been characterized to distinguish the three species of *Cannabis* which help drug enforcement units to determine the geographic source and the type of cultivar. Random Amplified Polymorphic DNA (RAPD) were the earliest genetic markers to explore the genetic variation in cannabis (Forapani et al. 2001, Hakki et al. 2003). The advent of the Amplified Fragment Length Polymorphism (AFLP) technique enabled higher resolution genetic fingerprinting with reproducible results (Peil et al. 2003,

Hakki et al. 2003, Datwyler and Weiblen 2006). Microsatellite DNA markers have also been developed for cannabis (Gilmore 2003). Cannabis demonstrates an exceptional capacity for clonal propagation and therefore, genetic markers can trace entirely clonally produced plant material.

Spectral characteristics of cannabis

The published studies examining the spectral signature of cannabis are limited in number and often contradictory in nature regarding the actual detectability of cannabis amidst other vegetation. In general all healthy green vegetation has the same general spectral properties (i.e. the way in which it reflects and absorbs light across wavelengths) (Figure 13.1).

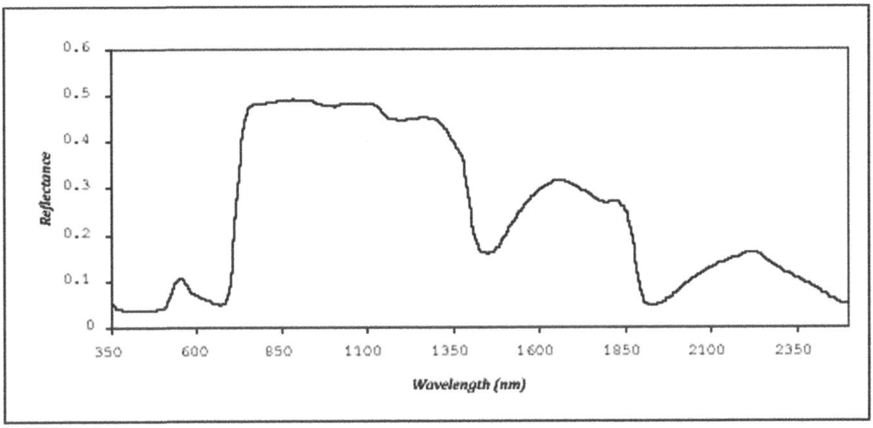

Figure 13.1 The spectral response of healthy green vegetation.

The region centered around 550nm is known as the *green peak* in vegetation spectra and is representative of photosynthetic pigments such as chlorophylls a and b and photoprotection pigments associated with the xanthophyll cycle (Gamon et al. 1992, Guo and Trotter 2004, Stylinski et al. 2002, Sims and Gamon 2002). Healthy, green vegetation has strong absorption in the red wavelengths (620-700nm) and high reflectance in the near infrared. The inflection point between the two is referred to as the *red-edge* and can be related to foliar nitrogen and chlorophyll content (Cho and Skidmore 2006). The plateau in the near infrared region is also a characteristic of vegetation reflectance spectra (Gates et al. 1965); it is predominantly controlled by internal structure at the leaf level (Asner 1998, Gates et al. 1965) and is also influenced by leaf area index (total leaf area per ground area), water content, plant physiology and stress at the canopy level (Asner 1998). The challenge therefore, in the location of illicit cannabis is separating its signature from the surrounding vegetation.

One of the earliest publications examining the spectral properties of cannabis is Daughtry and Walthall (1998). In that study, the reflectance and transmittance of leaves from several varieties of *C. sativa* were compared to the reflectance and transmittance of other vegetation native to the East Coast of the United States. Both sides of the leaves were examined along with the effect of the application of nitrogen fertilizer. Differences between strains of cannabis were found to be minimal. Differences in the spectra of the cannabis and the leaf spectra of seven tree species and eight herbaceous species were observed however (Daughtry and Walthall 1998).

Walthall et al. (2003) describe that the most likely reason for the unique "hazy emerald-green" reflectance of cannabis reported by trained aerial spotters is due to specular reflectance from the waxy cuticle layer of the leaves and from scattering due to microscopic structures on the leaf surfaces. The scattering of blue sky-light was hypothesized to add to the green reflectance (i.e. green peak) inherent in green vegetation to create an emerald-green quality to the spectral signature of cannabis. Thus, Walthall et al. (2003) state that in clear conditions, the blue component of the reflectance will be stronger than under cloudy conditions where green reflectance and internal leaf elements would be dominant. The contrast of the "emerald-green" appearance of the cannabis may be enhanced by the introduction of fertilizer and elimination of water stress especially if other vegetation is stressed due to a lack of water, nutrients or is subject to other conditions such as pests. The canopy architecture of cannabis was hypothesized to be the cause of the "hazy" effect when the plants are seen from a distance. In contrast to Daughtry and Walthall (1998), no significant differences were observed between the leaf reflectance of different strains/varieties, leading to the conclusion by Walthall et al. (2003) that THC content has little effect on reflectance. Examination of cold-stage electron micrographs indicated that the leaves are covered with patches of aligned rods, only a fraction of a visible wavelength of light in diameter and multiple wavelength dimensions long (Walthall et al. 2003). The contribution of the rods and a waxy substrate beneath the rods were found to contribute to the preferential scattering of blue light (Walthall et al. 2003).

In ongoing surveys, the United Nations Office on Drugs and Crime (UNODC) has been using satellite imagery to monitor the growth of illicit crops such as cannabis, opium and coca (UNODC 2005a-d). Currently, methodologies employed in the surveys conducted in the different countries are not standardized, but follow similar principles of exploiting the phenological differences between the crops and other vegetation. Multispectral satellite imagery (i.e. SPOT, IKONOS, Quickbird), containing only a few bands sensitive to radiation spanning from the blue to shortwave infrared wavelengths, is the type of imagery most often used in the UNODC surveys due to its relatively low cost and high repeat acquisition. The illicit crop plantations in these countries are generally large in size and limited efforts are made to hide them in comparison to plantations in North America which are considerably smaller and in many cases significant efforts have been made by the growers to make their sites difficult to locate; posing a more difficult detection problem. Castro-Easu et al. (2006) illustrate the effect of the environment on vegetation spectral properties. ElSohly et al. (2006) found that the chemical composition of cannabis is altered by its environment. Therefore, it is possible to presume that the environment in which the cannabis plants are grown will effect their spectral signatures, potentially allowing for their discrimination from other vegetation.

Cannabis biological control measures

A significant amount of resources are spent every year to seize and destroy illicit drug cannabis growing operations. In some cases, deterrents have been tried in order to minimize the chances of recurring harvests, however, chemical and manual methods have been minimally effective as long-term controls (Tiourebaev et al. 2001). Use of conventional herbicides on cannabis growing operations, a common method in certain countries, is expensive both in terms of manpower and resources yet the plants are fairly resistant to most commercial herbicides which under some environmental conditions triggers a stress reaction in cannabis to raise the levels of THC.

In general, biological control measures of pests and weeds fell out of favor in the 1950s when a new range of chemical herbicides, pesticides, and fungicides became available. Over time these chemical control measures waned in effectiveness; the targets developed resistance, the chemicals were found to be expensive, adversely effecting non-target hosts, or not to be effective enough on the targets themselves (McPartland 2000, McPartland 1996). In light of these findings, natural predators and pathogens of the pests and weeds were re-examined for potential use as biological control measures.

There are a number of plant pathogens that attack weeds in general, but only a few have shown to be virulent enough to control weeds. While the biological control of cannabis pathogens has proven successful, the use of cannabis pathogens to control cannabis has not been effective (Tiourebaev et al. 2001); cannabis is often referred to as "*the weed with no enemies*" (McPartland et al. 2000, McPartland 1996, 1997). However, while cannabis is exceptionally pest-tolerant it is not pest-free. There are over 100 diseases and 300 insect pests described on cannabis, but less than a dozen cause noteworthy economic losses (McPartland et al. 2000, McPartland 1996, 1999b, 2000). In the case of cannabis all known pathogens that affect drug producing plants also affect industrial hemp plants. Thus, aggressive extermination protocols for the drug plants will also destroy a valuable industrial fiber and oil-seed crop (Thompson et al. 2007, McPartland 1999a).

Traditional biological control seeks to reduce the target weed population to a low level rather than complete extermination. Reduction without eradication is acceptable for most agricultural weeds, but is unacceptable for "zero tolerance" drug control, which seeks the *complete eradication* of a crop (McPartland 1999a). The epidemics required to eradicate entire plant populations are more frequently observed in monocultures that lack genetic diversity and when there is little physical distance between susceptible plants (Thompson et al. 2007). This is a potential weakness of cannabis crops; the plants are often monocultures and are physically spaced as tightly as the environmental conditions allow maximizing production and profits, yet evading detection. Epidemic pathogens are not common in nature since survival of the pathogen depends upon survival of the host. Total eradication of the host weed would not benefit the pathogen and such virulence is strongly selected against in nature (Gressel et al. 2007, Thompson et al. 2007).

Potential biological controls – Fungi

Research into the creation of fungal pathogens that destroy drug plants, including cannabis, that have been published date back to 1998. The fungi were genetically engineered to be of the 'epidemic' type of potency (McPartland 1999a). However, genetically transformed fungi are genetically unstable, mutate easily and are fraught with unpredictable environmental pitfalls. Exotic pathogens can readily spread from their intended targets to other organisms (Gressel et al. 2007, McPartland 1999a). And, once these pathogens are released into the environment, they cannot be recalled (McPartland 1999a). Furthermore, because these mycoherbicides are created to be fungicide resistant means it would be very difficult to eradicate them if they were to spread to non-target hosts such as industrial cannabis (McPartland 1999a). While there are a number of fungal species that can have severe effects on cannabis, only one has been identified as having the most potential as a mycoherbicide; *Fusarium oxysporum* (McPartland et al. 2000, McPartland 1999a).

F. oxysporum, occasionally referred to as Agent Green, is a fungal pathogen that causes *Fusarium wilt* disease in more than a hundred species of plants. *F. oxysporum* has several specialized forms – known as *formae specialis* (f.sp.) – that infect a variety of hosts causing different diseases. There is even one for cannabis; *F. oxysporum f.sp. Cannabis* (McPartland et al. 2000). However, even these specialized forms are not limited to their preferred host, and will affect susceptible neighbouring plant species.

Symptoms of infection in cannabis include yellowing, stunted growth, leaf curling, root discoloration, and loss of structural integrity in the upper portion of the plant (Tiourebaev et al. 2001). In one study it was argued that the various *F. oxysporum f.sp. Cannabis* pathogen strains were host-specific and will not negatively impact other plant species. This host-specificity allows the mycoherbicide to be applied to weed infestations within a crop or within a natural area, where it should leave the non-target host alone (Tiourebaev et al. 2001). These strains were evaluated for virulence on *C. sativa* (susceptible, positive control), tomato (*Lycopersicon esculentum*), corn (*Zeamays*), wheat (*Triticum aestivum*), beans (*Phaseolus vulgaris*), and potato (*Solanum tuberosum*). The authors however did not include data on what impacts these strains had on non-target hosts. In this study the most virulent strains of *F. oxysporum* showed symptoms on the cannabis plants two weeks after inoculation, while others showed effects after 6 weeks (Tiourebaev et al. 2001). Growing time for field plants is usually around 15-16 weeks, therefore depending on *when* in the growing stage the field is sprayed, the crop may be harvested before the mycoherbicide has had time to effectively eradicate the crop. A range of infection rate varied from 12%-66% of the target host (Tiourebaev et al. 2001). The actual average number infected across all test plots were about 1/3 of the total crop. It was not stressed in the report that infection with *F. oxysporum* does not necessarily mean rapid death of the plant. The researchers emphasized that the *F. oxysporum* can survive in the soil for many years, preventing re-establishment of the weed population, however when they tested their most virulent strains the following year, the majority had only minor effects on the new crop (Tiourebaev et al. 2001).

The genetically modified mycoherbicide approach can in theory totally eradicate a field of drug plants if given enough time to take effect, and inoculation over a succession of a few weeks (Tiourebaev et al. 2001). This approach, however, utilizes a delivery system similar to that of chemical herbicides – such as flying over fields while releasing the control agent. Thus the mycoherbicide approach, compared to the current chemical herbicide strategy, is equally expensive, may require re-treatment of annual crops, and is not 100% effective (McPartland 1999a).

Arthropods and insects

Over 300 insect pests have been described on cannabis plants, of these only a couple dozen cause notable damage to cannabis plants and there are no insect species that have cannabis as the preferred host (McPartland et al. 2000). In fact cannabis has such a powerful chemical defense that cannabis products are used as insecticides to protect other crops (McPartland 1997).

The Unites States Department of Agriculture set up a five-year study to determine the best insect species to use for biological control of cannabis by assessing the impact these pests have on the target plants. Five species were identified as potential control measures (USDA 2005): 1) The weevil *Cardipennis rubripes* 2) The weevil *Rhinoncus percarpus* 3) The flea beetle *Psylloides attenuata* 4) The hemp stem-borer *Grapholitha delineana* and 5) The hemp sawfly, *Trichiocampus Cannabis* (USDA 2005).

Most damaging to cannabis are the Borers, especially the European Corn Borer (ECB) (*Ostrinia nubilalis*) and the Hemp Borer (*Grapholita delineana*) (McPartland et al. 2000). Host plants of the ECB originally were hemp and hops, but they tend to prefer corn. The ECBs are moths that lay eggs on crops, these eggs develop into larvae that chew or 'bore' their way through the leaves, flowers and stems of the plant. On cannabis, 5-12 larvae can destroy a plant. The Hemp Borer, also known as the Hemp Moth, is slightly less virulent than ECB- each larva consumes about 16 cannabis seeds, and approximately 40 larvae will kill a cannabis seedling in ten days (McPartland et al. 2000; McPartland 1996). Both late season ECBs and Hemp Borers affect the top third of the plant, especially the flowering parts. In severe infestations Borers can destroy 80% of a crop's flowering top and 41% of seed crop (McPartland et al. 2000). However these two species of Borers will also attack Hops (*Humulus lupulus),* and therefore are not good candidates for biocontrol measures (McPartland 1999, McPartland 1996).

The Hemp Flea Beetle (*Psylliodes attenuata*) is another relatively prolific pest of cannabis, the larvae burrow into roots and adults eat leaves and flowering tops. The weevils *Ceutorhynchus rapae* and *Rhinocus pericarpius* bore in to the stem of plants causing harm but are generally not lethal to cannabis. However they do destroy hops (McPartland 1999, McPartland 1996). The Hemp Saw fly (*Trichiocampus Cannabis*) is not native to Europe or North America but is common in China where it has had significant impact on the industrial cannabis growing operation. Nevertheless it is easily treated with common, readily attainable chemical pesticides (McPartland 1999b).

The USDA project was abandoned in 2004, when it was concluded that none of the selected control insects had a high enough potency to warrant their destructive potential of non-target hosts, primarily hops, corn and rapeseed; Turner (1985) estimated that 21% of biocontrol insects intentionally introduced into North America have spread to non-target native plants (McPartland,1999a, USDA 2005).

Plants

Cannabis produces chemicals that limit the growth of other plant species nearby (McPartland et al. 2000), in other words cannabis fields do not need extensive weeding because they provide their own herbicide (McPartland 1997). There are two true plants that can outgrow and smother cannabis; Bamboo species and Giant Ragweed (*Ambrosia trifida)* (McPartland et al. 2000). If bamboo or ragweed is applied to the fields when the cannabis plants are still in the seedling stage (about 10-25 days), the bamboo or ragweed will catch up and overtake the growth of the cannabis and smother the field at around 10-15 weeks, or just prior to the crops' maturation for harvest (McPartland et al. 2000). Giant Ragweed is a well known agricultural weed, especially by corn and soybean farmers, and therefore is not a logical choice for reintroduction into areas where multi-decade long efforts to exterminate it have taken place (McPartland et al. 2000). Bamboo is used in China as a form of cannabis control, but in a large number of cases the bamboo became the next weed to control as it is a very prolific plant that is virtually impossible to eradicate once it is established.

Broomrape *(Orobanche ramose*) has been called the "only really serious enemy to hemp" (McPartland et al. 2000). However it is also a serious enemy to other plants such as tomato, eggplant, potato, cabbage, coleus, bell pepper, sunflower, celery, and bean, making it a dangerous control measure to use in field conditions. In tomatoes it will normally cause 75% crop loss, in sunflowers 90%, while in other plants severe infestation can cause total crop failure (McPartland et al. 2000). Broomrape is a parasitic plant, because it lacks chlorophyll it cannot photosynthesize and is thus completely dependent on other plants for survival. Once attached to a host, broomrape robs its host of water and nutrients, eventually killing it (McPartland et al. 2000). Broomrape is a serious agricultural pest, and much effort has been put towards containing and controlling its spread across agricultural areas. Ironically broomrape is best controlled by *F. oxysporum* – the same fungi used to control hemp growth (McPartland et al. 2000).

One method of controlling cannabis involves using another cannabis species. This method is not found in any scientific literature, but has made its way into grey journals and white books among the cannabis growing community. Rival growers sometimes try to either steal or destroy each other's crops in order to maximize value and profits of their own crop. One method that has had some success is planting industrial cannabis plants in a field of drug cannabis plants. The industrial cannabis strains tend to grow faster and taller than the drug strains. The industrial cannabis controls in two ways: 1) the higher growth smothers the slower growing drug plants and 2) the industrial cannabis male plants pollinate the drug cannabis female plants. Pollination lowers the THC levels and therefore lowers the value of the crop. Secondly the low THC industrial cannabis male plants are breeding with the high THC drug females, so the seeds from the crop are useless for the next growing operation because the offspring would be relatively low THC plants and have little value.

Animals

Animals are well known pests of outdoor and indoor cannabis growing operations. While the total effects of animal pest on annual crop harvest is overall insignificant, in individual growing areas, a combination of pests or even one species of animal pest can decimate the entire crop (McPartland et al. 2000, McPartland 1996, 1999b, 2000).

Birds pose a threat to cannabis seeds and there are anecdotal descriptions of flocks of bird descending on freshly sown fields and consuming virtually every seed (McPartland et al. 2000, McPartland 1996), however seeds will still germinate after passing through the gastrointestinal tract of the bird, provided they were not cracked (McPartland et al. 2000). Wild deer and rabbits cause damage to seedlings, and in years or areas with no other pasture, will consume and destroy the entire fields of cannabis crop (McPartland et al. 2000). Industrial cannabis farmers lose about 7% of their crop to birds feeding on seeds and deer feeding on seedlings (McPartland 1999b).

Cattle, mules, donkeys and horses all can graze on the flowering tops of plants (McPartland et al. 2000, McPartland 1999b). Some breeds of dogs also consume cannabis, especially the flowering tops and can create problems for indoor growers who use the dogs as security to protect the crop from theft and sabotage (McPartland et al. 2000). Sheep, goats and most species of cattle prefer cannabis species to many grass species and will selectively seek and consume it in a mixed field (McPartland et al. 2000). Goats and sheep consume the *entire* plant with no ill effects (McPartland et al. 2000). One goat can graze one acre of cannabis down to 'golf course evenness in 30 days' (McPartland et al. 2000). A small herd of goats can decimate an entire field of mature plants in less than 2 days. There have been anecdotes of illicit growers in Hawaii utilizing goats to sabotage their competitors' crops. Using livestock to control feral cannabis is commonplace, but no published research has been found on using livestock to intentionally control cannabis growing operations.

Soil nutrient and contaminants

Many plant species cannot survive in conditions with a high concentration of heavy metal pollutants. Cannabis, however, hyper-accumulates elements or compounds from the soil and can tolerate high levels of contamination relatively well (McPartland et al. 2000). Growing in heavy metal contaminated soil, cannabis was found to be only minimally affected in most plant functions such as root development, plant growth and photosynthetic capacity even at levels of contamination that were lethal to most other plant species in the experiments (Linger et al. 2005, McPartland et al. 2000). Linger et al. (2005) found that cannabis plants treated with high levels of cadmium had better germination rates than the controls. In other plants, photosynthesis and cellular respiration are particularly affected by heavy metals and therefore, makes them more vulnerable to other control measures and mechanisms (Citterio et al. 2003).

Other common drug producing plants such as *Erythroxylum coca* (Coca) and *Papaver somniferum* (Opium) do not have the same resistance to heavy metals as cannabis (Citterio et al. 2003). Aerial spraying of fields with herbicide containing cadmium, copper, nickel and other metals, are effective in controling some plant species but have been found to be only minimally effective on cannabis (Citterio et al. 2003).

The tolerance of cannabis to contamination has been exploited in industrial uses to clean up contaminated soils. Campbell et al. (2002) found that the plants significantly reduced the concentration of chrysene and benzo[a]pyrene, two polycyclic aromatic hydrocarbons in a clay soil. Cannabis has also been successfully used to remove lead, zinc and cadmium contamination from soils (Kos and Lestan 2004). The amount of heavy metals extractable by cannabis in contrast to other plants varies across studies. In one study Kos et al. (2003) found the potential uptake of lead amounted to 26.3kg/ha. They caution however, that full environmental remediation is unlikely to be achieved with one single crop. In an innovative application at the time, in 1998, Bast Crops, Phytotech, and Consolidated Growers and Processors successfully used industrial cannabis to remove soil contaminants near Chernobyl (Guterman 1999). The means through which the plants cope with the heavy metal uptake is still largely unknown but thought to be a series of chronic stress adaptation mechanisms at the molecular level (Bona et al. 2007).

Salt is one compound that cannabis does not tolerate (McPartland et al. 2000). The salt content in ocean spray is enough to ruin an entire crop, which is one reason why it is rare to find outdoor cannabis growing operations near the coastline. Spraying saline solution onto fields may be an effective method of crop eradication. Salting fields may be a cost effective option for permanently (10-15 years) ruining a cannabis grow-up, while still allowing saline-tolerant plants to grow (McPartland et al. 2000). Once the plants have taken up the salt, the damage is virtually irreversible.

This same ability of cannabis plants to hyper-accumulate heavy metals that has been exploited in soil remediation can also become a health concern for consumers of cannabis from the illicit market. There are virtually no rigorous standards among the growers and the soil/growth-media in which the plants are grown vary depending both on logistics and personal preference.

Figure 13.2 and Table 13.3 illustrate the concentrations of 21 common soil elements from samples taken at several large commercial illicit grow-ops in Eastern Canada. In Canada, drug cannabis can be found planted directly into the soil or planted in containers. Sometimes growers use specialized growth media, fertilizers, herbicides or insecticides, but the application of these products is not consistent among sites. This inconsistency in the composition of the growth media can be seen in Table 13.3 and Figure 13.2. The amount of uptake by cannabis of the various elements depends on several factors from the age of the plants to their overall stress level. Nevertheless, in a soil matrix with a greater amount of elements available, the uptake will be more than in soils that do not contain the elements. This variety in the composition of the growth media becomes a health concern to the consumers in cases where the growers apply too much chemicals to the soil (or grow cannabis in contaminated soil, for example abandoned factory or industry land) which can be taken up by the plants and subsequently consumed. Of particular concern is prolonged consumption of cannabis products from contaminated sites, especially to individuals whose health may be otherwise compromised.

Conclusion

This chapter has outlined the unique characteristics of cannabis as well as the various efforts surrounding biological control. Although the acceptance of different species of cannabis is still controversial, three main varieties have been shown: *C. sativa, C. indica, C. ruderalis*, and are actively being used in breeding programs to produce news strains with specific characteristics.

From an ecological perspective, cannabis is a relatively hardy plant. However, it does have specific needs and characteristics that can be exploited by growers. These same needs and characteristics can also be employed by law enforcement agencies to optimize searches and the detection of illicit cannabis grow operations. In this regard, cannabis plants contain several unique chemical compounds which

Table 13.3 **Concentration of common soil elements from commercial cannabis operations, natural forest soil and two popular growth media mixes [*]**

Sampling Site	Copper (PPM)	Lead (PPM)	Zinc (PPM)	Nickel (PPM)	Cobalt (PPM)	Manganese (PPM)	Iron (%)	Strontium (PPM)	Vanadium (PPM)	Calcium (%)	Phosphorus (%)
Eastern 1	19 ± 2.0	12 ± 2.0	53 ± 6.0	6 ± 0.6	4 ± 0.6	502 ± 53.8	0.90 ± 0.07	40 ± 3.8	21 ± 1.5	0.9 ± 0.10	0.1 ± 0.01
Eastern 2	28 ± 0.6	6 ± 0.6	91 ± 7.0	10 ± 1.0	5 ± 0.0	201 ± 32.9	0.48 ± 0.06	60 ± 3.0	16 ± 0.6	2.3 ± 0.20	0.7 ± 0.08
Eastern 3	10 ± 0.0	8 ± 0.6	35 ± 1.0	8 ± 0.6	5 ± 0.0	604 ± 32.5	1.09 ± 0.03	24 ± 1.0	23 ± 1.0	1.1 ± 0.01	0.1 ± 0.00
Eastern 4	18 ± 0.0	17 ± 1.2	99 ± 1.0	6 ± 0.0	3 ± 0.6	398 ± 11.9	0.87 ± 0.02	29 ± 0.6	15 ± 1.0	1.2 ± 0.02	0.9 ± 0.00
Eastern 5*	17 ± 0.0	12 ± 1.5	141 ± 0.6	17 ± 0.6	10 ± 0.0	588 ± 12.1	2.26 ± 0.03	24 ± 0.0	49 ± 0.6	0.5 ± 0.01	0.08 ± 0.00
Eastern 6*	15 ± 0.6	10 ± 1.7	69 ± 2.0	19 ± 0.6	11 ± 0.6	517 ± 36.0	2.44 ± 0.08	22 ± 0.6	52 ± 2.0	0.4 ± 0.01	0.08 ± 0.00
Eastern 7	6 ± 0.6	11 ± 1.5	48 ± 0.6	7 ± 0.0	5 ± 0.6	1,081 ± 27.1	1.32 ± 0.02	51 ± 6.6	28 ± 1.0	0.9 ± 0.04	0.16 ± 0.00
Forest	14 ± 3.6	10 ± 0.0	27 ± 7.9	3 ± 1.5	4 ± 1.7	187 ± 55.8	0.99 ± 0.28	28 ± 9.5	27 ± 7.6	0.5 ± 0.15	0.04 ± 0.01
High Organic	7 ± 2.3	15 ± 1.2	15 ± 1.2	1 ± 0.0	1 ± 0.0	133 ± 6.4	0.09 ± 0.00	60 ± 1.5	1 ± 0.6	1.5 ± 0.10	0.2 ± 0.00
Potting Mix	62 ± 5.7	15 ± 1.0	140 ± 14.9	9 ± 1.0	2 ± 0.6	294 ± 36.5	0.64 ± 0.08	57 ± 5.9	14 ± 1.5	1.6 ± 0.17	0.4 ± 0.06

Sampling Site	Lanthanum (PPM)	Chromium (PPM)	Magnesium (%)	Barium (PPM)	Titanium (%)	Aluminum (%)	Sodium (%)	Potassium (%)	Sulfur (%)
Eastern 1	40±4.4	11±1.5	0.19±0.02	103±12.1	0.04±0.01	0.62±0.07	-	0.10±0.01	0.21±0.02
Eastern 2	6±3.8	15±1.2	0.75±0.08	81±3.5	0.03±0.00	0.33±0.04	0.02±0.00	0.66±0.07	0.32±0.02
Eastern 3	11±0.6	14±0.6	0.51±0.00	75±2.7	0.04±0.01	0.85±0.03	0.04±0.00	0.41±0.01	0.26±0.00
Eastern 4	9±1.2	9±0.0	0.42±0.01	102±6.9	0.02±0.00	0.60±0.02	-	0.18±0.01	0.14±0.00
Eastern 5*	36±0.6	31±0.6	0.55±0.01	140±1.2	0.12±0.00	1.85±0.01	0.02±0.00	0.20±0.00	-
Eastern 6*	23±0.6	32±1.2	0.64±0.01	153±4.0	0.13±0.00	2.14±0.07	0.02±0.00	0.26±0.01	-
Eastern 7	23±1.2	16±0.0	0.42±0.01	148±3.5	0.03±0.00	1.09±0.02	-	0.24±0.00	0.12±0.01
Forest	2±0.6	5±2.5	0.36±0.12	35±5.6	0.04±0.01	1.03±0.27	0.04±0.02	0.45±0.16	0.08±0.03
High Organic	1±0.0	1±0.0	0.24±0.01	24±1.0	0.01±0.00	0.04±0.00	0.05±0.01	2.04±0.03	0.41±0.02

[*] The numbers denote the average with one standard deviation for the concentration of the elements in either parts-per-million (PPM) or percent (%) as indicated in the table. N = 3 for the calculation of each average and standard deviation value. Planting *Cannabis* outdoors in soil (without pots) is a relatively common occurrence on the West Coast of Canada. The "Forest" sample illustrates the composition of forest soil in an area of Western Canada that is known for a high density of such grow-ops. Sampling sites with a * are at the same large commercial growing operation in Eastern Canada. The High Organic and Potting Mix samples are growing media commonly found in Western Canadian grow-ops. A value of – indicates the concentration of that element was below the detection threshold.

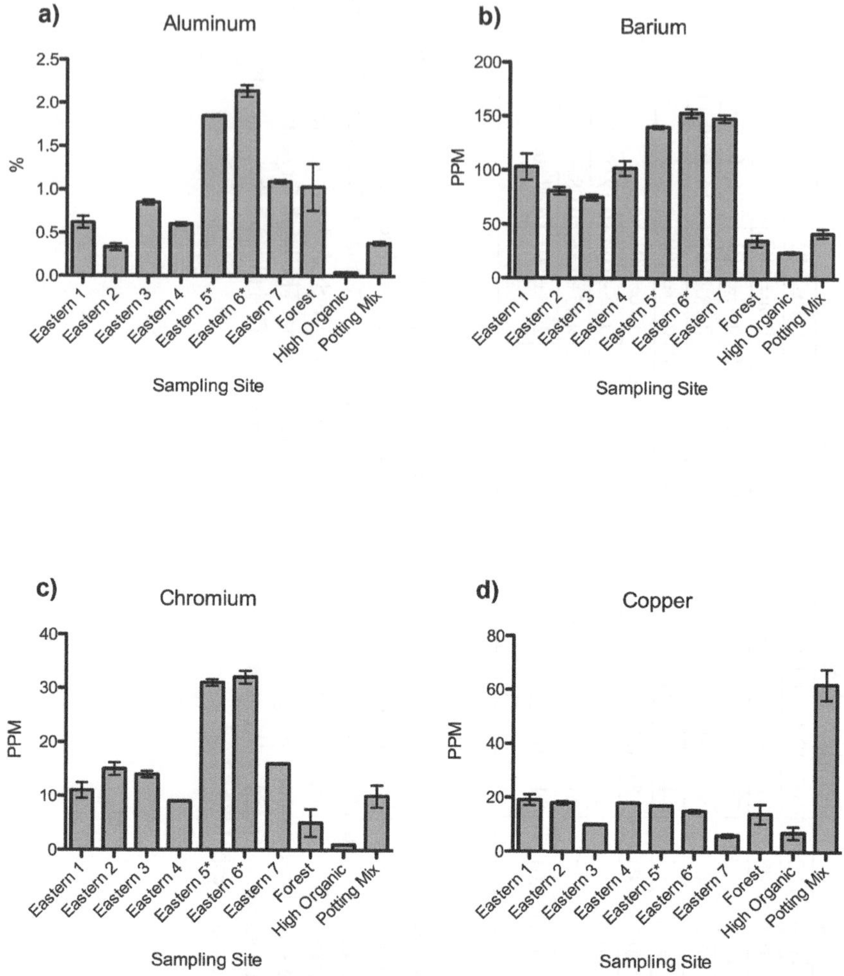

Figure 13.2 Mean ± one standard deviation of the concentration of aluminum, barium, chromium, copper, lanthanum, lead, manganese and zinc from commercial Cannabis operations, natural forest soil and two popular growth media mixes[*].

[*] Planting *Cannabis* outdoors in soil (without pots) is a relatively common occurrence on the West Coast of Canada. The "Forest" sample illustrates the composition of forest soil in an area of Western Canada that is known for a high density of such grow-ops. Sampling sites with a * are at the same large commercial growing operation in Eastern Canada. The High Organic and Potting Mix samples are growing media commonly found in Western Canadian grow-ops.

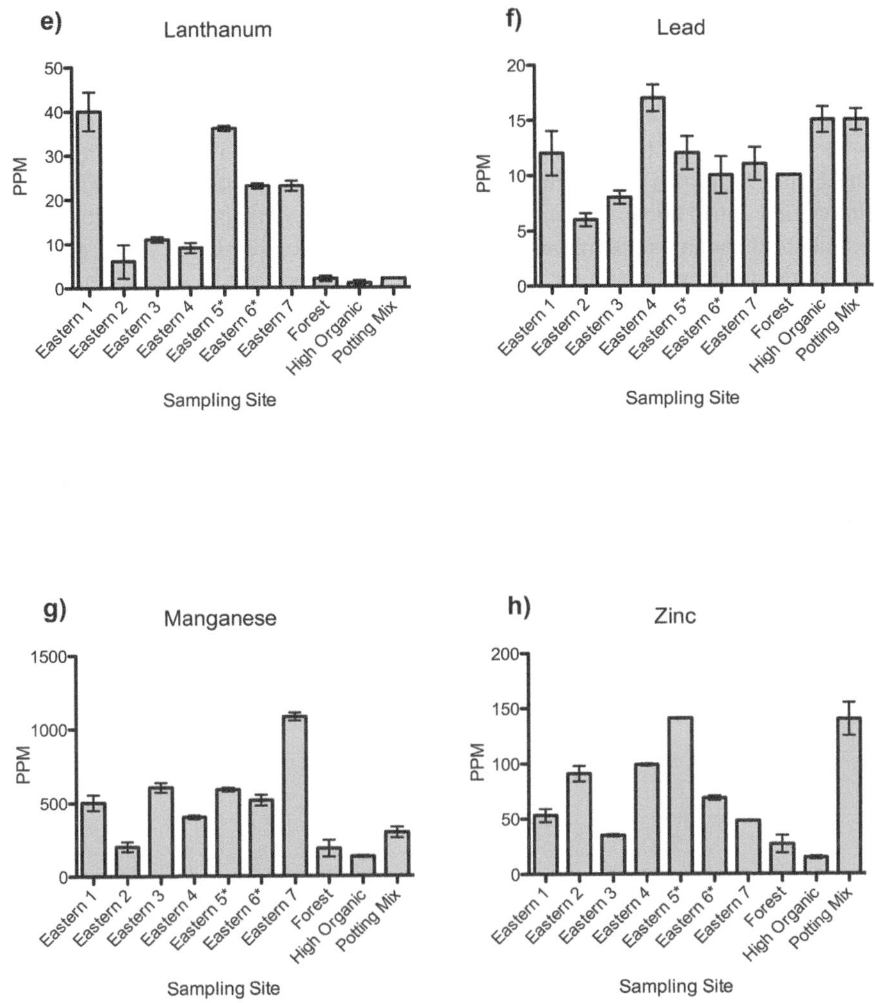

Figure 13.2 cont.

may in part be contributing to their unique spectral characteristics. It has also been shown that both age and environment affect the chemical composition of the plants, allowing for the development of chemical fingerprints.

It is also important to emphasize that the area of cannabis genetics is a relatively new area of research but is expanding as breeders seek to exploit the most desired traits in their plants. By understanding the drivers behind the unique spectral signature of cannabis, remote sensing technology could be better exploited to locate the illicit outdoor grow operations that exist in North America. These operations present a more difficult problem for law enforcement agencies as they are typically smaller with more effort made by the growers to conceal their site. This is in contrast to other countries in the world where illicit crop plantations are very large in size and minimal efforts are made to hide them.

Research has shown that biological control of cannabis is inherently difficult as the plant is very tolerant and has the ability to thrive in contaminated soils. These characteristics make cannabis an effective plant for soil remediation. Most biological control agents that are detrimental to drug cannabis are also detrimental to industrial cannabis (hemp) and other agricultural crops and therefore, cannot be used at the landscape scale for drug cannabis eradication.

Finally, the ability of the cannabis plants to hyperaccumulate heavy metals and other elements may become a health concern for consumers as they may be exposed to chemical contaminants from the cannabis products they consume. The real possibility exists for growers to apply excessive chemicals to the soils that can be taken up by the plants and unknowingly be consumed by individuals emphasizing the need for education and regulation of cannabis production.

List of references

Asner, G.P. 1998. Biophysical and biochemical sources of variability in canopy reflectance. *Remote Sensing of Environment*, 64, 234-53.

Brenneisen, R. 2006. Chemistry and analysis of phytocannabinoids and other cannabis constituents, in *Marijuana and the cannabinoids*, edited by M.A. ElSohly. Totowa, NJ: Humana Press, 17-50.

Campbell, N.A. and Reece, J.B. 2007. *Biology*. Pearson / Benjamin Cummings.

Castro-Esau, K.L., Sanchez-Azofeifa G.A. et al. 2006. Variability in leaf optical properties of Mesoamerican trees and the potential for species classification. *American Journal of Botany*, 93, 517-30.

Cho, M.A. and Skidmore, A.K. 2006. A new technique for extracting the red edge position from hyperspectral data: the linear extrapolation method. *Remote Sensing of Environment*, 101, 181-93.

Citterio, S., Santagostino, A. et al. 2003. Heavy metal tolerance and accumulation of Cd, Cr and Ni by Cannabis sativa L. *Plant and Soil*, 256, 243-52.

Clarke, R.C. and Watson, D.P. 2006. Cannabis and natural Cannabis medicines, in *Marijuana and the cannabinoids*, edited by M.A. ElSohly. Totowa, NJ: Humana Press, 1-15.

Datwyler, S. and Weiblen, G. 2006. Genetic variation in hemp and marijuana (Cannabis sativa L.) according to amplified fragment length polymorphisms. *Journal of Forensic Science*, 51, 371-75.

Daughtry, C.S.T. and Walthall, C.L. 1998. Spectral discrimination of Cannabis sativa L. leaves and canopies. *Remote Sensing of Environment*, 64, 192-201.

ElSohly, M.A. 2002. Chemical constituents of Cannabis, in *Cannabinoids-Pharmacology, Toxicology, and Therapeutic Potential*, edited by F. Grotenherman and E. Ruso. New York, NY: Haworth Press, 27-36.

ElSohly, M.A., Standford, D.F. et al. 2006. Chemical fingerprinting of Cannabis as a means of source identification, in *Marijuana and the cannabinoids*, edited by M.A. ElSohly. Totowa, NJ: Humana Press, 51-64.

Faeti, V., Mandolino, G. et al. 2006. Genetic diversity of Cannabis sativa germplasm based on RAPD markers. *Plant Breeding*, 115(5), 367-70.

Flachowsky, H., Schumann, E. et al. 2008. Application of AFLP for the detection of sex-specific markers in hemp. *Plant Breeding*, 120(4), 305-309.

Forapani, S., Carboni, A. et al. 2001. Comparison of hemp varieties using random amplified polymorphic DNA markers. *Crop science*, 41, 1682-9.

Gamon, J.A., Penuelas, J. et al. 1992. A narrow-band spectral index that tracks diurnal changes in photosynthetic efficiency. *Remote Sensing of Environment*, 41, 35-44.

Gates, D.M., Keegan, H.J. et al. 1965. Spectral properties of plants. *Applied Optics,* 4(1), 11-20.

Gilmore, S. and Peakall, R. 2003. Isolation of microsatellite markers in Cannabis sativa L. (marijuana). *Molecular Ecology Notes,* 3(1), 105-7.

Green, G. 2005. *The Cannabis breeder's bible: The definitive guide to marijuana genetics, Cannabis botany and creating strains for the seed market.* San Francsico, CA: Green Candy Press.

Gressel, J., Meir, S. et al. 2007. Approaches to and successes in developing transgenetically enhanced mycoherbicides, in *Novel Biotechnologies for Biocontrol Agent Enhancement and Management,* edited by M. Vurro and J. Gressel. Dordrecht: Springer, 297-306.

Guo, J. and Trotter, C.M. 2004. Estimating photosynthetic light-use efficiency using the photochemical reflectance index: variations among species. *Functional Plant Biology,* 31, 255-65.

Hakki, E., Uz, E. et al. 2003. Genotyping of Cannabis sativa L. accessions from Turkey using RAPD and AFLP markers. *Journal of Forensic Science*, 136, 31-41.

Health Canada 2006. *About hemp and Canada's hemp industry*. Available at: http://www.hc-sc.gc.ca/hc-ps/substancontrol/hemp-chanvre/about-apropos/index-eng.php [accessed: 20 August 2010].

Kalacska M. and Bouchard M. 2010. Using police seizure data to estimate the size of an outdoor cannabis industry. *Police Practice and Research: An International Journal.* First published on 7 April 2011. DOI: 10.1080/15614263.2010.536722

Kalacska M. and Bouchard M. 2010. Using police seizure data and hyperspectral imagery to estimate the size of an outdoor cannabis industry. Police Practice and Research: An International Journal. First published on 7 April 2011. DOI: 10.1080/15614263.2010.536722

Linger, P., Ostwald, A. et al. 2005. Cannabis sativa L. growing on heavy metal contaminated soil: growth, cadmium uptake and photosynthesis. *Biologia Plantarum*, 49(4), 567-76.

McPartland, J.M. 1996. Cannabis pests. *Journal of the International Hemp Association,* 3(2), 52-55.

McPartland, J.M. 1997. Cannabis as repellent and pesticide. *Journal of the International Hemp Association*, 4(2), 87-92.

McPartland, J.M. 1999. Killing Cannabis with mycoherbicides. *Journal of the International Hemp Association,* 6(1), 4-8.

McPartland, J.M. 1999. A Survey of Hemp Diseases and Pests, in *Advances in hemp research*, edited by P. Ranalli. New York, NY: Food Productions Press, 109-32.

McPartland, J.M. 2000. Biological Control of Hemp Diseases and Pests. Paper presented at the *Third International Symposium: Bioresource Hemp*. Wolfsburg (Germany), 13-16th September, 2000. Available at: http://www.nova-institut.de/secure/mcpartland-2-e.pdf [accessed: 25 October 2010].

McPartland, J.M., Connell, R. et al. 2000. *Hemp diseases and pests : management and biological control*. New York, NY: CABI Publisher.

Mechoulam, R. and Gaoni, Y. 1967. Recent advances in the chemistry of hashish. *Fortshritte der chemie organischer*, 25, 175-213.

Mediavilla, V. and Steinmann, S. 1997. Essential oil of Cannabis sativa L. strains. *Journal of the International Hemp Association*, 4, 80-82.

Moliterni, C.V.M., Cattivelli, L. et al. 2004. The sexual differentiation of Cannabis sativa L.: A morphological and molecular study. *Euphytica*, 140, 95-06.

Novak, J., Zitterl-Eglseer, K. et al. 2001. Essential oils of different cultivars of Cannabis sativa L. and their antimicrobial activity. *Flavour and Fragrance Journal*, 16(4), 259-62.

Peil, A., Flachowsky, H. et al. 2003. Sex-linked AFLP markers indicate a pseudoautosomal region in hemp (Cannabis sativa L.). *Theoretical and applied genetics,* 107(1), 102-9.

Sakamoto, K., Shimomura, K. et al. 1995. A Male-Associated DNA Sequence in a Dioecious Plant, Cannabis sativa L. *Plant and Cell Physiology*, 36(8), 1549-54.

Schultes, R.E., Klein, W.M. et al. 1974. Cannabis: an example of taxonomic neglect. *Botanical Museum Leaflets,* 23(9), 337-67.

Sims, D.A. and Gamon, J.A. 2002. Relationships between leaf pigment content and spectral reflectance across a wide range of species, leaf structures and development stages. *Remote Sensing of Environment*, 81(2-3), 337-54.

Stylinski, C.D., Gamon, J.A. et al. 2002. Seasonal patterns of reflectance indices, carotenoid pigments and photosynthesis of evergreen chaparral species. *Oecologia,* 131(3), 366-74.

Thompson, B., Kirkpatrick, M. et al. 2007. Genetically enhancing the efficacy of plant pathogens for control of weeds, in *Novel Biotechnologies for Biocontrol Agent Enhancement and Management*, edited by M. Vurro and J. Gressel. Dordrecht: Springer, 267-76.

Tiourebaev, K.S., Semenchenko, G.V. et al. 2001. Biological Control of Infestations of Ditchweed (Cannabis sativa) with Fusarium oxysporum f.sp.Cannabis in Kazakhstan. *Biocontrol Science and Technology,* 11(4), 535-40.

United Nations Office on Drugs and Crime 2005a. *Maroc, enquête sur le Cannabis 2004*. Geneva, Switzerland: United Nations.

United Nations Office on Drugs and Crime 2005b. *Afghanistan, Opium Rapid assessment survey*. Vienna, Austria: United Nations.

United Nations Office on Drugs and Crime 2005c. *Myanmar Opium survey*. Vienna, Austria: United Nations.

United Nations Office on Drugs and Crime 2005d. *Colombia, Coca cultivation survey*. Vienna, Austria: United Nations.

United Nations Office on Drugs and Crime 2006. 2006 *World drug report, part 1: analysis*. Vienna, Austria: United Nations.

USDA 2005. *Classical Biological Control of Narcotic Plants- Annual Report 2005.* The Exotic and Invasive Weeds Research Unit: United States Department of Agriculture-Agricultural Research Service.

van der Meer, F. 1999. Physical principles of optical remote sensing, in *Statistics for remote sensing*, edited by F. van der Meer and B. Gorte. Boston: Kluwer Academic Press, 27-40.

Walthall, C.L., Daughtry, C.S.T. et al. 2003. *What do we know about spectral signatures of illegal Cannabis cultivation?* Beltsville, MD: USDA-ARS Hydrology and remote sensing laboratory.

Chapter 14
The Seizure Rate of Cannabis Crop Eradication Operations in New Zealand, 1998-2009[1]

Chris Wilkins and Paul Sweetsur

Introduction

New Zealand is believed to have been self sufficient in the domestic supply of cannabis since the early 1990s (Staff 1988, Yska 1990, NDIB 2007, Newbold 2000). The smuggling of cannabis sticks from Thailand in the 1970s was gradually replaced by the domestic cultivation of cannabis during the 1980s to the point where cannabis supply is now thought to be entirely meet by local cultivation. New Zealand's geographical isolation, small population and strong border protection make the smuggling of bulky illegal drugs, such as cannabis, across the border both costly and risky and hence bestow a natural advantage on domestic cannabis cultivation (New Zealand Customs 2002).

Large scale commercial outdoor cannabis cultivation occurs in a number of rural regions in New Zealand including the Bay of Plenty, Eastern District and Northland (Staff 1988, Yska 1990, Walker et al. 1998). A number of factors have contributed to making outdoor cannabis cultivation a popular illegal cash crop in New Zealand including the mild climate, the ready availability of isolated bush and forest land to conceal crops, the ingenuity of the local people, and the limited economic opportunities in some rural areas (McLaughlan 1996, Walker et al. 1998, Wilkins and Casswell 2003). In some economically depressed rural

1 We would like to thank the New Zealand National Drug Intelligence Bureau (NDIB), New Zealand Police, the Dunedin Multidisciplinary Health and Development Research Unit and the Christchurch Health and Development Study at the University of Otago for providing data for this chapter. The analysis in this chapter drew on data from the 1998, 2001, 2003, 2006 and 2009 New Zealand National Household Drug Surveys (NZNHDS). The 2006 and 2009 NZNHDS were funded by the National Drug Policy Discretionary Fund (NDPDF). The 2003 NZNHDS was directly funded by the New Zealand Ministry of Health. The 1998 and 2001 NZNHDS were funded by contestable research grants from the Health Research Council (HRC) and partially by direct funding from the New Zealand Ministry of Health.

towns the money from cannabis cultivation is now an important source of seasonal income (Walker et al. 1998).

The principal response of the New Zealand Police to the illegal cultivation of cannabis since the early 1980s has been to conduct annual cannabis crop eradication operations, currently known as the National Cannabis and Crime Operation (NCCO)[2] (NDIB 2007). The NCCO involves the use of fix winged aircraft and helicopters to spot and destroy cannabis plants and is conducted in most rural districts in New Zealand. The NCCO regularly detects over 1,000 cannabis plots, destroys over 100,000 cannabis plants and arrests hundreds of offenders, as well as recovering firearms and stolen property.

Some commentators have expressed scepticism about the effectiveness of the NCCO (Drug Policy Forum Trust 1998, Dawkins 2001, NORML 2001). However, an early attempt to quantify the effectiveness of the NCCO in the late 1990s indicated the operation achieved a fairly high seizure rate, particularly when compared to the seizure rates reported for other drug types in other countries (Wilkins et al. 2002a).

While seizures rates are imperfect measures of the effectiveness of drug enforcement (see Reuter et al. 1988), they are superior to merely reporting the total number of seizure incidents or the total quantity of a drug seized. Seizure rates place the quantity of a drug seized in the wider context of the size of the illegal market for the drug (see Sutton and Maynard 1994). This is important as larger seizures of a drug may not necessarily represent increased enforcement effectiveness if the total size of the illegal market for the drug is growing at a faster rate than seizures. Conversely, smaller seizures of a drug may not necessarily represent decreased enforcement effectiveness if the total size of the illegal drugs market is shrinking at a faster rate than seizures.

An interesting research question is therefore, how has the cannabis seizure rate of the NCCO changed over the past ten years, and what are the implications for its future effectiveness. There has been some progress with the methodology and data available to calculate the cannabis seizure rate of the NCCO over the past decade or so which further supports the case for a return to this topic. The aim of this chapter was therefore to estimate the cannabis seizure rate of the NCCO for the years 1998, 2001, 2003, 2006 and 2009.

Method

The seizure rate for a drug is simply the total quantity of a drug seized by the authorities divided by total quantity of the drug produced (see Sutton and Maynard 1994, Wilkins et al. 2002a). The total quantity of a drug produced is the quantity seized plus the quantity which is not seized. Drug enforcement

2 The operation has previously been known as the 'Annual National Cannabis Recovery Operation' and the 'National Cannabis Eradication Programme' (NDIB 2007).

agencies are generally able to provide good statistical data on the quantity of a drug type they have seized each year. The principal challenge with calculating seizure rates is to estimate the quantity of a drug which is not seized by the authorities. Drugs which are not detected by the authorities are eventually consumed by drug users. National population drug surveys which measure the level of drug use in the general population can therefore potentially be used to estimate the total quantity of a drug consumed and not seized by the authorities.

General population survey methodology

The New Zealand National Household Drug Survey (NZNHDS) interviews a random national sample of people living in households in New Zealand using a Computer Assisted Telephone Interview (CATI) facility (see Wilkins and Sweetsur 2008). A CATI system allows for close supervision of interviewers to ensure the collection of quality data, and allows a high number of call-

Table 14.1 Characteristics of the New Zealand National Household Drug Survey (NZNHDS), 1998-2009

Survey wave	Age range (years)	Sample size (number of people)	Response rate (%)
1998	15-45	5,475	79
2001	15-45	5,504	80
2003	13-65	8,245	68
2006	13-45	2,010	69
2009	13-45	2,040	64

Source: Wilkins and Sweetsur 2008

backs to be completed at relatively low financial cost. The NZNHDS contacts respondents up to 10 times per interview shift on different days and times of the week in an effort to reach those seldom at home. NZNHDS surveys have been completed using the same CATI methodology in 1998, 2001, 2003, 2006 and 2009. The age range and sample sizes of the different NZNHDS surveys have changed from wave to wave in response to funding and research priorities (see Table 14.1). There has been some decline in the response rate of the NZNHDS over the past ten years due to an increase in commercial telephone marketing in New Zealand, but the response rates achieved still compare well with national drug surveys conducted in other countries.

Measures of cannabis consumption

The NZNHDS collects particularly comprehensive data on cannabis consumption when compared to national population drug surveys conducted around the world (see Wilkins et al. 2005). The NZNHDS not only collects data on the prevalence of cannabis use (i.e. whether a respondent has used cannabis in the previous 12 months), it also collects data of the frequency of cannabis use and the quantity of cannabis consumed. Respondents are asked how many times they have used cannabis in the previous 12 months, and how much cannabis they would consume on a typical occasion. The interviewer is provided with coded answers for number of joints and grams of cannabis. The New Zealand Institute of Environmental Science and Research (ESR) has previously estimated that an average cannabis joint in New Zealand contains 0.5 grams of cannabis (Bates 1998). To account for the fact that cannabis is commonly consumed in groups (see Wilkins et al. 2002), survey respondents are first asked how many people they typically shared a cannabis joint with. If the respondent indicates they typically used cannabis in a group they are then asked how many people they would typically smoke cannabis with and how much cannabis the group would typically use. The quantity of cannabis smoked by the group is divided by the number of members in the group to obtain the amount smoked by the individual respondent. The cannabis consumption data can therefore be a fraction of a joint as a single joint is often shared by a group of people. There was limited funding to conduct the 2006 NZNHDS and as a result only the prevalence and frequency of cannabis use questions were asked and no questions were included on the quantity of cannabis used. To calculate the 2006 estimates we used the mean quantity of cannabis consumed on a typical occasion from the 2009 survey.

Population estimates of cannabis consumption

To calculate the population estimates of cannabis consumption we multiplied the mean frequency of cannabis use by the mean quantity of cannabis used on a typical occasion by the weighted number of last year cannabis users in the survey by a population factor. The population factor is the population in a given year divided by the sample size of the NZNHDS in the same year. We wanted to calculate the most comprehensive estimate for each year so we used data from the 2003 survey (which had the widest age range, 13-65 years old) to extend the age range of all the estimates to 13-65 years old. The 2003 NZNHDS was used to determine the ratio of the prevalence of cannabis use among 46-65 year olds and 13-14 years olds compared to 15-45 year olds. This ratio was used to expand out the estimates by dividing the total quantity of cannabis consumed by those aged 15-45 years old by the ratio and then multiplying this result by the population aged 13-14/46-65 years old divided by the population aged 15-45 years old. All our estimates are produced with the 95% Confidence Interval.

This process can be illustrated with the estimation of total cannabis consumed in 2006. Using the 2003 data, the prevalance of cannabis use was 6 times greater among 13-45 years olds than 46-65 year olds. The New Zealand population in 2006 aged 46-65 years old was 969,540 people. The 13-45 year old population in 2006 was 1,978,080 people. The quantity of cannabis consumed by the population aged 13-45 years old in 2006 was 13,530,295 grams. The quantity of cannabis consumed by 46-65 year olds in 2006 was (969,540/1,978,080)*(13,530,295/6) = 1,105,294 grams. The total quantity of cannabis consumed by 13-65 year olds in 2006 was therefore 13,530,295 grams + 1,105,294 grams = 14,635,589 grams.

Accounting for underreporting of cannabis use

A limitation with estimates of illegal drug consumption made using general population survey data is that survey respondents tend to underreport illegal drug use (MacCoun and Reuter 2001). Respondents may be reluctant to report the full extent of their illegal drug using behaviour as they are concerned about attention from the authorities, their personal reputation or they may simply have difficulty recalling their drug use episodes with precision.

Methodological studies in the United States which have examined the level of survey underreporting of illegal drug use in population household drug surveys have found underreporting varies considerably according to the type of drug in question (see Fendrich et al. 2004, Harrison et al. 2007). Drug types which are more widely accepted and which attract fairly light legal penalties, such as cannabis, are associated with much less survey underreporting than drug types which attract heavier legal penalties and are associated with higher levels of social stigma, such as heroin, cocaine and methamphetamine (see Fendrich et al. 2004, Harrison et al. 2007). Fendrich et al. (2004) found 78% of respondents in a household survey who tested positive for cannabis use using urine, hair and oral fluid tests had earlier self-reported using cannabis use in the past 12 months. In contrast, only 23% of those testing positive for cocaine use and 20% of those testing positive for heroin use had self-reported use in the past 12 months. Unfortunately there has been no similar New Zealand study of the level of underreporting of drug use by the NZNHDS.

An alternative approach to accounting for survey underreporting which we have used in previous New Zealand calculations (see Wilkins et al. 2002b) is to compare levels of self-reported drug use from the NZNHDS with levels of self-reported drug use from New Zealand Longitudinal Studies which also ask about drug use. Longitudinal studies repeatedly interview the same birth cohort of individuals on an ongoing basis over many decades from a very young age all the way through to adulthood. This allows researchers to build a high level of trust and rapport with respondents which is likely to result in more truthful responses to sensitive issues such as illegal drug use. New Zealand has two established longitudinal studies; the Dunedin Longitudinal Study and the Christchurch Longitudinal Study, which have gained an international reputation for high quality research on cannabis use (see

Room et al., 2008). The Dunedin and Christchurch study samples are both urban samples from the general population in their respective cities.

The Dunedin Longitudinal Study consists of a study sample of 1,037 individuals born in Dunedin between 1 April 1972 and 31 March 1973 at the Queen Mary Maternity Hospital (Dunedin Multidisciplinary Health and Development Research Unit (DMHDRU) 2010). It is conducted by the Dunedin Multidisciplinary Health and Development Research Unit at Otago University in Dunedin. The Dunedin Longitudinal Study has repeatedly interviewed the same birth cohort sample over a number of decades; the birth cohort was last interviewed at age 32 years. The participants were asked whether they had used 'marijuana/ hashish' in the past year.[3] The Christchurch Health and Development Study (CHDS) has been conducted for more than 30 years (University of Otago Christchurch 2009). The study sample consists of 1,265 individuals born in Christchurch during mid 1977. The participants were asked whether they had used 'cannabis (marijuana, grass, pot, dope)' in the past 12 months.

We accounted for underreporting of cannabis use in the NZNHDS by comparing the last year prevalence of cannabis use from the NZNHDS with the last year prevalence of cannabis use from the Dunedin and Christchurch longitudinal studies for corresponding ages and years of surveying (Table 14.2 and 14.3). The last year prevalence of cannabis use was lower in the NZNHDS than in both the Dunedin and Christchurch longitudinal studies. Consequently, we calculated the percentage of the longitudinal results for cannabis prevalence achieved by the NZNHDS for the four available points of comparison. For example, last year

Table 14.2 Comparison of the prevalence of cannabis between the NZNHDS and the Dunedin Longitudinal Study

Study	Last year prevalence of cannabis	n
1998-1999 Dunedin Longitudinal Study 26 year olds	51.1%	980
1998 NZNHDS 24-28 year olds	22.3%	790
2004-2005 Dunedin Longitudinal Study 32 year olds	37.4%	972
2003 NZNHDS 30-34 year olds	16.2%	921

Source: S. Ramrakha, Dunedin Multidisciplinary Health and Development Research Unit (personal communication, 21 October, 2009).

3 S. Ramrakha, Dunedin Multidisciplinary Health and Development Research Unit (personal communication, 21 October, 2009).

Table 14.3 Comparison of the prevalence of cannabis between the NZNHDS and the Christchurch Longitudinal Study

Study	Last year prevalence of cannabis	n
1998 Christchurch Longitudinal Study 21 year olds	46.8%	1265
1998 NZNHDS 19-23 year olds	34.7%	693
2001 Christchurch Longitudinal Study 24 year olds	47.8%	1265
2001 NZNHDS 22-26 year olds	28.5%	708

Source: J. Horwood, Christchurch Health and Development Study (personal communication, 17 November, 2009).

cannabis use among 24-28 year olds in the 1998 NZNHDS survey was 43.6% of that of 26 year olds in the Dunedin 1998-1999 Longitudinal Study (i.e. 22.3% vs. 51.1%). We then took the mean of these four results for the four points of comparison [(43.6+43.3+74.1+59.6)/4 = 55.15%] to arrive at the underreporting factor which was used in the calculations (i.e. 100/55.15 (1.81).

Converting cannabis consumption into cannabis plants

The success of the NCCO is measured in the number of cannabis plants detected and destroyed in each annual operation. Consequently, to calculate the seizure rate for the NCCO we must convert the total grams of cannabis consumed in a year from the survey results to an equivalent number of cannabis plants by dividing by the mean yield of a cannabis plant. Cannabis is sold by traditional British imperial weights in New Zealand, despite New Zealand adopting the metric system many decades ago. Under optimal growing conditions a single cannabis plant is capable of producing up to one pound of cannabis in a season (Walker et al. 1998, NDIB 2007). However, these yields are only possible under very controlled horticultural conditions, such as with indoor cultivation techniques and cloned high yield female plants (De Launey 1996, ABCI 2001).

Cannabis plants grown outdoors are often subject to harsh growing conditions including extreme weather conditions (i.e. excessively wet winter months or dry summer months), poor soil conditions, weed infestation, and are vulnerable to predation by insects, rats, goats and possums (Staff 1988, Walker et al. 1998, Te Runanga o te Rarawa, 1995, Wilkins and Casswell, 2003; see also Kalacska et al., this volume). The sophistication of outdoor cannabis cultivation efforts, and consequently the expected yield of the cannabis plants grown, also varies considerably (Staff 1988, McLaughlan 1996, Walker et al. 1998, Te Runanga o te Rarawa 1995). At one extreme cultivators merely scatter cannabis seeds or plant cannabis seedlings in isolated bush land and then leave them to fend for themselves, only returning at harvest time. At the other extreme cannabis cultivators build irrigation systems, utilise fertiliser and pesticides, provide protection against predation, and conduct regular visits to ensure the ongoing good health of cannabis plants. The New Zealand Environmental and Science and Research (ESR) agency has measured the mean weight of dried flower-head material from cannabis plants seized during the NCCO (ABCI, 2001). They found the weight of flower-head material on female cannabis plants ranged from 0.5-268 grams, with a mean yield of 40.2 grams – or approximately 1.4 ounces (i.e. 1 ounce = 28.3 grams). The ESR point out the NCCO is conducted in the months before cannabis plants reach full maturity and consequently their findings are likely to underestimate the true yield of outdoor cannabis plants to some extent. There has been no further research of the yield of mature outdoor cannabis plants in New Zealand to inform our assumptions, so we assumed a yield of two ounces per cannabis plant to take account of some additional maturing of plants.

Results

Table 14.4 presents the characteristics of cannabis consumption in New Zealand from the 1998, 2001, 2003, 2006 and 2009 NZNHDS surveys. Note, the different survey waves sometimes involve different survey age ranges and this prevents direct comparisons in these instances. In 2009, 16% of New Zealanders aged 13-45 years old had used cannabis in the past 12 months. Those who had used cannabis in the past year in 2009 had used it on a mean number of 78 times in the past year, had consumed a mean of 0.48 grams of cannabis on a typical occasion and consumed a total of 37 grams of cannabis each over the past year.

Table 14.5 presents the different age components used to calculate the total quantity of cannabis consumed among the New Zealand population aged 13-65 years old for 1998-2009. In 2009, 11,749,019 grams of cannabis was consumed by 13-45 year olds and 1,033,380 grams of cannabis was consumed by 46-65 year olds which adds up to a total consumption figure of 12,782,399 grams of cannabis consumed by 13-65 year olds. The 95% Confidence Intervals indicate there is some variation in these estimates. The total consumption estimate for 2009 of 12.8 million grams of cannabis had a lower 95% Confidence Interval of 9.1 million grams and an upper 95% Confidence Interval of 16.5 million grams.

Figure 14.1 suggests there was a considerable increase in the total quantity of cannabis consumed in New Zealand during the years 1998-2006. The total quantity of cannabis consumed in 2006 is approximately twice as much as the total quantity consumed in 1998. A great deal of the increase in cannabis consumption occurred between 1998 and 2003. The consumption of cannabis declined by 12%

Table 14.4 Patterns of cannabis consumption in the New Zealand population, 1998-2009

	1998	2001	2003	2006	2009
Age range (years)	15-45	15-45	13-65	13-45	13-45
Prevalence of use in past 12 months (%)	19.9	20.3	15.3	17.0	16.0
Mean frequency of use in past 12 months (times)	50.3	74.6	78.4	84.0	77.7
Mean amount used on a typical occasion (grams)	0.37	0.31	0.41	0.48*	0.48
Total amount used in past 12 months (grams)	18.4	23.5	32.4	40.2	37.3

* The 2006 NZNHDS did not include questions on the quantity of cannabis consumed on a typical occasion so we used the data from the 2009 NZNHDS

Table 14.5 Population estimates of total annual cannabis consumption in New Zealand population, 1998-2009

	1998	2001	2003	2006	2009
Total grams consumed (15-45 years old) (95% Confidence Intervals)	6,435,742 (5,662,977, 7,208,506)	8,302,648 (7,127,737, 9,477,560)	-	-	-
Total grams consumed (13-45 years old) (95% Confidence Intervals)	-	-	-	13,530,295 (9,932,826, 17,127,763)	11,749,019 (8,329,722, 15,168,316)
Total grams consumed (13-14/ 46-65 years old) (95% Confidence Intervals)	624,335 (549,368, 699,301)	880,308 (755,735, 1,004,880)	-	-	-
Total grams consumed (46-65 years old) (95% Confidence Intervals)	-	-	-	1,105,294 (809,080, 1,395,145)	1,033,380 (732,637, 1,334,122)
Total grams consumed (13-65 years old) (95% Confidence Intervals)	7,060,077 (6,212,345, 7,907,807)	9,182,956 (7,883,472, 10,482,440)	13,889,960 (11,230,576, 16,549,344)	14,635,589 (10,741,906, 18,522,908)	12,782,399 (9,062,359, 16,502,439)

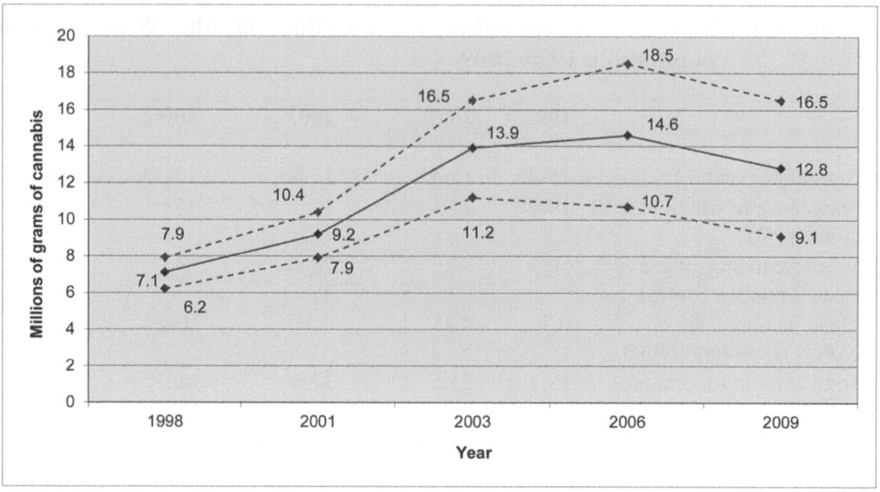

Figure 14.1 Total grams of cannabis consumed annually among those aged 13-65 years old in New Zealand (95% CI) (millions of grams), 1998-2009

in 2009 compared to 2006. However, total cannabis consumption in 2009 is still 80% higher than the 1998 figure.

Table 14.6 presents the calculation of the seizure rate of the NCCO for the years 1998, 2001, 2003, 2006 and 2009. The first step is to convert the total quantity of cannabis consumed in grams into an equivalent number of cannabis plants by using the assumed mean yield of an outdoor cannabis plant of two ounces per plant. The number of cannabis plants consumed is then increased by the underreporting factor for cannabis use for the NZNHDS (i.e. 1.81).

The New Zealand National Drug Intelligence Bureau (NDIB) was able to provide statistics on the total number of cannabis plants destroyed during the NCCO for the years 1998, 2001, 2003, 2006 and 2009. Figure 14.2 shows there was some variation in the number of cannabis plants destroyed by the NCCO from year to year. The number of cannabis plants destroyed during the 2001 NCCO was 43% lower than the number of plants destroyed in the 1998 NCCO. The total number of cannabis plants destroyed in the 2003 NCCO was 6% higher than the 2001 NCCO, and the 2006 NCCO destroyed 3% more cannabis plants than the 2003 NCCO. Finally, there was a 20% increase in the number of cannabis plants destroyed in 2009 NCCO compared to the 2006 NCCO. The number of cannabis plants destroyed in the 2009 NCCO was still 24% less than the number of plants destroyed in 1998 NCCO.

The number of cannabis plants destroyed during the NCCO is added to the number of cannabis plants consumed in a given year to obtain the total number of cannabis plants cultivated in a given year. The seizure rate is then simply the total number of cannabis plants seized during the NCCO divided by the total number of cannabis plants cultivated. Figure 14.3 shows the highest seizure rate achieved by the NCCO during the years we examined was in 1998 (45%). The seizure rate of the 2001 NCCO was 40% lower than the 1998 NCCO. The seizure rate for the 2003 NCCO was 22% lower than in the 2001 NCCO. The seizure rate of the 2006 NCCO was 5% lower than the 2003 NCCO. Finally the seizure rate increased by 30% in the 2009 NCCO compared to the 2006 NCCO. The cannabis seizure rate in the 2009 NCCO was still 42% lower than the seizure rate of the 1998 NCCO.

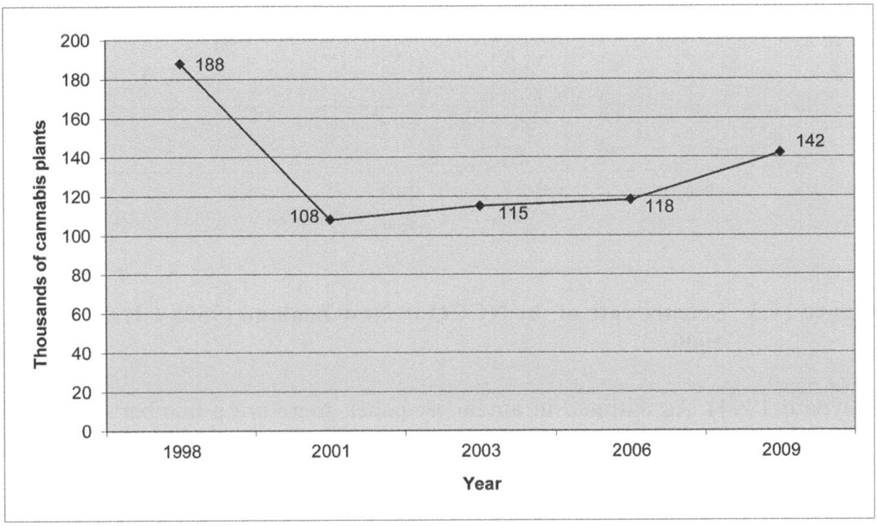

Figure 14.2 Total number of cannabis plants seized during the NCCO in New Zealand (thousands of plants), 1998-2009

Source: National Drug Intelligence Bureau (NDIB) (Personal communication, 4 February, 2010).

Discussion

The NCCO is a key response to the illegal cultivation of cannabis in New Zealand. An aerial cannabis crop eradication programme has been conducted annually in New Zealand under various operational guises since the early 1980s (NDIB 2007). In this chapter we have attempted to provide some measure of the effectiveness of the NCCO by calculating the cannabis seizure rate of the operation for the years 1998, 2001, 2003, 2006 and 2009.

The first point to acknowledge is that seizure rates achieved by the NCCO are remarkable high when compared to seizure rates referred to the literature. For example, the seizure rate for heroin achieved by the United Kingdom Customs Service was estimated to be just over 10% in 1985 before it declined to around 5% in the period 1986 to 1988, before rising to almost 10% in 1990 (Sutton and

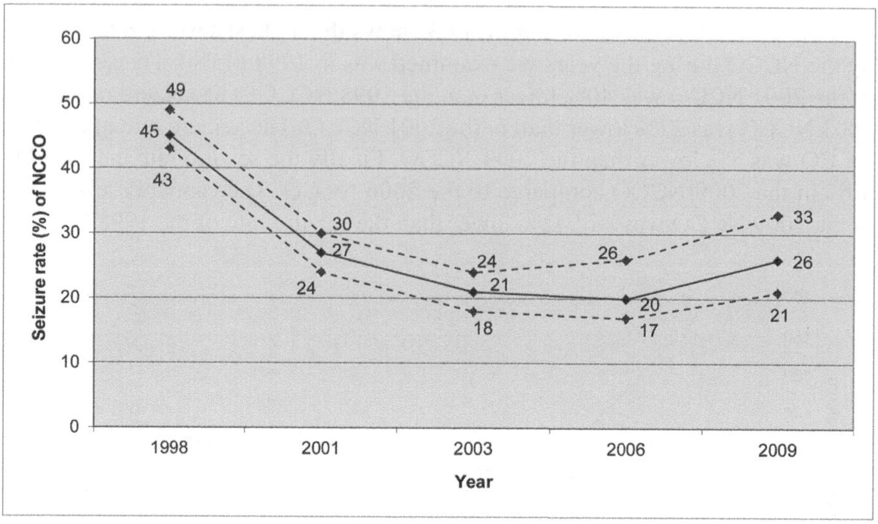

Figure 14.3 Seizure rate of the NCCO in New Zealand (95% CI) (%), 1998-2009

Maynard 1994). As outlined in an earlier paper, there are a number of reasons why we might expect the NCCO seizure rate for cannabis to be higher than seizure rates for other drugs in other countries (see Wilkins et al. 2002a). Firstly, cannabis plants are much bulkier than processed heroin or cocaine and hence are more vulnerable to detection and seizure. Secondly, all the cannabis used in New Zealand is cultivated within New Zealand's borders and consequently is directly accessible to New Zealand Police drug enforcement operations. In contrast, most of the cannabis consumed in the United States is cultivated in Mexico and is therefore beyond the jurisdiction of the United States authorities (Reuter 1997). Thirdly, New Zealand is widely held to have very low levels of governmental corruption and this supports the effectiveness of drug enforcement operations. The 2009 Transparency International Survey of government corruption found New Zealand government agencies to be the least corrupt out of 180 countries measured (Transparency International 2009).

As discussed in the introduction to this chapter, calculating drug seizure rates puts the quantity of a drug seized by the authorities into the wider context of the size of the illegal market for the drug. Seizure rates thus provide valuable insight into the effectiveness of drug enforcement and trends in the effectiveness of drug enforcement. If we only considered the number of cannabis plants destroyed each year by the NCCO as the measure of success of the operation, we might conclude that after a significant fall in the number of cannabis plants destroyed in 2001 there has been a gradual return to operational success. The number of cannabis plants destroyed by the NCCO in 2009 approaches the high point in cannabis plant

Table 14.6 Seizure rate for cannabis of the of NCCO in New Zealand, 1998-2009

	1998	2001	2003	2006	2009
Total grams consumed (13-65) (95% Confidence Intervals)	7,060,077 (6,212,345, 7,907,807)	9,182,956 (7,883,472, 10,482,440)	13,889,960 (11,230,576, 16,549,344)	14,635,589 (10,741,906, 18,522,908)	12,782,399 (9,062,359, 16,502,439)
Total number of plants consumed (95% Confidence Intervals)	124,736 (109,759, 139,714)	162,243 (139,284, 185,202)	245,406 (198,420, 292,391)	258,579 (189,786, 327,260)	225,837 (160,112, 291,563)
Under reporting factor	1.81	1.81	1.81	1.81	1.81
Total number of plants consumed (accounting for under reporting) (95% Confidence Intervals)	225,772 (198,664, 252,882)	293,660 (252,104, 335,216)	444,185 (359,140, 529,228)	468,028 (343,513, 592,341)	408,765 (289,803, 527,729)
Number of plants seized (NCCO)	187,577	107,868	115,445	118,457	141,780
Total number of plants cultivated (95% Confidence Intervals)	413,349 (386,241, 440,459)	401,528 (359,972, 443,084)	559,630 (474,585, 644,673)	586,485 (461,970, 710,798)	550,545 (431,583, 669,509)
Seizure rate (%) (95% Confidence Intervals)	45 (43, 49)	27 (24, 30)	21 (18, 24)	20 (17, 26)	26 (21, 33)

seizures achieved in 1998. The seizure rates calculated for the NCCO indicate quite a different picture.

The highest cannabis seizure rate for the NCCO was achieved in 1998 (i.e. 45%) and in all the subsequent years of the operation (2001, 2003, 2006, 2009) the seizure rate of the NCCO remained between approximately one half and two thirds of the seizure rate achieved in 1998. The seizure rate of the 2009 NCCO was 42% lower than the seizure rate achieved by the 1998 NCCO. This result is due to the fact that the total quantity of cannabis consumed in New Zealand over the period examined increased at a faster rate than the increase in the number of cannabis plants destroyed by the NCCO.

This finding poses the question of why seizures of cannabis plants made by the NCCO were not able to keep pace with the rate of increase in cannabis use in New Zealand. There are a number of possible explanations. Firstly, there appears to have been a decline in the financial budget allocated to cannabis crop eradication operations over this time with implications for the scope of the operation. In a recent report on cannabis in New Zealand the NDIB explained that in 1997/1998 there was a 'significant reduction' in funding for cannabis crop eradication operations and as a consequence the budget for the 2006 NCCO was '30% less than the 1994 cannabis crop eradication operation' (NDIB, 2007, p.56-57). The NDIB report identifies several rural districts which were vulnerable to exploitation by outdoor cannabis cultivators but were no longer covered by the NCCO due to constraints on flying time. The New Zealand Police have indicated that, as a matter of policy, they do not release the budget for the NCCO as they do not want to alert the criminal fraternity to the scope of the operation. This prevents any more detailed investigation of this factor, but it could potentially be an important explanation for the decline in the seizure rate of the NCCO.

Secondly, the effectiveness of the NCCO is also impacted by operational factors and wider strategic priorities for drug enforcement. The operational success of individual NCCO are affected by a range of variables including the suitability of the weather for flying, mechanical breakdown of aircraft, aerial and other operational accidents, and the level of district police support for the operation (NDIB, 2007). In 2005 a fixed wing aircraft involved in the NCCO crashed resulting in the deaths of a police officer and a pilot and this resulted in the operation being suspended for several weeks. The success of the NCCO in different regions is also influenced by the priority placed on the operation by individual District Police Commanders. The national budget for the NCCO covers the expense of helicopter and fixed wing aircraft nationwide, but Police District Commanders decide the level of police time and resources dedicated to the operation. Police District Commanders also influence the extent of cannabis crop eradication operations in their regions in a more indirect way by managing the level of resources dedicated to collecting intelligence on the location of cannabis plantations in their area. The allocation of flying time for the NCCO is based on the level of advanced intelligence on the location of cannabis crops in a region. If intelligence on cannabis cultivation is weak in an area then less flying time is allocated to cannabis crop eradication in an area. The priority placed on cannabis crop eradication by Police District Commanders is influenced by wider strategic priorities for drug enforcement. New Zealand experienced a significant increase in methamphetamine use and domestic methamphetamine manufacture during the early 2000s (see Wilkins et al. 2002c), and this increase in methamphetamine related activity was linked to violence crime, family violence, property offending, mental health problems and environmental contamination (see New Zealand Police Commissioner quoted in Stevens 2002, Wilkins 2002). The New Zealand Police subsequently placed a high priority on disrupting the emerging methamphetamine market (see New Zealand Police 2009) and it is conceivable that in a context of constrained resources that this took some focus away from cannabis crop eradication.

Thirdly, cannabis cultivators, like international drug smugglers, are likely to adopt strategies to counter the effectiveness of drug enforcement tactics such as aerial cannabis crop eradication (see Reuter et al. 1988). Outdoor cannabis cultivators in New Zealand have responded to the risk of aerial detection in a number of ways including by dispersing cannabis plants over larger areas rather than planting them in single dense blocks, utilising camouflage netting, dispersing cannabis plants in maize fields, planting cannabis plants in long single rows, and suspending cannabis plants off the ground in large trees with dense canopies (NDIB 2007, Walker et al. 1998). It is possible that the adoption of these counter strategies has spread among cannabis growers over time and this has contributed to a decline in the effectiveness of the NCCO in recent years.

Fourthly, a final possible factor in the declining seizure rate of the NCCO is the emergence of indoor cannabis cultivation in New Zealand. Indoor cannabis cultivation (both soil and hydroponic cultivation) emerged in New Zealand in the late 1990s / early 2000s. While no complete statistics exist on the share of total cannabis production accounted for by indoor cultivation methods in New Zealand, partial figures presented by the NDIB for 2006 suggest that indoor cannabis cultivation may be roughly responsible for at least 15% of the cannabis produced in New Zealand (NDIB 2007). Indoor cannabis cultivation is of course carried out inside of buildings and hence cannot be detected from the air. The emergence of indoor cannabis cultivation thus represents a challenge to the future effectiveness of the NCCO at controlling cannabis cultivation in New Zealand.

We acknowledge a number of limitations with our estimates. Firstly our adjustment for survey underreporting of cannabis use in the NZNHDS is by necessity fairly approximate. The longitudinal surveys we utilised to calculate the level of survey underreporting of cannabis use in the NZNHDS may themselves suffer from a degree of underreporting. The longitudinal surveys are conducted in specific urban cities in the South Island of New Zealand and the level of cannabis use in those locations may differ from the level of cannabis use in the whole of New Zealand. Unfortunately there are no methodological studies available which can provide a more precise indication of the level of underreporting of cannabis use in the NZNHDS. A higher level of underreporting of cannabis use in NZNHDS than we assumed in our analysis would reduce the seizure rates achieved by the

NCCO. Secondly, we were required to make an informed estimate of the average yield of mature cannabis plants grown outdoors in New Zealand. The NDIB have indicated that they believe our assumption of an average yield of two ounces per cannabis plant is 'conservative' (NDIB 2007, p.57, footnote 75). Furthermore, the NDIB believe the yield of cannabis plants has increased considerably since the mid 2000s due to an increase in the sophistication of horticultural techniques largely brought about by the emergence of indoor cultivation techniques, and these horticultural techniques are now widely applied to outdoor cannabis cultivation. However, it is difficult to ascertain the extent to which the emergence of these advanced cultivation techniques has increased the *average* yield of cannabis plants grown outdoors. While some outdoor cannabis growers may well have adopted these advanced horticultural techniques, many others may persist with fairly low intensity approaches as described earlier in this chapter. Without further evidence of a change in the average yield of cannabis plants grown outdoors in New Zealand it was difficult to justify the adoption of a different yield figure. Higher average yields for cannabis plants than we assumed would increase the seizure rate of the NCCO. We have requested further evidence from the NDIB to inform our understanding of the average yield of outdoor cannabis plants in New Zealand.

To conclude, our chapter suggests that cannabis crop eradication operations are fairly effective, at least in the New Zealand context, but their effectiveness may be being eroded by counter measures developed by cannabis cultivators and as a result of changes in the cannabis cultivation sector, that is, the emergence of indoor cannabis cultivation (see also Potter, this volume). An important question that we were unable to answer with our present information was, are these operations cost-effective, that is, do the social benefits of these operations justify their cost.

List of references

Australian Bureau of Criminal Intelligence 2001. *Australian illicit drug report 1999–2000*. Canberra: Australian Bureau of Criminal Intelligence.

Bates, M. 1998. *Interim report on the toxicology of herbicides proposed for application to cannabis plants.* Porirua: Kenepuru Science Centre, Institute of Environmental Science and Research.

Dawkins, K. 2001. Cannabis prohibition: taking stock of the evidence. *Otago Law Review*, 10, 39–89.

De Launey, C. 1996. The real value of a cannabis plant. *Alternative Law Journal*, 21, 127-30.

Drug Policy Forum Trust 1998. *New Zealand should regulate and tax cannabis commerce.* Wellington: Drug Policy Forum Trust.

Dunedin Multidisciplinary Health and Development Research Unit (DMHDRU) 2010. *Welcome to the Dunedin Multidisciplinary Health and Development Research Unit (DMHDRU)*. Available at: http://dunedinstudy.otago.ac.nz/ [accessed: 12 November 2009].

Fendrich, M., Johnson, T., Wislar, J., Hubbell, A. and Spiehler, V. 2004. The utility of drug testing in epidemiological research: results from a general population survey. *Addiction*, 99, 197-208.

Harrison, L., Martin, B., Enev, T. and Harrington, D. 2007. *Comparing drug testing and self-report of drug use among youths and young adults in the general population.* [Office of Applied Studies, Substance Abuse and Mental Health Srevices, US Department of Health and Human Services]. Available at: http://www.oas.samhsa.gov/validity/drugTest.pdf. [accessed: 28 January 2009].

MacCoun, R. and Reuter, P. 2001. *Drug war heresies: learning from other vices, times and places*. Cambridge: Cambridge University Press.

McLaughlan, M. 1996. Gone north: on the cannabis trail. *North & South*, November, 117–23.

National Drug Intelligence Bureau (NDIB) 2007. *'New cannabis': The cornerstone of illicit drug harm in New Zealand.* Wellington: New Zealand Government.

Newbold G. 2000. *Crime in New Zealand.* Palmerston North: Dunmore Press.

New Zealand Customs Service 2002. *Review of Customs Drug Enforcement Strategies 2002. Project Horizon Outcome Report*. New Zealand Customs Service, Wellington.

New Zealand Police 2009. *New Police Illicit Drug Strategy to 2010*. Wellington: New Zealand Police.

NORML 2001. *Submission to New Zealand Parliamentary Health Select Committee Inquiry into Health Issues and Legal Status of Cannabis*. Auckland: National Organization for the Reform of Marijuana Laws.

Reuter, P. 1997. *The mismeasurement of illegal drug markets: the implications of its irrelevance.* Santa Monica, CA: Rand Corporation.

Reuter, P., Crawford, G. and Cave, J. 1988. *Sealing the borders: the effects of increased military participation in drug interdiction.* Santa Monica, CA: Rand Corporation.

Room, R., Fisher, B., Hall, W., Lenton, S. and Reuter, P. 2008. *The global cannabis commission report.* Oxford: Beckley Foundation.

Staff, B. 1988. A report from cannabis country. *North & South*, April, 103–109.

Stevens, M. 2002. Police hope big speed bust will strangle supply. *Dominion Post.* 8 August, 9.

Sutton, M. and Maynard, A. 1994. *Trends in the cost-effectiveness of enforcement activity in the illicit heroin market, 1979–1990.* University of York: Centre for Health Economics.

Te Runanga o te Rarawa 1995. *Cannabis project report.* Wellington: Te Puni Kokiri.

Transparency International 2009. *Corruption Perceptions Index 2009.* Available at: http://www.transparency.org/policy_research/surveys_indices/cpi/2009/cpi_2009_table [accessed: 25 March 2010].

University of Otago Christchurch 2009. *Christchurch Health and Development Study – Introduction.* Available at: http://www.chmeds.ac.nz/research/chds/index.htm [accessed: 20 November 2009].

Walker, L., Cocklin, C. and Blunden, G. 1998. *Cannabis highs and lows: sustaining and dislocating rural communities in Northland.* Auckland: University of Auckland, Department of Geography.

Wilkins, C. 2002. Designer Amphetamines in New Zealand: Policy Challenges and Initiatives. *Social Policy Journal of New Zealand*, 19 (December), 14-25.

Wilkins, C. and Sweetsur, P. 2008. Trends in population drug use in New Zealand: Findings from national household surveying of drug use in 1998, 2001, 2003 and 2006. *New Zealand Medical Journal*, 121, 61-71.

Wilkins, C., Bhatta, K. and Casswell, S. 2002a. The Effectiveness of Cannabis Eradication Operations in New Zealand. *Drug and Alcohol Review*, 21, 369-374.

Wilkins, C., Bhatta, K. and Casswell, S. 2002b. A Demand Side Estimate of the Financial Turnover of the Cannabis Black Market in New Zealand. *Drug and Alcohol Review*, 21, 145-51.

Wilkins, C., Bhatta, K. and Casswell, S. 2002c. The emergence of amphetamine use in New Zealand: findings from the 1998 and 2001 national drug surveys. *New Zealand Medical Journal*, 115(1166), 256-63.

Wilkins, C. and Casswell, S. 2003. Cannabis cultivation and organised crime in New Zealand. *Contemporary Drug Problems*, 30 (Winter), 757-77.

Wilkins C., Casswell S., Bhatta, K. and Pledger, M. 2002. *Drug use in New Zealand.* University of Auckland: Alcohol & Public Health Research Unit.

Wilkins, C., Reilly, J., Pledger, M. and Casswell, S. 2005. Estimating the dollar value of the illicit market for cannabis in New Zealand. *Drug and Alcohol Review*, 24, 227-34.

Yska, R. 1990. *New Zealand green: the story of marijuana in New Zealand.* Auckland: David Bateman.

Chapter 15

Keeping Down The Weeds: Cannabis Eradication in the Developed World[1]

Gary R. Potter

Introduction

Cannabis cultivation is prohibited under international law. The 1961 Single Convention on Narcotic Drugs calls on signatory states to limit the cultivation of cannabis (alongside the coca bush and the opium poppy) and to destroy any existing illegal plants[2]. The 1988 UN Convention against Illicit Traffic in Narcotic Drugs and Psychotropic Substances requires states to make cultivation of the three major "narcotic" plants[3] a criminal offence. Under this framework, drug crop eradication has been a key strategy in supply-reduction efforts in global drug control efforts. The 1998 UN General Assembly Special Session (UNGASS), working under the slogan "A Drug Free World, We Can Do It", reaffirmed "the need for a comprehensive approach towards the elimination of illicit narcotic crops" and welcomed "the United Nations Drug Control Program… with a view to eliminating or significantly reducing the illicit cultivation of the coca bush, the cannabis plant and the opium poppy by the year 2008" (UNGASS 1998, paragraphs 18 and 19). However, in 2008 the United Nations Office on Drugs and Crime admitted that "global trends indicate that the world has fallen short of these goals" (UNODC 2008a). With specific reference to cannabis, the 2008 World Drug Report implicated 172 countries and territories in cannabis production in

1 The author would like to thank Martin Bouchard, Aili Malm and Tom Decorte for comments on earlier drafts of this chapter, and all those present at the Copenhagen meeting for help in developing the original idea.

2 Some cultivation is permitted for research purposes, and non-drug varieties of hemp (which is cannabis by another name) are cultivated for food, fibers and other industrial uses (but see Potter 2010, on the drug content of hemp).

3 In some of the literature, and much of the international legislation, the term 'narcotic' is used to describe cannabis, opium and coca (and their derivatives). Strictly speaking cocaine and cannabis are not narcotics. Nevertheless, I shall follow the terminology of the international documents and use the word narcotic interchangeably with drug when discussing the three plants or their products.

2007 (UNODC 2008b: 96), demonstrating the truly global nature of contemporary cannabis cultivation.

From the perspective of eradication efforts this globalization represents a failure in two dimensions. Cannabis cultivation *continues in many countries* that have been subject to concerted eradication efforts and that have a long history as source countries in the international market (see, e.g. chapters by Afsahi and Klein, this volume). In these countries, eradication efforts have obviously failed. Cannabis cultivation has also *expanded into other countries* across both the developing and, increasingly, the developed world. It may even be the case that eradication efforts have been one factor in encouraging the spread of cultivation to new countries (see e.g. Farrell 1998, Weisheit 1992). The globalization of cannabis cultivation means eradication efforts, if stated goals are still to be pursued, must be directed within most countries of the world. It also means that many Western nations have had to recognize drug cultivation as a domestic problem rather than as an overseas one (Potter 2010a, 2010b, c.f. Pearson and Hobbs 2001).

Ultimately, whether in the developed or the developing world, the eradication of cannabis plants and the policing of the offence of cultivation are dependent on the detection of grow sites: discovery of the plants is a necessary precursor to destroying them or to prosecuting the grower. A second (and sometimes overlooked) element to successful eradication is the prevention of cultivation from occurring in the first place. However with large scale cultivation of cannabis occurring (and expanding) in so many countries around the world, clearly neither detection nor prevention is straightforward.

The aim of this chapter, then, is to consider the challenges to the eradication of cannabis cultivation around the world. We pay particular attention to the challenges posed by indoor cultivation in the developed world, drawing on the situation in the UK as a case-study. We start (section two) with a brief consideration of the literature on cannabis cultivation around the world, focusing on the problems associated with the policing of cultivation. Section three draws on ongoing empirical research to explore cannabis cultivation in the UK. In both the literature and the empirical research we find that certain aspects inherent to the nature of cannabis cultivation make detection and eradication problematic. These difficulties are exacerbated by the various "adaptive responses" employed by cannabis growers to avoid or minimize the impact of law enforcement efforts (Farrell 1998). Section four considers these findings to illustrate the difficulties inherent in cannabis eradication efforts, whether in the developing or developed world, arguing that the difficulties involved in cannabis eradication are inherent in the act of cultivation, not the geographical or socio-economic context in which it occurs. The conclusion (section five) considers the implications of this analysis – the essence being that cannabis eradication efforts, especially if measured in absolute terms (i.e. against the stated goal of elimination of *all* illegal cultivation), are unlikely to ever be anything more than moderately successful.

Global difficulties in eradicating cannabis

Drug crop eradication in the developing world

International drug crop eradication efforts have met with limited success regardless of which narcotic plant is targeted (UNODC 2008a, 2008b, 2009, Farrell 1998). Although the focus in this chapter is cannabis in the developed world, particularly when grown indoors, a brief consideration of the difficulties encountered in eradication efforts around the world is illuminating. Failure is largely blamed on the geographical, economic, social and political conditions in the countries and regions where narcotic crops have usually been grown, and on growers employing adaptive responses to militate against the risks associated with eradication efforts. We now consider these two sets of problems, *initial conditions* and *adaptive responses*, in more detail.

The recent expansion of cannabis cultivation in the developed world aside, drug crop cultivation is usually associated with the developing world. The countries most heavily implicated in growing drug crops are often characterized by internal unrest or a lack of effective state control over large parts of the country. Regardless of socio-political conditions, cultivation often occurs in remote or underdeveloped areas (Farrell 1998, Clemens 2008, Vellinga 2004, del Olmo 1998).

From the perspective of eradication efforts, the result is that drug crops can be hard to detect (and hard to destroy if they are detected), especially where local resistance combines with geographical inaccessibility. The economic attractiveness of drug crops to local peoples and armed groups, and the fact that they can grow in conditions unsuited to other agricultural crops, means that even when crops are successfully destroyed the incentive remains for further cultivation efforts in the future (Farrell 1998, Mansfield and Sage 1998).

When eradication efforts do have some initial success, another set of problems emerge. Farrell (1998), in reviewing the evidence from UN sponsored eradication efforts, identified a number of "adaptive responses" employed by drug cultivators in the face of eradication efforts. Firstly, if crops are lost, growers and traffickers may put more effort into extracting and refining drug products from the remaining plants. In this way drug production levels can remain high even when cultivation levels drop, as we saw earlier. Those involved in farming drugs may also try to prevent or off-set the impact of eradication through engaging in "both violent and non-violent protests, the camouflaging of crops against aerial observation through inter-cropping [i.e. dispersing drug crops amongst other crops], and the removal of cultivation to more remote and protected areas. However, the main response to periodic [i.e. expected] eradication is anticipatory planting of larger areas of crops" (Farrell 1998: 402). We may also recognize examples of adaptive responses where drug growers have engaged in armed resistance, or have employed bribery and corruption to discourage state interference (see Dorn et al. 2005).

As well as adaptive responses employed by individual growers, evidence suggests that where cultivation is successfully eradicated in a particular area or country it is often compensated for by increased cultivation and production elsewhere. Globally, levels of production of the major plant-based drugs have remained stubbornly high and remarkably steady in the face of eradication efforts and international policy (Farrell 1992, UNODC 2008a, 2008b, 2009).

Specific difficulties in cannabis eradication

With the spread of cannabis cultivation to other countries, including many industrialized nations, many of the conditions associated with narcotic crop cultivation in the developing world do not apply. The question therefore arises as to whether the difficulties in cannabis eradication are related primarily to contextual (geographical, socio-economic, political) conditions, or whether they are inherent in the act of cannabis cultivation itself. A consideration of the factors that make cannabis eradication particularly difficult will, hopefully, provide some insights into how best to respond to the emergence of cultivation in an increasing number of nations, including many Western ones.

Cannabis differs from other narcotic crops in a number of ways. It is a hardy and versatile plant and will grow across a wide geographical area (UNODC 2009, Leggett 2006, Booth 2003). Cannabis can be grown in small quantities and still be viable as a drug crop because the return per plant is high and because it needs no chemical refining and little processing of any sort (UNODC 2009, Potter 2010a, Adler 1993, Kilmer et al. 2010). It is widely grown indoors, further increasing the geographical range over which it can be cultivated. The viability of smaller-scale production over a large portion of the globe means "the point of diminishing returns is quickly reached in ferreting out smaller grows" (UNODC 2009: 174); eradication aimed at relatively small and dispersed "grows" is neither practically nor economically viable, nor is it particularly effective.

Unlike the other two major narcotic plants, cannabis cultivation occurs on a commercial scale in an increasing number of industrialized nations. This has happened in part because of the options for cultivating over a wider geographical area but there are other factors to be considered too. Import substitution[4] in Western cannabis markets has been explained in economic terms, highlighting factors that have made domestic production an attractive and viable alternative to importation (Potter 2008, 2010a, 2010b, Bouchard 2007, Jansen 2002, Weisheit 1992). One such factor may be drug eradication and law-enforcement efforts directed elsewhere (Potter 2010a, Weisheit 1992, UNODC 2009, Farrell 1998). Weisheit, for example, suggests that anti-smuggling efforts on the Mexican border in the 1960s and the spraying of *paraquat* on cannabis plantations in Mexico in the 1970s may have both played a part in encouraging domestic cultivation in the US (Weisheit 1992: 47).

4 The economic term for expanded domestic production in commodity markets traditionally dependent on importation of a product.

Whether or not import substitution is in some way encouraged by eradication efforts elsewhere it certainly brings new challenges, not least in increasing the number of countries where eradication efforts are needed. The emergence of extensive outdoor cultivation in countries such as Canada, the US, Australia and New Zealand clearly undermines the idea that cultivation is inherently linked to underdeveloped countries or those suffering political instability.

However the basic problems are essentially the same. Literature on rural, outdoor cannabis cultivation in the US suggests that such cultivation often occurs in relatively poor, remote agricultural or wilderness areas (Weisheit 1992, Katz and Whitaker 2001, Clayton 1995, Hafley and Tewksbury 2001). As such cannabis cultivation is particularly economically attractive (especially to those with agricultural skills and equipment) and can be hard to detect and eradicate, with geographical remoteness complemented by tight-knit local populations showing opposition to outside interference. US growers also employ tactics such as camouflage of cannabis with other crops, or the use of booby traps or armed guards (although these latter two may be directed more at other criminals than at law enforcement agencies) (ibid.). Elsewhere in North America the planting of what we might think of as "sacrificial crops" has been reported, with growers planting in the same place year after year even though the crops are always eradicated. The presumption is that the growers know that the police have to divert time and energy to any such plantation making it less likely that they will have the resources available to detect and destroy other crops.[5]

All of the features discussed here show clear similarities to the factors militating against eradication in the developing world. Geographical remoteness plays a part, which itself relates to the versatility of the cannabis plant. Local economic conditions make cannabis cultivation attractive; local socio-political conditions can help protect growers from eradication efforts conducted by outsiders. Growers demonstrate techniques in protecting their plants from eradication, and strategies for compensating for any crops that are eradicated. However some of the underlying causes are different in important ways. Cannabis cultivation is not just a problem of the developing world, and so cannot be thought of simply in geo-political terms, although even within the industrialized world we may see links to rural under-development.

The problem of indoor cultivation in the UK

The question to be considered in this section is whether similar hindrances to eradication efforts are encountered in the context of the predominantly urban, indoor cultivation found in the UK (Potter and Dann 2005, Potter 2010b). Indoor cultivation clearly throws up challenges that are different from those relating to outdoor cultivation, whether occurring in the developed or developing world. Indoor

5 Margaret Kalacska (personal communication, 18 May, 2009).

cultivation has been seen in itself as an adaptive response by some commentators. Bergman (2002, cited in Jansen 2002) suggested that indoor cultivation took off in the US in the 1970s in response to harsher anti-cannabis laws. Bouchard (2007) demonstrates how indoor growers "face lower enforcement-related risks" than outdoor growers, even when the former were growing larger numbers of plants. Moving to indoor cultivation clearly makes sense as an adaptive response (see e.g. Wilkins, this volume). Others explain the move towards indoor cultivation more in terms of embracing the opportunities opened up by indoor cultivation techniques than a direct response to eradication efforts against outdoor cultivation (e.g. Potter 2008, 2010b, Jansen 2002, Leggett 2006), but it is obviously the case that indoor cultivation makes detection harder. The opportunity to reproduce ideal growing conditions and to cultivate all year round also allows growers to maximize drug production within any area given over to cultivation (Potter 2010b, Leggett 2006), demonstrating further the attraction of growing indoors.

Researching cultivation in the UK

This section draws on data from ten years of research in the UK. From 2000-2006 the author was engaged in gathering data for a PhD dissertation. Since completing the doctorate, fieldwork has continued, focusing on cannabis growers in different geographical localities as the author has lived in different cities around the UK.

The research was ethnographic in its overall approach, involving interacting with cannabis growers in their day-to-day lives, visiting their grow rooms, observing their cultivating activities, participating in harvest, witnessing occasions of drug use and drug distribution, and talking to growers about these (and other) aspects of their lives. For the PhD, over 50 cannabis growers were interviewed and observed in depth; countless others were met, observed or chatted to as and when opportunities arose. To give a more balanced picture of cannabis cultivation in the UK interviews were also conducted with representatives from the Police and the Forensic Science Services, and with other expert witnesses.

Since the initial graduate project, more cannabis growers, users and dealers have provided data through observation, conversation and interview as opportunities have arisen. The author has also conducted follow-up research with many of the original sample. Alongside the ethnographic data, online data sources have also been utilized with observation and interviews being carried out via cannabis-related email distribution lists and online discussion forums. Finally national and local newspaper articles have also provided data on cannabis cultivation.

While none of the data sources used are representative in terms of their coverage of cannabis cultivation and cannabis cultivators, together they provide a broad and informative picture of cannabis cultivation in the UK. The final sample is skewed towards smaller scale cannabis growers (although these are often still commercially oriented) as larger scale growers and those more linked to organized crime were harder to gain access too. Nevertheless, such growers did feature in the study. The data is qualitative rather than quantitative: it illustrates the range of approaches to cannabis cultivation that exist in the UK, but is not suited to accurate estimates of the prevalence of the different approaches encountered. For further discussion of the methodological issues, including limitations to the sample, see Potter 2010b.

The nature of cultivation in the UK

It is, of course, impossible to be sure of the extent of cannabis cultivation in the UK, but a number of indicators suggest that domestic cultivation has increased significantly over the last two decades and probably accounts for well over half of the UK cannabis market (see Potter 2008, 2010b, for a discussion of various indicators). Elsewhere I describe the range of cannabis growers encountered in the research in some detail (Potter 2010b); a brief summary of those involved, their methods and their motivations, will suffice here.

Cannabis growers come from a broad range of socio-economic backgrounds and are involved in cultivation to different degrees, ranging from those growing a single, one-off plant for personal satisfaction to those involved in cultivating millions of pounds worth of cannabis over a number of years. Growers employ both indoor and outdoor cultivation methods, but indoor growing, often incorporating high-tech methods (as described below), is more common (see also Hough et al. 2003).

Although profit is a key motivator for many cannabis growers, it is not the sole motivational "driver" (Dorn et al. 2005) encouraging involvement in cultivation. Many growers in the UK (as elsewhere in the world) do not seek any financial return from their activities at all, growing instead for personal use, to share with friends, to avoid the illicit market, for ideological reasons associated with cannabis, or out of medical necessity (Hough et al. 2003, Potter 2010b; see also Decorte 2008 and Hakkarainen and Perälä, this volme). Many other growers do make money, but are motivated primarily by non-financial reasons. They find they can profit on the side, but did not originally engage in growing for financial reasons and would continue growing if the financial benefits were removed (Weisheit 1992, Potter and Dann 2005, Potter 2010a, 2010b, Hough et al. 2003).

Those growing primarily for commercial reasons are common, but are probably a minority of all growers. Commercial growers can operate on a small scale, making a few hundred or thousand pounds a year just from growing a handful of plants in a space as small as a cupboard or a spare room. Equally, there are many examples of those who make hundreds of thousands or even millions of pounds from cannabis cultivation, using domestic, agricultural and industrial buildings to accommodate their operations.

Growers may seek to make money out of some perceived "need" – to supplement otherwise meager incomes, or to pay a pressing expense. Or they may seek to make money for personal gain that can only be described as "greed". However even when financial gain is important, growers may still be motivated in part by non-financial drivers – ideological affiliation to cannabis (for both its narcotic and non-narcotic properties) is common amongst even the most commercially minded growers (Potter 2010b, see also Caesar 2009).

Detection avoidance and UK cultivators

> Andrea,[6] a student in her twenties, began considering cultivation as a business venture in 2008. Caring for her sick mother and two younger siblings, Andrea's motivation can be seen as partly altruistic. The intention is to fund the family until she finishes studying and can embark on a suitably lucrative career. She went into partnership with an acquaintance already experienced in cannabis cultivation, Max, who provided equipment, expertise and the cuttings to get started. Growing in Andrea's house, they started with a few dozen plants spread over a number of rooms. The grow-op was a hydroponic operation utilizing high-powered indoor lights. Ventilation systems were rigged up and rooms blacked out. After a few weeks the smell became noticeable from outside the flat. Wary of her neighbors either reporting her to the police or (equally worrying in her view) robbing her of her cannabis, Andrea decided to destroy all but a small number of plants in her own bedroom. "I should have used a carbon filter. We'll get one before we start again, after my exams", she told me. Recently diagnosed with cancer she also told me she would try to get her GP to indicate his support of her use of cannabis for therapeutic purposes, allowing her to argue medical necessity in mitigation should she ever get busted. "I've never smoked cannabis, and still don't intend to, but if you've got cancer, you may as well exploit it!" However she also said, in the same conversation, "I'm prepared to do time." She offered to take me round her grow-op, but only when Max was absent as she feared he would disapprove of her even discussing it with anyone, yet alone bringing them round for a look! [Series of interviews conducted October 2009 to August 2010]

Cannabis growers take active steps to avoid detection, seeing law-enforcement activity as one risk among many that threaten the successful cultivation of cannabis. As a case-study, Andrea illustrates a number of points about cultivation and risk avoidance. She knew the risks involved, recognizing the possibility of being caught and of receiving a custodial sentence, but also that the police were not the only people to be wary of (there are numerous instances where cannabis growers have suffered at the hands of other criminals). She recognized potential sources of risk – the smell of the plants, excessive heat and powerful lighting that might arouse suspicion. Her growing partner at least had some recognition of the risks associated with careless talk, although Andrea was happy to trust a relative stranger with her secret. She sought to minimize the chances of getting caught through utilizing (or preparing to utilize) methods to counter sources of risk, and knew about techniques such as using a carbon filter to neutralize smell. She also

6 Names have been changed.

sought to minimize the consequences of getting caught through keeping only a minimal number of plants when she felt the risk of detection to be unacceptably high, and through pre-planning a slightly bogus but believable defense of medical use.[7]

> There are fifteen plants in Brian's attic (sixteen if you include the "mother" plant from which all the others originated as cuttings), producing around 100 ounces of cannabis every 3 months and earning Brian around £40,000 or more a year. The entrance to the attic looks like it hasn't been disturbed for years. There is no ladder to the hatch; to enter you must scramble up. You enter into an attic that, at first glance, looks like a mostly empty space with a few boxes strewn around. It is not immediately obvious that the space is smaller than it should be: the false wall is very convincing. Inside the inner room is bright, hot and smelly, although none of these things are noticeable from the floor below. Even just before harvest time, which is when the plants are at their most pungent (and when I visited) the smell is only really noticeable if you are expecting it. Desk fans keep the air circulating within the room and a powerful extractor fan channels air through a home-made carbon filter and out through the chimney. The electricity for all the hardware is taken straight from the mains, bypassing the meter, although Brian has resisted the temptation to supply the rest of the house in similar fashion. The watering system involves recycling the waste water where possible, topped up in part by rain-water, placing minimal demands on the domestic supply. Brian jokes that he off-sets this by washing less! In the heavy winter of 2009/10 Brian was concerned when the snow on his roof melted before that of his neighbors. When a neighbor commented on this, Brian muttered something about his landlord (who never came round so long as the rent was paid on time, and who would have found that his key mysteriously wouldn't fit the lock if he had come unannounced) being too mean to get roof insulation (the loft was actually very well insulated). To be on the safe-side he suspended growing operations for a few months, and is now looking to move house. [Two interviews and one grow-site visit, October 2008 to May 2010]

Brian's story further illustrates the ways in which growers can and do successfully minimize the risk of detection – and how aware they are of potential sources of risk in the first place. Many growers make false walls and secret doors or concealed cabinets for their plants. It is common to utilize plumbing or electrical skills to their advantage, or to employ sympathetic handymen to help set-up their systems. In more professional, more commercially oriented operations, carpenters, builders and electricians may be on a permanent retainer or be central members of the criminal organization. Equipment such as carbon filters and materials for

7 Medical necessity is not a legal defense for cannabis use or cultivation in the UK, but there are examples of medical users getting lighter sentences, or of juries returning 'not guilty' verdicts (see Potter 2010b).

insulating against loss of heat, light and smell can be purchased online or from the same shops and mail-order companies that supply lights, pumps and other cultivation equipment. Alternatively the internet, books and magazines – and more experienced growing acquaintances – can provide instructions on how to make such equipment and otherwise secure ones grow-op. Potential giveaways like unusual patterns of utility consumption and snow-free roofs can be accounted for with a little planning and bravado. Unwanted visitors (of which landlords are only one category) can be discouraged.

> Jonah has featured in previous discussions (Potter and Dann 2005, Potter 2010b), but his career has further developed. Jonah has been involved in growing "Well over a million pounds worth" of cannabis over the years (much more since recording this quote) although "God knows where the money has gone!" Yet Jonah has not had anything other than a few baby plants in pots in his own house for most of that time "not with my daughter living with me. I couldn't take that risk". Instead Jonah always gets involved with growing with other people. A favorite strategy is to help other, novice, growers get started. Jonah provides equipment and expertise – and cuttings (he breeds his own varieties) and the partners provide the space to grow. At the end of the first successful harvest, Jonah takes half as payment for advice. At the end of the second, Jonah again takes half, but the partner gets to keep the equipment and carry on alone (keeping their entire future crops) if they wish. Such partnerships usually involve around ten plants, but with Jonah involved in upwards of 20 partnerships (or franchises) at a time, the amount of cannabis that he helps grow – and receives a share of the profits from – is considerable. He also offers his services as an "expert" to more experienced growers who are experiencing difficulties, for a fee (in cannabis or cash), of course! Recently (early 2010) Jonah announced his "temporary retirement". Hearing through the local media, and "through the grape-vine", that the local police were stepping up their anti-cultivation efforts, he decided to suspend his activities until things "quieten down". But, he says, "I'll be back!" [Field notes and interviews, October 2003 to May 2010]

Andrea's friend Max seems to operate in a similar way to Jonah – involved in a number of small to medium sized grow-ops in a variety of different properties. The approach is not uncommon (see Potter 2010b, Potter and Dann 2005), and we can recognize three different elements of his approach that militate against the impact of detection.

Firstly, any given grow-op is kept to a relatively small size in terms of the number of plants. Growers recognize that they are less likely to receive a meaningful sentence (the benchmark for most growers is avoiding a custodial sentence) if they have a smaller number of plants (even though a few large plants can produce more cannabis than a larger number of smaller plants, and can still provide substantial financial returns) (ibid.; see also Lenton, this volume). This aspect – minimizing the impact of detection – is always a hot topic on online discussion boards and email distribution lists. Advice, which includes input from people with knowledge of court cases in this area, includes minimizing the number of plants, avoiding having any obvious "dealing paraphernalia", avoiding spreading cultivation over more than one room or location, and avoiding a set-up that looks too professional or geared up for long-term production. Growers recognize that they can utilize a grow-op that would appear, to the forces of law and order, to be non-commercial (and therefore unlikely to result in custody) for commercial purposes. Growing ten plants at a time, for example, can still net an experienced grower tens of thousands of pounds a year.

Secondly, situating a grow-op on someone else's property minimizes the chances of being held to account. If any of Jonah's or Max's partners get busted, they will be the ones facing legal proceedings, while the brains behind the business (Jonah or Max in our examples) are shielded. I met growers who had served time in prison for a grow-op that was largely the responsibility of someone else, but who had protected the identity (whether through genuine loyalty, or through fear of repercussions) of that someone else.

Thirdly, by utilizing a number of different grow-sites, possibly with a number of different partners, the impact-minimization of growing on a small scale and growing on another's property can be maintained, whilst still engaging in a significant level of cultivation. Using a multi-site approach means also that even if a site is detected, and the plants confiscated, the grower does not lose all of their investment. Many large scale commercial operators benefit from this multi-site approach, and some growers sent to prison for cultivating hundreds or even thousands of plants have taken some comfort from the fact that other grow-ops remained undetected, with the profits (hopefully) waiting for them at the end of their sentence.

The inherent problems with cannabis eradication

In the UK many cannabis growers are motivated by financial reasons, but cannabis cultivation is not particularly connected to poverty, or an absence of alternative economic activity, or rural underdevelopment, as it is in the examples from both the developing and developed world we discussed in section two. With most cultivation taking place indoors, cannabis growing is not a rural or remote activity. Cultivation is widely reported in many urban centers and can hardly be said to take place in areas where the authorities have little control. Clearly none of the major factors cited as making drug crop eradication in developing countries so problematic are relevant to the case of indoor cultivation in the developed world.

Having said this, there are fundamental similarities between the practical difficulties facing eradication efforts whether directed at indoor or outdoor cultivation. Cannabis can be grown more or less anywhere, and does not need to be grown on a particularly large scale to be economically viable (UNODC 2009, Kilmer et al. 2010). Economic viability is not the only motivation for growing anyway, which further increases the attraction of small-scale growing – and the number of people who are willing to become involved. Nevertheless the potentially vast profits associated with large scale cultivation remain, and such patterns of cultivation are found in a wide range of countries.

Growers in all contexts can be seen to take active steps to minimize the chances of detection. Indoor growers can take this to a particular extreme. Growers can also be seen to minimize the impact of detection. In the UK the concern, for the grower, is as much on avoiding prison as on the actual loss of the crop, but the point is that growers take steps to minimize the impact of getting caught. The criminal law and criminal justice system do not deter them from growing; instead they encourage the grower to think about how best to tailor their cultivation in response to the legal context. This in itself is an adaptive response and further demonstrates how the rational actions of cannabis growers combine with the characteristics of cultivation that make it easy and attractive to grow, to make cultivation a difficult target for eradication or policing efforts.

Conclusions

It was suggested in the introduction that eradication efforts depend on the detection of plants being cultivated, and the prevention of future cultivation. With cannabis being so easy to grow, prevention is clearly difficult. With potentially high profits to be made from cultivation, there is no shortage of potential cultivators – especially when we also consider the various non-financial reasons for growing cannabis. Cannabis can be grown almost anywhere and is easy to conceal, especially with indoor growing techniques. What is more, whether grown outdoors in the developing world or indoors in the developed world, cannabis cultivators take active steps to make detection more difficult, and to lessen its impact if it does occur.

The conclusion to be drawn here is that cannabis eradication seems to be an increasingly unattainable goal. Years of global efforts have failed to eradicate cultivation in those nations more usually associated with drug production. Here the blame has often been placed on geographical inaccessibility, local economic conditions, and social, political and even military difficulties. The emergence and spread of indoor cultivation in urban areas in the developed world clearly demonstrates that such contextual conditions are only tangential to the problems of cannabis eradication. Rather, the real problems facing the goal of eradication are inherent in the act of cultivation itself.

There is no shortage, as is clear from the global evidence, of willing participants in the act of cannabis cultivation. Cannabis is primarily grown as a drug product: cannabis is the world's most popular illicit drug (UNODC 2009) and there is no shortage of demand. Cannabis is cultivated because it is financially attractive, but it is also cultivated by many people who are not motivated by profit. Cannabis is also easy to cultivate, can be grown almost anywhere, and can be easily hidden.

Large scale cultivation can, seemingly, take place in well-policed western cities as easily as in remote underdeveloped regions of the world. Those motivated to grow cannabis are also motivated to take steps to protect their growing operations.

It might be argued that most eradication efforts are directed against larger commercial rather than non-commercial cannabis growers and those growers motivated by non-financial reasons do not represent a failure of an eradication policy. However, the international law criminalizes *all* cannabis cultivation (with some legal exceptions for medical, industrial and scientific purposes), whether or not it is commercial. Further, it is not possible to completely separate out commercial and non-commercial cultivation: many growers initially motivated by non-commercial goals become involved in commercial cultivation (sometimes on a large scale), and commercial cultivators, especially those spreading their operations over multiple smaller sites, may be able to effectively hide their commercial intent and claim to be non-commercial (or small-scale commercial) cultivators.

The point is not simply that non-financial motivation *makes* eradication an unobtainable goal (although under the current strict, zero-tolerance global policy regime, this is an important point). Rather, the situations discussed in this chapter (with similar situations found throughout the Western world), represent further challenges to a UN policy goal that the world is already struggling to achieve. Evidence from around the world demonstrates how eradication efforts directed at large scale cultivation in the developing and the developed world have met with limited success. The UK evidence discussed in this chapter illustrates not just how non-financial growers further undermine the absolute goal of eradication, but also how adaptive responses of urban indoor growers (spreading efforts over multiple smaller grow sites *and* improved protection of individual grow sites) represent a further significant challenge even to the narrower goal of eradication of commercially oriented cultivation.

List of references

Adler, P. 1993. *Wheeling and Dealing: An Ethnography of an Upper-Level Drug Dealing and Smuggling Community* (2nd edition). New York: Colombia University Press.

Bergman, D. 2002. Made in the U.S.A. Hoe Amerikaanse kwekers de Nederwiet uitvonden [Made in the U.S.A. How American cultivators invented the Dutch weed]. *Essensie*, 65, 42-46.

Booth, M. 2003. *Cannabis: A history.* London: Doubleday.

Bouchard, M. 2007. A capture-recapture model to estimate the size of criminal populations and the risks of detection in a marijuana cultivation industry. *Journal of Quantitative Criminology*, 23, 221-41.

Caesar, E. 2010. The Secret Cannabis Kings. *Sunday Times Magazine*, 28th March 2010. Available at: http://www.mapinc.org/drugnews/v10/n229/a02.html [accessed: 10 April 2010].

Clayton, R.R. 1995. *Marijuana in the "Third World"*: Appalachia, U.S.A. London: Lynn Rienner.

Clemens, J. 2008. Opium in Afghanistan: Prospects for the Success of Source Country Drug Control Policies. *Journal of Law and Economics*, 51(3), 407-32.

del Olmo, R. 1998. The Ecological Impact of Illicit Drug Cultivation and Crop Eradication Programmes in Latin America. T*heoretical Criminology*, 2, 269-78.

Dorn, N., Levi, M. and King, L. 2005. *Literature Review on Upper Level Drug Trafficking*. Home Office Online Report 22/05. London: Home Office. Available at www.homeoffice.gov.uk/rds/pdfs05/rdsolr2205.pdf. [accessed: 9 April 2010].

Farrell, G. 1998. A global empirical review of drug crop eradication and United Nations' crop substitution and alternative development strategies. *Journal of Drug Issues*, 28(2), 395-436.

Hafley, S.R. and Tewksbury, R. 2001. The rural Kentucky marijuana industry: organization and community involvement. *Deviant Behavior*, 16(3), 201-21.

Hough, M., Warburton, H., Few, B., May, T., Man, L-H., Witton, J. and Turnbull, P.J. 2003. *A growing market: The domestic cultivation of cannabis*. York: Joseph Rowntree Foundation.

Jansen, A.C.M. 2002. *The economics of cannabis cultivation in Europe.* Paper presented at the 2nd European Conference on Drug Trafficking and Law Enforcement. Paris, 26th and 27th September, 2002. Available at http://www.cedro-uva.org/lib/jansen.economics.html. [accessed: 9 April 2010].

Katz, R. and Whitaker, S. 2001. Explaining accommodation and resistance in Kentucky. *Crime, Law an Social Change*, 35(4), 295-318.

Kilmer, B., Caulkins, J.P., Pacula, R.L., MacCoun, R.J. and Reuter, P.H. 2010. *Altered State? Assessing How Marijuana Legalization in California Could Influence Marijuana Consumption and Public Budgets*, Santa Monica, CA: RAND Corporation.

Leggett, T. 2006. Review of the world cannabis situation. *Bulletin on Narcotics*, 58 (volumes 1 and 2).
Mansfield, D. and Sage, C. (1998) Drug Crop Producing Countries: A Developmental Perspective, in *The Control of Drugs and Drug Users*, edited by R. Coomber. Boca Raton, Florida: CRC Press, 161-182.
Pearson, G. and Hobbs, D. 2001. *Middle market drug distribution*, Home Office Research Study 227. London: Home Office.
Potter, G. 2008. The growth of cannabis cultivation: Explanations for import substitution in the UK, in *Cannabis in Europe: Dynamics in perception, policy and markets*, edited by D.J. Korf. Lengerich: Pabst Science Publishers, 69-86.
Potter, G. 2010a. You Reap What You Sow: Profit, Pleasure and Pain in Domestic Cannabis Cultivation, in *Pleasure, pain and profit. European Perspectives on Drugs*, edited by T. Decorte and J. Fountain. Lengerich: Pabst Science Publishers, 134-51.
Potter, G. 2010b. *Weed, Need and Greed: a study of domestic cannabis cultivation.* London: Free Association books.
Potter, G. and Dann, S. 2005. Urban crop circles: Urban cannabis growing in the north of England, in Cocktails and dreams: *Perspectives on drug and alcohol use*, edited by W. Palacios. Upper Saddle River, New Jersey: Pearson Prentice Hall, 89-109.
UNGASS 1998. *Political Declaration and Action Plan against Money Laundering 10th June 1998*, New York. Available at: http://www.imolin.org/imolin/en/ungadec.html [accessed: 10 September 2010].
UNODC 2008a. *UNGASS – ten years on.* Vienna: UNODC. Available at: http://www.unodc.org/documents/wdr/WDR_2008/ungass_E_PRINT.pdf [accessed: 10 September 2010].
UNODC 2008b. *Annual Report*, 2008. Vienna: UNODC.
UNODC 2009. *Annual Report*, 2009. Vienna: UNODC.
UNODC 2010 *Afghanistan Cannabis survey 2009*. Vienna: UNODC. Available at: http://www.unodc.org/documents/crop-monitoring/Afghanistan/Afghanistan_Cannabis_Survey_2009.pdf [accessed: 10 September 2010].
Vellinga, M. (ed.) 2004. *The Political Economy of the Drug Industry: Latin America and the International System.* Gainsville, Florida: University Press Florida.
Weisheit, R.A. 1992. *Domestic Marijuana: A neglected industry.* New York: Greenwood Press.

Chapter 16
Emerging Trends in Cannabis Cultivation – and The Way Forward

Martin Bouchard, Gary R. Potter and Tom Decorte

On November 2, 2010 the citizens of California were asked to vote on Proposition 19 – the Regulate, Control, and Tax Cannabis (RCTC) proposition – which would have legalized the possession and cultivation of cannabis for citizens over 21 years old, and allow the state to regulate and tax the sale of cannabis in licensed establishments. Although it didn't pass, the mere fact that such a proposition was seriously considered in a major US state is notable. The legalization of cannabis would, to say the least, considerably change the landscape of cannabis consumption and cultivation in the US, but also for other countries directly or indirectly affected by the change (e.g. Mexico, Canada). If such a proposition were to materialize, it would provide extensive material for another book.

As demonstrated in a recent volume on this very issue, discussion over possible change in cannabis policy is happening across the world (Room et al. 2010). Over the past decades, several countries have seen changes to the traditional approaches of criminal prohibition of cannabis use. In the Netherlands and several US states, less punitive cannabis use control regimes were implemented in the late 1970s. More recently, reforms have been implemented or proposed in an increasing number of countries in the European Union, Oceania and the Americas. In February 2009, a Latin American Commission on Drugs and Democracy, co-chaired by former presidents of Brazil, Mexico and Colombia, called for an examination of the decriminalization of possession of cannabis for personal use. Mexico, Argentina, Brazil and Ecuador are expected to take new decriminalizing steps (Jenkins 2009). Most of these reforms seem to be occurring within the bounds set by the international drug control treaties, but several authors have also discussed measures which would in one way or another move beyond the limits of the current international drug control regime (see Room et al. 2010 for a comprehensive review).

However, the global prohibitionist regime is probably not at immediate risk, and there are also some steps in the opposite direction. For example, Møller (2009) recently showed how the Danish government cracked down on the Christiania cannabis market in Copenhagen after years under a regime of relative tolerance. In 2009 the British government increased the severity of penalties available for cannabis possession, reversing an easing of penalties that occurred in 2004. Room et al. (2010) describe the heterogeneity and complexity of the alternative cannabis control regimes that have evolved in different countries in recent years, ranging from "depenalization" (i.e. prohibition with cautioning or diversion), "decriminalization" (prohibition with civil penalties) to "de facto legalization" (e.g. prohibition with an expediency principle) or "de jure legalization", and the differences in how they might be enforced locally or regionally. But while a number of countries have implemented reform measures aimed at controlling the *use* of cannabis, fewer have addressed the issue of cannabis *supply* activities.

Whatever way forward is chosen globally, or by any individual country, no sound policy decision should be taken without knowledge of the markets involved, including the role played by cannabis cultivation – the necessary first link in any cannabis supply chain. In other words, any projections of the impact of legislative changes need to be rooted in as detailed as possible knowledge of the present. This book represents a detailed overview of "the present" of cannabis cultivation around the world. In this concluding chapter, we identify the emerging themes from the book. This exercise allows us to comment on the reasons why cannabis cultivation has spread worldwide, although no such proposition can be more than tentative before we accumulate more research on cannabis cultivation where causes can be isolated. We contribute by making a few suggestions on the way forward for research to be able to better understand the phenomenon at hand. We close with a discussion on the policy implications of the work presented in this book.

Emerging themes

The trade-offs between the costs and benefits of cannabis cultivation in traditional producer nations were made clear by the first two contributions of this book. In traditional producer nations, such as (but by no means limited to) the ones described by Afsahi (Morocco) and Klein (Caribbean), cannabis cultivation clearly provides some economic and social benefits. However there are problems attached, including criminality, environmental damage and the loss of traditional economic activities. Some of these problems appear to be made worse by policies of eradication and criminalization. It is also suggested from these first two contributions that increased cultivation in the industrialized countries relates to reduced cultivation in traditional places. Whether successful eradication in traditional countries has contributed to increased cultivation in the developed world, or whether increased developed-world cultivation has led to less demand driving traditional cultivation and hence apparent eradication successes, or some combination of the two, is not clear. We suspect it is a bit of both. Reduced cultivation in traditional producer nations may be good in terms of reducing environmental damage, but also has a negative impact on local economies. Where there are alternatives (e.g. cocaine), less demand for cannabis may encourage other drug trafficking or other types of criminality.

Future research should focus on these issues in particular. The first step in that regard would be to encourage the development of systematic data collection and measures aimed at comparing the costs and benefits of various policy regimes, but also of various alternative economic activities. Most urgent, however, is the realization by local authorities and Western nations that policy responses to production in those countries should be considered in much different terms than elsewhere.

Moving beyond the traditional producer countries of the developing world we see that cultivation is widespread and spreading ever wider: it truly is a global phenomenon, and is also increasingly localized. In fact, the most important emerging trend from part II is arguably one of *democratization* of the cannabis cultivation industry. First the democratization from traditional producing countries to industrial countries like the US (Weisheit, this volume) and then to countries like Denmark and Finland, which appear to have experienced the emergence of domestic cannabis cultivation later than others (Dahl and Asmussen; Hakkarainen and Perälä, this volume). We also see democratization across types of grower: this book treated of medical growers (Dahl and Asmussen), small cultivators seizing an opportunity to entirely avoid illegal market channels and produce a quality product for their own benefit (Decorte; Arana and Montañés Sánchez, this volume) and even to organized criminals who see in the cultivation industry an opportunity to make tangible monetary profits (Bouchard and Nguyen; Malm et al., this volume).

Given the range of approaches, of growers, and of motivations, it is not easy (though it might be tempting, and it might be a step in the right direction) to draw a line between "good" and "bad" growing – one that recognizes the varying degrees of commercial intent and criminal involvement. Commercial growing can be small-scale, especially when non-commercial growers realize they can sell their surplus or are offered money when they try to give gifts (see, e.g., Potter 2010). Growers can progress through careers, becoming more (or less) commercial and more (or less) professional. Many will be content with cultivating very small amounts for their own consumption. The problem, at the moment, is that *all* growers are largely dealt with the same (in policy, if not necessarily in practice) so it is hard to concentrate efforts on "bad" growing. At the very least, a reflection on the opportunities for differential enforcement for different types of cannabis cultivation is warranted. Policy models where (very) small-scale cultivation is tolerated – what MacCoun and Reuter (2001) termed the "Alaska model" – exist, and have not been shown to increase harms where implemented.

The first two chapters of part III provide case-studies on two jurisdictions that have experimented with the toleration of small-scale cultivation (a feature also of the Spanish study that closes part II). One argument for this type of decriminalization has been to remove the criminal (particularly the organized criminal) element from cannabis supply (see also Decorte 2010a). Although the Dutch model has long been seen as somewhat successful in this respect, recent concerns over the increased involvement of organized crime in cannabis cultivation have undermined this particular argument and led to increased official efforts to target a cultivation industry which had previously been tolerated (Korf, this volume). Such concerns over the possibility of (organized) criminals managing to exploit official tolerance to cultivation were important in shaping the Western Australian Cannabis Infringement Notice scheme and contributed to a situation where the degree of official tolerance towards cultivation is so narrowly defined as to have failed to make any significant impact on the wider cannabis market (Lenton, this volume).

Across most of the world the dominant policy response to cannabis cultivation is eradication efforts. But cannabis is not an easy plant to eradicate for a number of reasons. It grows almost anywhere – indoors and out – and as such cultivation can be hard to detect in the first place. The plant is resistant to many biological and chemical agents (Kalacska et al., this volume) which makes eradication difficult. Even where significant quantities of the crop are destroyed it may not have much impact on the wider market, particularly when cultivators have had time to respond to eradication efforts (Wilkins and Sweetsur, this volume). Those who grow cannabis can be seen to engage in adaptive responses to eradication efforts by employing tactics to minimize both the chances of detection (and, hence, eradication) and also the impact on their cultivation efforts if plantations are detected by the authorities (Potter, this volume, but see also Farrell 1998; Gallupe, Bouchard and Caulkins 2011). Difficulties in drug-crop eradication efforts in traditional producer nations have been well documented; it seems that similar – and new – difficulties confront eradication efforts but also policies of official tolerance in the industrialized world.

To recap, we can summarize the emerging themes of the book in three statements. Cannabis cultivation is spreading around the world with implications not just for those countries where it is an emerging phenomenon, but also those countries whose traditional position as major exporters is being undermined. Cultivation in the industrialized world is heterogeneous: whilst traditional (or even organized) criminals are often involved, attracted by the money, we must recognize the role of growers motivated by non-financial and even ideological or altruistic concerns. Responses to cultivation have limited success: we see that conservative, zero-tolerance eradication efforts and more liberal, harm-reduction decriminalization policies fail to satisfactorily tackle either the problem of cannabis cultivation itself or the related difficulties of criminal involvement in the cannabis trade.

A provisional explanation of the spread of cannabis cultivation

The aim of this conclusion is not just to identify the trends emerging from the research presented in this book, but also to analyze and explain them. Here we take the opportunity to draw not just on the preceding chapters but also years of empirical research on cannabis cultivation around the world to establish the existence of a few solid patterns. The global spread of cultivation may be summarized in these three points:

1. Cultivation initially spread from the developing to the developed world, and continues to spread in both.
2. Although we clearly notice early and late bloomers, the development of the industry appears to occur similarly in each country, with a prevalence of small scale cultivation in an experimental phase, followed quickly by the growth of a commercial segment of the market where criminal elements co-exist with otherwise law-abiding citizens in a deeply heterogonous industry.
3. Law enforcement agencies are in reactive mode and have difficulty following the upward trend, let alone curbing it.

The grand question is, as always, "why". After uniting the worldwide experts under the umbrella of a single book, each combing the literature on cultivation, and each contributing a few pieces of the puzzle, we feel that there is no better opportunity to take stock and venture a few propositions that might explain the spread of cannabis cultivation in so many countries around the world. But first, a few disclaimers. We do not think that there is necessarily a single, simple explanation for the growth of the industry in every country. Rather, we feel that there are most likely a number of factors that are at play, and that their unique combination and interaction in any given setting may provide a likely explanation for the growth in the local cultivation industry. We also believe that the reasons for the rise of cannabis cultivation in the first phase for the first group of non-traditional cultivating countries (e.g. Canada, The Netherlands, the US) may be substantially distinct from the reasons explaining the rise in the later group (e.g. Scandinavia). For one thing, a crucial communication channel like the World Wide Web, a vital source of information, equipment and even cannabis seeds for many growers (Potter 2008, 2010), was only widely adopted in the later phase. In other words, while it can be hypothesized that the Internet has contributed to the spread of cultivation in some countries, no such argument can be made for the reasons why the industry was booming in British Columbia or parts of the US as early as the mid 1980s (Bouchard 2007, Weisheit 1992). Yet, this book has shown that the phenomenon is sufficiently universal to warrant an effort at an explanation that may be general enough to be applied to most countries.

To be sure, we focus our proposition on the second phenomenon – the fact that cultivation is found almost everywhere (the spread, as opposed to the birth of cultivation). Yet we make an effort, where appropriate, to link our description to the first phase of the spread of cultivation. In a nutshell, we see the spread of cannabis cultivation as *a convergence of opportunity and sustained demand for the (local) product to go alongside an ever growing supply of motivated offenders and relative failure of policy to prevent the spread.* Each part of this proposition is important and needs to be briefly explained.

Opportunity The simplest explanation for the spread of cannabis cultivation is that the knowledge and technology became available to everyone willing to make a trip to the local garden shop. Bouchard and Dion (2009) demonstrated that the first hydroponic shop in Quebec, Canada, opened as early as 1969, decades before one could order equipment from the Internet. Of course the knowledge to grow cannabis did not necessarily follow the availability of technology. Before the Internet, knowledge slowly spread from person to person, from group to group through underground communication channels (books, magazines, word-of-mouth) and pockets of hippie communities. Locations where such communities were found in larger concentrations would find some cannabis cultivation going on, but the quality and reputation of the product was poor compared to the imported product (Warner 1986). This all changed with the spread of herbicide paraquat by US authorities, creating incentives for cannabis entrepreneurs to look elsewhere, including local groups.

Development in varieties of cannabis produced paralleled the development in local production, which enhanced the reputation of domestically grown cannabis for early bloomers. In other words, late bloomer countries (and growers) have a higher likelihood of starting further along the learning curve. The important point is that cannabis cultivation became *possible* for anyone willing to invest some time in learning the fundamentals. The growth of the Internet obviously made the knowledge available to all, and speeded up the learning process, as well as increased exposure of the activity. Grow guides and grow shops were facilitators to the diffusion of the activity around the world. This does not mean that person to person knowledge transfer is ineffective, or unnecessary. Bouchard and Nguyen (this volume), for example, showed that first hand, person to person knowledge transfer and mentoring is more likely to lead to successful commercial cultivation than indirect sources, with Potter (this volume, see also Potter 2010) also demonstrating the role of experienced mentors in introducing new people to cultivation. The important point for our purposes is that the plant can be grown for profit anywhere, and the knowledge necessary to do so is just as ubiquitous.

Sustained demand Surely, there would no incentives to cultivate cannabis without the assurance that there is a market for it. After a decline in the 1980s, the worldwide trends in cannabis use have been either stable or on the rise, creating incentives for increased production (UNODC 2008, 2009). In addition, the benefits of cannabis for medical purposes, or the improved quality and variety of the product have helped create new markets where they did not exist before. As one would expect, this growth in demand parallels almost perfectly the growth in production in developed countries. Both phenomena undeniably feed upon each other (Bouchard 2007).

Sustained supply of motivated offenders As seen above, a remarkable feature of the cannabis market is its widespread consumption among all age ranges and social classes. A rarely underlined consequence of that feature is the stimulation of cannabis cultivation among otherwise conventional elements of the population. It is only natural that otherwise law-abiding citizens would find ways to obtain supply through other channels than the criminal market. A consequence of this is that cannabis cultivation is in some places as firmly rooted and widespread as cannabis use itself. In Quebec, for example, Bouchard (2007) estimated that close to 1% of the 15+ population was involved in cannabis cultivation. A recent self-report survey showed that these proportions are even higher in a few rural regions where the cultivation industry became one of the premier employers for a significant proportion of the population, including adolescents (Bouchard et al. 2009).

Avoiding contacts with drug dealers and other criminal elements is only one of the many motivations of cannabis growers reported in this book, and elsewhere (e.g. Weisheit 1992, Potter 2010, Decorte 2008, 2010b). Because the motivations are as varied as the populations of cannabis growers, it is no surprise that there has been no shortage of motivated individuals ready to try their luck at cannabis cultivation. In fact, the diversity of reasons why people grow cannabis goes way beyond the usual motivations for crime involvement. In this book only, we saw how some growers are involved for intangible reasons, like a love for growing (as well as using) the plant (see e.g. Hakkarainen and Perälä; Bouchard and Nguyen, this volume). The fact that cannabis has the potential to provide benefits for certain medical conditions attracts a segment of the population into the cultivation industry that may not otherwise be involved (Dahl and Asmussen, this volume). Avoiding the criminal market may not simply be a symbolic statement; as Decorte (this volume) shows, it may also be a matter of taste, as many Belgian growers report becoming involved out of dissatisfaction with the quality of the commercial product they find in the market. Still other growers view their involvement as a social or political message (Hakkarainen and Perälä; Arana and Montañés Sánchez, this volume).

Then, of course, there are the commercial motivations of the rest of the growers. Undeniably, there is money to be made in this industry, although growers may become disappointed with the actual level of profits after all expenses have been covered (Bouchard and Nguyen, this volume). Money is a powerful motivation for many individuals who are involved, and it shall continue to be one as long as this remains an illegal, but in-demand, industry.

Relative failure of drug policy to prevent or stop the spread This part of the proposition is not so much a statement on the "war on drugs" as it is simply an observation *post facto* that whatever policy was in place before the rise of the cannabis cultivation industry, it has not been preventing its development. The cultivation industry has been blooming in repressive and tolerant countries alike, without distinction. While this statement is perhaps generally true, it does not mean that there are no nuances to be made in the stories of specific countries and contexts. The industry may have developed in a different form, sooner, or later in regime X than expected under regime Y. Yet, the universal nature of the current cultivation industry makes such finer analyses less imperative. The important point is that forces other than official cannabis policies are at play, and at one point are likely to take over. Cannabis cultivation may be too easily done, the demand for the product, the knowledge and techniques too widespread to expect something different.

Research implications

We have already made one key point here: research into the expansion and nature of cultivation in the developed world needs to consider not only the impact on those countries and their cannabis markets, but also the impact on traditional, developing-world, producer nations and on international patterns of cultivation and distribution of cannabis. However it is clear that it is the emergence and spread of cannabis in the developed world that is still relatively new and relatively poorly understood.

Although it is rarely possible to fully exhaust a research domain, the one area where the most work has been done is on typologies of growers, especially on the motivations of cannabis growers around the world. A lot has been learned from that work, most importantly on the wide variety of cannabis growers (which mirrors, a similar diversity of cannabis users). One way forward for research would be to follow the careers of those growers who would never have been involved in a criminal activity had it not been for cannabis cultivation. The specific question to be answered is whether involvement in the cultivation industry has had any impact on exposure to other criminal opportunities which may not have been available otherwise. Progression and regression in cultivation careers, and the factors affecting those movements, should be a fruitful area for future research. Related to this point, serious research should be devoted to measuring the effect of involvement in cannabis cultivation on the frequency and quantity of cannabis consumed, or more generally on the variations in the harms associated with consumption. It could be, for example, that growing cannabis for personal use increases consumption while, at the same time, decreases the overall harms associated with cannabis use. This is likely to be so if a) the cannabis consumed is of a milder and/or organic variety; b) more generally of a type better suited to the effects one is looking for (e.g. for medical purposes or a particular type of "high"); or c) one avoids the criminal markets and reduces risks of rip-offs or other victimization. Researchers who benefit from longitudinal research designs are invited to incorporate questions about the timing involvement in cannabis cultivation over the life course, as well as questions about the effect of involvement on consumption.

The succession of case studies from different countries around the world also emphasizes the need for comparative research examining the impact of various policies on the structure of the cannabis cultivation industry. Updating the work of Peter Reuter (1983) on the consequences of illegality for criminal organizations in the context of the worldwide heroin trade, Paoli, Greenfield and Reuter (2009) recently proposed that variations in *effective illegality* had an impact on the size and operations of illegal enterprises around the world. The work of Afsahi and Klein in this volume suggests a clear divide between the developed and developing world in the dynamics of drug production where the potential for corruption and selective enforcement remains a powerful driving force affecting the size and shape of the cannabis industry. However, much less is known on the more subtle variations in regimes affecting the developed countries. This issue is important because drastic changes in policies are unlikely to occur. If it so happens that small changes in policy (e.g. the tolerance of small-scale cannabis cultivation) have an influence on cannabis market participants, then it becomes worth exploring those options and the nature of their consequences. While the argument is made that tolerance of small-scale cannabis cultivation may remove the necessity for many users to obtain their supplies from illegal channels, how much of such transfer effectively occurs upon a change in policy remains unknown.

More research is also needed on the issue of medical marijuana. Too little is known beyond the perception, by users, of physiological and psychological benefits from cannabis consumption. An interesting issue raised by Dahl and Asmussen, and one that should be part of that research agenda is whether certain varieties of cannabis are more effective than others for certain conditions (*Indica* vs. *Sativa*), as well as the comparative advantage of cannabis over alternatives – including an examination into side effects and addiction potential. The legal status of those users and growers is blurry in most instances, and is worthy of empirical attention. Regulation mechanisms to ensure quality and continued supply of the product but also compliance with legal agreements are for the most part unknown.

Several systems of cannabis supply regulation have been proposed in different countries, and research on their effectiveness would be of international interest. In the Netherlands, Canada and Switzerland for example, government sponsored committees have recommended provisions for state-regulated cannabis availability, including provision for licensed retail outlets. Both the proposed systems and the pragmatic, social and political reasons why they were not implemented may be worth studying (Room et al. 2010). There are also a few working examples of cannabis supply regulation worth looking at, such as the state-authorized bhang shops in Indian states Uttar Pradesh, Rajasthan, Madhya Pradesh, Uttarakhand and Orissa, and the "cannabis social clubs" which seem to have gained legal recognition and legitimacy in Catalonia and the Basque country. Other operating models for regulated cannabis availability are the state-sanctioned existing distribution systems for medical cannabis users, e.g. in Canada, the United States and the Netherlands. The fact that they are limited to the special sub-population of medical cannabis users does not make them uninteresting as research objects for questions related to regulation regimes for cannabis availability and supply to a broader population.

Other research priorities might be to focus on patterns and prevalence of cannabis cultivation, especially in other countries not covered in this book (particularly African and Latin American countries, but also other European countries such as France and Germany, and central and eastern Europe), and in other traditional producer countries (Mexico, Lebanon, Pakistan, Afghanistan, India). As mentioned above, more research also needs to be done into the effects of different systems of penalizing cannabis cultivation on both cultivation and usage patterns (both within, and in surrounding regions where the change has occurred).

Policy implications

This book also naturally leads to a discussion of policy options in the face of a still growing worldwide cannabis cultivation industry. No chapter truly assessed the consequences of a change in policy, or provides enough material for strong recommendations on our part. What the collective effort does suggest, however, is the need for a serious reflection on the manner in which policy intervenes and handles participants in this industry. If nothing else, this book has convincingly shown that seeing the cultivation industry as a one-dimensional phenomenon is a mistake. Examples of depictions of the cultivation industry as an "organized crime" phenomenon are just as common as images of an industry dominated by small-time growers and plant lovers strictly in it for "intangible rewards" (Weisheit 1991) and a cheap-yet-quality cannabis product. Instead, the heterogeneity of participants in the industry is probably the most robust finding of research on cannabis cultivation. Such variability in involvement makes policy recommendations so important yet so delicate at the same time. Can policy truly reflect the heterogeneity of the industry and if so, how would that operate in practice?

One option that has been applied in different yet related contexts is to formally recognize the variations in the level of tolerance for one type of involvement compared to another. The Dutch regime which created a clear divide between cannabis and harder drugs by tolerating the sale and use of cannabis in licensed establishments is an example of this. In the context of cannabis cultivation (in other countries) this would mean recognizing a difference between small-scale cultivation for personal use and cultivation for commercial purposes. This kind of regime has been experimented with before in one form or another, as illustrated in a few contributions in this volume (Lenton, Korf, Arana and Montañés Sánchez). Formalized tolerance of small scale cultivation would presumably entail setting some kind of limit on the number of plants under cultivation and/or the total amount of cannabis produced. Supplying to others would either be strictly prohibited, or severely limited. Cultivation for medical purposes might be considered as a separate issue in that there are stronger arguments and more public sympathy towards medical use than recreational use. If medical cultivation was dealt with separately by policy then there would presumably need to be guidelines on who was allowed to grow how much on behalf of whom. There would also need to be decisions as to what medical conditions are recognized, and how a medical user gets permission to grow.

Tolerance of individual growers, whether strictly for medical use or for a wider concept of personal use, could separate out the more serious criminals and links to other crimes with an argument that legalized small-scale cultivation could undermine the wider illegal market (Decorte 2010a). However the chapters by Korf, Lenton and Potter show that criminals can be adept at utilizing individual small-scale cultivation efforts (whether or not officially tolerated) as part of a larger, organized criminal enterprise. But toleration of those who grow for personal use, medical or "ideological" reasons gives those with such motivations a way to source cannabis without recourse to the black market – and may encourage a greater respect for the law for such users (and those who sympathize with them). There might also be benefits for policing efforts with some clear indications of how best to target resources.

The issue of whether this model (the "Alaska model" of MacCoun and Reuter 2001) would indeed lead to more harms than benefits is important, and perhaps the one criterion against which to base such decisions. In the end, how one projects the consequences of this regime may depend on whether one believes this to be a small or drastic change in policy. Research into the effect of relatively small changes in policy such as de facto decriminalization showed that it had little effect on the prevalence of use, one way or another (MacCoun and Reuter 2001, Room et al. 2010). There are reasons to believe that a similar situation can be expected for tolerance of small scale cannabis use, but again we lack any systematic research documenting the impact of such changes on the dynamics of the cannabis industry after they were made. We strongly believe that if any changes should be made to policy, they should be documented and analyzed by pre-post research designs with solid prevalence indicators at both the demand and supply levels. Any such changes should also not be drastic enough that one cannot revert back to the initial state in case of obvious increases in harms related to change in regime. Policy discussions that go further than such a model are certainly welcome, as no indicators suggest that the status quo is working well enough in any country to make such reflections fruitless. It would be imprudent for us to go further in suggesting policy changes as this is not the purpose of this book, or of any parts of it. We simply hope that the book does provide a solid empirical base to feed future policy discussions on this issue, and to orient empirical research on the directions it should go to actually provide more solid answers to the issues raised in these pages.

List of references

Bouchard, M. 2007. A capture-recapture model to estimate the size of criminal populations and the risks of detection in a marijuana cultivation industry. *Journal of Quantitative Criminology*, 23, 221-41.

Bouchard, M. and Dion, C.B. 2009. Growers and facilitators: probing the role of entrepreneurs in the development of the cannabis cultivation industry. *Journal of Small Business and Entrepreneurship*, 22(1), 25-38.

Bouchard, M., Alain, M. and Nguyen, H. 2009. Convenient labor: the prevalence and nature of youth involvement in the marijuana cultivation industry. *International Journal of Drug Policy*, 20(6), 467-74.

Decorte, T. 2008. Domestic marihuana cultivation in Belgium: on (un)intended effects of drug policy on the cannabis market, in *Cannabis in Europe: dynamics in perception, policy and markets*, edited by D.J. Korf. Lengerich, Pabst Science Publishers, 69-86.

Decorte, T. 2010a. The case for small-scale domestic cannabis cultivation. *The International Journal of Drug Policy*, 21(4), 271-75.

Decorte, T. 2010b. Small scale domestic cannabis cultivation: an anonymous web survey among 659 cannabis cultivators in Belgium. *Contemporary Drug Problems,* 37 (Summer 2010), 341-70.

Farrell, G. 1998. A global empirical review of drug crop eradication and United Nations' crop substitution and alternative development strategies. *Journal of Drug Issues,* 28(2), 395-436.

Gallupe, O., Bouchard, M., and Caulkins, J. 2011. No change is a good change? Restrictive deterrence in illegal drug markets. *Journal of Criminal Justice*, 39, 81-89.

Jenkins, S. 2009. The war on drugs is immoral idiocy. We need the courage of Argentina. *The Guardian*, 3 September. Available at: http://www.guardian.co.uk/ commentisfree/2009/sep/03/drugs-prohibition-latin-america. [accessed: 29 October 2010].

MacCoun, R. and Reuter, P. 2001. *Drug war heresies: learning from other vices, times and places*. Cambridge: Cambridge University Press.

Møller, K. 2009. Police crackdown on Christiania in Copenhagen. *Crime, Law, and Social Change*, 52(4), 337-45.

Paoli, L., Greenfield, V. and Reuter, P. 2009. *The world heroin market: can the supply be reduced?* New York: Oxford University Press.

Potter, G. 2008. The growth of cannabis cultivation: Explanations for import substitution in the UK, in *Cannabis in Europe: Dynamics in perception, policy and markets*, edited by D.J. Korf. Lengerich: Pabst Science Publishers, 69-86.

Potter, G. 2010. *Weed, Need and Greed: a study of domestic cannabis cultivation.* London: Free Association books.

Reuter, P. 1983. *Disorganized Crime: The Economics of the Visible Hand.* Cambridge, Mass.: MIT Press.

Room, R., Fischer, B., Hall, W., Lenton, S. and Reuter, P. 2010. *Cannabis policy: moving beyond stalemate*. Oxford, UK: Oxford University Press.

UNODC 2008. *Annual Report, 2008.* Vienna: UNODC.

UNODC 2009. *Annual Report, 2009.* Vienna: UNODC.

Warner, R. 1986. *Invisible hand: The marijuana business*. New York: Beech Tree Books.

Weisheit, R.A. 1991. The intangible rewards from crime: The case of domestic marijuana cultivation. *Crime and Delinquency*, 37(4), 506-27.

Weisheit, R.A. 1992. *Domestic Marijuana: A neglected industry*. New York: Greenwood Press.

Index

References to diagrams are in **bold**

For Product Safety Concerns and Information please contact our EU representative GPSR@taylorandfrancis.com Taylor & Francis Verlag GmbH, Kaufingerstraße 24, 80331 München, Germany